Drawing and Illustrating Architecture

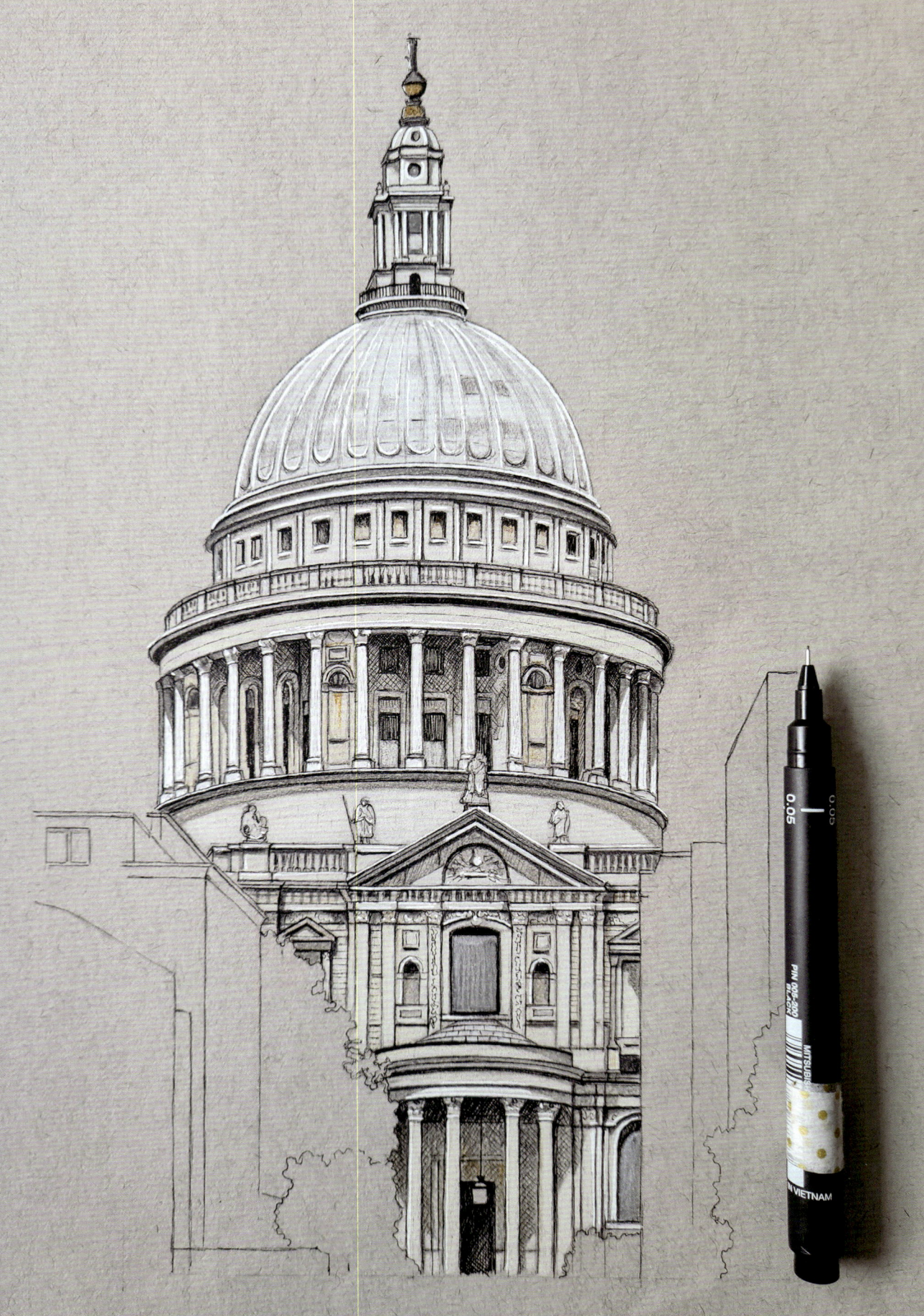

Drawing and Illustrating Architecture

A Step-by-Step Guide to the Art of Drawing and Illustrating Beautiful Buildings

DEMI LANG

rockynook

Drawing and Illustrating Architecture:
A Step-by-Step Guide to the Art of Drawing and Illustrating Beautiful Buildings
Demi Lang
www.demilang.com

Project editor: Jocelyn Howell
Project manager: Lisa Brazieal
Marketing coordinator: Katie Walker
Cover and interior design: Frances Baca
Layout: Kim Scott/Bumpy Design

ISBN: 979-8-88814-041-3
1st Edition (2nd printing)
© 2024 Demi Lang

Rocky Nook Inc.
1010 B Street, Suite 350
San Rafael, CA 94901
USA

Image Attributions:
Page 82, Radcliffe Camera: David Iliff, CC BY-SA 3.0 DEED
<https://creativecommons.org/licenses/by/2.5/deed.en>, via Wikimedia Commons
Page 140, Figure 6.113: Artur Opala, CC BY 3.0 <https://creativecommons.org/licenses/by/3.0>,
via Wikimedia Commons
Page 178, Big Ben and Houses of Parliament, London, UK: © S.Borizov/Shutterstock

www.rockynook.com

Distributed in the UK and Europe by Publishers Group UK
Distributed in the U.S. and all other territories by Publishers Group West

Library of Congress Control Number: 2023934964

This book is printed on acid-free paper.
Printed in China

For my dad, who I know is looking down from the stars and watching over me with a look of astonishment on his face x

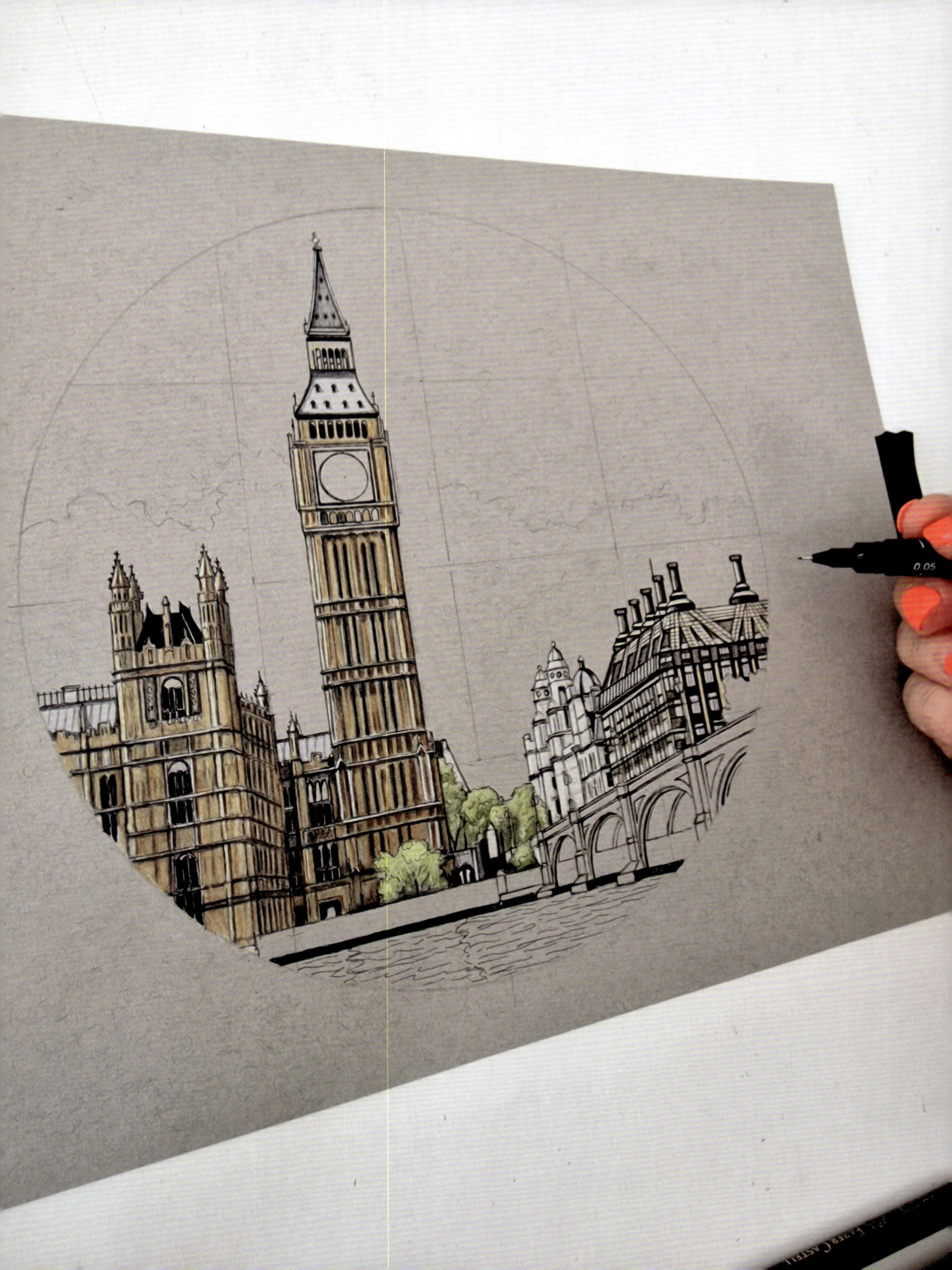

Contents

Acknowledgments

With amazing gratitude and thanks to my wonderful husband, Steve, for your love, help, and support. Thank you for encouraging me to get back up when I became overloaded, which was often!

To my mum, Sheila. For encouraging my creativity and giving me never-ending support. Thank you for allowing me to make a mess on the kitchen table with my paints and pens when I was small—it paid off in the end! To my uncle Rob for teaching me to draw the sun, trees, and the sky when I was little. All these moments ignited the initial sparks of creativity and created special, treasured memories.

To my daughters: Darcey, for all your technical support over the years, and to Sasha, for your calm kindness and for letting me talk things through.

Also, to my lifelong friends for your love, belief, and support along the way. Amy, thank you for believing in me and telling me I could do it! Without your belief, encouragement, and girl power right at the beginning, there would be no book! Thank you for helping me grow.

With massive thanks to the awesome team at Rocky Nook for guiding me through the process. Thank you, Jocelyn, for making sense of my manuscript! Thank you, Ted, for your enthusiasm and encouragement and for giving me this amazing opportunity. Forever grateful.

Finally, thank you from the bottom of my heart to anyone who has bought this book or taken my online class. Good luck on your artistic journey, you are helping to make the world a more beautiful place!

Introduction

Drawing is like meditation to me; the hours slip by me with no recognition of time.

First, I want you to know that I am not an architect and have no formal training in the field. This is a question I get asked a lot. I simply have an absolute passion for drawing beautiful architecture. Something about the way sunlight touches a building ignites my creativity and leaves me inspired to put pen to paper as soon as possible! I am in awe of grand buildings and architectural details and the architects and craftsmen who designed and built them.

I have always been creative, and my mum encouraged this as a child. Art was my only real interest and the only thing I was vaguely good at. After leaving school I went on to study graphic design in college. It was there that I first discovered artists such as David Hockney and his iconic painting *The Splash* and the amazing art and stories of the Pre-Raphaelites, and my interest and passion for the arts grew.

Apart from art at school and that two-year course that taught me the basics of graphic design (before computers!), my drawing skills are completely self-taught. One valuable skill I took away from that course was how to make sure things were put straight on a page with simple tools. This has been an essential skill that I still use for my work today.

I believe that just like with any other skill, with dedication and lots of practice, anyone can learn to draw. As is true for any subject or vocation in life, there will always be varying levels of ability, but with continued practice, as the months and years go by, you will be able to look back and observe your progress and see how far you have come. Your personal style will also evolve and develop, and you will discover what you enjoy sketching most. Draw and sketch subjects that appeal to you so you can't wait to get started!

I try to draw every day, even if it's only for ten to thirty minutes. Of course, this is not always possible; sometimes I'm busy with life and family, but it's always at the back of my mind like an itch I need to scratch. If too much time passes without getting to scratch the itch, I start to feel discontented, like something is missing—which it is!

I find art in general and creating very relaxing, like meditation and the sense of accomplishment from creating something makes me feel good. Like any chosen practice or hobby, it is a daily dose of self-care and time for yourself.

Even when time and energy are limited, doing just one thing can open up the creative pathways to doing the next thing.

I love exploring towns and cities, and when you look closely at a building there are so many details that you don't see straight away. I like to look closely and imagine the stonemasons and architects from yesteryear who painstakingly designed, carved, and built these magnificent buildings in a way that is rarely seen today.

When you are drawing you see the world with different eyes. By stopping and closely observing, you see things you never would have noticed. When you are in urban surroundings, remember to always look up! Towering above you are often magnificent windows, rooftops, and chimneys that go unnoticed.

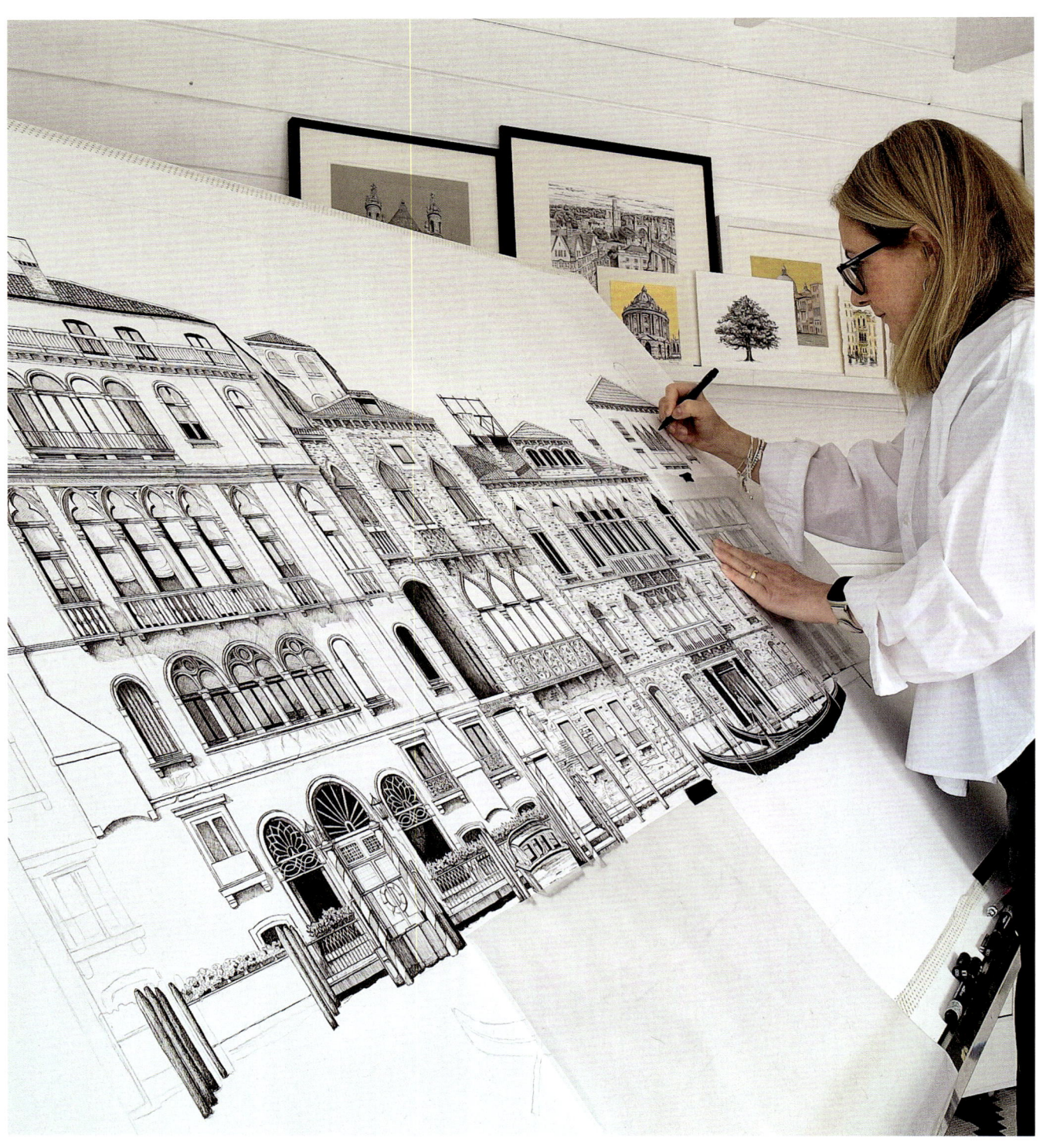

I am excited to teach you what I have learned from observing others and have taught myself over the years through dedicated practice, with many highs and lows along the way.

I have drawn and painted so many different subjects and experimented with so many different mediums over the years, but I found my passion drawing and illustrating beautiful architecture. My work is all drawing-based and often combines many mediums. Much of my work is mixed media, which you will see in this book, combining pencil and ink to create vibrant, realistic architecture illustrations. After much trial and error with different mediums and techniques, I have discovered that it's what I enjoy and what I am best at.

The beauty of drawing is that you can do it anywhere, whether it is on location, seated at a table, at a drawing board, or in a comfy chair.

In this book, my aim is to teach you my way of doing things. It is not necessarily the "classic" or "right" way of doing things, as I have no formal training. It is just what I do and it works for me, so I'm sure it will work for you! My goal in these pages is to share my techniques and teach you how to accurately draw and illustrate architecture. If the projects in this book seem overwhelming at first glance, please don't be put off. Slow down and patiently go through each step, one by one. Detailed drawing is time-consuming and does require patience, but the results will be worth it!

All the reference photos for the projects in this book are available in a downloadable PDF at

rockynook.com/drawing-illustrating-architecture

Alternatively, if you don't want to use the photos provided, you can always choose your own photo to work from and apply the principles within this book to it. For instance, you may wish to draw your own home or a building that has a special significance to you.

Whether you follow this exactly or whether it triggers your own creative spark, I hope that you learn some new techniques, feel inspired, and enjoy your creative journey.

Be patient with yourself. Learning to draw is no different to learning other new skills—a new language, for instance—these things take time and effort, but the rewards will be worth it!

Inside this book there are chapters on art materials and setting up, the basics of my drawing methods, and the techniques I use to complete a whole drawing from start to finish. This is followed by a series of individual projects, each with a step-by-step guide to help you work through them.

Please remember that your artwork is your very own and the steps here are a guide to get you started. Always draw in a way that you enjoy and that makes you happy. It will be harder in the beginning as you are learning and developing the techniques, but over time and with practice your style will evolve and it will get easier!

I wish you the best of luck, and remember, progress requires time, patience, dedication, and lots of practice!

Demi

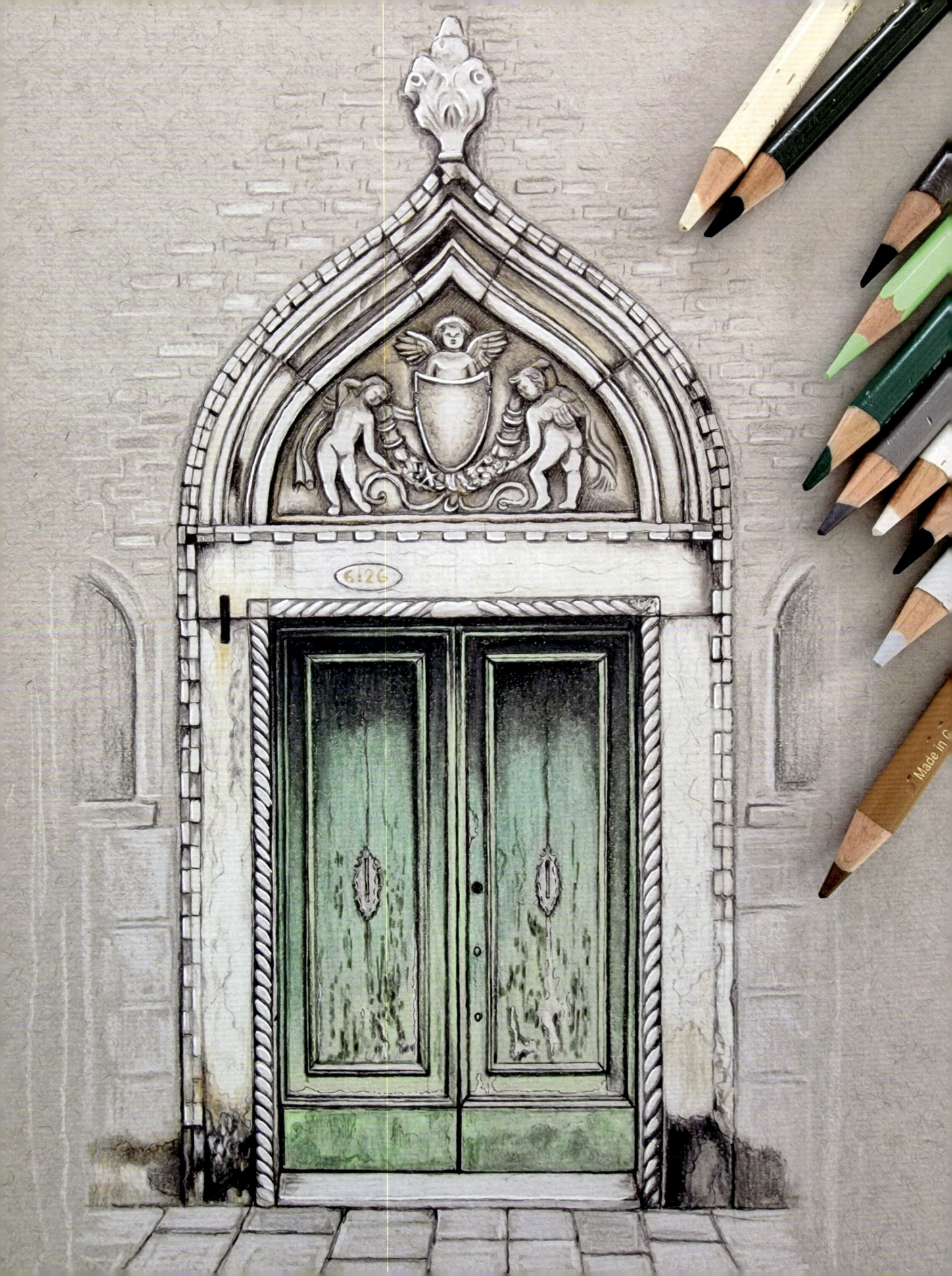

PART ONE

Materials and Techniques

In Part 1 of this book, I begin by walking you through the essential art materials you will need to get started on the projects within the book, followed by tips for setting up and organizing your workspace. This is information I've gathered through years of trial and error as an artist, so I'm simply sharing with you what I have learned works well.

Next, we'll look at how to build a photo reference library, which will be useful for your future projects and is a fun way to spend some time appreciating the world around you. We'll also discuss the benefits of sketching. I love to explore with a sketchbook in hand.

In chapter 3, we'll get into bit of art theory. This is important information to understand because it is the foundation of the drawings featured in this book, so it's worth taking the time to read through it. For instance, throughout the book I talk about the contrasts between light and dark and how these elements impact the final outcome of a piece of art.

In chapter 4, you will learn the three different methods I regularly use to draw out a picture: the grid method, freehand sketching, and working from a printout or digital screen. If you plan to use one of these methods, you will need to pay particular attention to this section before moving on to the projects in Part 2 of the book. You'll also learn some basic drawing techniques and how to layer coloured pencils to create a drawing full of texture and rich colour!

There is a lot of information to take in, so you may find it useful to look through everything once, and then re-read relevant parts whenever necessary as you work through the book.

My biggest piece of advice is to take your time and enjoy the process of creating your drawings. Playing with the colours and fineliners and learning what you can do is very satisfying, so have fun!

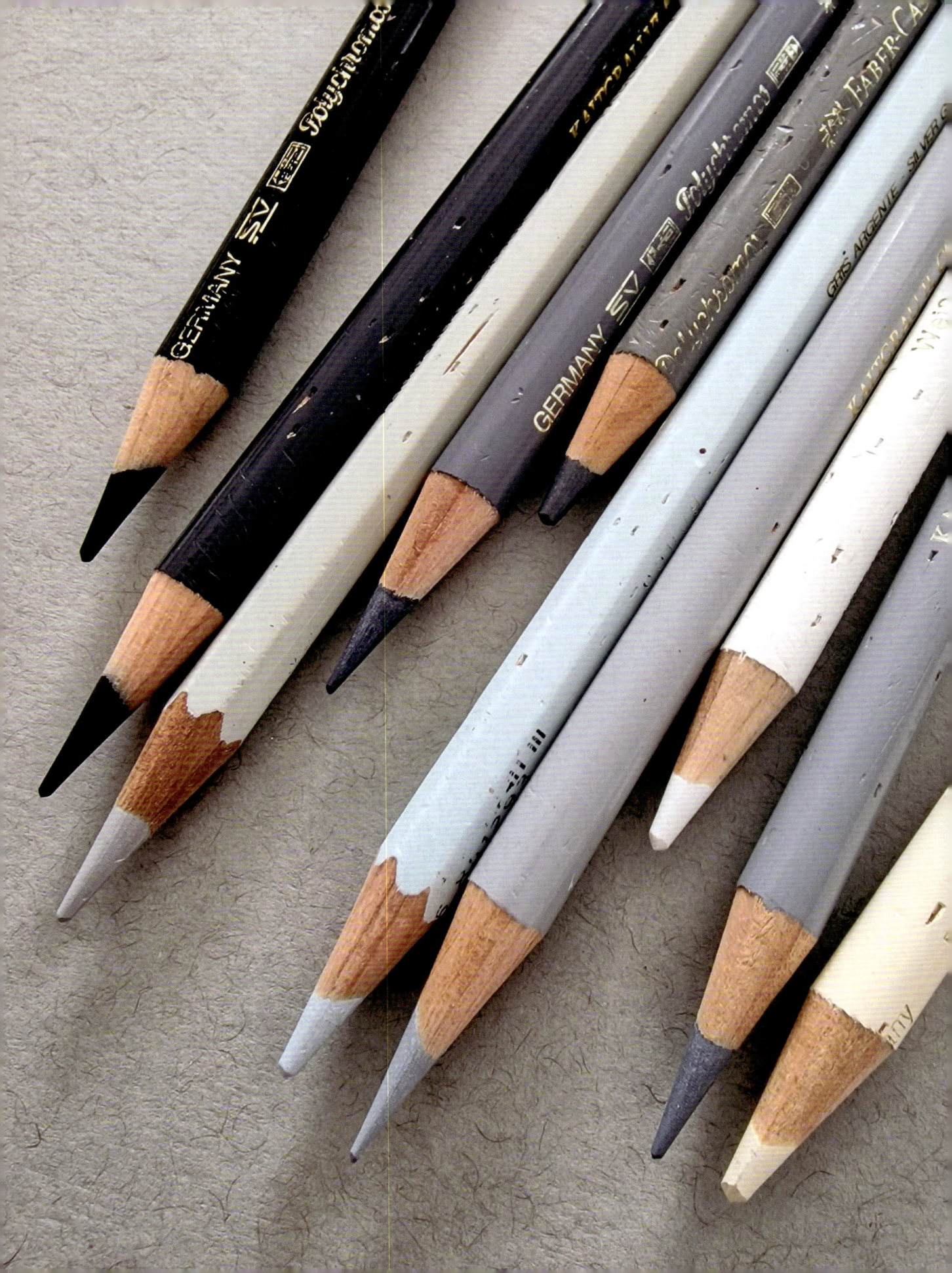

CHAPTER ONE

Art Materials and Workspace

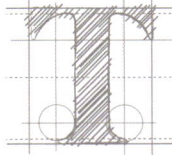

This chapter covers all the art supplies you will need to work on the projects in this book. After many years of trial and error, I have found the specific types and brands that work best for me, so what follows is a basic guide of my choices to get you started. I'm sure you will find what works best for you and what your budget allows you to spend. The good news is you don't have to spend a fortune! There is an array of different options available to suit all budgets.

The costliest items are good-quality coloured pencils. I have built up my collection slowly by buying individual colours as I needed them—I have never bought an expensive set. Big sets also often contain colours that you will never use. I started by buying a few colours at a time, focusing first on my monochrome collection. I do enjoy experimenting with new products, so I am always on the lookout for something new to try.

What matters more than expensive art materials are dedication and lots of practice!

You can do just as much with a sharp, inexpensive regular graphite pencil as you can with an expensive mechanical pencil. However, the benefit of a mechanical pencil is that you don't have to stop to sharpen it. The point is always sharp, which helps with precision and a consistent weight line.

The exact tools you use are a personal choice. There is so much to choose from in art shops and in online stores. That said, below is a list of the absolute essentials you will need to follow the techniques I use in this book, followed by a more detailed breakdown of everything. Anything beyond the items on this list is optional.

- ▶ Toned grey or tan paper (I use grey throughout the book)
- ▶ White cartridge or watercolour paper
- ▶ White highlighting pen
- ▶ Sharp HB pencil (preferably mechanical)
- ▶ Black 0.05mm fineliner pen
- ▶ Coloured pencils that are quite soft and blend well
- ▶ Blender
- ▶ Eraser
- ▶ Ruler
- ▶ Set square (also known as a triangle)
- ▶ Pencil sharpener
- ▶ Masking tape or washi tape

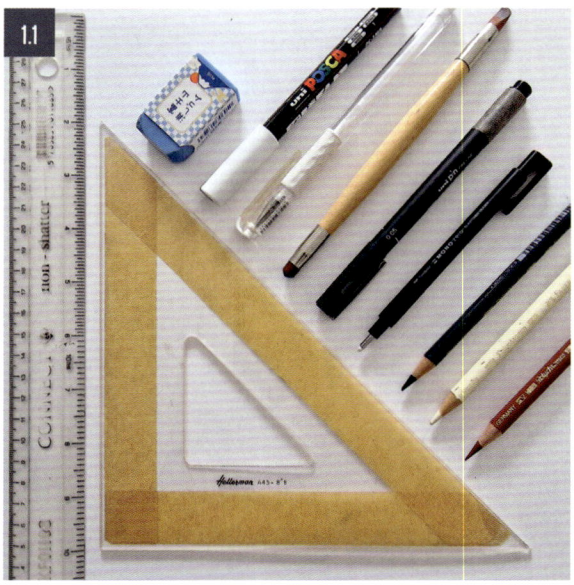

DRAWING PENCILS

A drawing always starts with the humble graphite pencil. There are so many different types of pencils available, but you don't need anything expensive or fancy—unless, of course, you want to invest in something special. The most important aspect of any pencil you use is that it is sharp!

I choose to use a mechanical pencil because it gives fantastic precision and it doesn't need sharpening; you just have to replace the lead inside when it runs out.

There is an amazing variety of mechanical pencils available to buy, from very expensive and nice-looking ones to simple, less-expensive options. They actually all do the same job! Even the cheapest pencil can give you years of service and is endlessly refillable. I have broken a few expensive pencils by accidently dropping them, which resulted in bent nibs and made them unusable, so I don't buy anything too expensive.

Something I always look for is a pencil that has an eraser on the end for making quick and convenient corrections.

You can buy refill packs of the lead in different sizes. A good size to choose for detailed drawing is 0.3mm or 0.5mm.

Pencil Grades

All graphite pencil comes in different grades, on a scale from hard to very soft. The softer the lead is, the darker its marks will be, whereas a harder, firmer lead will create lighter lines and shading.

Softer leads have a B grading with a number next to it to indicate how soft the lead is, with B being slightly soft and 9B being extremely soft. At the other end of the scale are harder leads with an H grading. In the same way as with the B grades, the numbers go as far as a 9H, which is extremely hard.

In the middle of both of these scales is the HB pencil, which is neither too hard nor too soft. I generally use this grade for drawing out because it doesn't smudge or make a mess and I can create clear, firm lines.

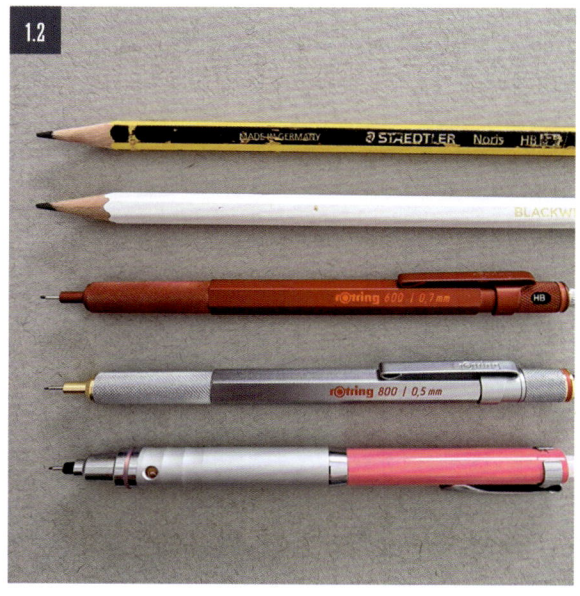

For more loose and sketchy drawings, I use a 2B graded pencil, which is slightly softer and allows me to be more expressive.

FINELINER PENS

Fineliner pens are a type of fine fibre- or plastic-tip pen that can be used for drawing and sketching (**FIGURE 1.3**). The tips are usually quite robust and don't bend or break very easily. They are a great choice for drawing because you can find ones that are relatively cheap and they are most often disposable.

My favourite drawing pen is the highly economical Uni-Ball Pin drawing pen, which contains waterproof and fade-proof pigment ink. This is a nonnegotiable pen feature for me, as I want my work to last a lifetime, and the ink in this pen is archival. I also don't want the ink to run if I use another medium, such as watercolour paint, on top of it. This ink will not smudge if it gets wet.

Another excellent pen that is widely available is the Sakura Pigma Micron drawing pen.

You can buy fineliner pens in many different nib sizes, each of which creates a different line weight (**FIGURE 1.4**). In other words, a 0.05mm pen nib will create a very fine line, compared to a 0.8mm pen nib, which will create a much broader line.

Throughout this book I use a Uni-Ball Pin 0.05mm pen. These pens are disposable but last quite a long time. I find that I get a lot of good drawing miles from just one pen. I keep the older pens for a while when they start to fade to create lighter shading.

COLOURED PENCILS

There are many different brands of coloured pencils available, of varying quality. You can buy them in beautiful sets in metal tins and expensive special wooden boxes. I have only ever bought them as single pencils and have built up my collection over a few years.

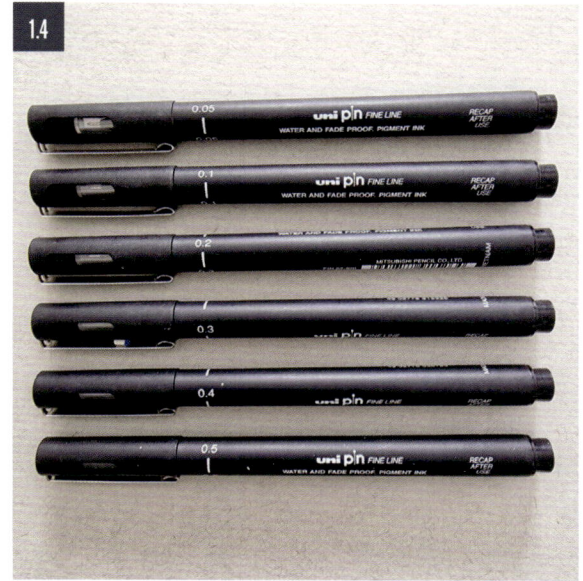

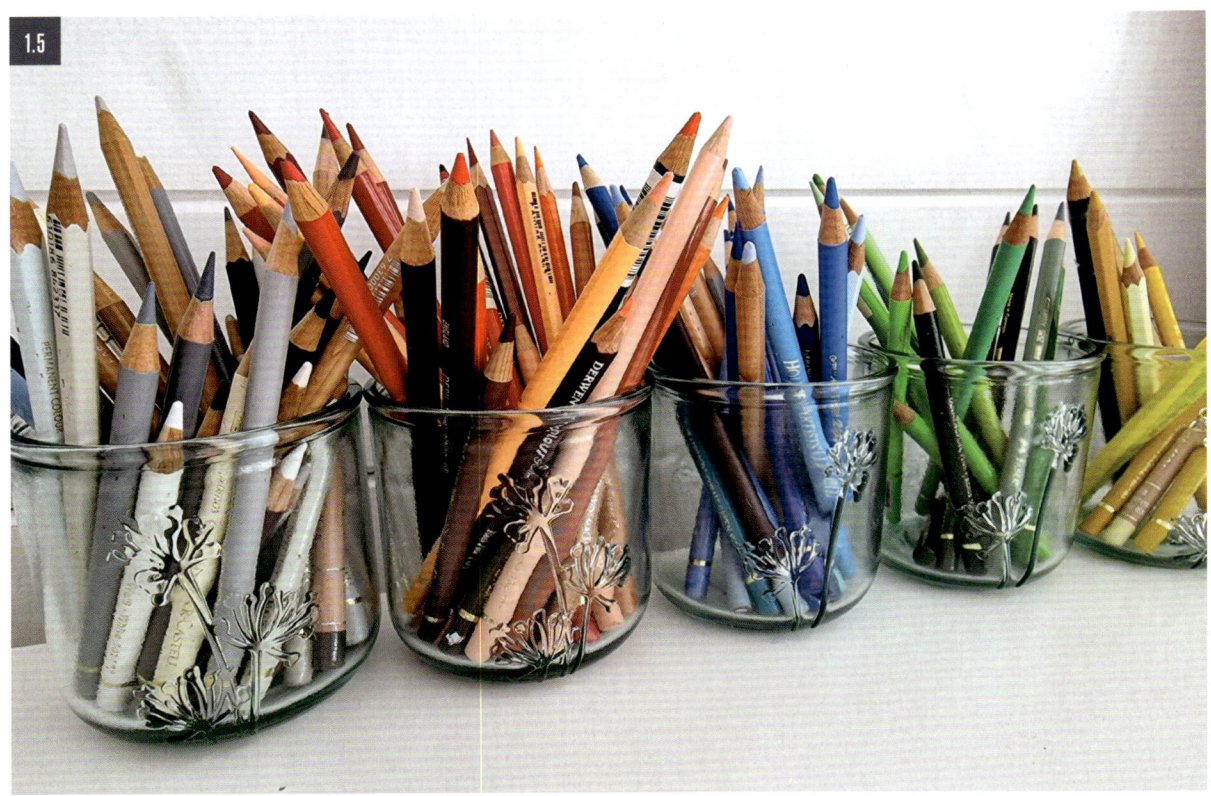

I have a core set of colours that get used and replaced continuously, and other colours I couldn't resist buying that rarely get used but are nevertheless beautiful to have and occasionally use.

Here are the main qualities I look for in a pencil:

▶ It must be smooth and creamy and blend easily.
▶ The colour must be lightfast, bright, and vivid.
▶ It must layer well and be capable of creating rich, opaque colour.

Most of my pencils are from the artists' quality brand Faber-Castell Polychromos. I have settled on consistently using this brand because the pencils tick all the boxes for my requirements. They are also readily available from many online stores and local art shops.

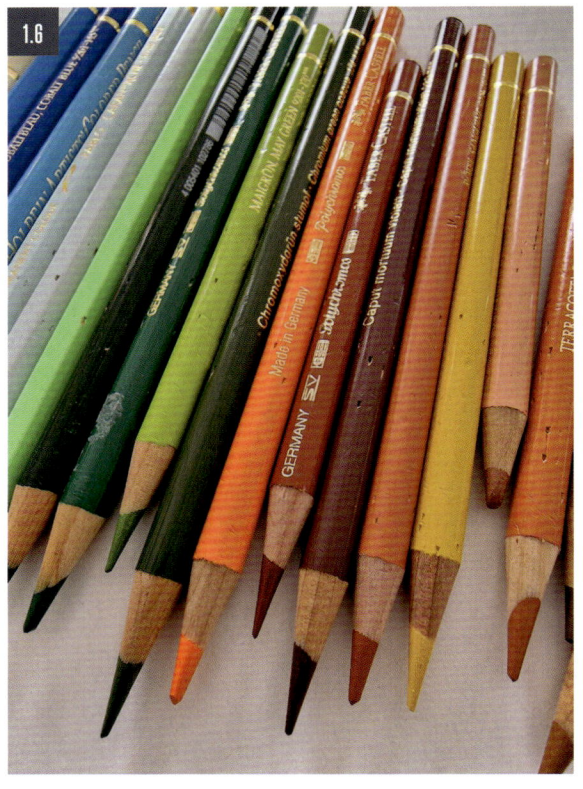

These pencils have oil pastel lead that blends really well. The lead is highly resistant to breaking, can be sharpened, and is capable of holding a sharp point, which is essential for detailed work. They also come in a huge range of lightfast and vivid colours that are smudge proof and water resistant.

My other favourite brands that I use in combination with the Polychromos are Pablo pencils by Caran d'Ache and Holbein pencils. Both of these brands tick all my boxes and have beautiful, soft, opaque colours.

Other popular pencil brands are Prismacolor and Luminance 6901, which is also made by Caran d'Ache.

BLENDERS

I use a double-ended, rubber-tipped pastel blender for blending and pushing my pencil colours together (**FIGURE 1.7**). This is a useful tool designed for use with soft pastels, but I find it works really well with coloured pencil too. I like the way that I can push the pencil colours deep into the tooth of the paper and create a smooth finished surface.

You can also buy specialist blending pencils that do the same job.

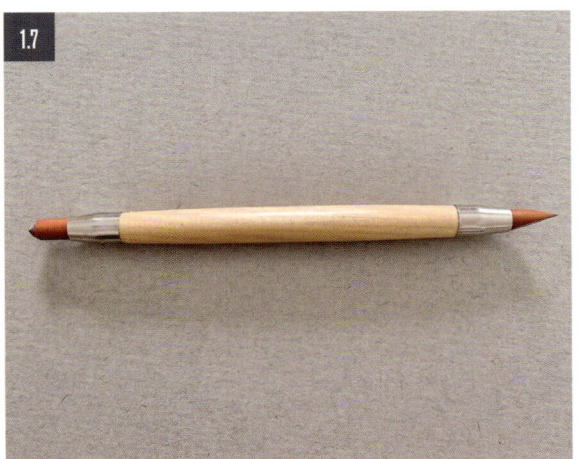

PAPER

Toned paper

My favourite paper to use for drawing is toned paper. I either use toned grey or toned tan paper—throughout this book I use toned grey.

I use toned paper because it allows me to use a greater range of tonal values in my drawings. When using a white pencil or pen on toned paper, the colour will stand out clearly, but on white paper you will be unable to see it at all.

There are many toned papers available, but my go-to paper of choice is one made by a company called Strathmore. It is a nice shade of mid-grey and is smooth and 100% recycled. It is a good thickness and can take a lot of work and pencil layers without buckling.

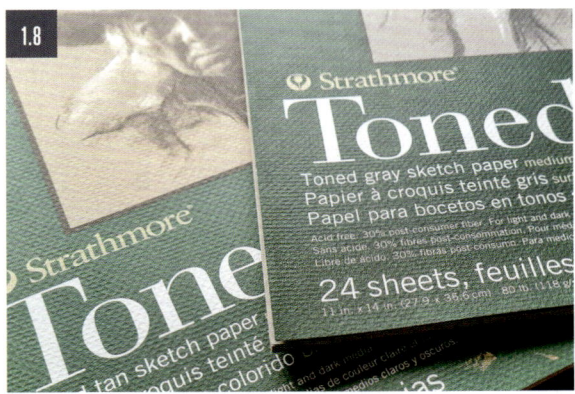

White Paper

You will need a sheet of white paper to draw on for the black-and-white drawing project in chapter 5.

A heavyweight cartridge paper or smooth, hot press watercolour paper works well for this purpose. Choose a nice-quality paper that is thick enough that it won't warp or buckle when you work on it. You'll want it to stay nice in case you decide to put your finished work into a mount/matt or frame.

You will also need an extra single sheet of either clean white paper or tracing paper to keep under your hand to separate it from the drawing surface while working. This is essential to keep your work clean and prevent smudging.

WHITE HIGHLIGHTING PENS

I regularly use white ink pens to add bright highlights to details within my work. You'll notice that they feature in most of the projects in this book.

White gel pens with a fine nib are great for this purpose. I use a gel pen called the Pentel Hybrid Gel Grip K118. It has a nice fine nib that is great for detail and it is inexpensive. Sakura is another great brand of gel pens.

Another great choice of opaque, white pen is a fine-nibbed white paint pen. I use the finest-nib pen by Posca. The white ink lays down nicely and is a very bright white.

Both types of pens have a tendency to clog up sometimes. If this happens, run the nib back and forth on a separate sheet of paper to get the ink flowing.

ERASERS

Erasers are an essential tool for getting rid of unwanted graphite pencil lines or coloured pencil work. I keep a few different erasers in my studio, including standard rectangle-shaped ones plus a fine-tipped retractable one that you hold like a pen. These are perfect for erasing specific areas

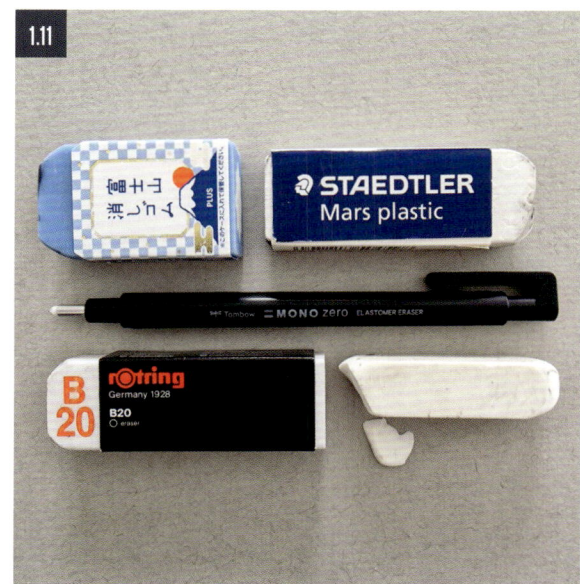

with good precision so you don't mess up the surrounding area. You can also target and erase very small details quickly and easily. Tombow makes a great one called the Mono Zero eraser. This is not essential but very useful.

> ➤ Another great way to erase a precise area is to cut a thin slice off a big eraser and use the resulting thin edge to erase.

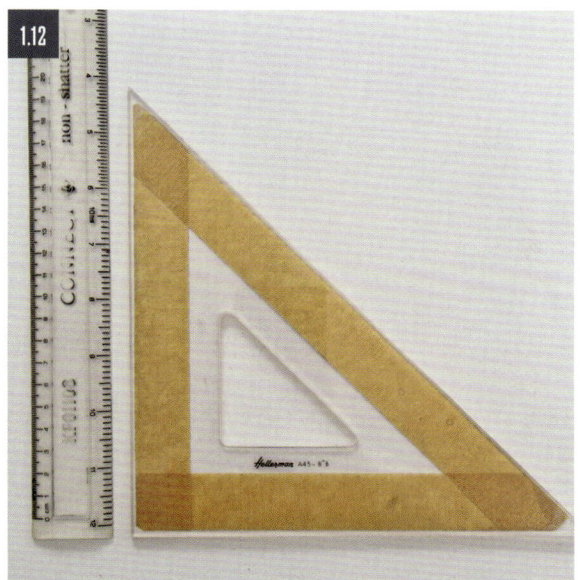

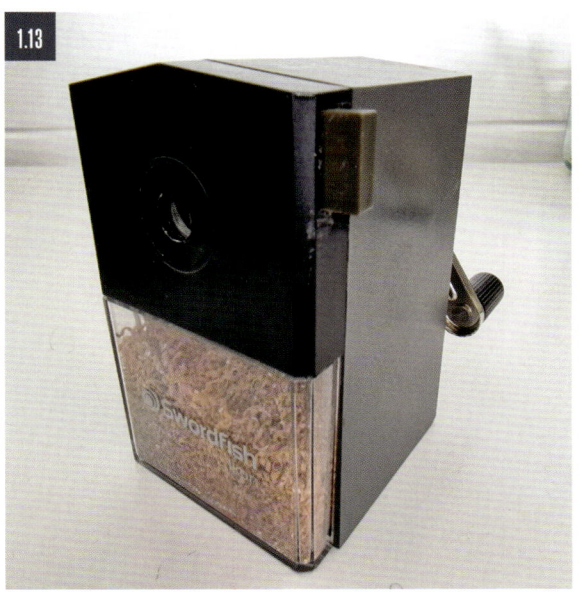

RULER

An essential part of my drawing kit is a 30cm ruler. I prefer to use a clear one so I can see what is going on underneath.

SET SQUARE (TRIANGLE)

A set square, or triangle, is a clear, plastic drawing tool to help you measure accurate straight lines at different angles. I use one throughout this book to draw perfectly positioned 90-degree vertical lines.

To do this, position an edge of the set square against either a ruler or a horizontal baseline that you have already drawn, and draw a vertical line along the other edge. You can also line the set square up with the horizontal baseline of your paper, and then draw along the other vertical edge.

PENCIL SHARPENER

A good pencil sharpener is essential to keep the points of your pencils nice and sharp. These come in all shapes and sizes, and I have used and discarded many over the years. I now only use a desktop manual pencil sharpener called the Swordfish Ikon (**FIGURE 1.13**). I've never had a problem with it, and it creates perfect point every time! You can also buy replacement blades for it.

I am sure you can buy sharpeners that are very similar, but after finding this to be excellent I stopped looking any further.

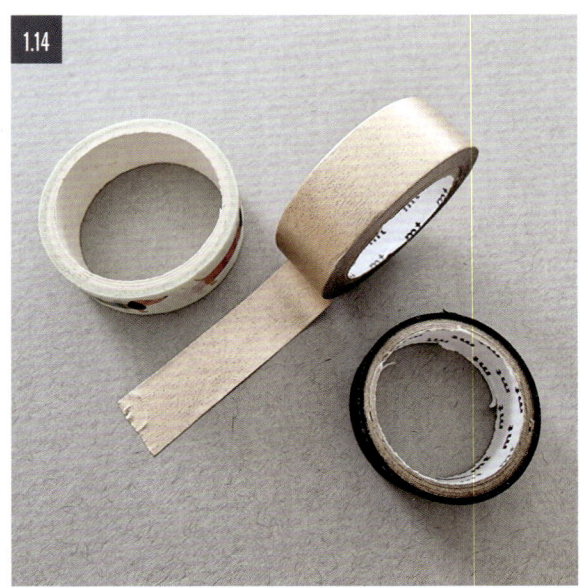

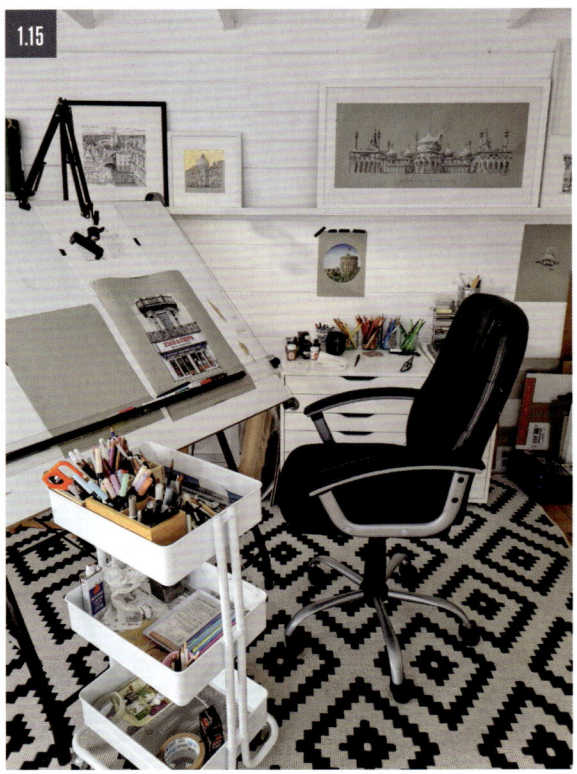

MASKING TAPE OR WASHI TAPE

Masking tape and washi tape are lightly adhesive tapes to be used for holding your paper in place on your work surface. I recommend choosing one that is low tack, easy to remove, and doesn't leave a residue behind or damage your paper. Washi tape also comes in many pretty colours and designs!

SETTING UP

Before you start drawing, it's important to set up your workspace. Gather everything you will need for each project and make sure your equipment is nice and clean.

I always clean my working area before I start a new project. I also like to organise and tidy up my pens and pencils. Going through this ritual puts me in the right frame of mind to start something fresh and new: clear workspace, clear mind!

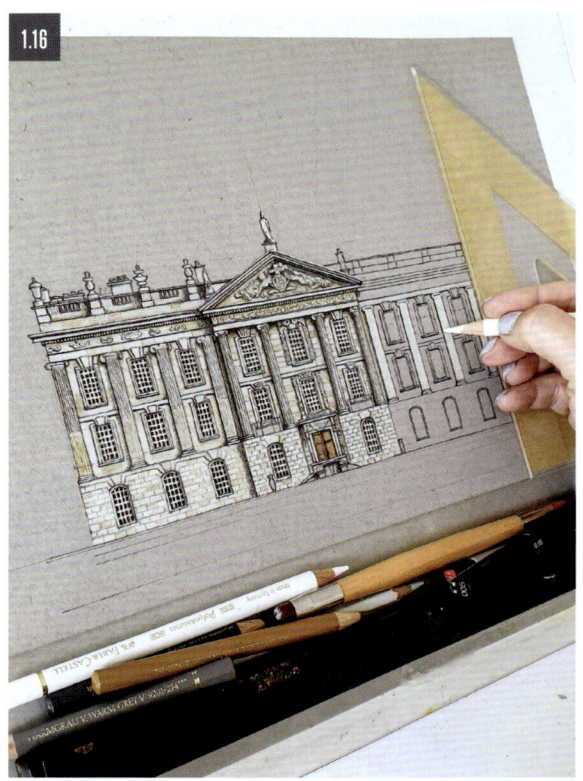

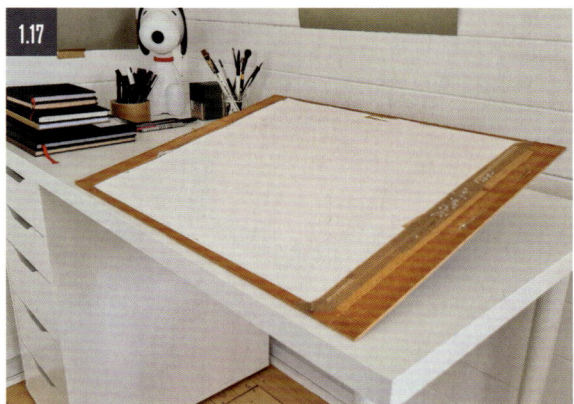

Deciding where you will set up and work is important too. Make sure that you have good, natural light or have a decent lamp nearby. If you are right-handed, ideally the light source should be on the left of you so that your right hand doesn't cast a shadow on your artwork, and vise versa if you are left-handed.

I work at a large A0 drawing board that I inherited from brother. You can buy small versions of these that you can place on top of a desk or table. Some have parallel rulers across them, which makes the drawing out process much easier.

> ➤ I realise it's not possible or practical for everyone to have a drawing board. A great alternative is to make your own workstation by stacking a few books on top of each other on your desk or table, and then placing a piece of board across the height of the books to create a slanted work surface (**FIGURE 1.17**).

YOUR FINISHED WORK

Once you have completed your beautiful artwork, you need to store it carefully so the surface doesn't get spoiled. You can buy special spray fixatives to help preserve the surface, although I find that with good quality pencils, if the surface is blended well,

the colours don't move anyway. I would say that fixative is an optional extra, but I do use it just to be sure.

Store your finished artworks in a drawer, folder, or portfolio to keep them in good condition, preferably with some paper slotted between each work. Glassine paper is a specialist paper used for this purpose. It is an excellent choice to protect your artwork.

If you frame your artwork, it's best not to place it in direct sunlight on the wall. Avoiding sunlight will keep the colours within the work fresh and vibrant. You can get specialist framing glass that has UV filters in it, but it is more expensive.

Again, these are all recommendations to get you started. Over time, you will also discover your own favourite supplies and what works for you! I can't stress enough that creating great artworks is not about having expensive supplies. The most important factor will always be the effort you put in, plus the magical ingredients of patience and practice, practice, practice!

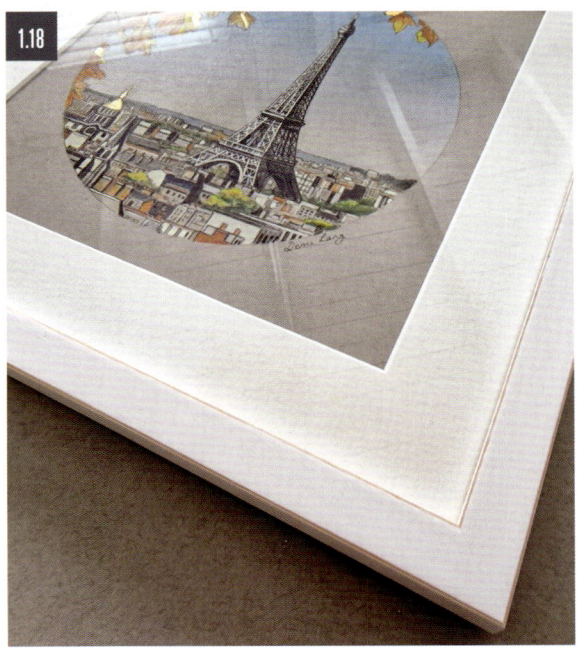

COLOURS USED IN THIS BOOK

All the colours are Faber Castell Polychromos unless otherwise stated in brackets.

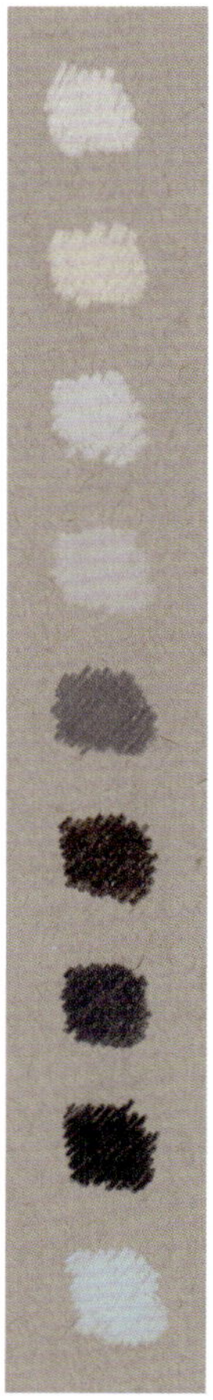

White

Ivory

Silver Grey (Pablo)

Cold Grey I

Warm Grey IV

Dark Sepia

Paynes Grey

Black

Bluish Pale (Pablo)

Sky Blue (Holbein)

Middle Phthalo Blue

Cobalt Blue

Light Green (Pablo)

May Green

Permanent Green

Hookers Green

Chromium Green Opaque

Chrome Oxide Green

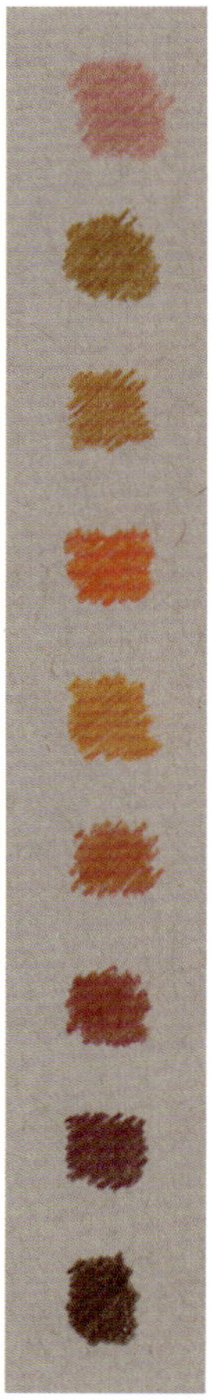

Cinnamon

Brown Ochre

Burnt Ochre

Orange Glaze

Terracotta

Sanguine

Indian Red

Caput Mortuum Violet

Burnt Umber

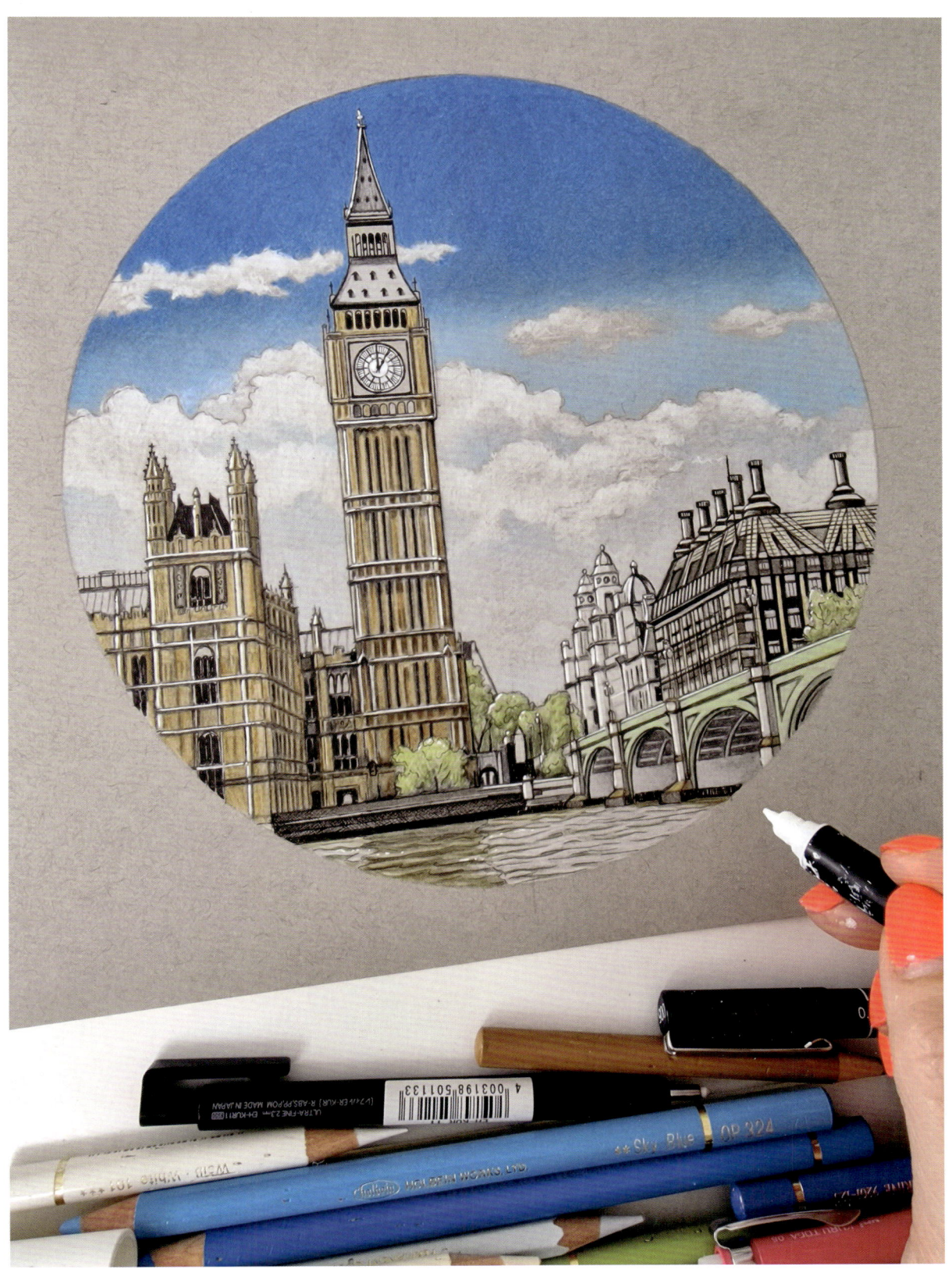

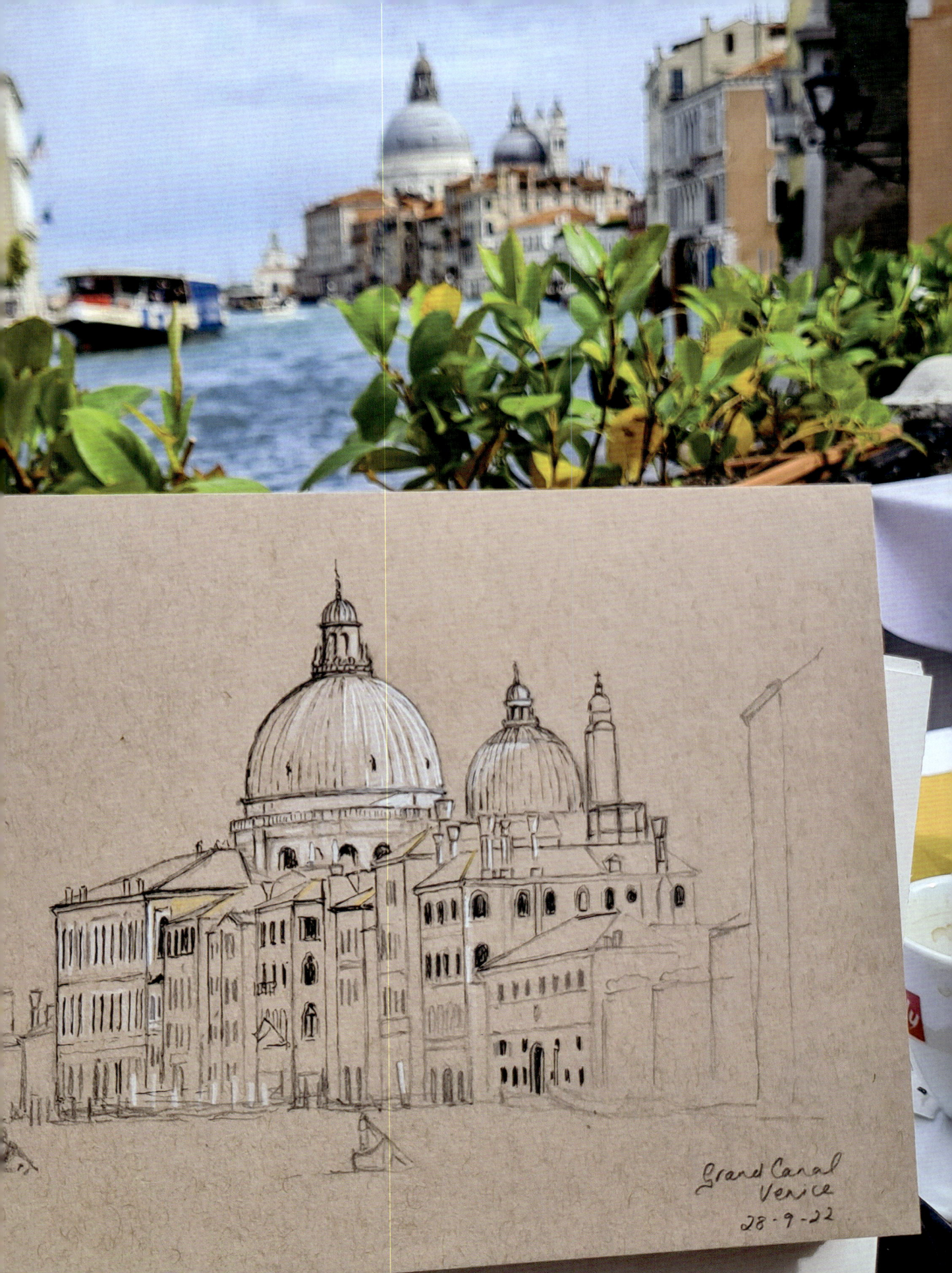

Grand Canal
Venice
28-9-22

CHAPTER TWO

Sketching and Building a Photo Reference Library

In this chapter we are going to discuss the benefits and pleasures of using sketchbooks and the value of creating a photographic reference library.

SKETCHING

Most of my work is done on my A0 size drawing board in my studio, but I also like to sketch outside on location and I do so whenever I can. However, because of the high level of precision and details in my art, it's not practical for me to draw a complete picture outside, so I spend many hours inside at my drawing board working and listening to podcasts and audiobooks to keep me focused and pass the time as I beaver away on my art. I will do a quick sketch on location when I have time and the weather allows, but this is not always possible.

If you have time to sketch on-site, it is an absolute bonus. It is not only an enjoyable practice, but it will also help you become familiar with your subject matter and its location. As you take in the beauty of your subject, you can make colour notes and identify the direction of light from the sun and any shadows that are formed. You can then use your memories of the day and other information you've collected along with your sketches and any photos you've taken to create your complete artwork back at home.

A sketchbook can also provide a lovely memory and visual diary of a holiday or day trip. Remember to add in the names of the places you sketch as well as dates and times. It's great to look back at these recordings over the years and remember the places you have visited.

Materials for Sketching

Sketchbooks can be any size you want depending on what suits you and your travels best (**FIGURE 2.1**). They range in price and paper quality as well. Paper quality is very important and something I never compromise on. I always choose a sketchbook with a good-quality, heavyweight paper so it won't buckle or warp with any medium I might use on it, although I usually stick to just pen or pencil. A good choice is watercolour paper or a heavyweight cartridge paper, and toned papers tend to

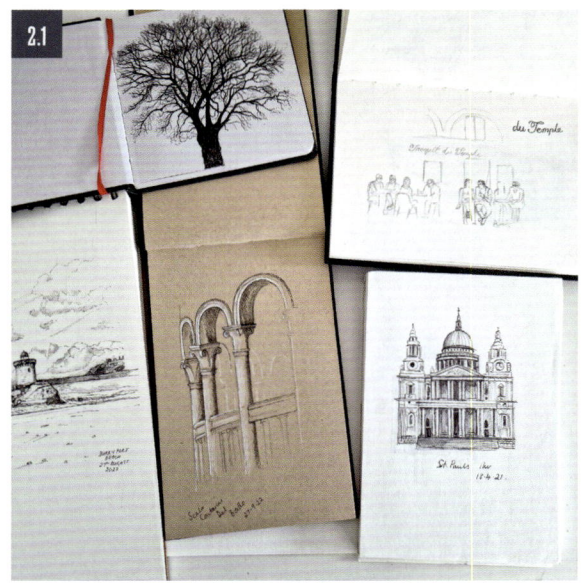

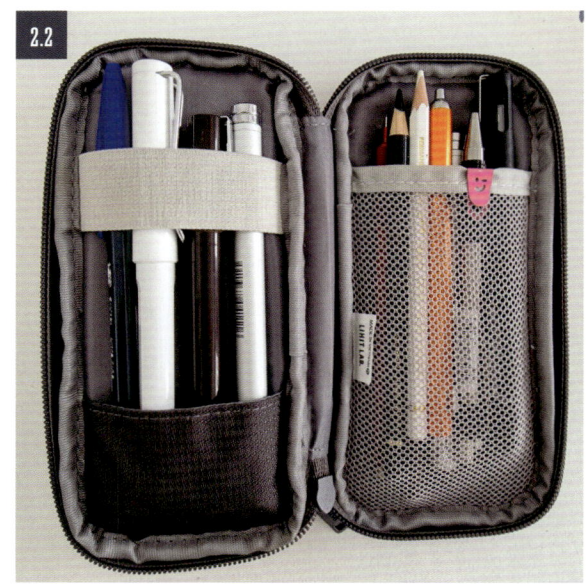

be quite thick. One of my first choices for a sketchbook is one containing toned paper, and I prefer it to be hardbound so that I can rest it on my lap or a wall.

I often have a lot of special or very useful pens stuffed in my pencil case, plus an eraser and a ruler (**FIGURE 2.2**). However, if I want to keep my bag light for travelling, I will just take my favourite and essential basic kit, which includes a mechanical pencil, a black fineliner, a white pencil to mark in any highlights created by the sun, and an eraser. I will fit these into the smallest pencil case I have and, along with my sketchbook, this is all I will need.

If you don't sketch already, it might be something you would enjoy. People will stop and look at what you are doing and may want to talk to you and ask questions. Try not to be shy, and say thank you to any compliments. You may even get lucky and sell your finished sketch!

Sketchbooks can also be used at home to just practice or doodle and to experiment with mark-making or trying out new pens and pencils. Enjoy the process and have fun!

BUILDING A PHOTO REFERENCE LIBRARY

As I have already mentioned, although I love my sketchbooks and enjoy sketching on-site, my main source of reference is my photo collection, which I have built over time by taking photos when I am out and about visiting places that are of interest to me.

This usually involves walking around cities and towns looking for interesting architecture or visiting a stately home. There are so many amazing buildings in England, like Blenheim Palace and Chatsworth House, but no matter where you are in the world, there are beautiful buildings to draw. My day trips are an important part of my life and something I enjoy very much. Although it's not always possible to visit the places we create our art from, I much prefer it because I can really study and gain a greater understanding of my subject.

Working from photographs is sometimes the only option available—for instance, if you are working on a commissioned artwork and the subject

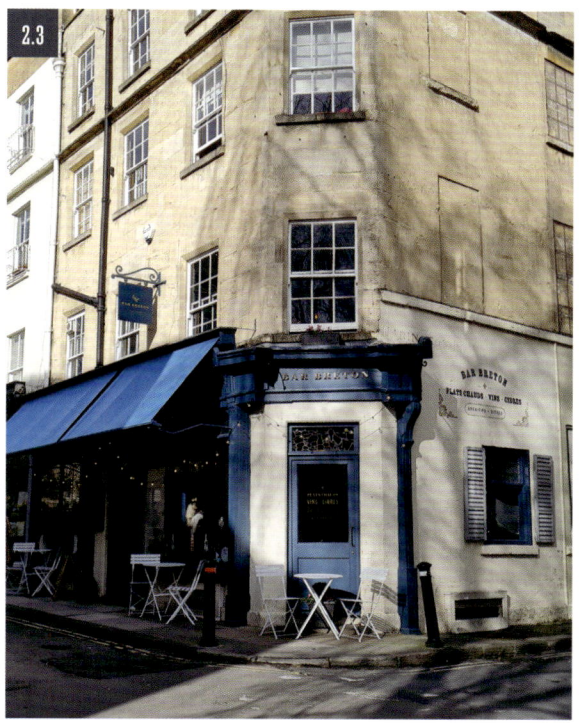

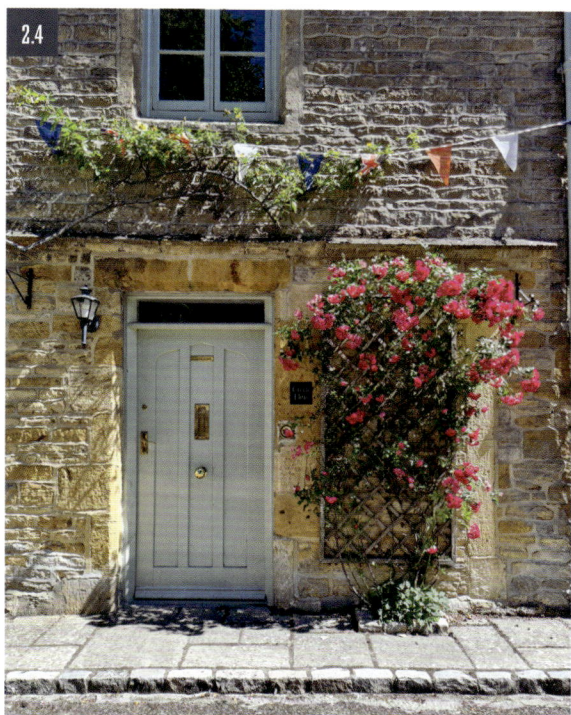

is on the other side of the world, you likely won't be able to visit the site. In these cases, I ask for as many photos to be supplied as possible to help me gain an understanding of the building and its surroundings.

Collecting Reference Photos

I have been collecting photos to use as reference for my artwork for many years. I keep my photos in folders on my computer or print them out so whenever I need an image to draw from there is a collection of my own photos ready for me to dip into. Keeping a collection of photos can help to inspire and inform your artistic work, and it's fun to browse through them when you are looking for fresh ideas. I find this especially useful if I am going through a time where I am feeling uninspired, although this is rare!

One of my favourite pastimes is exploring a new place on a sunny day and wandering around snapping away at the architecture bathed in sunlight.

On one of these trips, I might take a hundred photographs that I will go through at a later date, deleting bad ones and keeping the best for future reference. I can't explain the excitement of discovering a beautiful piece of architecture, knowing it will become a drawing at some point in the future.

Walking the streets and alleyways of towns and cities, you can find so much inspiration and reference to work from. Imagine the vibrant lettering of a shop sign or the dappled light falling across a busy café scene complete with tables and chairs and people chatting and enjoying the sunshine (**FIGURE 2.3**).

At any turn, on any street, you might find an interesting wooden door surrounded by elaborate stone carvings, an ornate window with flowers and shutters (**FIGURE 2.4**), or a magnificent church window. The possibilities are endless! Photograph and draw what excites and inspires you. This is especially helpful if the subject matter is complex and will be challenging to draw.

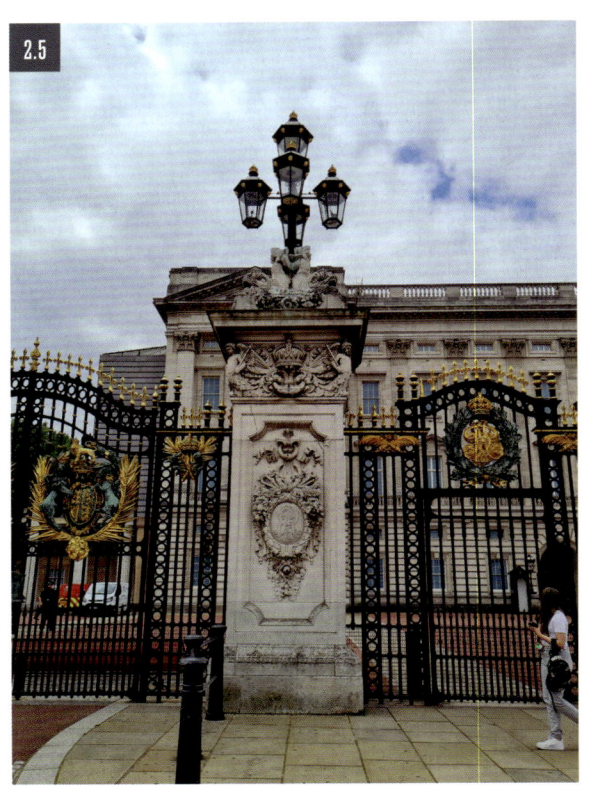

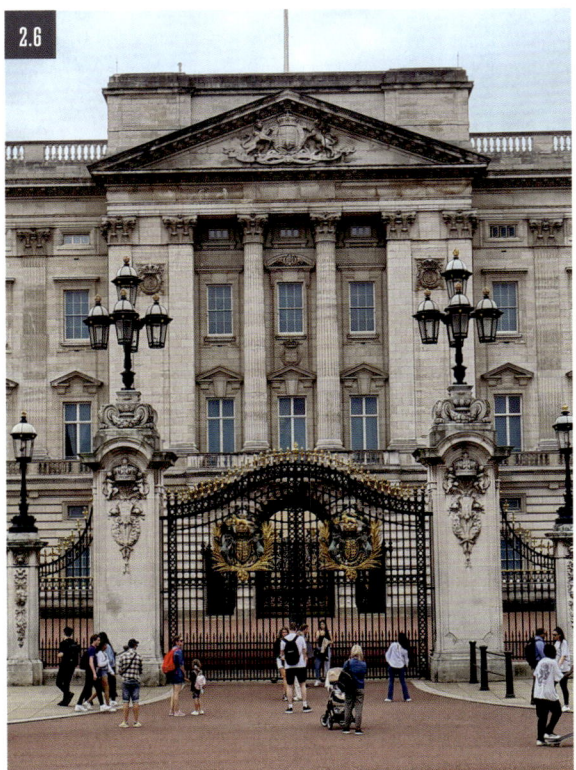

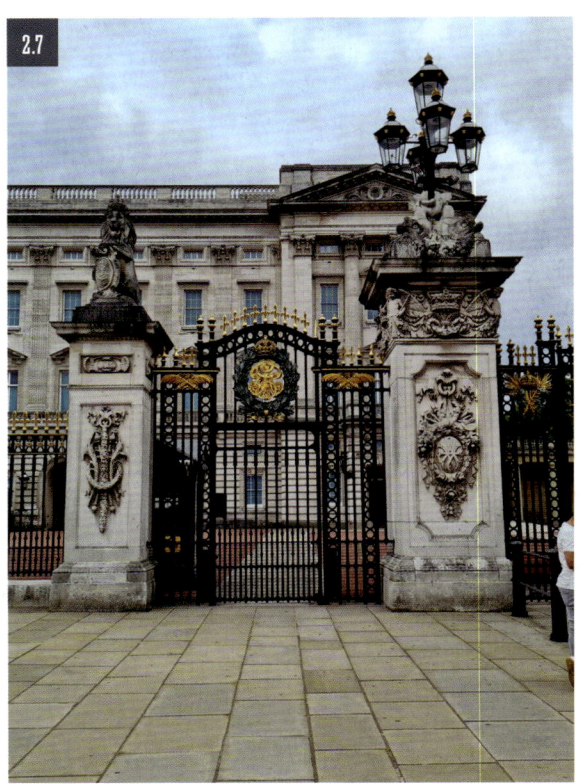

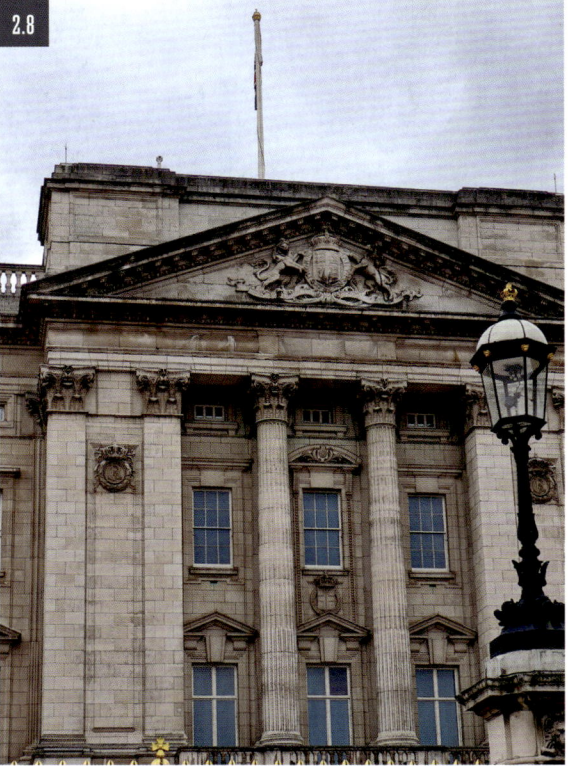

Having lots of patience will sometimes be necessary when you're out and about taking photos. For instance, sometimes you'll have to wait for a crowd of people to move out of the way of your view of the subject matter, or for the hidden sun to come out from behind a big fluffy cloud. You might then have only seconds to get the shot you want before the sun disappears again or another person walks in to block your view.

A good example of this is a recent trip I took to Buckingham Palace in London. I walked up and down the length of the front elevation of the palace trying to get a clear photograph of each section whilst dodging the many tourists. I didn't end up capturing the best photos and the light was very bad, but the closeup reference of architectural details has been useful for other projects, and I was able to study the intricate architectural details on the central pediment for use in another project (**FIGURES 2.5–2.8**).

I will usually try and make these trips during the sunnier months of the year so that I have lots of reference photos to take me through the dark English winter months when good photo opportunities are minimal.

For me, it's important to have a good photo to work from, as this is where it all begins. It's the beginning of an idea and hopefully I will have captured some good shadows. If you can't get out and take your own photos or you want to draw subjects you can't get to, there are many photo-sharing websites online, although it's important to ensure you don't breach any copyright rules. You can also find great photos to work from on Pinterest.

Choosing High-Quality Reference Photos

Working from high-quality reference photos is important for a great end result, and it makes the creative process much easier. The image should be as crystal clear and sharp as possible. If the photograph isn't in focus and the details are blurry, it will be much more challenging to create a good drawing. I find that holding my breath as I take the photo helps to keep my camera steady so I can capture a clear photograph. Look for spots on which you can rest your camera or smartphone, like a wall or table, or use a tripod if you have one.

Although the photographic reference is only a starting point, being able to see the subject matter clearly and understand the location of the reference will really help with the process. Because photographs are two-dimensional, you can't always get a full sense of a building from a single image. By visiting the building in person, you can gain an understanding of its size and scale in relation to other buildings, trees, and people that surround it. It's helpful to take some extra photos of these surroundings that you can look at back at home to put things into context.

Try to take your photos straight on, from a frontal perspective, so that the lines of the building façade are as vertical as possible. This becomes more difficult with taller buildings, in which case, I suggest moving farther away from the subject to gain a straighter perspective.

To improve the colour and clarity of photos quickly and easily, I use the "enhance" button in my smartphone's photo-editing function.

As we are talking about the clarity of photos, it is worth mentioning that a reference photo printed from a computer will lose its sharpness and clarity, making it more difficult for you to see the details. These printouts are great for drawing grids on top of the image to help with the drawing process, but it is also a good practice to work from a digital screen (computer, tablet, etc.) alongside the printout. This way, you have the best of both worlds and can zoom in on details on the screen, and then view the building as a whole on the printout.

Large Subjects and Small Details

Sometimes your subject matter will cover a large area. If the building you want to draw is very wide or you want to draw an entire street, I recommend walking along the width of the building or street and stopping at regular intervals to take photos of each section straight on. You can then piece the individual photos together to make up the entire building.

I recommend zooming in and photographing individual architectural details as well. You often can't see all the details that are needed in just one photo of the subject, so it's really useful to take lots of closeups (**FIGURES 2.9** and **2.10**). Then when you are back home in your workspace, you have all the references you need to create a great artwork with lots of concise details.

You must be able to see architectural details to create a realistic drawing. If you can't see the small details, you will have to make them up. This is often the case with large buildings where some of the details are high up or you can't zoom in enough. In these cases, you will have to "suggest" details with loose lines that roughly indicate the shapes you can see (**FIGURE 2.11**). The ultimate goal is to include as much detail as you can to create

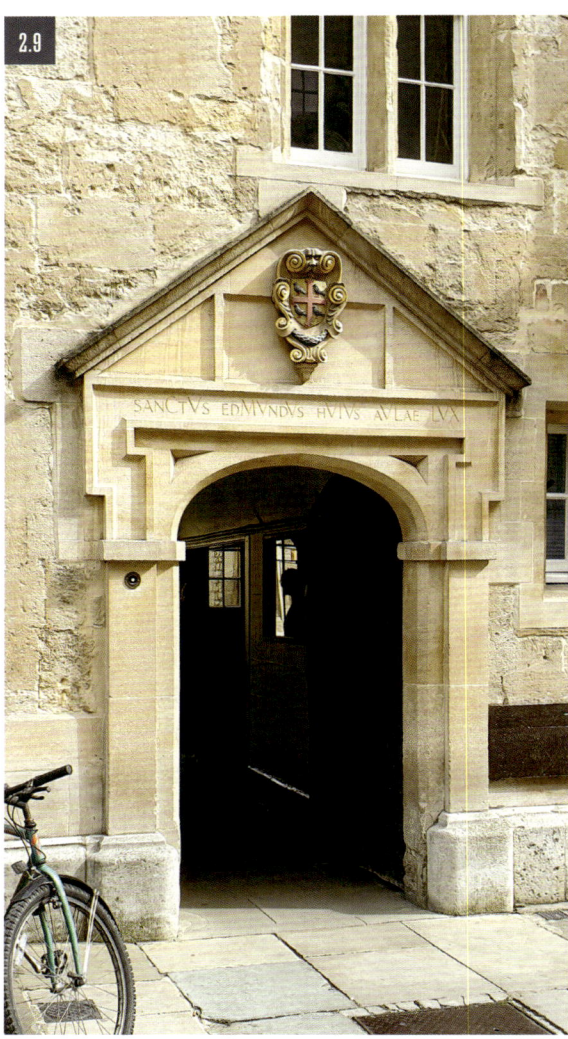

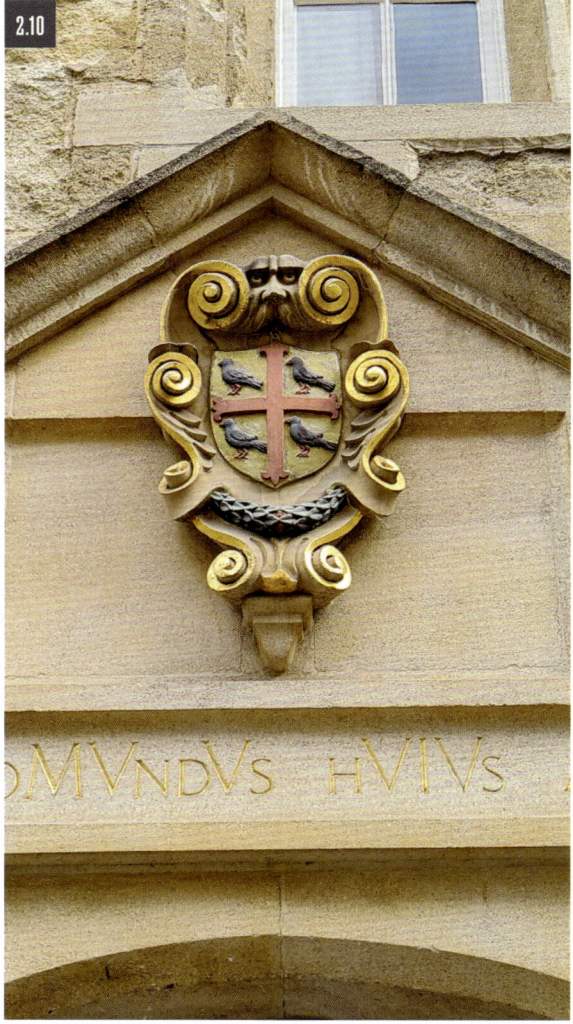

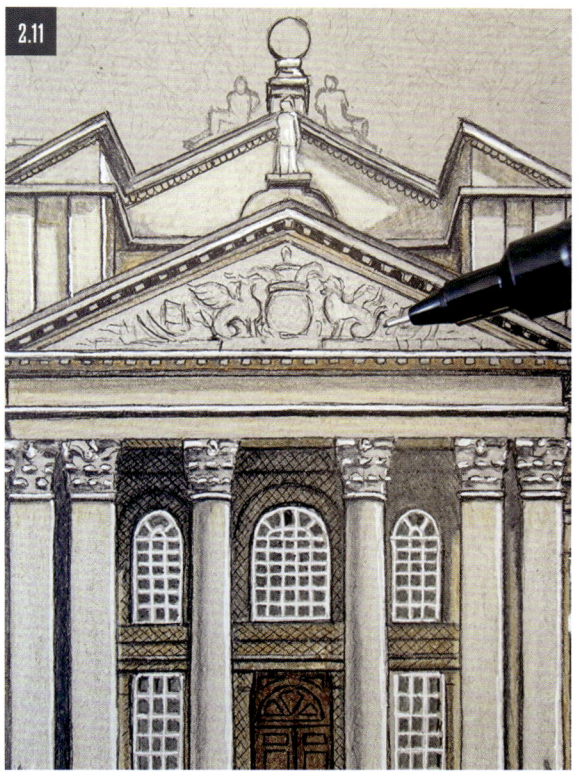

the best drawing possible. The more detailed the reference photo is, the easier the drawing process will be.

Lighting

Another important consideration when taking photos is the lighting on the scene. The best photos are taken in bright, clear conditions, and even better photographic results can be achieved when the sun is shining. This is especially important in the realistic art that I focus on where the best results can be achieved with photographs that have good strong shadows. I talk about this a lot more in chapter 3 under the section titled "Pop Point" (page 46).

Shadows will change shape and appear differently throughout the day depending on how high the sun is in the sky, so if you want a shadow to be in a particular place, you may have to return at a different time of day. Multiple factors will affect this, including the time of year and weather conditions. You can only learn this from observation.

I am more of an opportunist and usually grab good photographic opportunities as they occur, although I do sometimes go back to the same spot when there is a particular shadow I want to capture, such as a perfectly crisp shadow across a door. Sometimes luck is involved. If the conditions are right and you see something beautiful that you might like to draw, take your camera out and snap away!

It is possible to work from well-lit, clear photos that don't have shadows as well (**FIGURE 2.12**). You can make use of the dark shadows in the crevices where the different elements of a building meet up by accentuating them and focusing on the details available to you.

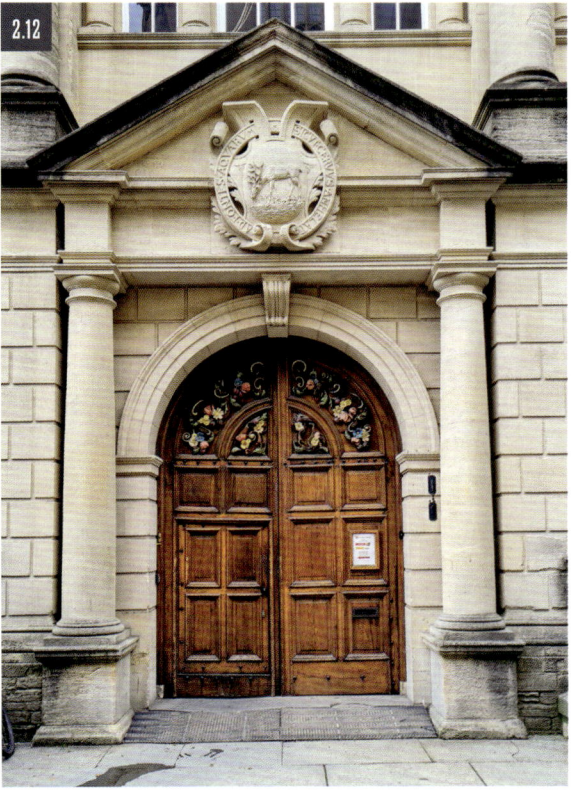

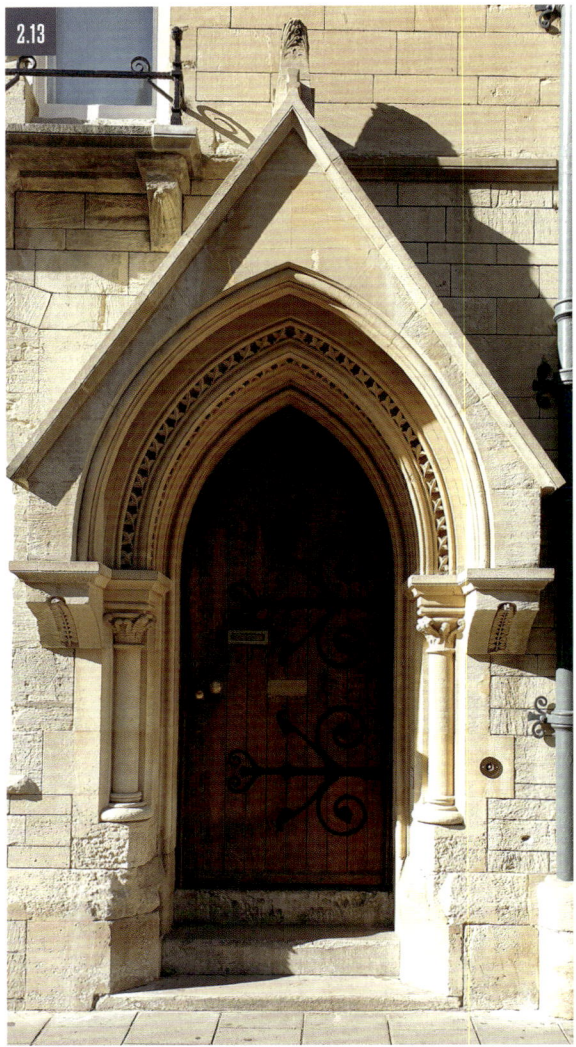

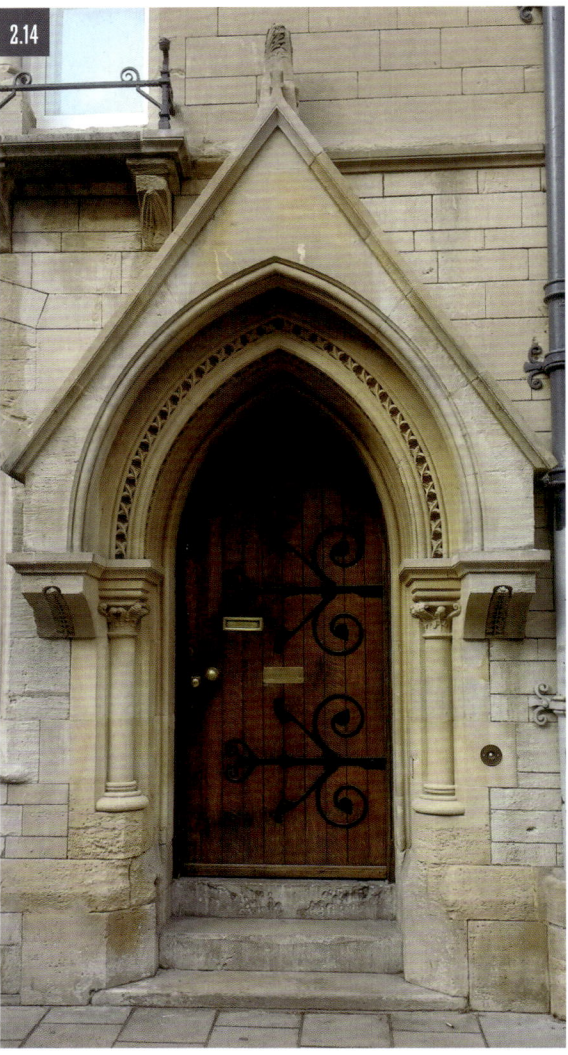

In other words, almost anything is possible if you maximise the good parts of the photographic reference that is available to you, but it will always be of benefit to have the best reference possible. For instance, I wouldn't work from a photo taken on a gloomy rainy day, as it just wouldn't work without some brightness and clarity. On the other hand, photographs taken in the snow can make for very beautiful pictures, especially if you're working on toned paper where you can use white pencil to indicate the snow.

Take a look at **FIGURES 2.13** and **2.14**, which show a reference photograph taken on a bright sunny day alongside a photo of the same door taken on a dull, gloomy day. These photos illustrate how capturing the light and shadows will help you create the best picture. The photo taken on the bright day has lots of fantastic shadows that would give a drawing some extra magic, whereas the photo taken on the dull day with no shadows looks quite flat. Again, you could work from the photo without shadows, but the one with shadows will give you extra-special results. You can also combine texture with crosshatching and cool colours in the bold lines of the shadows to give your work more life and interest.

The world is alive with architectural drawing material, particularly in cities and towns—you just have to go and seek it out. It's part of the art process and has become an enjoyable part of my life, and it might be something you enjoy too.

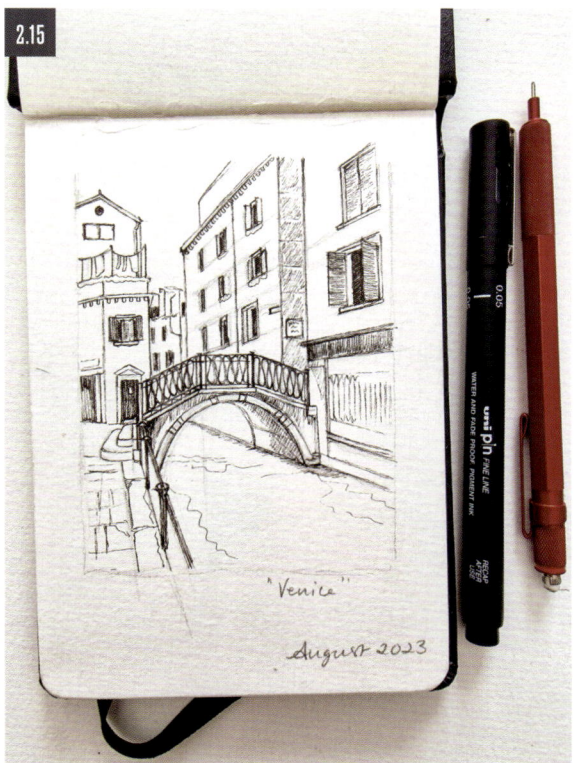

▶ Use your sketchbook to create a visual diary and lovely memories of your travels.

▶ Sketchbooks can be any size to suit your needs and can contain different types of paper. The choice is yours, but I wouldn't compromise on paper quality.

▶ Sketchbooks can be used anytime, anywhere for drawing, doodling, and practicing your skills.

▶ When out and about, take lots of photos for your reference library so you always have references readily available when creativity strikes.

▶ Remember to zoom in and take detailed shots of the buildings you're photographing.

▶ Photos should be well-lit, crystal clear, and sharp for best results. If the photograph isn't in focus and the details are blurry, it will be harder to create a good drawing.

▶ Take multiple photos, straight on, across the width of large buildings so that you can piece them together for more detailed shots to work from at a later time.

▶ Aim to take photos in sunny conditions where the light creates good shadows and highlights. Working from reference photos with these elements will enhance your work, as it creates greater depth and enables you to work towards creating a three-dimensional effect.

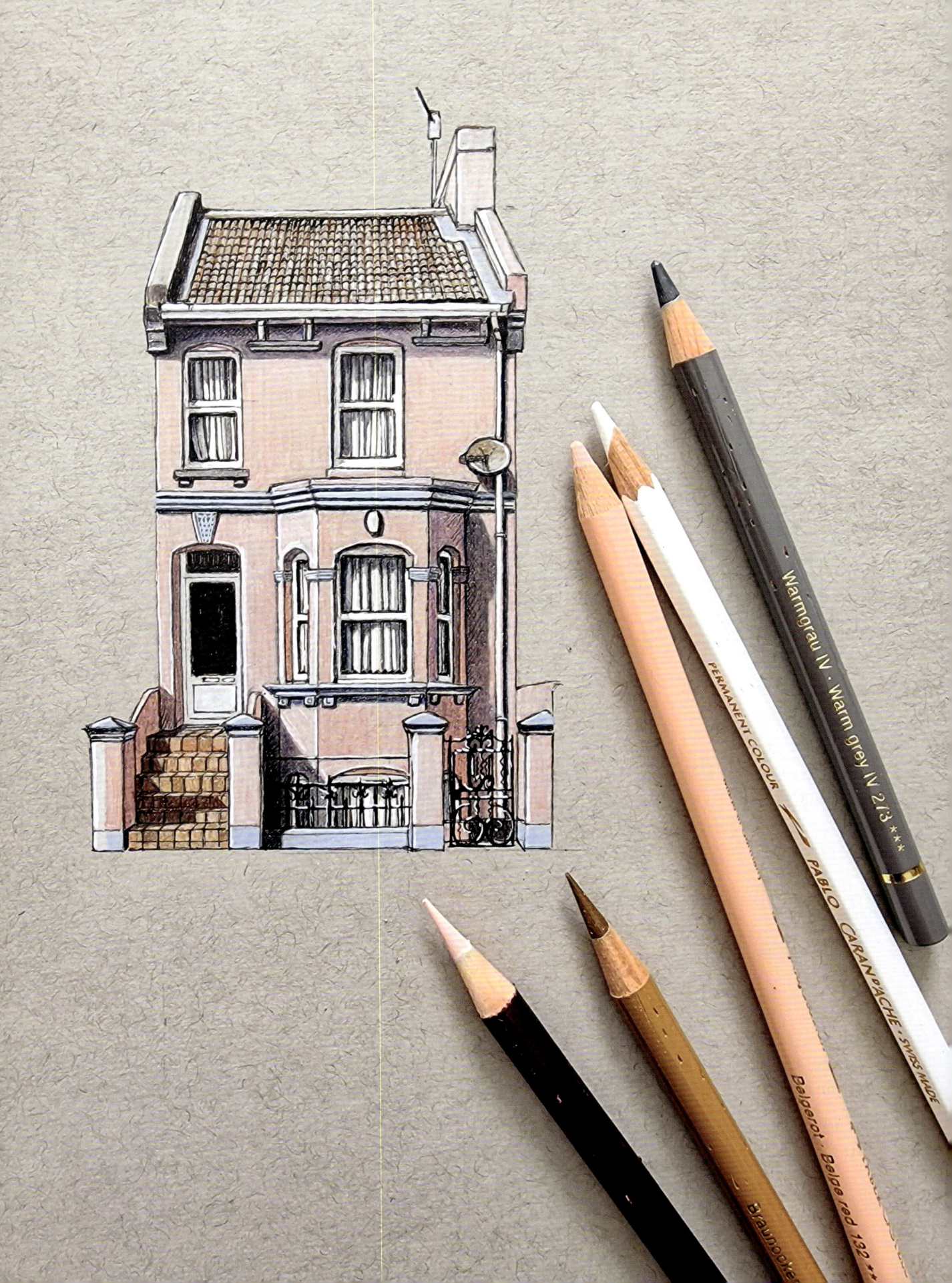

CHAPTER THREE

Art Theory and Techniques

In this chapter, we will look at the importance of tonal values, light, and shadow in a picture, and how they influence the overall look of an artwork. Having an understanding of these variables, and emphasizing the contrasts between them, will help you learn to "capture the light" in your artwork and create three-dimensional magic on a piece of paper.

Before we get into the details, I'd like to quickly go over the basic concepts of composition and perspective.

COMPOSITION

The composition of an artwork is the way in which the different elements contained within it are combined or arranged on the page. For the architecture illustrations in this book, I use what's called "central composition" throughout. This means I place the main subject in the central region of the page (**FIGURE 3.1**).

Central composition is a powerful way to draw attention to your subject and create a strong visual impact. When the main subject is right in the centre, it is very clear what you want the viewer to pay attention to.

My aim is for the focus to be on the beauty of the building as a whole, and then as the eye is drawn in further, for there to be strong emphasis on the shadows and highlights.

PERSPECTIVE

I don't concern myself too much with perspective (although I do understand the basics), as a lot of my sketches are frontal elevations. I just sketch what I see. However, if I am drawing a more complicated subject with some tricky perspective, I use the grid method to help me get the perspective just right. This is particularly useful for large-scale work. In **FIGURE 3.1**, you can clearly see the grid lines I've used to help me draw the complicated perspective lines of this artwork. See the section titled "Method 1: The Grid Method" in chapter 4 (page 55) for guidance on how to do this.

If you want to learn more about drawing perspective, there are some great books available that are

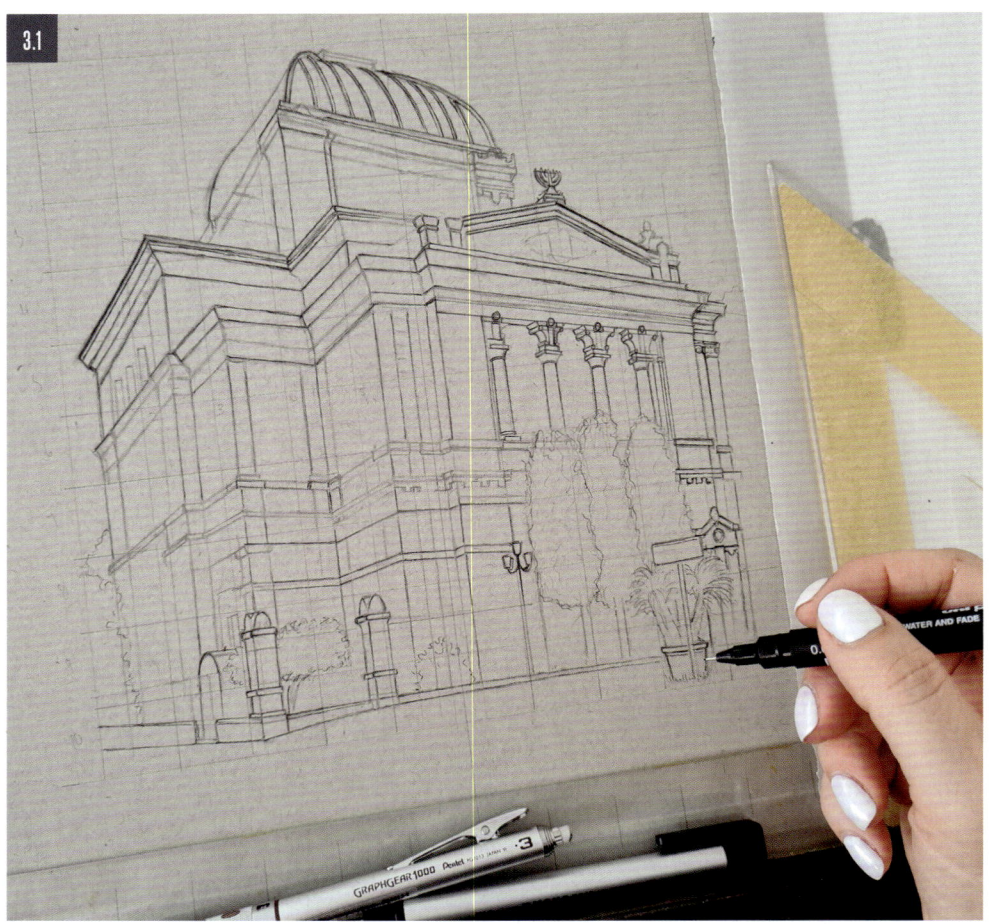

dedicated to this subject. I've included some recommendations in the list of resources on page 197.

TONES AND VALUES

Tonal value is one of the most important aspects to consider when creating great art. *Tone* just means how light or dark a colour appears to be on a tonal scale.

The tonal scale runs from white to black, and every colour has a tonal equivalent somewhere on the scale, so we use light colours to show where the light falls on our subject and darker colours to create shadows (**FIGURE 3.2**). Artists use this information to translate the light and shadows they see into different shades from the tonal scale, which then creates the illusion of a third dimension on the flat page.

Tonal Value Scales

Simply put, a tonal value scale is a strip of graded colours that run from white, the lightest value, through to the mid-tone values, and then onto black, the darkest value. This can be a useful tool to help you identify and understand light, middle, and dark tones more easily, and you can use it to check that the values in your drawing are correct. You may find it a useful exercise to make one of these yourself. This is easy enough to do: just draw some squares and fill them with the tonal colours

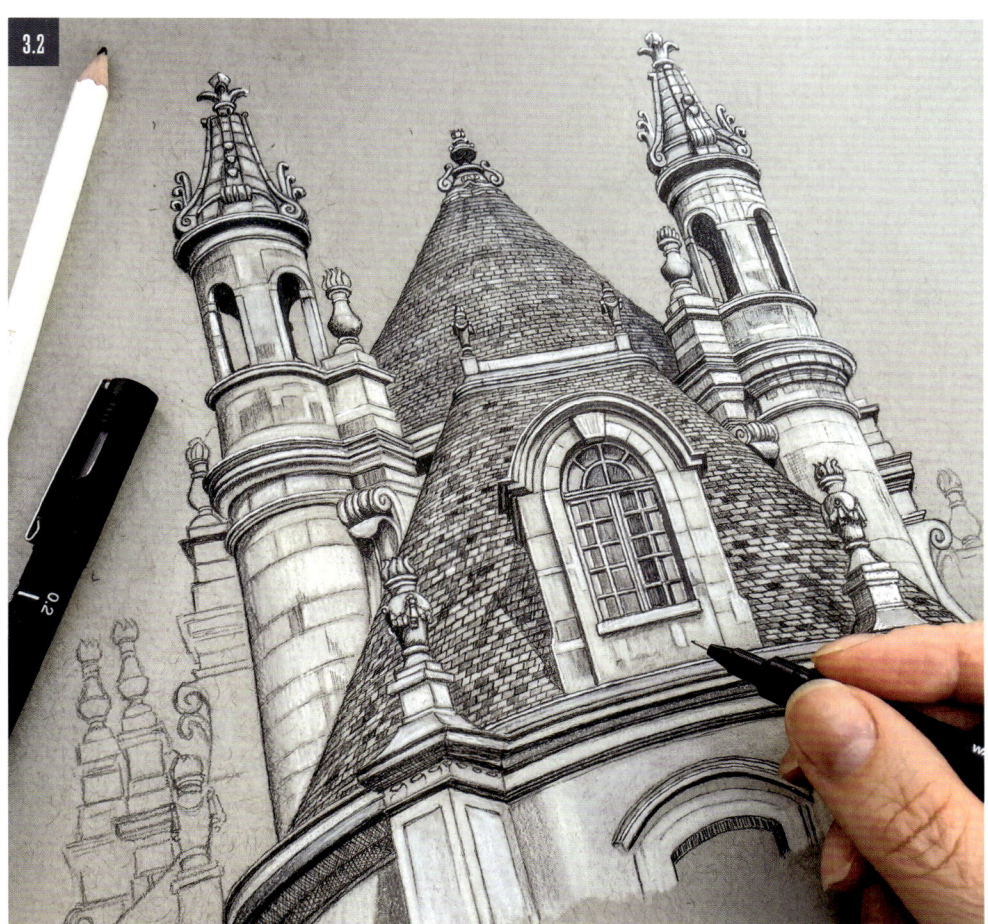

3.2

graduated from white to black using your pens and coloured pencils. Shown here are two tonal value scales, one on white paper (**FIGURE 3.3**) and one on grey paper (**FIGURE 3.4**), I made to demonstrate how you can see the lightest tones more clearly on toned paper than on white paper. You can use these scales to help you make your own.

I choose to use toned grey or tan paper a lot in my work because it has the added benefit of enabling me to see and use the lightest tones on the scale to my advantage. The brightest tone on the value scale, white, stands out predominantly against the toned grey and tan paper, imitating and creating the illusion of the light. This is an age-old way of working used by artists for centuries that I really enjoy. I hope you will enjoy it too.

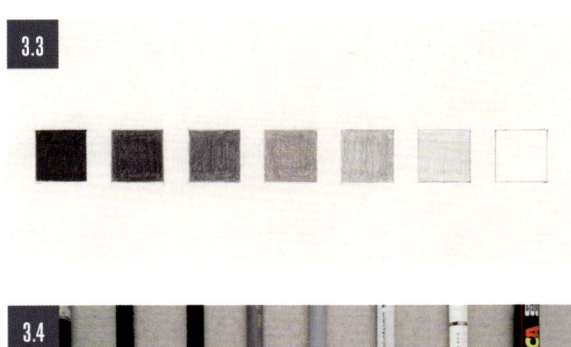

3.3

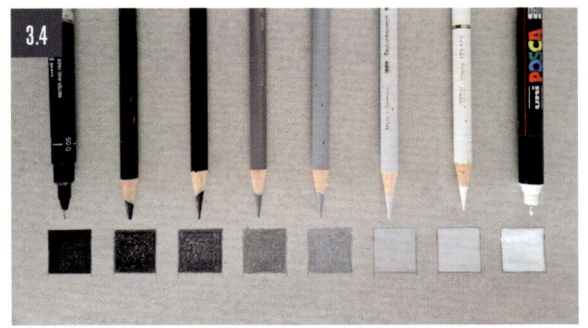

3.4

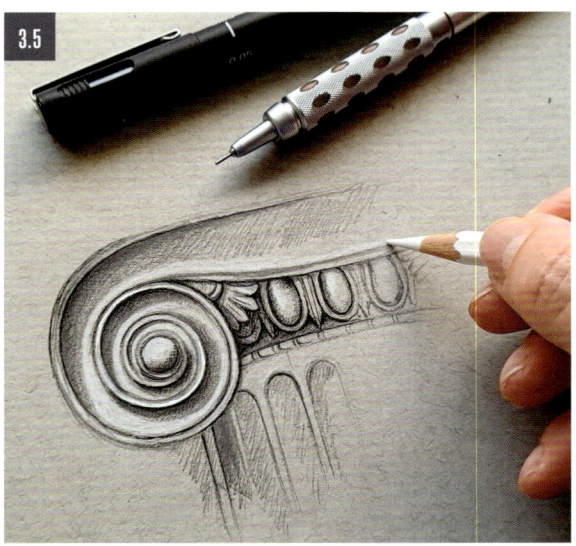

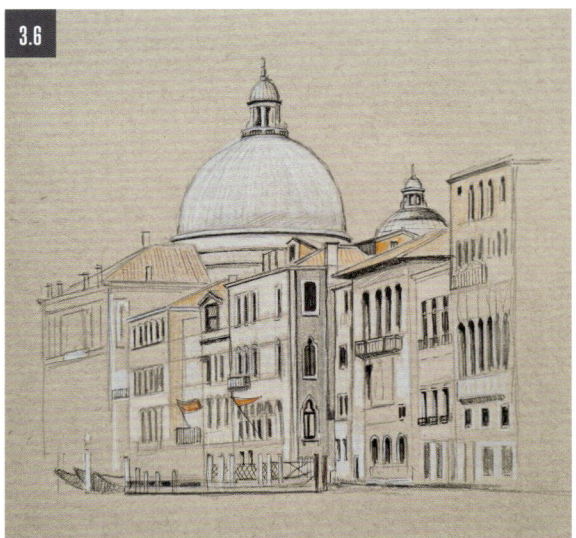

In **FIGURE 3.5** you can see how well the lightest tones stand out on the toned grey paper. The first swatch on the far right in **FIGURE 3.4**, is coloured with white Posca pen, which is very opaque. It is an incredibly bright white that I use to draw in and show the highest values in a picture (the highlights).

> ➤ Having a basic understanding of tonal values will help you capture a sense of light in your artworks.

Exploring Contrast

In any drawing, it is the value structure within it—in other words, the different contrasts between light, medium, and dark tones—that creates the illusion of light falling on the subject. If the tones used are too close together in value, the image won't stand out on the page, as there will be relatively little contrast. This kind of drawing is softer and gentler and has less impact. This is also the case for an artwork containing lots of different tonal values—there will be few areas of contrast. This works for certain styles of art, but not for the kind of high impact we want to create in architecture illustration. High-contrast images can be achieved by using fewer tonal values in between the strong black and white values.

In **FIGURE 3.6**, you can see an example of a slightly unfinished drawing I did of a scene in Venice. There aren't many contrasts in the tonal values at all. There is no shading on the dome, which makes it look flat, and the picture doesn't have high impact although the colours are soft and pretty.

Alternatively, contrast can be used to make your drawings more three-dimensional. Accentuating the light and shadows by using extremes in values (more light and dark values than middle values) will help you to create a more dynamic, high-contrast drawing.

A work that uses a smaller number of values will also have very high contrast. I often work with just a few values: white, mid-tone grey, and dark grey or black. **FIGURE 3.7** is a good example of a drawing I created using just a few tones from the tonal value scale. Although this drawing of Tempietto di Bramante is unfinished, it already has a three-dimensional quality.

It is by observing and then using different tonal values that we are able to see light and dark in an artwork. This then gives the drawing a three-dimensional quality, making the image stand out on the page.

Drawing and Illustrating Architecture

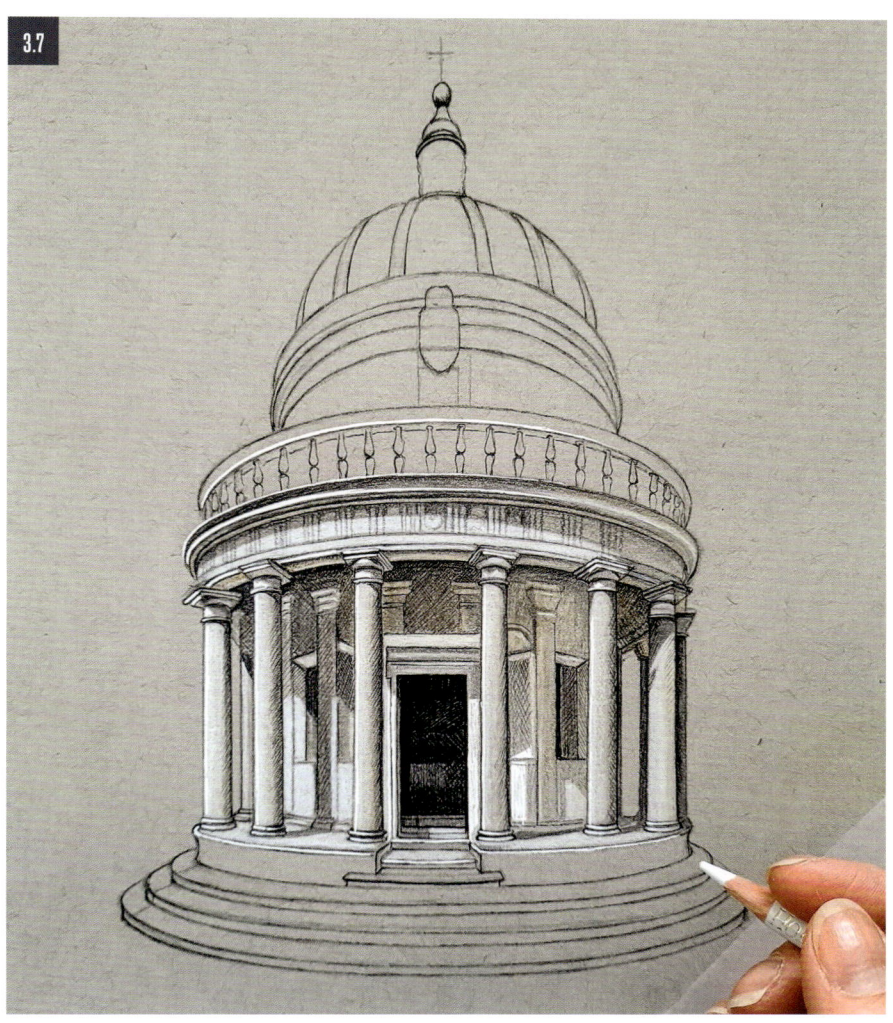

HIGHLIGHTS AND SHADOWS

Now let's look at light and shadows. The highlights and shadows are what visually define an object.

It is by adding highlighting and shading to a drawing that we can bring it to life and give it shape and form. Highlights and shadows give your artwork depth and dimension, taking it from a flat, lifeless image into a three-dimensional form.

Before you can draw the appropriate values that illustrate light and shadows correctly, it will help to be able to understand the basics of how light reacts when it hits an object.

The Light Source: This is the direction from which the strongest light originates—usually the sun. The placement of the light source affects every aspect of a drawing.

Shadows: These are the areas of an object that receive very little or no light.

Having areas of sharp contrast between light and shade in different parts of your subject matter will help to create a strong sense of perspective.

➤ The direction of the light source tells you where to draw the highlights and shadows.

In the diagram shown in **FIGURE 3.8**, you can see how the light falls from the light source onto an object and all the different types of shadows that are created. I've included this to give you an understanding of the importance of light and shadows and the role they play in realistic art.

The diagram names a lot of different shadows and highlights; there are those that are on the dark side as the object blocks the light from getting to them, and there are those on the light side that have the light source directly projected onto them.

Who knew that there are so many different names for shadows?

Centre Light: The area that faces most directly towards the light source.

Highlight: The reflection of the light source and the lightest light.

Form Light: The area that receives direct light.

Terminator: This area divides form light and form shadow.

Reflected Light: Light on the dark side of the form that is reflected onto the form by another surface.

Occlusion Shadows: Where two surfaces get close to each other, a dark shadow will form.

Penumbra: The softness around the shadow.

Cast Shadow: This shadow is the terminator projected on the ground.

Form Shadow: This is the part in shadow.

Core Shadow: As reflected light loses strength, it creates the core shadow.

Halftone: Form light is divided into halftones that darken as the form turns away from the light source.

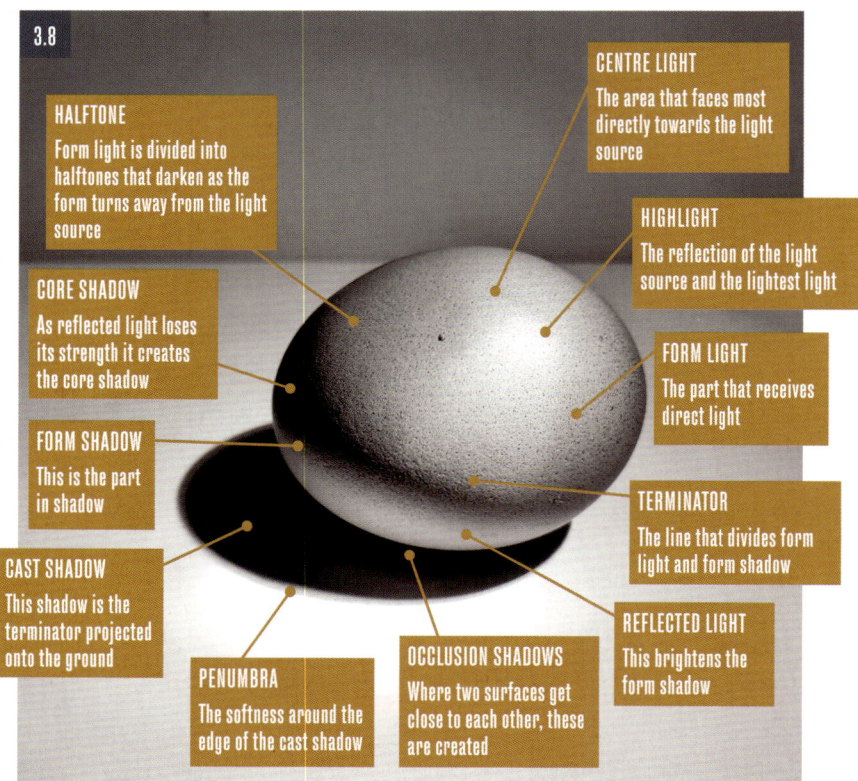

3.8

HALFTONE
Form light is divided into halftones that darken as the form turns away from the light source

CORE SHADOW
As reflected light loses its strength it creates the core shadow

FORM SHADOW
This is the part in shadow

CAST SHADOW
This shadow is the terminator projected onto the ground

PENUMBRA
The softness around the edge of the cast shadow

OCCLUSION SHADOWS
Where two surfaces get close to each other, these are created

CENTRE LIGHT
The area that faces most directly towards the light source

HIGHLIGHT
The reflection of the light source and the lightest light

FORM LIGHT
The part that receives direct light

TERMINATOR
The line that divides form light and form shadow

REFLECTED LIGHT
This brightens the form shadow

Light

In my work I tend to focus heavily on centre light and occlusion shadows, as using these two strong contrasts creates such high impact, which is what I am looking to achieve. My aim is to create a realistic drawing that jumps off the page. I want to capture the beauty and details of amazing architecture. I want to make a column shaft look round or create the illusion that you could walk through a door or archway (**FIGURE 3.9**).

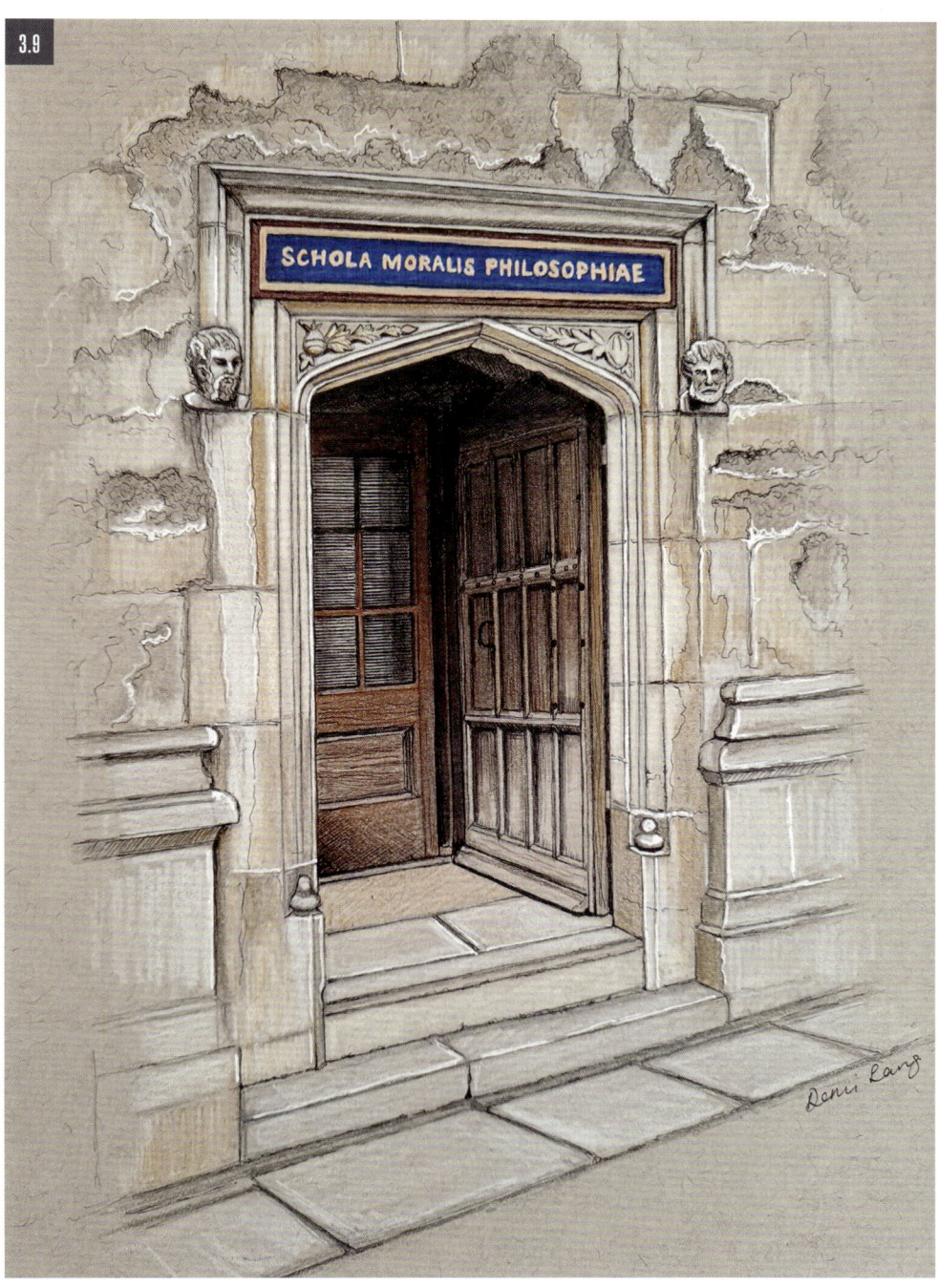

SCHOLA MORALIS PHILOSOPHIAE

When looking at objects or buildings, whether in real life or in photos, pay attention to how any shadows fall. And notice how strong the shadow is and its shape. How dark is it and is it graduated? How dark are the tonal values in the shadows? Where do they fall on the tonal value scale? Once you know where the shadows are you can work out where the light source is.

The strongest highlights come from the light source, which, as mentioned before, is usually the sun. Look for the direction of the light source. Where are the lightest values? Are there any strong highlights? Observe the direction the light source comes from as well, as this will help you put all the shadows in the correct place.

Here are some examples of photos from my own photo library with clearly defined, strong shadows.

In them, you can see the bold shadows created by the sun on beautiful, bright days in the Cotswolds and in Paris.

In **FIGURE 3.10**, the sun is high in the sky above the chimney pots, creating shadows on the left side of the candy-twist shafts and underneath the top edges. These shadow shapes add interest to a drawing.

In **FIGURE 3.11**, the sun directly impacts the right side of the structure and creates a well-defined, bold shadow all the way down the left side of the tower. Adding this shadow to a drawing would create a realistic three-dimensional shape, instantly making the artwork come to life.

FIGURE 3.12 is a photo I took in Paris of a typical French café. The photo has lots of depth and would make a great subject for a drawing with impact. There are a lot of mid-tone grey shadows in different areas across the whole photo, which then contrast beautifully with the cream-coloured stonework. The front-facing stonework is illuminated brightly by the sun as it hits the front of the building.

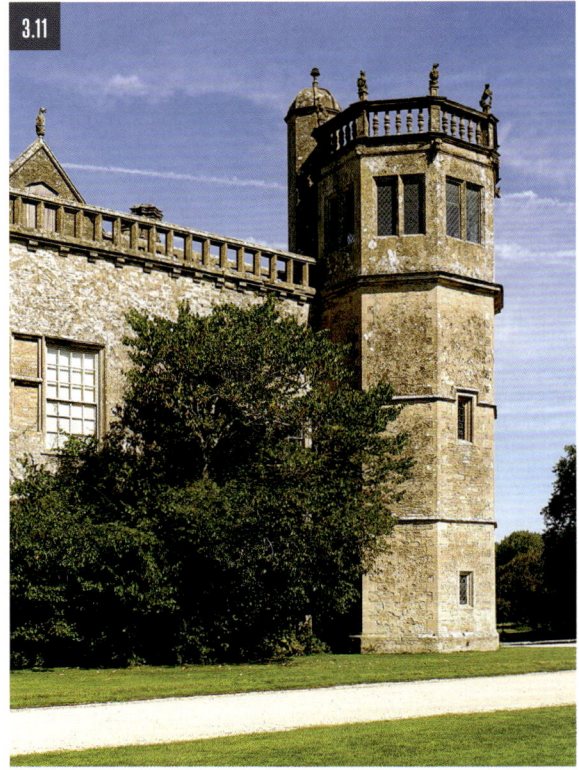

3.10

3.11

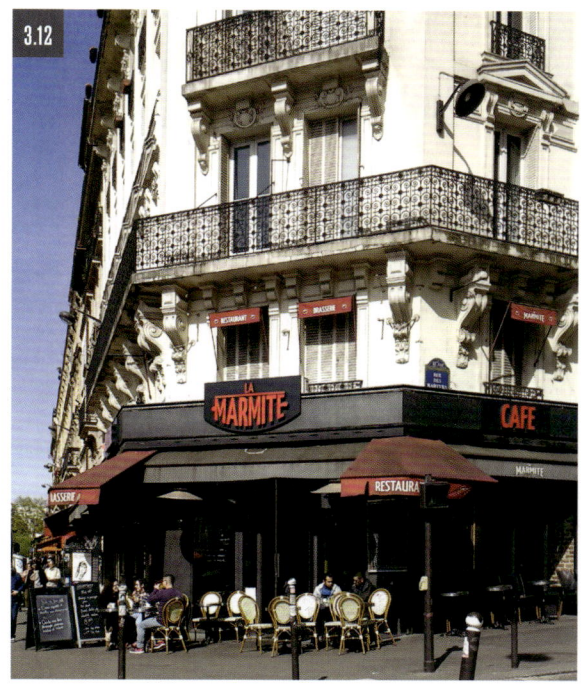

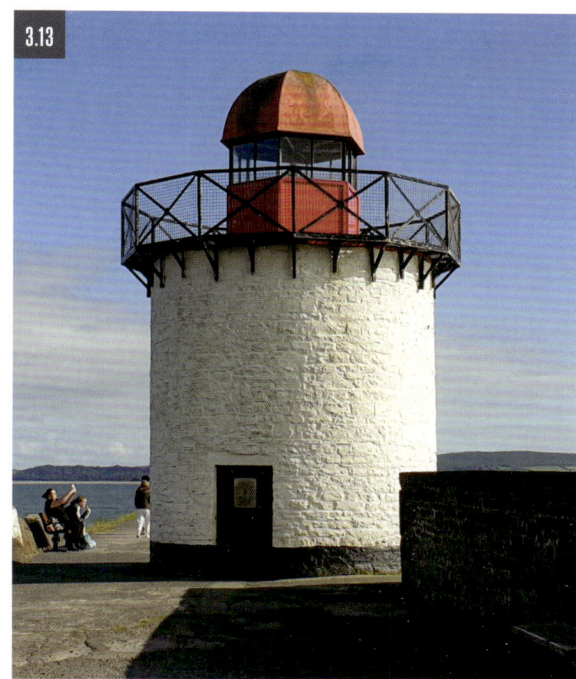

Further impact comes from the depth of the dark shadows under the café awnings. There are also other highlights around the tops of the chairs and tables.

In **FIGURE 3.13**, the sun impacts the lighthouse on the right side, creating a nice, graduated shadow consisting of mid-tones and light tones that travel around the circular shape of the building. If we replicated these tonal values with careful shading using coloured pencils, the end result would be a realistic three-dimensional drawing. The cherry on the top, so to speak, would be the added dark shadow on the left side of the lighthouse lantern, which further enhances the effects of the of the sunlight on the building.

Shading

It's important to remember that shadows aren't usually completely black. Be aware that photographs can sometimes make them look like they are. It's easy to make the mistake of blocking in large, dark, flat shadow areas without any reflected colour within them to add depth and interest.

In fact, shadows are often tinged with colours complementary to the colour of the object casting the shadow. I like to add interest to them by adding cool blues and violets or a gentle and warm yellow ochre near the edges. In **FIGURE 3.14**, you can see where I used a hint of violet in the bold shadows.

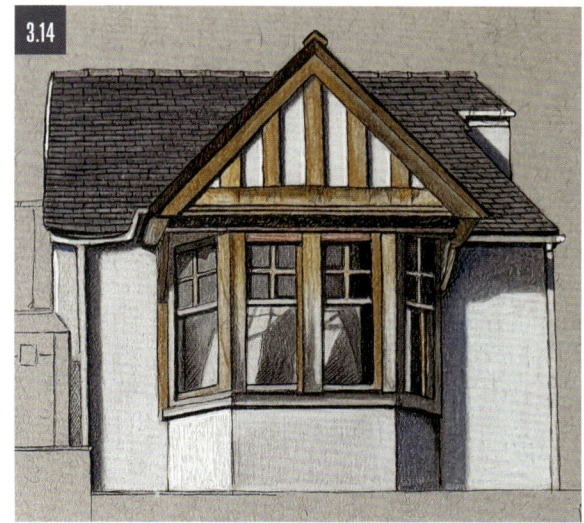

I also use crosshatching with a fineliner pen in combination with coloured pencil as a technique for varying the depth and darkness of the shading across the shadowed sections of a drawing (see **FIGURES 3.15–3.17**). The layers of coloured pencil are built up first, and then the crosshatched lines are laid down on top to create an interesting shadow.

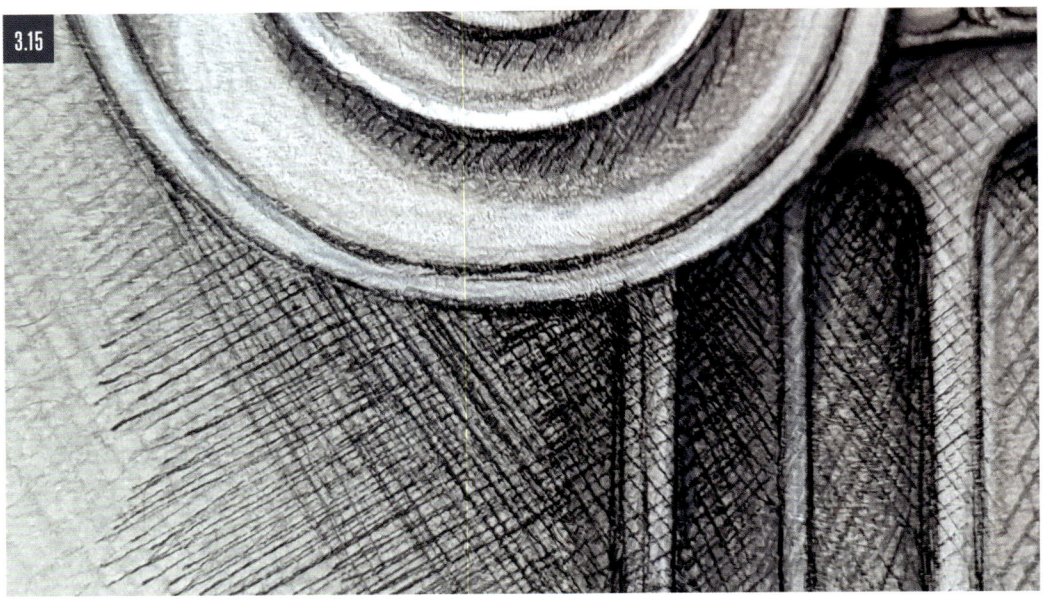

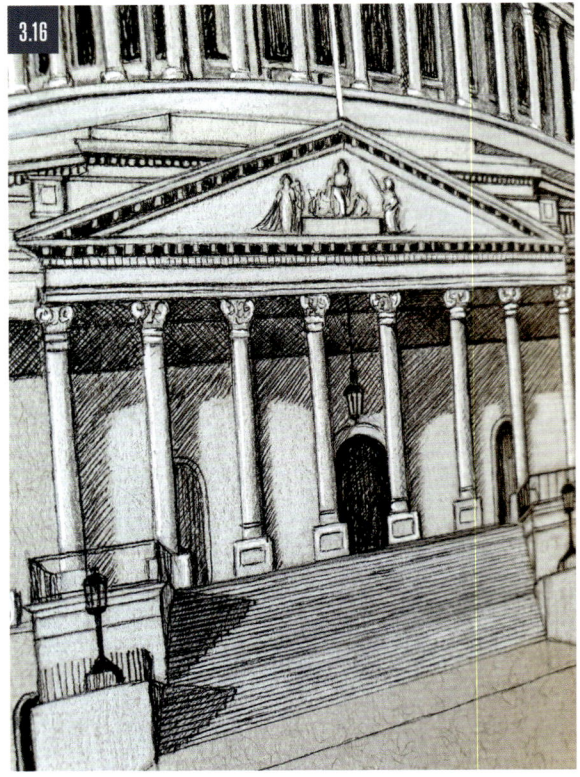

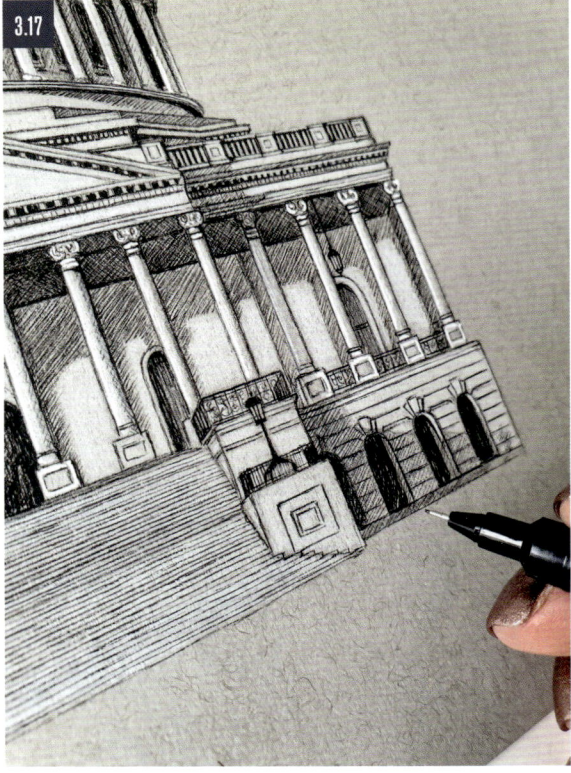

DRAWING TECHNIQUES

Crosshatching and Hatching

As mentioned in the previous section, crosshatching is a technique used by artists to create different tones and shading effects in a drawing. Basically, it is a series of parallel lines drawn at two angles that cross over each other to create the impression of light, shadow, and form (**FIGURES 3.18–3.20**). I use this simple and effective technique in all my work to build shaded areas and darken shadows.

Crosshatching is an excellent technique for creating strong, dark shadows and areas of interest. The closer the lines are together and the more they cross over each other, the darker the tone of the shading will be.

You can also graduate the placement of the lines to create toned effects. For instance, you would use a dense concentration of lines at the darkest park of a shadow, then gradually widen the placement of the lines across the shadow to its lighter edges (**FIGURE 3.21**).

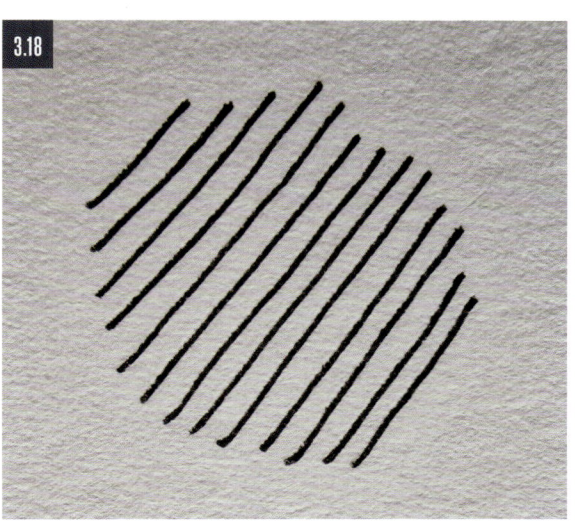

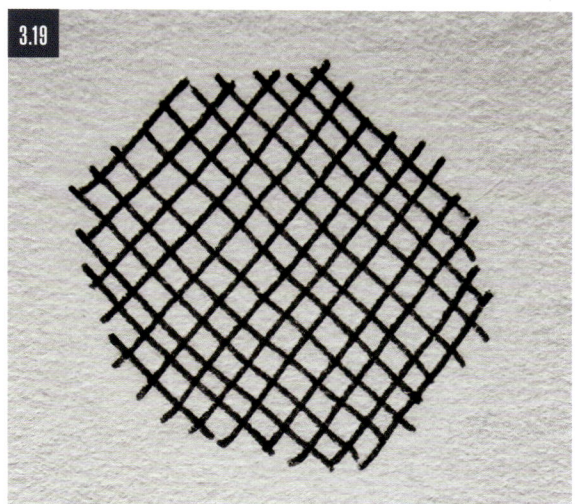

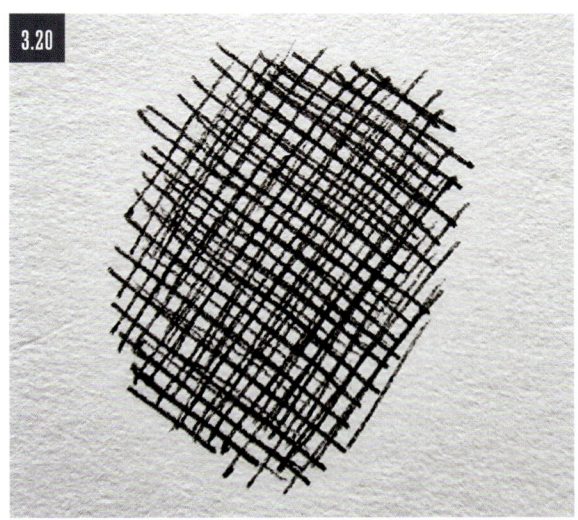

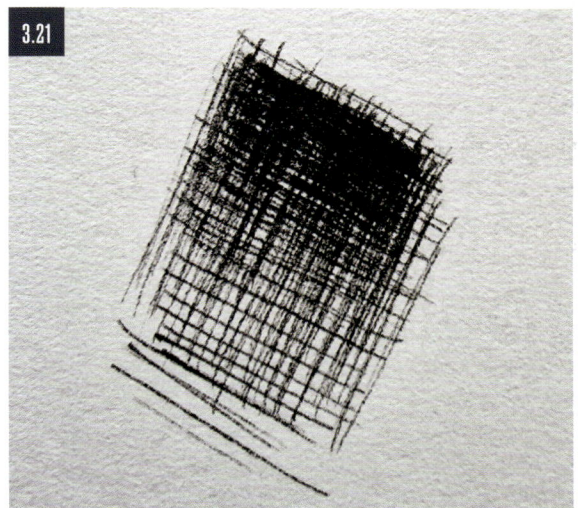

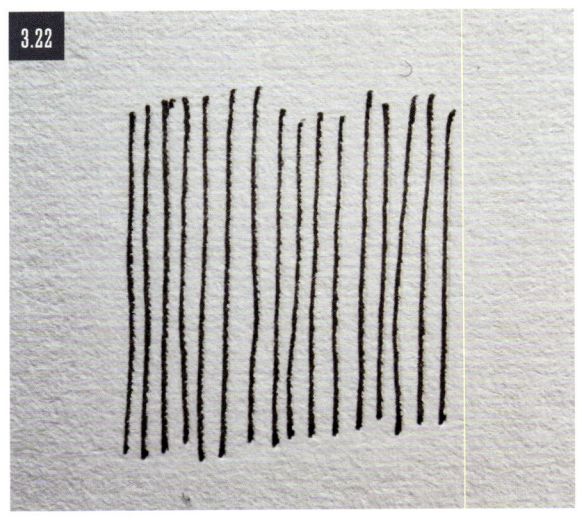
3.22

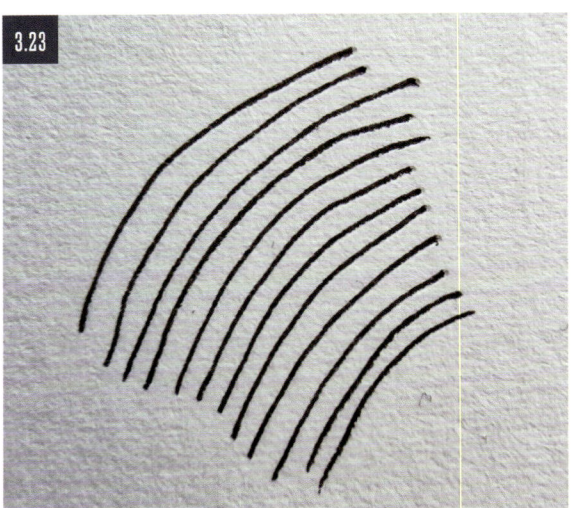
3.23

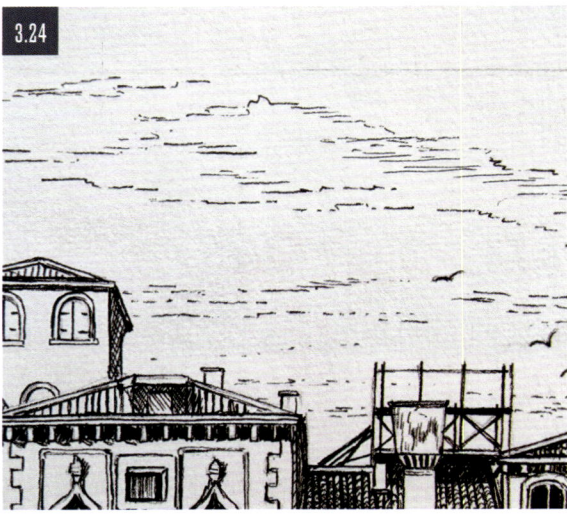
3.24

Hatching is the use of parallel lines that do not cross over each other (**FIGURES 3.22** and **3.23**). The lines can be straight or contoured to express tonal values and/or the shape and form of your subject matter. In the same way as with crosshatching, by increasing the quantity and thickness of the lines and decreasing the spacing between them, you can create a darker area in your drawing.

I find hatching lines to be useful for creating large areas of clouds (**FIGURE 3.24**). It is a really enjoyable way to draw.

How you choose to use hatching and crosshatching in a drawing is limitless. You can make these marks in any way you wish.

Ink On Top of Pencil

A key technique that I use in my work is to add crosshatching and hatching with a fineliner on top of my coloured pencil base layers (**FIGURES 3.25–3.27**). This creates a very attractive and interesting look. It also allows you to create varying degrees of tone and shading, plus add in any further details you may want to include, such as the cracks, marks, and textures on a wall.

The ink lines stand out well on top of the pencil colours, allowing you to define and accentuate the building shapes and details.

> ➤ You can rub out ink lines that have been drawn on top of coloured pencil, because the ink lines are sitting on top of the pencil base therefore, they can easily be erased off if you make a mistake.

When using this technique, its best to apply your fineliner on top of a surface that has already been burnished, and to move your fineliner lightly across the surface of the pencil to ensure that the pencil layer does not clog up the pen nib. If this does happen, scribble with the nib on a separate piece of paper to clear it up.

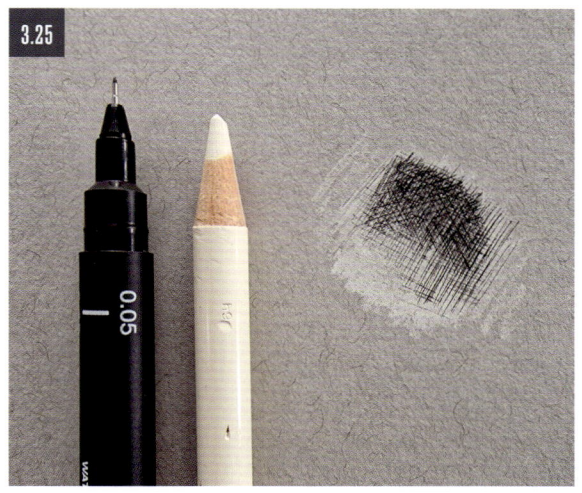

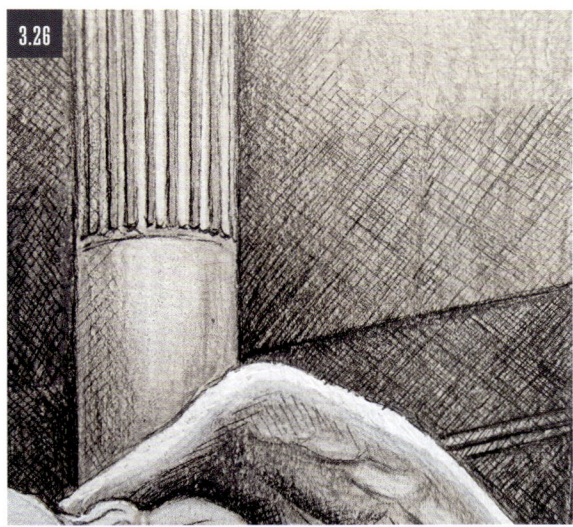

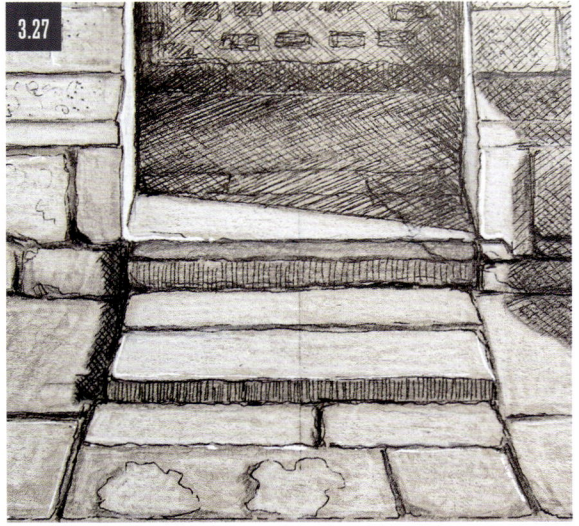

Coloured Pencils and Shading

Throughout this book I use the same technique of layering and blending with my coloured pencils to create varying hues, values, gradations, and textures. Let's look at the technique in more detail to enable you to create colour-rich drawings that pop off the page.

Layering pencil colours is the technique used for building up the saturation of colour in your drawing. It is also how you can create the forms of your subject matter by creating light, shadows, and different textures.

To achieve the best results, it is best to apply many light layers of colour, working with the lightest shades first, then moving onto the mid-tones, and then finally applying the darkest shades last. It is much easier to add dark colours over the top of light colours than it is to add light colours on top of dark.

To begin the process of building up layers of colour, start with a very light base of the first colour. Then simply add more and more layers until you achieve the colour you want. A single layer of colour is quite transparent, which is why it is necessary to keep adding more layers to deepen the richness and tone of the colour.

As a guide, I will normally use between four and six layers of colour to achieve a good rich colour, but I will keep working on an area until I achieve the desired colour. However, I do approach each new drawing with an open mind and don't count how many layers I am using, as each subject is a different and exciting challenge!

Using a blender is very useful, as it speeds up the process of layering and blending because you flatten out the surface colours more quickly.

> ➤ If you mess up and aren't happy with how the colour looks, you can always gently rub with an eraser to remove the top layers and then reapply.

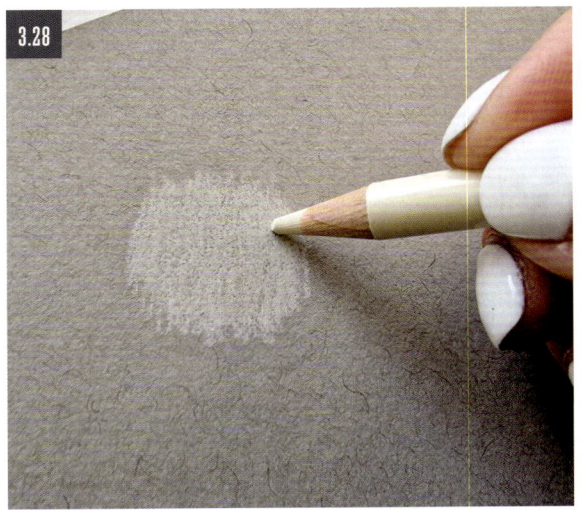

It is much better to deepen the colours slowly with thin layers than to apply one dense layer that can become greasy and unworkable. It is also more difficult to blend dense, heavily applied pencil lines together.

Building Layers

To create your pencil layers, begin by holding your pencil loosely on a side angle, and move the point in a light motion back and forth across the area to be coloured, using a light, consistent pressure and rhythm. This technique will create layers of even colour (**FIGURE 3.28**).

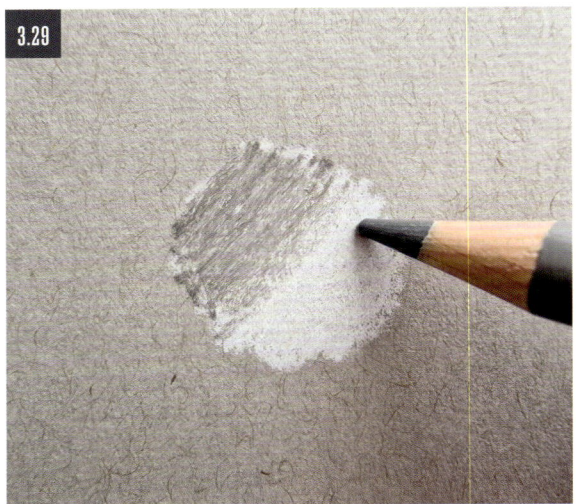

After you have applied some base layers, you can move onto adding any mid-tone layers (**FIGURE 3.29**).

You can use a firmer pressure in the final layers to blend and burnish the colours together to create rich, smooth colour with no graininess (**FIGURE 3.30**). The final layers are when you add the darkest colours to build depth and add more definition and details. You will need to apply a firmer pressure on your pencil in areas where you want to achieve a smooth finished surface. This can vary, as you may want to leave some areas, like a textured wall, without such a smooth surface.

To achieve the richest, smoothest layers, move your pencil around in small circular movements using a firm pressure (**FIGURE 3.31**). Keep the circles small and close together to effectively cover the area you are working on. This is called scumbling.

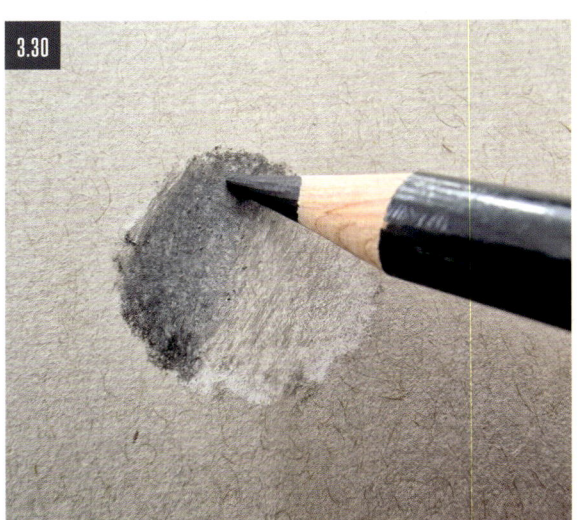

➤ Apply light pressure on your pencil for the base layers using a back-and-forth movement. Then use a firmer pressure in small circular movements for the details and final layers.

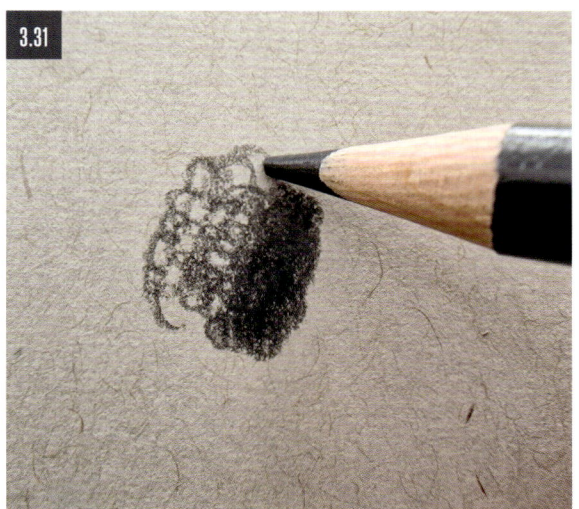

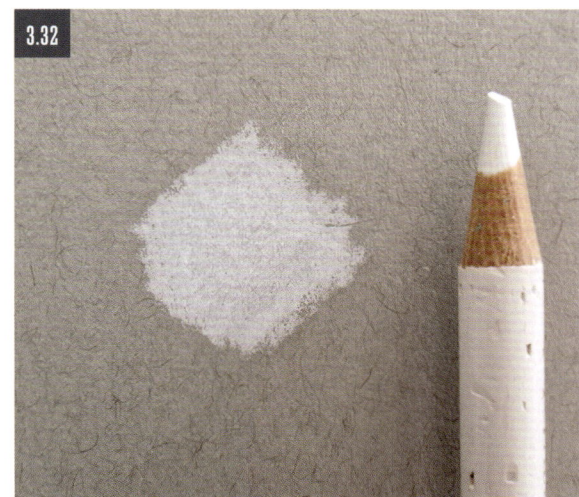

At the very end of the colouring and layering process, you can still apply lighter colours on top of the darkest colours to lighten or highlight areas that have become too dark, but the result will be subtle. These subtle differences can still be very useful and effective for any finishing touches, and they will elevate the colour of your work.

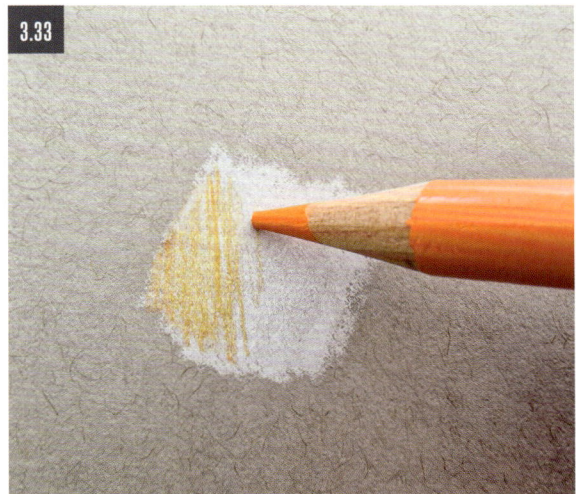

Depending on the area to be coloured, I often start with a foundational base layer of pure-white pencil. The white base layer lifts and brightens any subsequent layers, making the colour "pop" against toned paper. As it shines through the layers from underneath, the top layers glow!

When using this technique, to maximise the effect I will make the white base layers fairly opaque by applying three or more layers of the white pencil. Next, I will add the colour that I want to make to make glow. You can see in **FIGURES 3.32–3.34** that without the white base layer, the orange colour looks completely different.

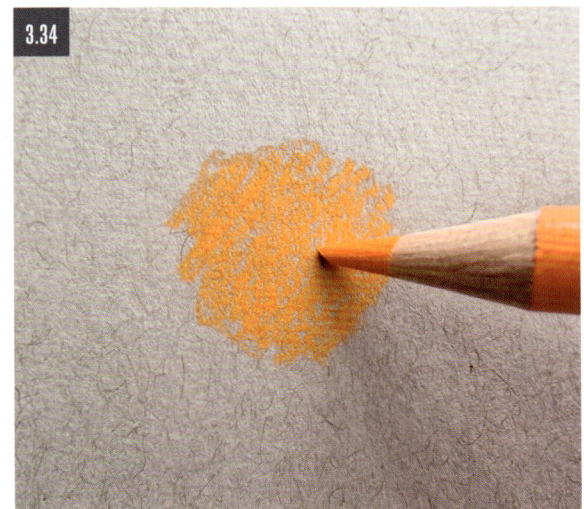

> ➤ Use light colours first for your base layers, then apply mid-tones, and finally apply the darkest colours.

Blending

Blending is a technique used to merge layers of pencil colours together to achieve a rich, smooth surface.

To blend the layers of coloured pencil together, I use an inexpensive pastel blender that I bought from an online art shop (**FIGURE 3.35**). There are also special blending pencils that you can buy, which work in the same way, but my favourite tool is the pastel blender.

The pastel blender has two supple rubber ends that I use to blend and push the pencil layers and colours together. All you need to do is gently rub the blender back and forth over the surface of the pencil layers (**FIGURE 3.36**). This will smooth out the colour and minimize any unwanted pencil lines or graininess as it pushes the pencil layers into the tooth of the paper. You only need to do this occasionally, in between applying layers when you see it is necessary and to smooth out the final top layers. You can also use the tool to blend more than one colour together when they meet (**FIGURE 3.37**).

If you don't have a blending tool, the colours will still blend together just from the pressure of the pencil point as it presses against the layers you are building.

I prefer to use a tool, as it really speeds up the process and gives me extra control over what I am doing. By using a blending tool, you are increasing the pressure on the surface of the colour, which flattens out the tooth of the paper to achieve a smoother colour-rich finish faster.

> ➤ Keep your pencils nice and sharp, as this will provide better control over the colour as it goes down.

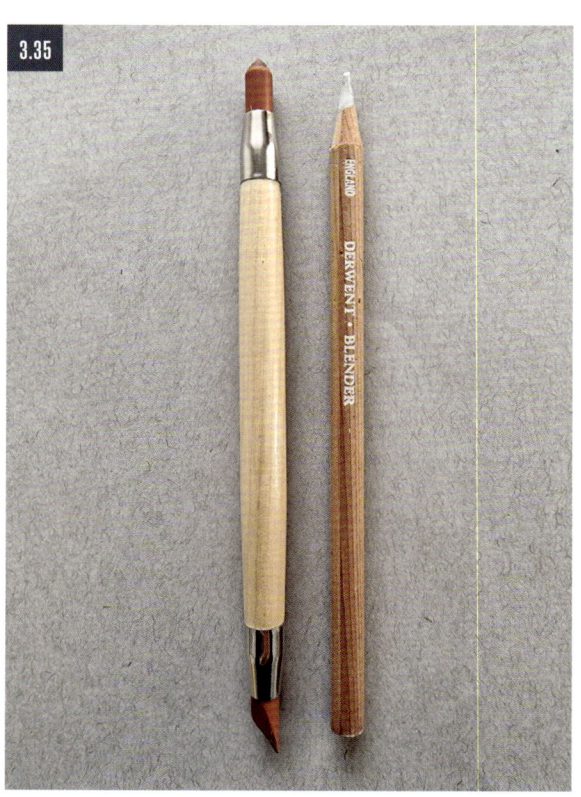

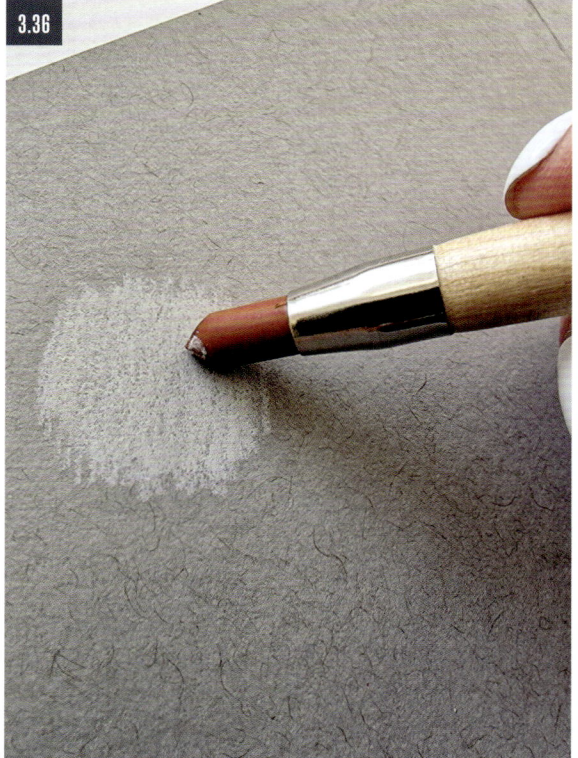

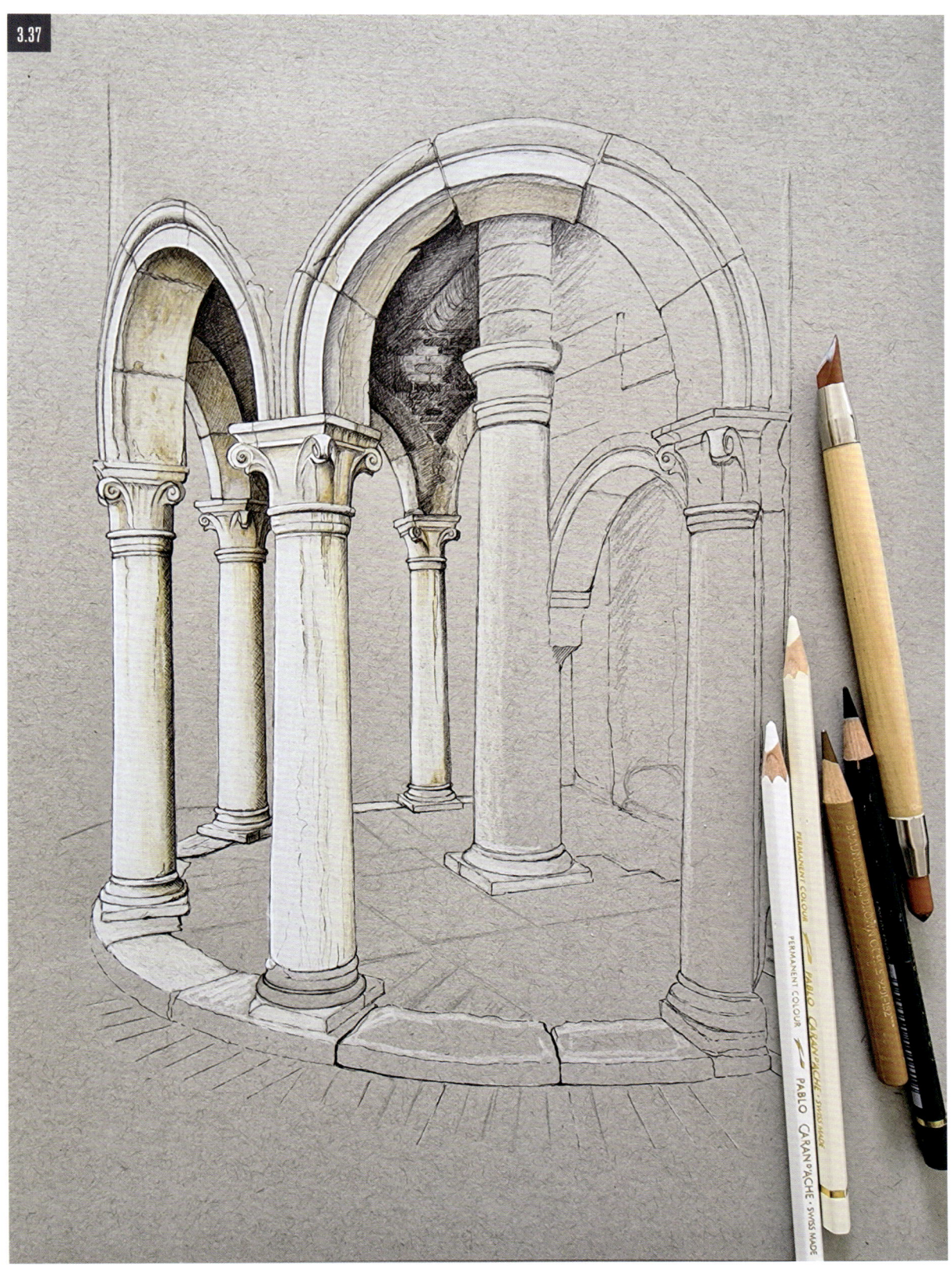

POP POINT!

There is a stage in a drawing that I call "pop point." This is a point I get to when the drawing suddenly comes to life and has a three-dimensional quality. I always get excited at this stage because it means the drawing is going to work! Unfinished sketches at this stage can sometimes be left as is—they have their own merit and beautiful look just as they are.

Achieving a good pop point begins with a really good reference photo where, for instance, there is a bright highlight, dark shadow, or strong contrast within the photo. You can further enhance this by upping the contrast in the photo before you begin. This can be done with the editing settings on most smartphones.

In the following sections I've included examples of photos for you to study and compare against each other—some with good light and shadows, and others not so good. You can also see the drawings I created from the good photos in various stages, and the moment I created a "pop point."

EXAMPLE 1 Royal Pavilion Brighton

Look at these two photos of the Royal Pavilion, Brighton (**FIGURES 3.38** and **3.39**).

Both photos were taken on the same day, but in the first one, the sun was hidden, so the photo looks dull and boring. If I'd used this to work from my drawing would have been dull and boring, too, and would have lacked shape and form.

Now compare it to the second photo, which I took when the sun came out. The dome of the Pavilion is brightly illuminated by the sun on the left side, and there are nice deep shadows that contrast beautifully with the white lattice work. Back in my studio I used this to my advantage and created this drawing of Brighton Pavilion. I emphasised

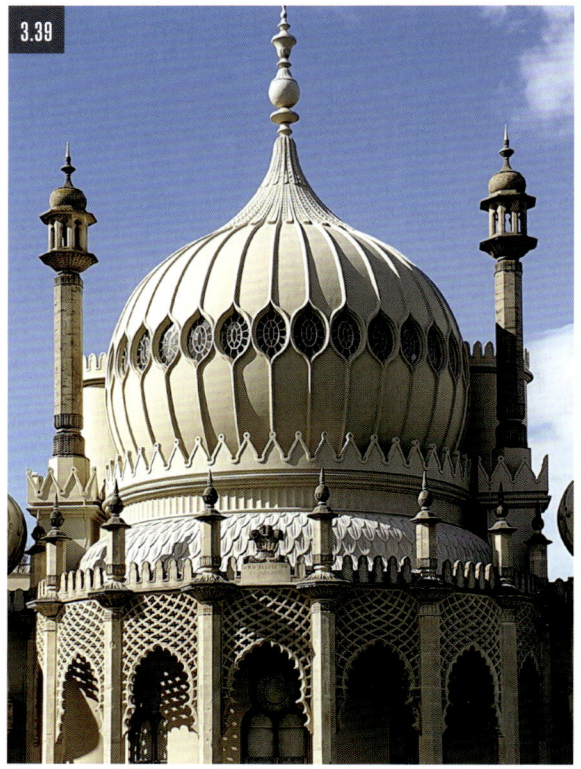

the centre light on the dome and the darker shadows, which created the overall three-dimensional effect and helped make the drawing pop on the toned grey paper (**FIGURE 3.40**). The finished drawing took over six weeks to complete (**FIGURE 3.41**).

It pays to be patient to get the right photos to work from. I plan a lot of my trips out to collect photos around the weather.

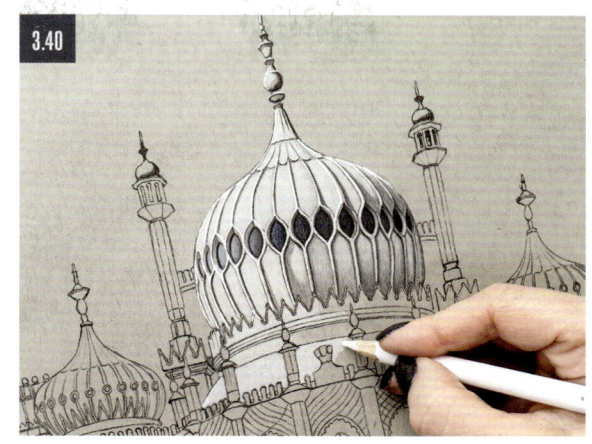

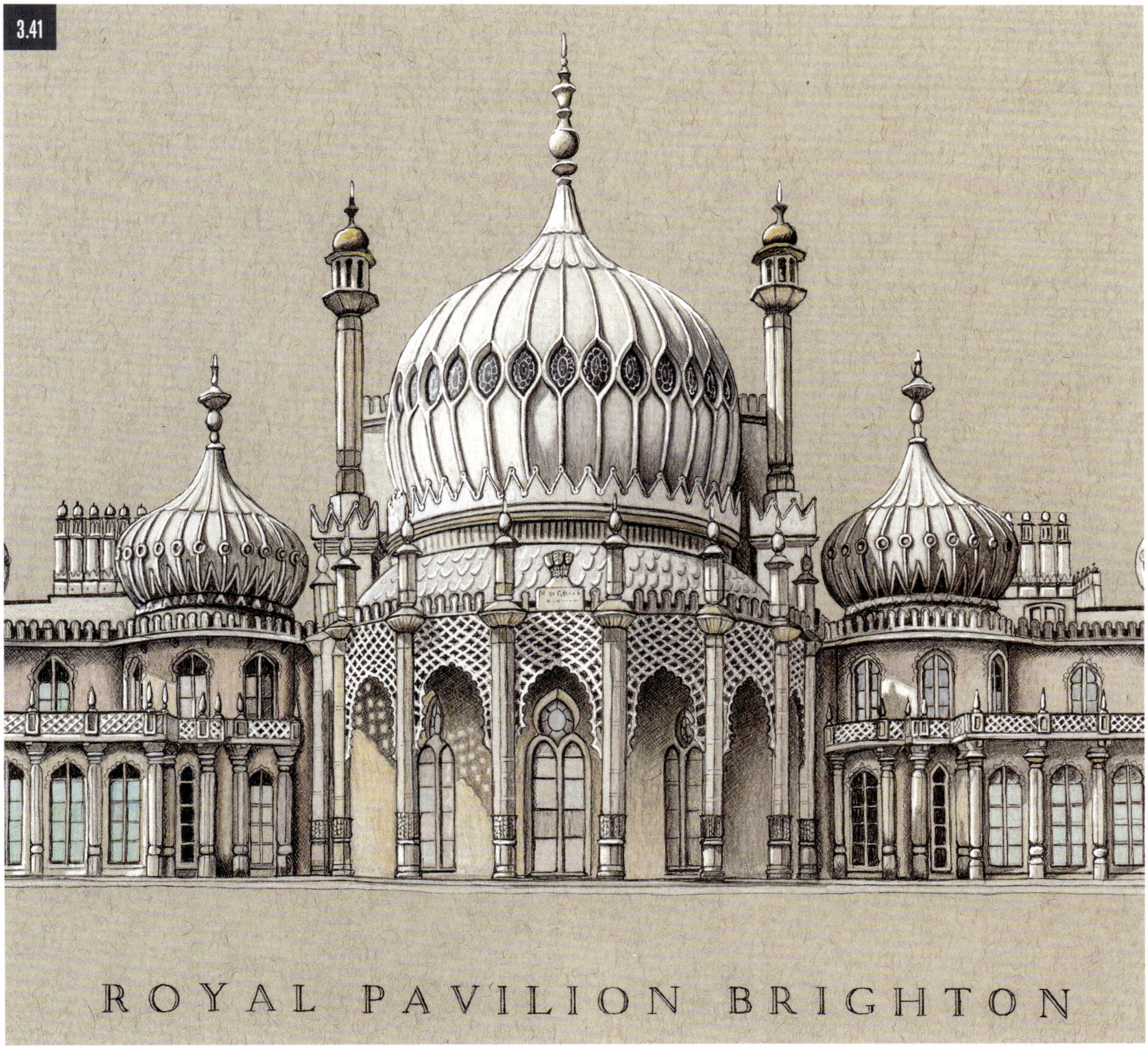

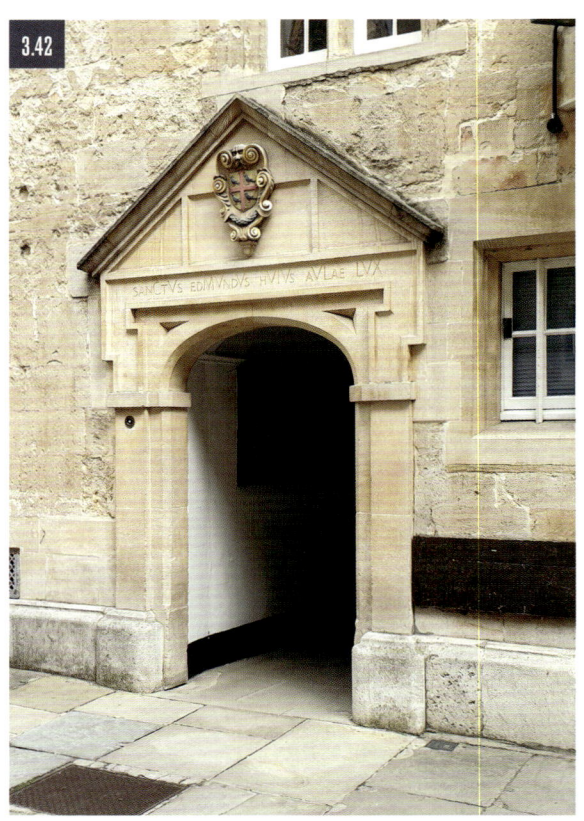

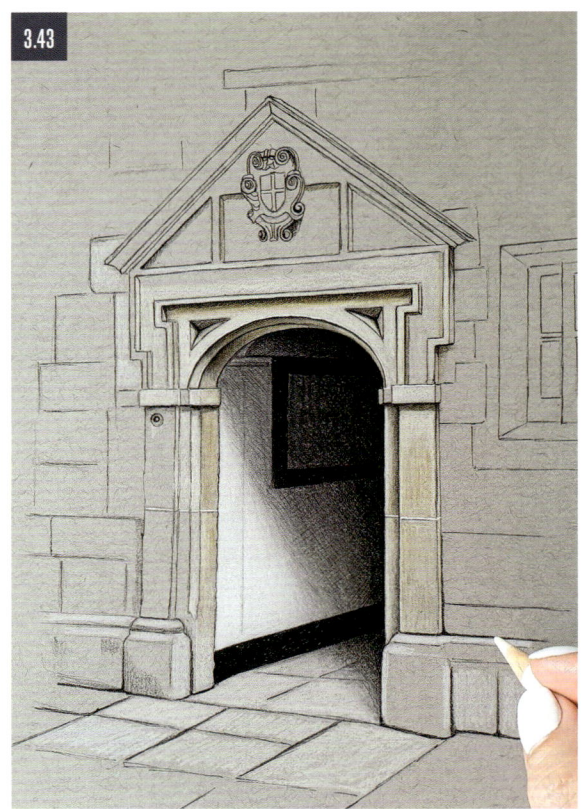

EXAMPLE 2 St Edmund Hall, Oxford

In this example of a photo I took in Oxford, it wasn't a particularly sunny day, but because there is still a strong contrast between the ivory-coloured stone-work and the darkness inside the archway, I was still able to create a "pop point." I created an illusion of depth on the paper by taking advantage of the strong contrasts in tonal values, which enabled me to create a powerful and dynamic drawing.

You can see in the images here the development of the drawing alongside the reference photo and the moment when I had created enough depth within the drawing for it to start to pop on the page (**FIGURES 3.42–3.44**).

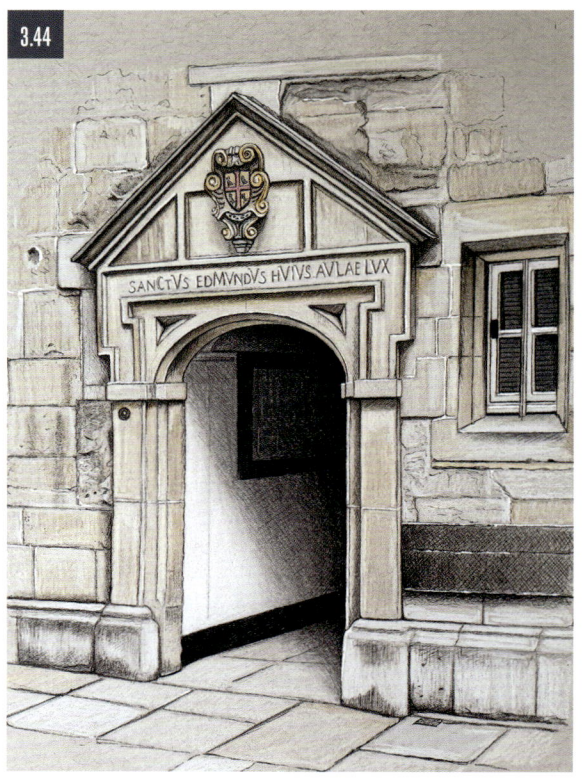

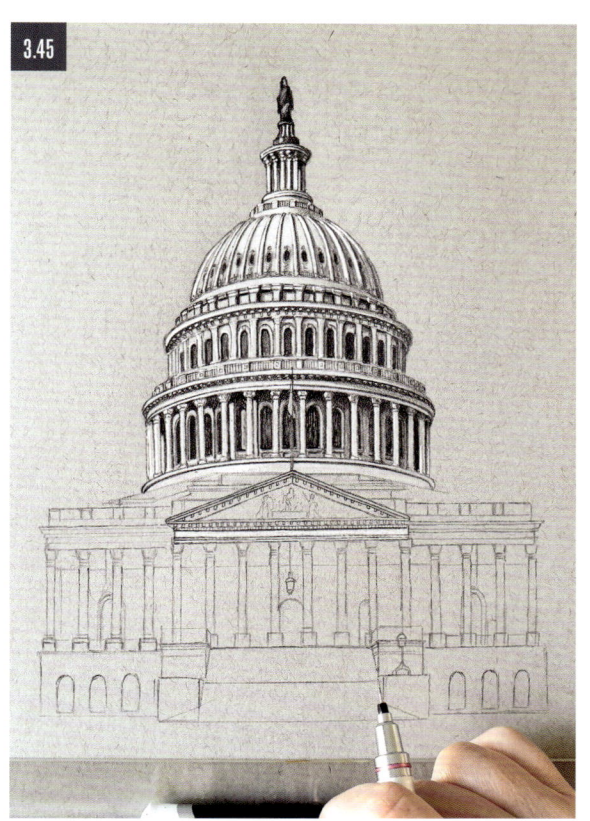

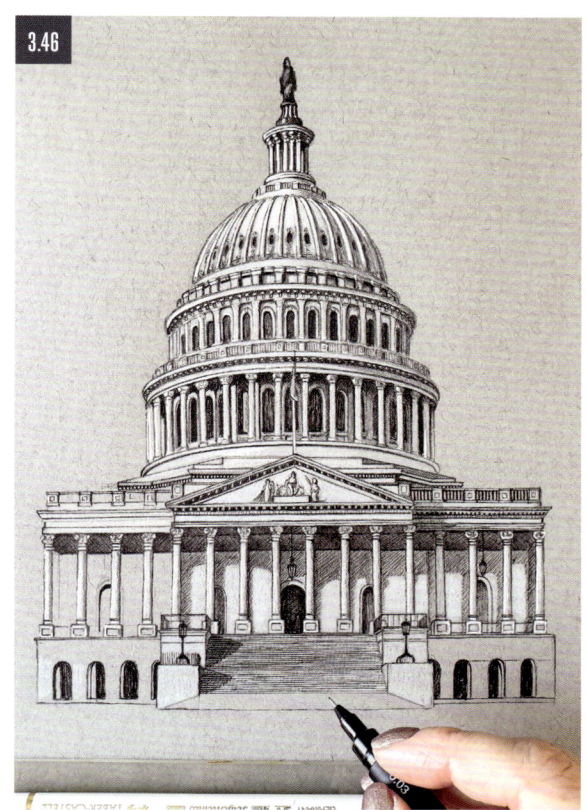

EXAMPLE 3 US Capitol Building

For this drawing I worked from a reference photo that I found on the internet, so I don't have it to share. The light in the photo was bright enough to create the deep shadows underneath the pediment of the building. The darkness of the shadows (**FIGURES 3.46** and **3.47**) contrast strongly with the pale coloured stone of the building that creates the "pop point." However, the drawing was already starting to become three-dimensional because of the dark shadows between the white columns and the gentle mid-tone shading on the right side of the dome.

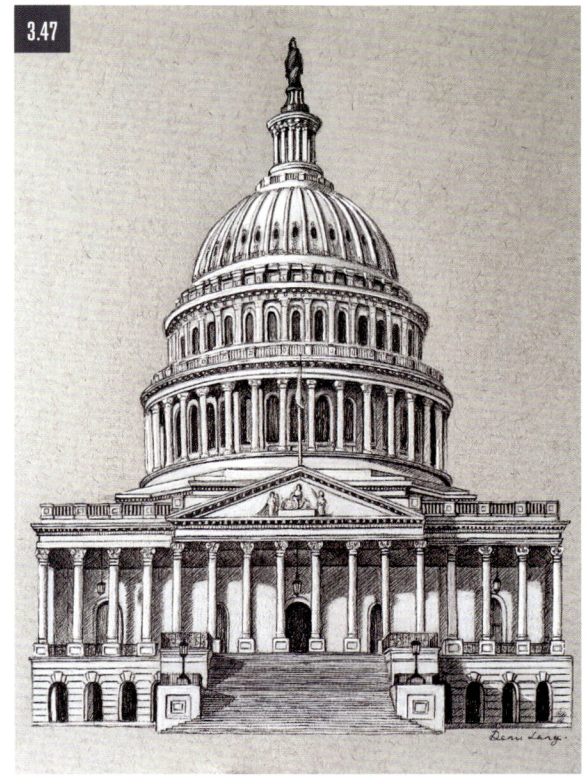

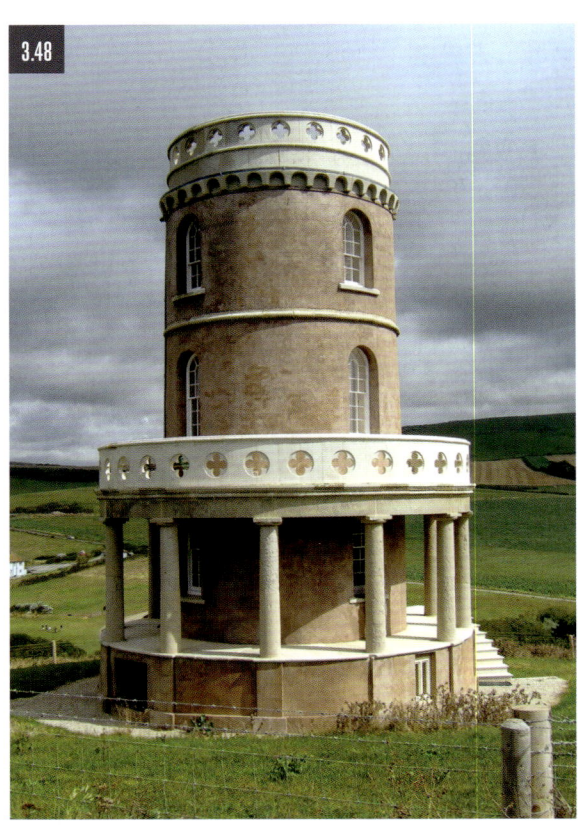

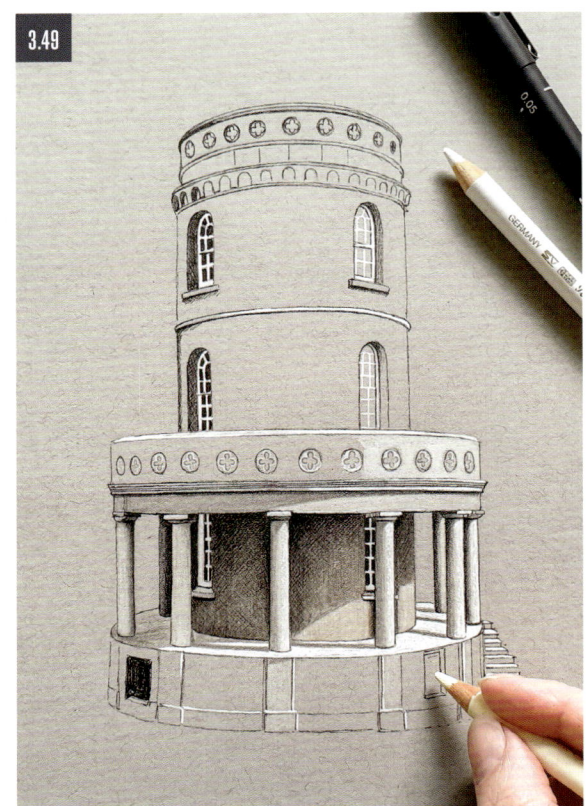

EXAMPLE 4 Clavell Tower

I came across this unusual folly while on holiday a few years ago (**FIGURE 3.48**). The folly sits on its own on the edge of a cliff next to the ocean, so the light was continuously changing with the rolling clouds. I stood there for quite a while until I managed to get the right photo with some perfect shadows that I could work from.

The sun is shining down from high on the right, hitting the columns on the right side and creating mid-tone shadows behind them on the left. As soon as I started to colour the columns with "light" and add in the shadows, the picture immediately started to pop (**FIGURE 3.49**)! The completed drawing is very three-dimensional because of the dramatic shadows and light (**FIGURE 3.50**). The graduated shadow around the cylindrical shape also helped to add extra depth.

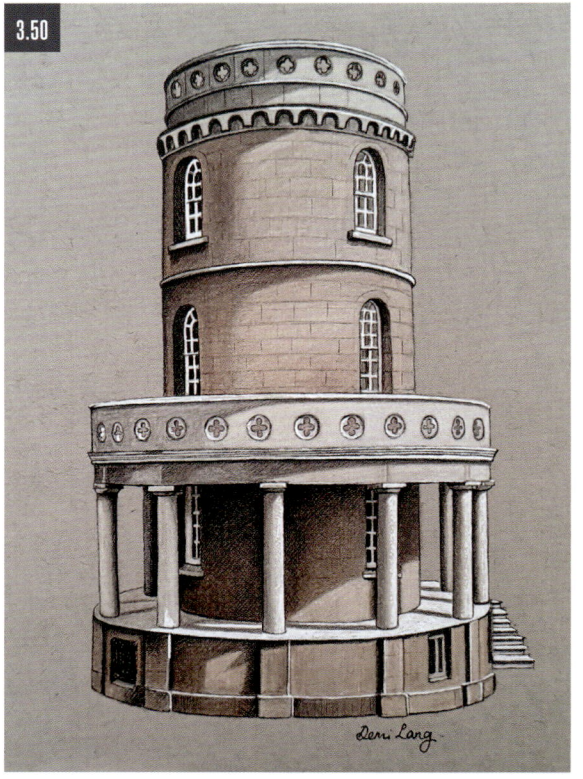

You should now have a little understanding about what I call "pop point" and how to achieve it. There is a lot to learn about tonal values, contrast, and shadows and highlights, plus colour, of course.

It may be challenging in the beginning to determine the different values for highlighting and shading in a photo, but the more you practice, the more you will learn and grow! It will become like a second language to you. In the next chapter, I'll show you how to complete your own colour drawing from start to finish!

TIPS TO REMEMBER

- ▶ Shadows are at their darkest when they are closer to the object at the point where two surfaces meet.
- ▶ Shadows are not all one colour—they have darker and lighter tones within them from reflected light. They are unlikely to be completely black.
- ▶ Shadows have darker values and highlights have light values.
- ▶ Start lightly when drawing in shadows and build up with more layers. It is easier to add more depth than to take away.
- ▶ Look for the light source so you can establish where to place shadows.
- ▶ Shadows aren't always really dark; it depends on how near or far they are from the light source and the strength of the light. They can even be quite subtle, like pale shadows in the snow or those on the edge of a shadow as it gets nearer to the light.
- ▶ Practice often. The more you practice, the more your skills will develop. You wouldn't expect to learn a new language overnight—it takes time and effort!

EXERCISE: EXPERIMENT WITH HIGHLIGHTS AND SHADOWS

Try this exercise to help you better understand how highlights and shadows are formed.

Position an object like a ball, apple, or egg on a flat white surface. Next, use a torch or lamp to shine light onto the object. Move the light around and observe how the shapes of the shadows and where they fall on the object change depending on the angle of the light source.

Pay attention to where the light hits the object and where it is at its brightest and also, where it is more diffused. See if you can spot the occlusion shadow (the darkest shadow) where the two surfaces of the object and the flat surface meet.

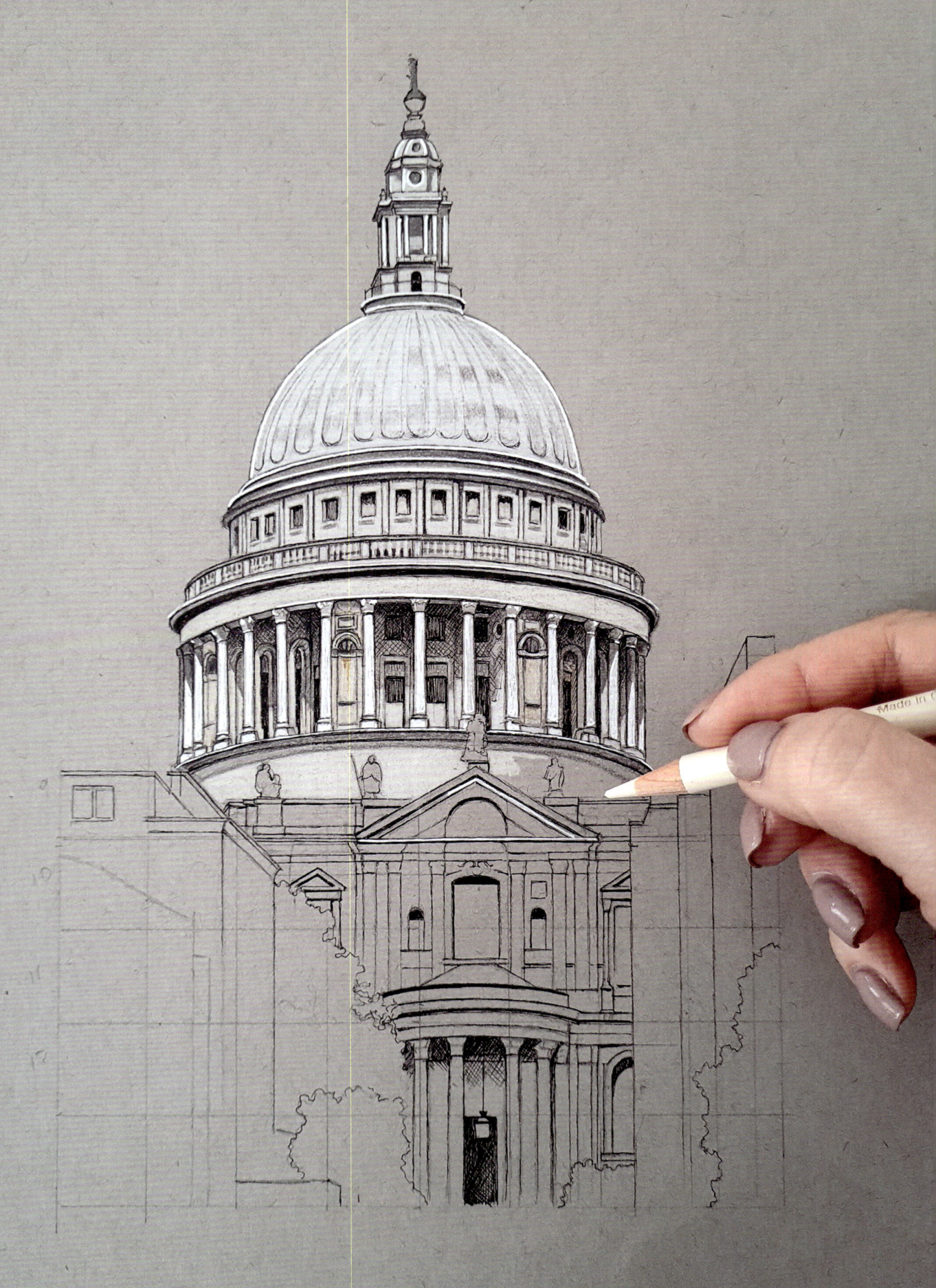

CHAPTER FOUR

Step-by-Step Process

In this chapter, I am going to show you step-by-step how to create a full colour drawing from start to finish using a reference photo I took of St Paul's Cathedral in London (**FIGURES 4.1** and **4.2**). It's a place I have visited and drawn many times and I'm still in awe of the size and beauty of the magnificent structure. The cathedral was designed by the highly acclaimed English architect Sir Christopher Wren and construction took place between 1675 and 1711. The dome dominates the London landscape and is still one of the highest in the world.

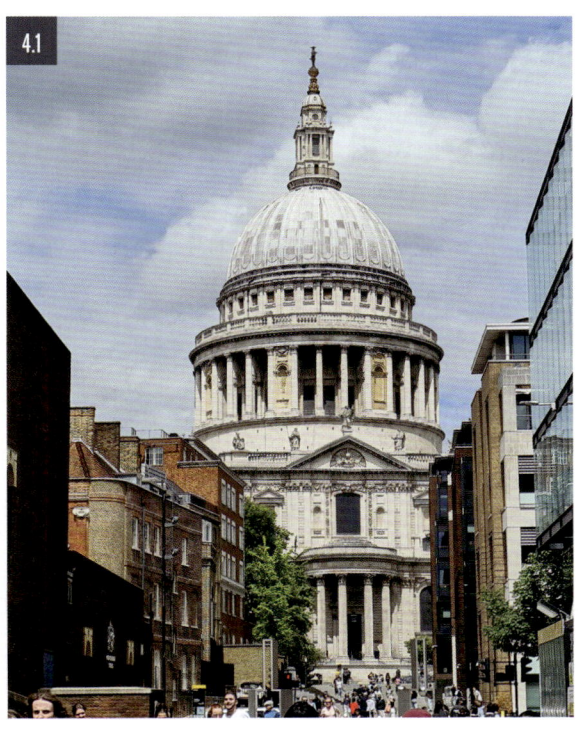

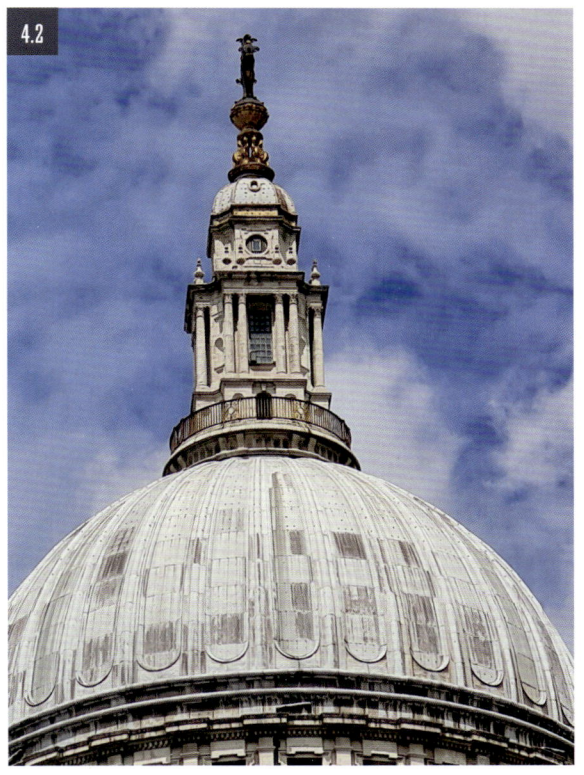

If you don't want to use this reference photo to draw from, look for something similar with a large dome.

I know it can sometimes be overwhelming when you have a blank page in front of you. Where do you start? It's often at this point we put our pencil down and put off starting something for another day, and then before you know it, the days have rolled into weeks! I know, I've been there, and I look back now and wish I hadn't given up. To help with this, I've broken the process down into easy-to-understand steps to make the process less daunting.

It all begins with a single line, then before you know it, the picture has progressed over many sessions!

I like to work in sections so that I feel like I am covering ground. For instance, one day I will aim to plan out a new drawing on the page, and another day I will add the ink lines. This way I make consistent progress without wearing myself out. I find that it's important to take regular breaks and give my eyes a rest too.

To demonstrate the process I use, I have chosen a clear, bright photograph of St Paul's Cathedral to work from because there are lots of details and powerful highlights that contrast dramatically with the dark shadows. This will help me create a good finished drawing.

I think of drawing as a puzzle—we have to observe the different shapes we see in front of us and find a way to fit them together, just like in a jigsaw puzzle.

It's worth taking the time to get the initial drawing just right so you don't run into problems later on. This is the first step. Once you have a good solid foundation of a drawing in place on your paper, it is much easier to confidently build the layers of colour on top. For me, this is the most time-consuming task of the whole process and I find it very satisfying once this is done, as I know the hardest part is over!

RECOMMENDED MATERIALS

- ▶ Toned paper
- ▶ Sharp pencil
- ▶ Black 0.05mm fineliner pen
- ▶ Coloured pencils: White 101, Silver Grey 002, Ivory 103, Brown Ochre 182, Warm Grey IV 273, Paynes Grey 181, Dark Sepia 9201-75
- ▶ White fine-nib Posca pen or white gel pen
- ▶ Eraser
- ▶ Ruler
- ▶ Set square, also called a triangle (optional)
- ▶ Blender

Step 1: CREATING YOUR PENCIL DRAWING (THREE METHODS)

The very first step of any artwork is to carefully sketch out your picture in pencil.

It can take a long time to do this, but once you have worked through the process and have a good drawing laid out and ready to colour, you will appreciate your hard work and achieve good results. It helps to be patient and accept that this initial part of the process will take a while. I often listen to audiobooks and podcasts when I'm doing this and the hours seem to fly by!

There are three methods I use for drawing my initial picture in pencil. The method I choose to use depends on the complexity of the subject I am working on and what size I want my finished picture to be.

I usually use one of the following three methods:

1. The grid method
2. Freehand sketching
3. Taking measurements from a printout or digital screen

Let's discuss each method in more detail.

METHOD 1 The Grid Method

Transfer your drawing or photo using a grid.

The grid method is an old and useful tool for creating accurate drawings by transferring your initial drawing or photograph onto a fresh sheet of paper for your final work. The subject matter will be properly sized and correctly positioned on the drawing paper, so it is an ideal method to use for complex and precise work no matter what stage you are at in your art journey. It can also be particularly useful when starting out to help you get the initial pencil drawing just right.

I often use the grid method to help me enlarge work, as the technique has the great advantage of allowing you to enlarge or reduce your subject matter as much as you like while still maintaining perfect proportions and accuracy.

The grid method is a simple process of drawing a grid of equal squares over your reference photo (or initial sketch), and then drawing another grid of equal squares onto your drawing paper. You then study and focus on each square individually and transfer the information you can see into the matching squares on your drawing paper.

To enlarge your drawing, you simply draw a grid of larger squares onto the paper you are going to draw on. For instance, if your grid squares on the reference photo are two centimetres wide, then to enlarge the picture, you might make the grid squares on your drawing paper four centimetres wide. Conversely, to reduce the size of the picture,

you would make the squares smaller on the drawing paper—for instance, one centimetre wide.

I have used this method for drawing some of my larger artworks, which have been up to a meter wide (**FIGURES 4.3** and **4.4**). The whole process took me many weeks, but it worked well and was worth the time and effort.

If you have good computer skills, you can digitally place the grid on your photo and print out the image to work from.

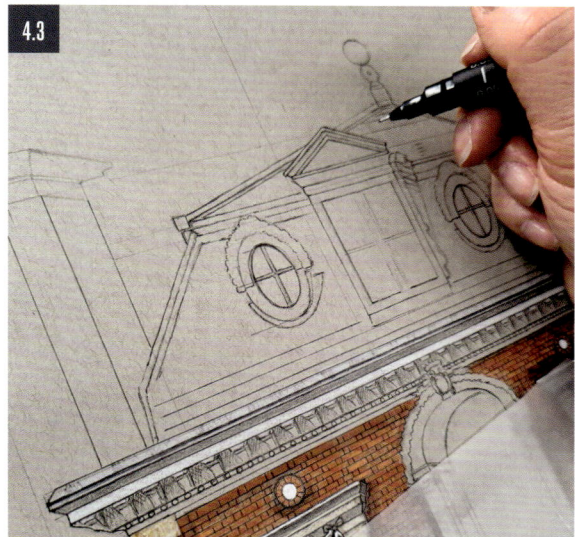

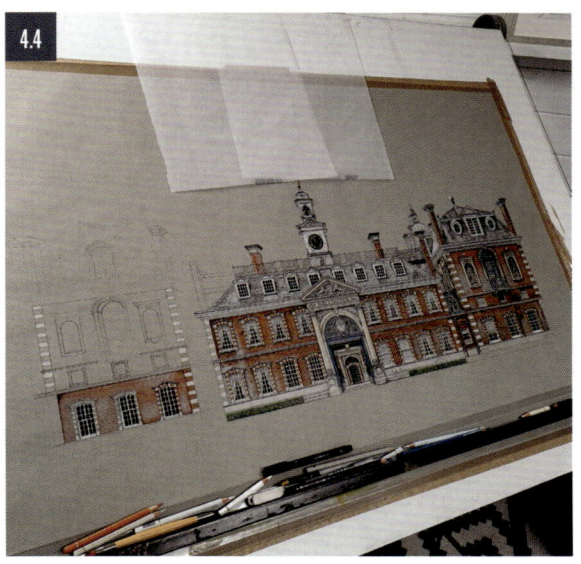

There are three main steps to drawing with the grid method.

Step 1: Choose the image, paper, and size

Choose the image (photograph) you want to draw from, the size you want your drawing to be, and the type of paper you wish to use. I am using my favourite toned grey paper here because I want the colours to really stand out (**FIGURE 4.5**). Print out the photograph onto which you will draw the squares; if you have already added the grid digitally, simply print it out.

Please note that for this to work you must use squares, not rectangles. This will keep your drawing to the same scale as the reference photo. Remember, the ratio should be 1:1.

Additionally, you must use the same number of squares on your reference photo and your drawing paper. For instance, if you use ten squares across and eight squares down on the printout, you should use the same number and orientation on your paper.

Step 2: Create the grid

To create the grid, you will need a pencil, ruler, and set square (optional) to draw a grid of equal squares onto your printout or photo. It's up to you what size the squares are, but I would suggest using a round number like one inch or three centimetres. For this demonstration I used two-centimetre squares on both my reference photo and drawing paper, so my drawing will be exactly the same size as the reference photo. It's worth remembering that the smaller the squares are, the easier it is to read and transfer any complex information from each square onto the drawing paper.

To begin, find and mark the central point of your page near the top of the image. You will use this central point as a marker and place equal squares on either side of it. Here I have used the very center of the tower as my central point (**FIGURE 4.6**).

Simply measure across the page and make small marks at regular intervals where each square will

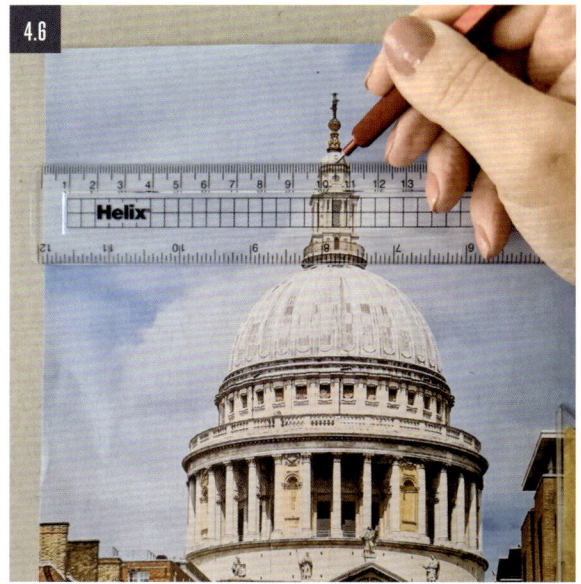

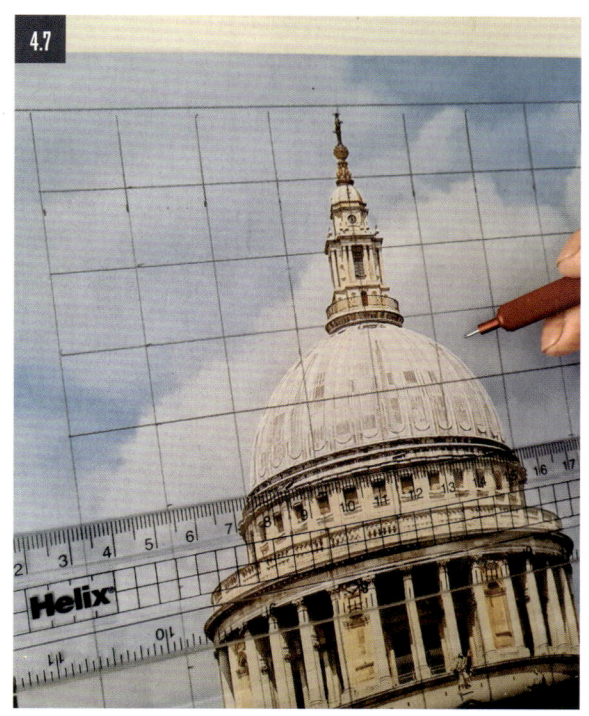

be. Then use the marks to guide you and draw in the vertical lines of the grid using a ruler and set square. Do this again down the left side of the photograph and draw in the horizontal lines (**FIGURE 4.7**).

When you have completed the grid, it is useful to number the squares across the top row and down the left column so you can easily identify which square you are working on (**FIGURE 4.8**).

Step 3: Transfer the image

The next step is to find the central point on your chosen drawing paper. Now draw a grid with an identical number of equal squares onto your paper using light pencil lines, just as you did on your printout (**FIGURE 4.9**). Try not to press too hard because you want to be able to erase the lines later on.

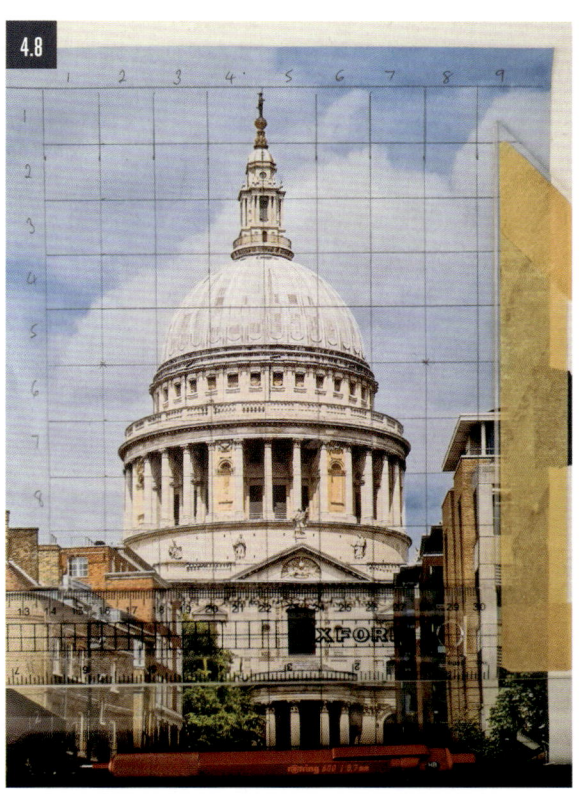

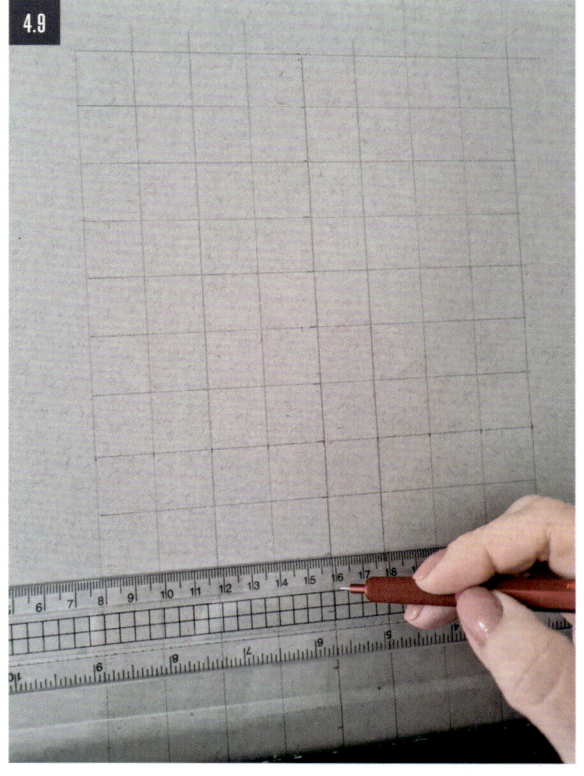

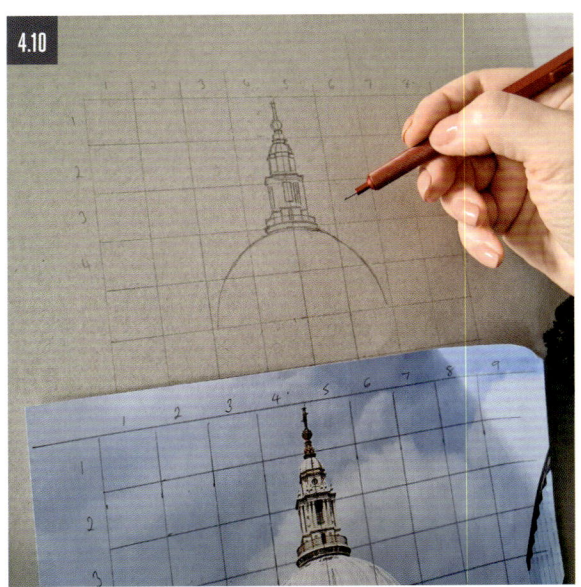

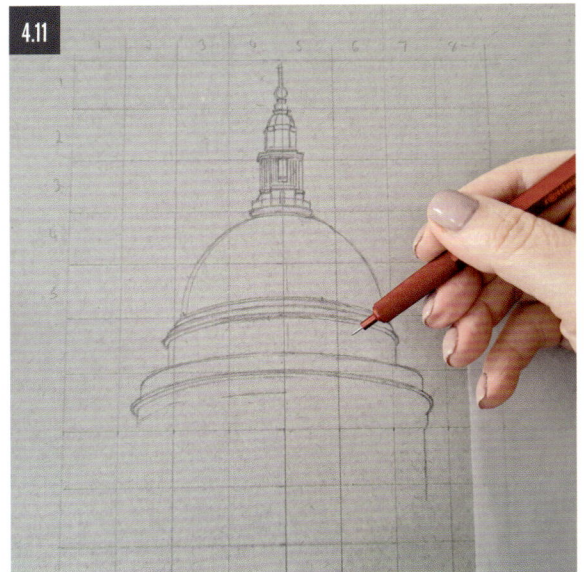

Working from left to right, begin transferring the information from each square on your printout onto the squares on your paper (**FIGURE 4.10**). Work carefully and at your own pace. Remember, it is better to get this right now. Look closely at your printout. Observe the shapes within each square and where the lines fall and meet within the box. Aim to duplicate this information, and your drawing will be well proportioned! Remember to place a sheet of paper under your hand to help keep your drawing clean (**FIGURE 4.11**).

At regular intervals, sit back and look at your work from a distance. It's easy to hyperfocus on one area, and it's only later when you sit back that you spot a mistake. Use your set square and ruler to check that your lines are straight (**FIGURE 4.12**). You can also use your ruler to measure the distances of lines within a square (**FIGURE 4.13**).

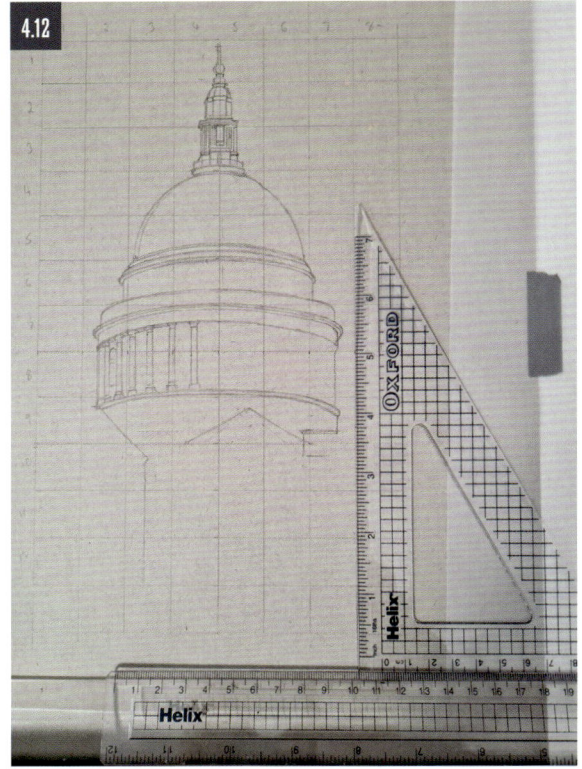

Continue this process until you have worked through each square and filled the entire page, completely transferring the image from the reference photo to the drawing paper (**FIGURE 4.14**). You don't have to add in every single tiny detail at this stage; you can always add more in later.

Drawing and Illustrating Architecture

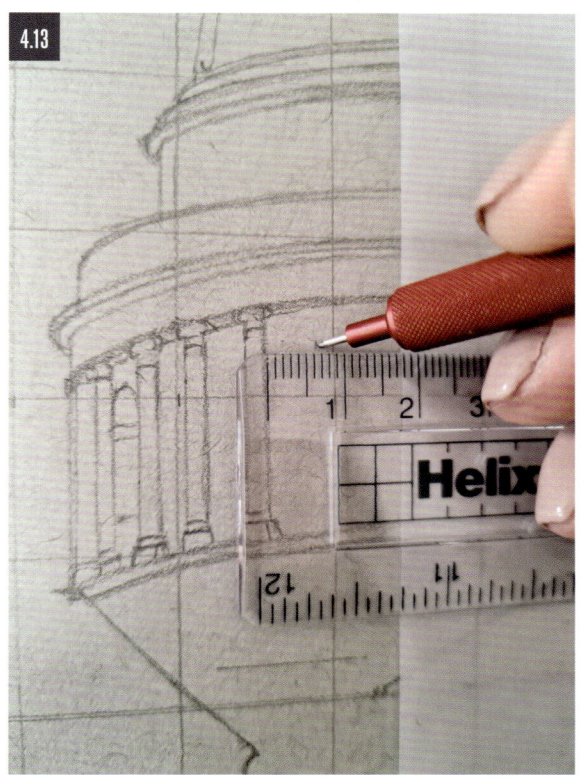

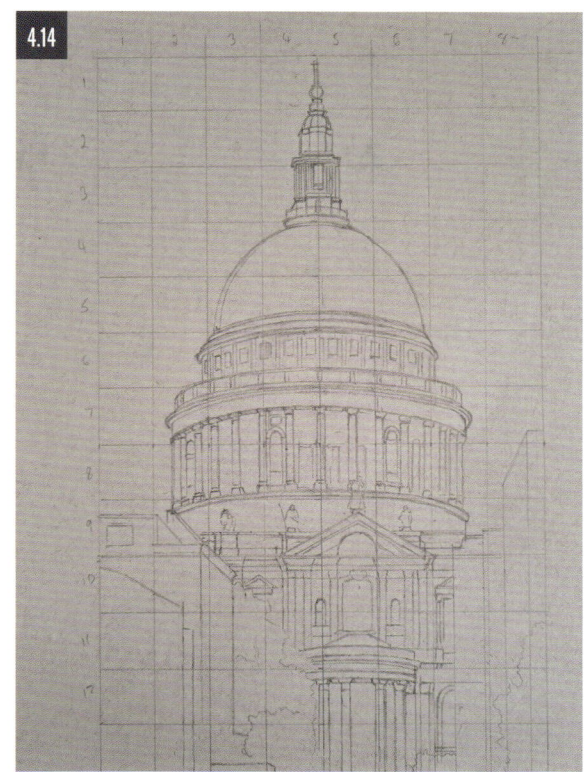

METHOD 2 Freehand Sketching

It's freeing and enjoyable to just sketch freehand, but if you are just starting out with drawing, it can be a bit of a challenge for complex drawings. Therefore, I recommend starting with one of the other two methods until you build more confidence. In the meantime, use a sketchbook to practice your drawing totally freehand. Sketchbooks are little works of art all on their own when they are filled with your drawings, and they are a great place to play around with your tools.

Freehand is my favourite way to draw if I am confident that I can achieve the accuracy I want with my chosen subject. Of course, not everything has to be entirely accurate—you can "suggest" shapes, buildings, and other elements of your subject. Your work is your own and very personal. I like to achieve realism and accuracy; that's just my way of doing things. You will find your own style and what works for you.

When you are freehand sketching, you are literally drawing what is in front of you, whether it be on the street or in a photo. I love sketching outside, but for most of my work, it's not possible because of the size and degree of accuracy required.

Since this book is studio-based, we'll talk about working from photos.

Step 1: Determine the composition

Think about the composition: where do you want the drawing to be on the page? For this drawing of St Paul's Cathedral, I want to plan a central composition in the same way I did with the grid method. As mentioned before, central composition is a powerful way to draw attention to your main subject. Things placed in the centre have a strong visual weight, so it will work very well for this drawing. To get started, measure all the way across your paper horizontally, then divide this

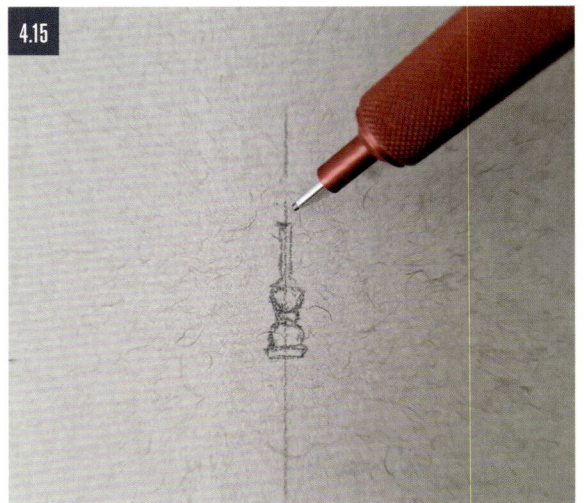

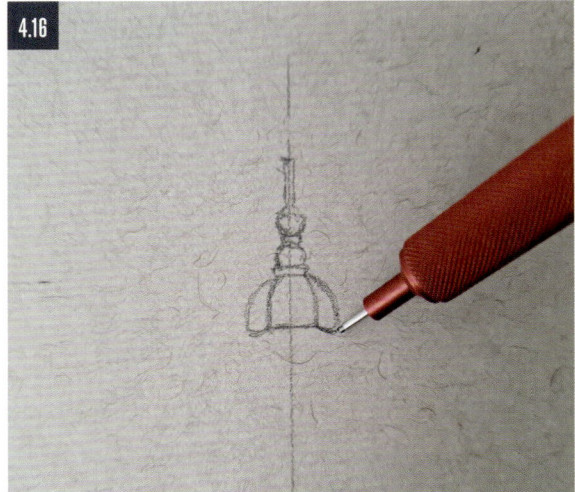

measurement in half and mark the central point. Do this again further down the page and join the two marks together with a vertical line. You can then use this central vertical line as a guide to position your drawing symmetrically on the page.

Step 2: Begin sketching

Now look at your reference photo and find the centre point there as well. Imagine where the image will be on your page. Sometimes it helps to lightly move your hand just above the paper as if you are drawing to help you visualise where your drawing will be.

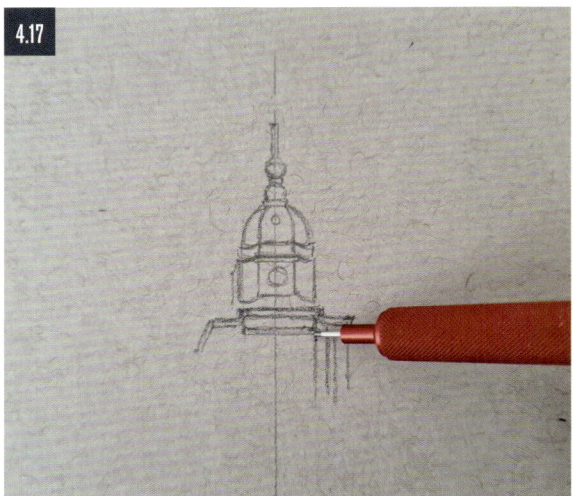

Begin lightly sketching the shapes above the lantern from the top centre point (**FIGURE 4.15**). Look at the shapes of the buildings and match up where the lines meet. Everyone has their own speed for this. I am slow and precise. Use light strokes of your pencil so you can easily rub out any unwanted lines. Take care not to press down too hard.

Connect each shape and line together as you move further down (**FIGURES 4.16–4.18**). Make sure your lines meet up in the correct places. It is as important to spend as much time observing your subject as it is to do the drawing.

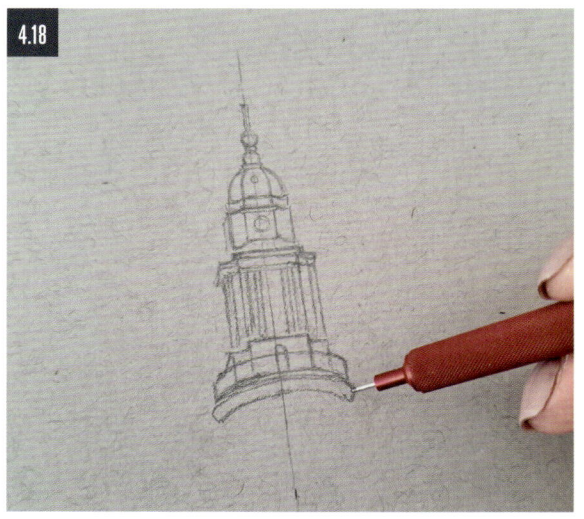

Drawing is copying the collection of lines and shapes that you see in front of you and piecing them together like a puzzle. I will remind you of this a lot throughout the book.

Make sure you regularly move yourself back away from your work every now and then, and look over your work to check that everything is well placed.

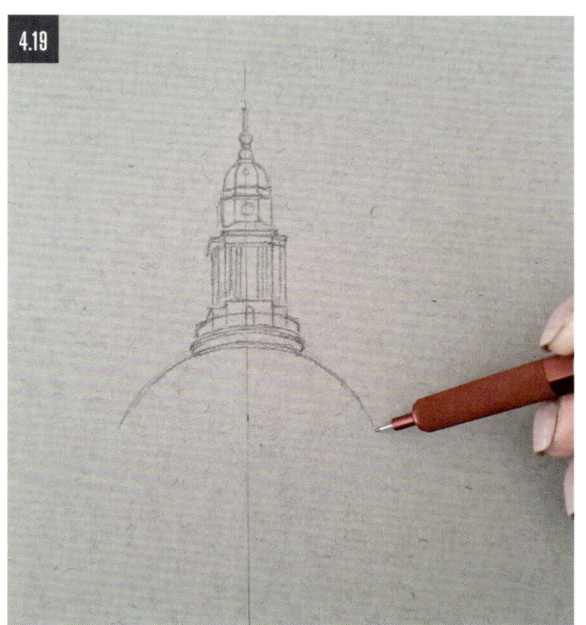

Step 3: Sketching the dome

Take extra care when drawing the dome, as it is the main focal point of the picture. Draw the curve shape down on the left and right sides, and then sit back and look closely to make sure that the lines are symmetrical (**FIGURE 4.19**).

You can use your ruler to help you do this by measuring across the width of the dome to the centre point and checking that the measurement is the same on both sides. Begin to mark in the baseline of the dome; this will also help you to judge that the shape of the dome is correct (**FIGURE 4.20**).

The idea at this point is to draw in the main shapes. You can add more details later with the fine nib of a fineliner pen.

Use your ruler to make sure that each side on the dome lines up. As you can see here, mine does not line up so I will erase the mistake and start again (**FIGURE 4.21**)!

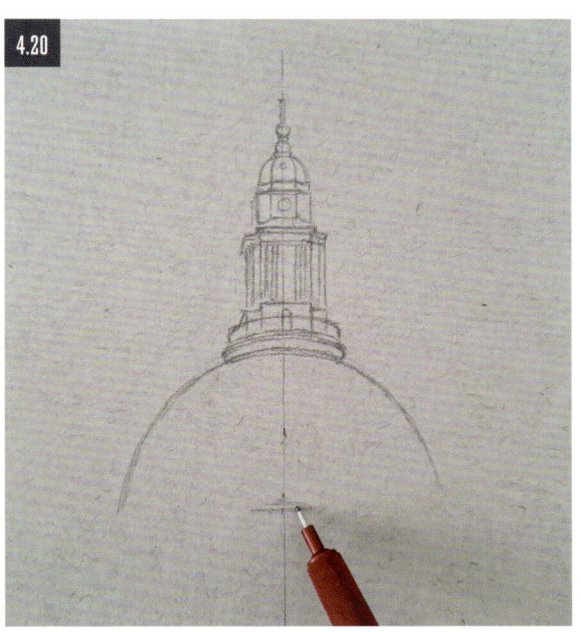

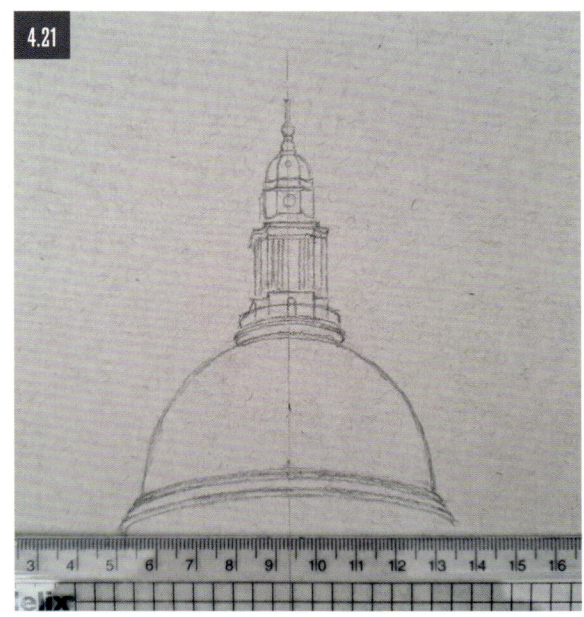

Now there is one well-placed ellipse across the width of the base of the dome, which you can use as a guide for the other ones that go underneath (**FIGURE 4.22**). Continue working downward until this section is finished (**FIGURE 4.23**).

Step 4: Columns, windows, and details

Now carefully mark in the columns (**FIGURES 4.24** and **4.25**). Use small pencil marks to space them out, and once you have checked visually that the marks are well placed, draw the lines in properly

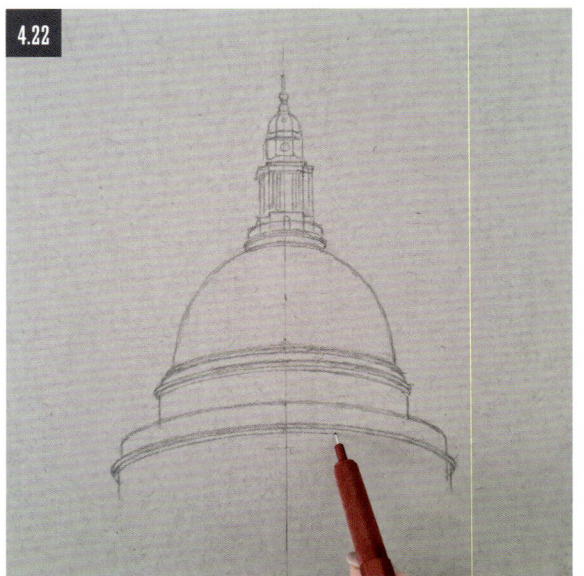

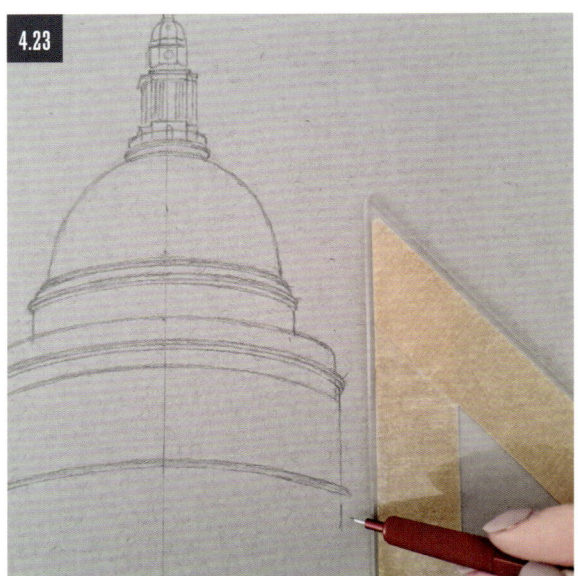

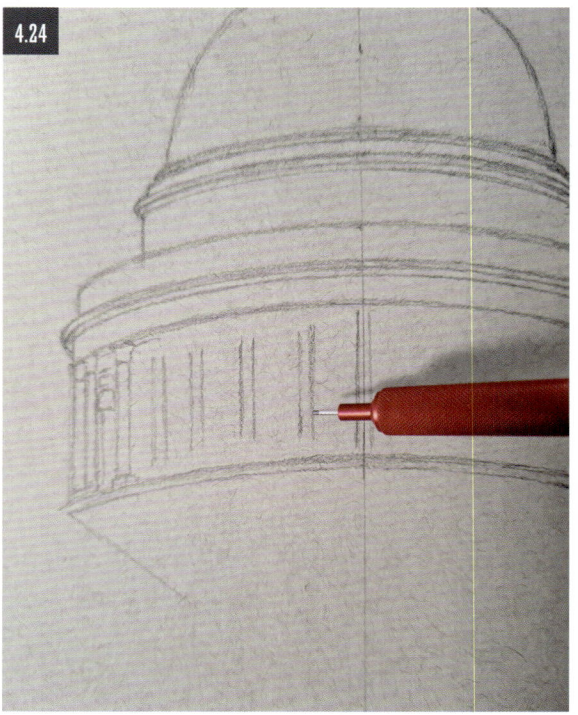

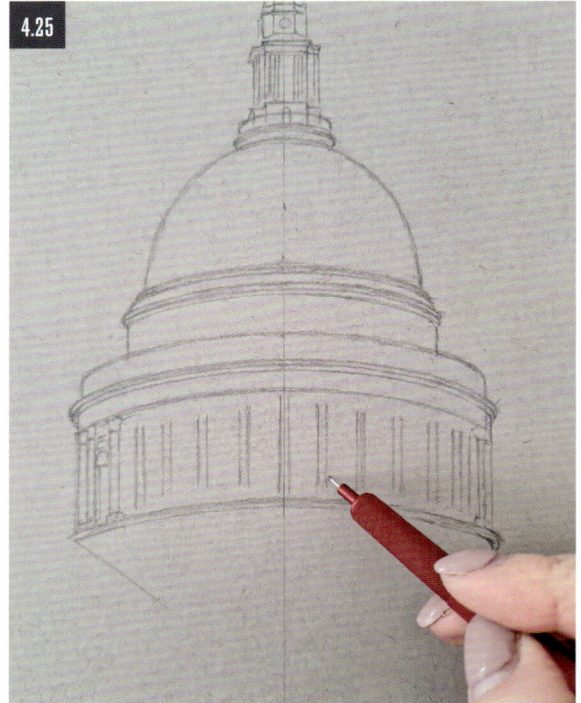

Drawing and Illustrating Architecture

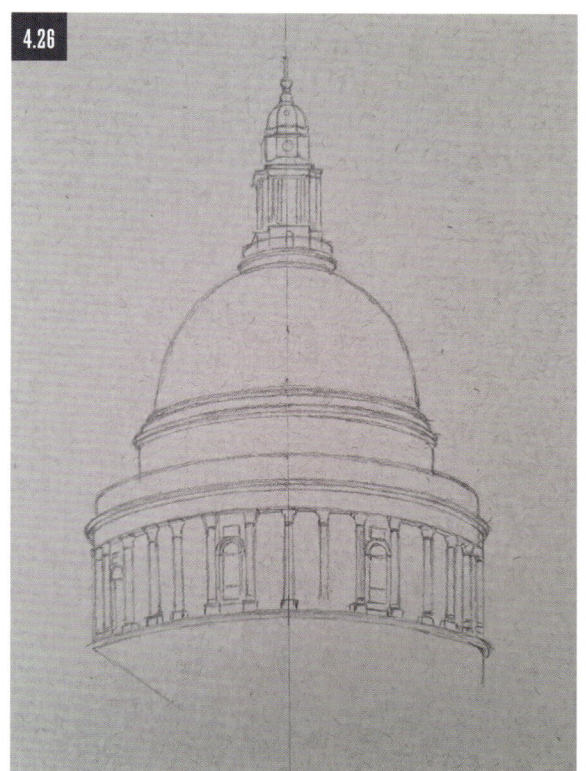

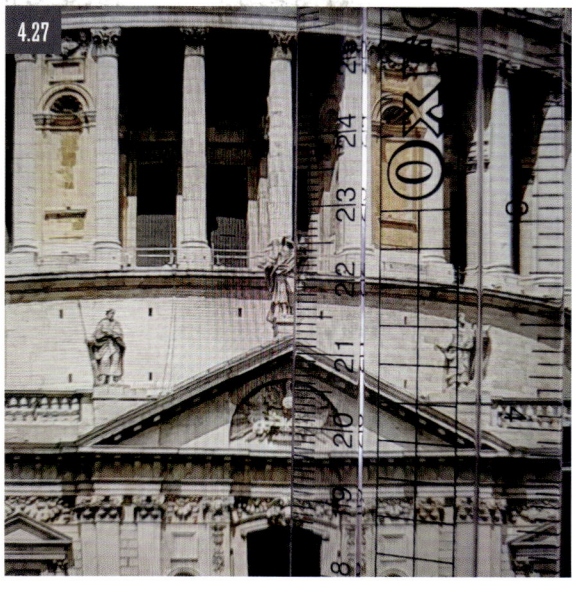

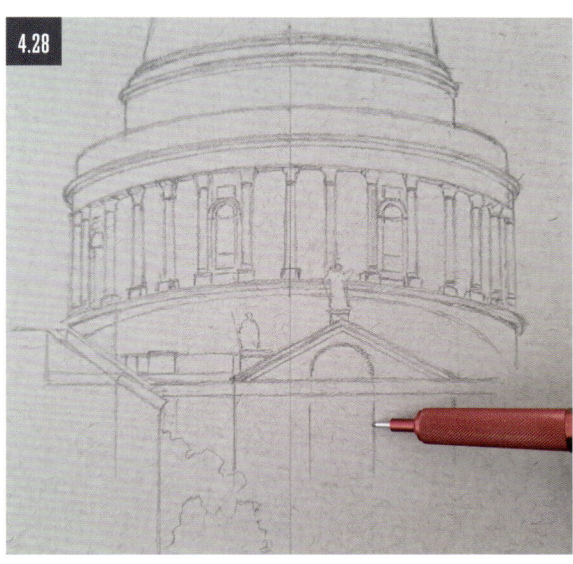

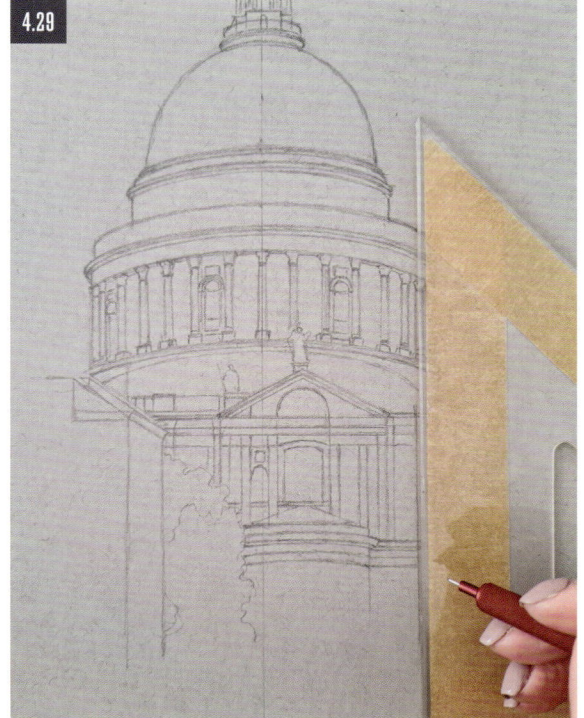

(**FIGURE 4.26**). Make sure to look at your reference picture regularly to help you gauge the space between them correctly. Notice that the distance between them gets smaller near the sides of the building. Getting this right will help create the illusion of depth.

Now that you have the columns in place, they can be used as markers to line up other vertical lines and areas of the building below (**FIGURES 4.27** and **4.28**). Regularly check that everything is straight using your ruler and set square (**FIGURE 4.29**).

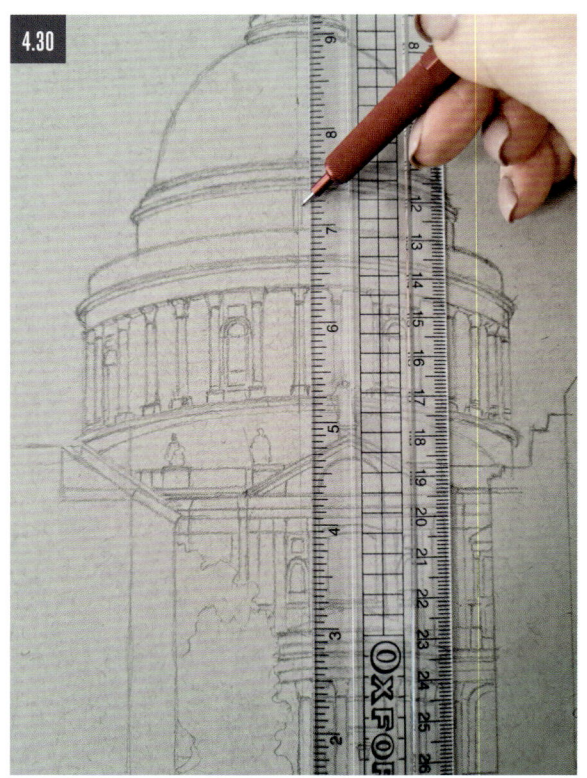

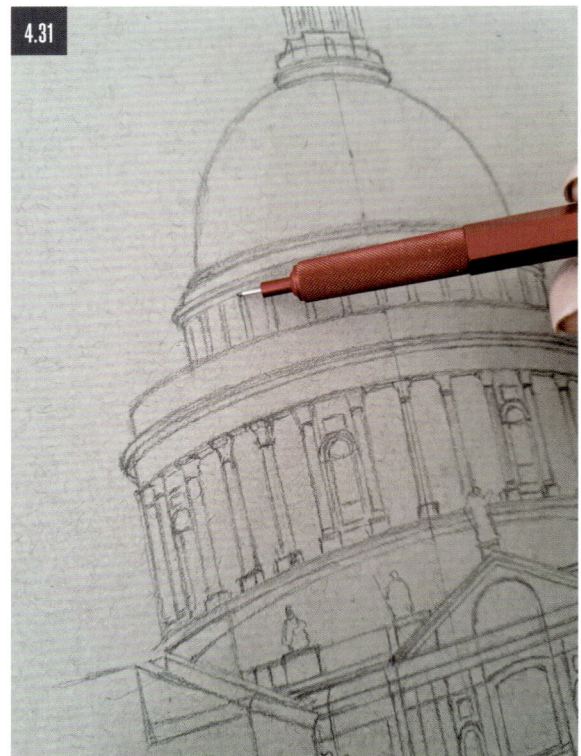

Continue to work down the building, piecing the shapes and lines together until you get to the bottom.

Look back over your drawing and see if there are any other details that you want to add at this stage. Here I am using the columns as markers to add in more details and the windows above them (**FIGURES 4.30** and **4.31**).

Well done if you have gotten this far—remember, practice makes perfect!

The initial pencil drawing is the hardest part. If you take the time to create a strong foundation for your work, you won't run into trouble further down the line. It is better to spend time getting it just right at the beginning.

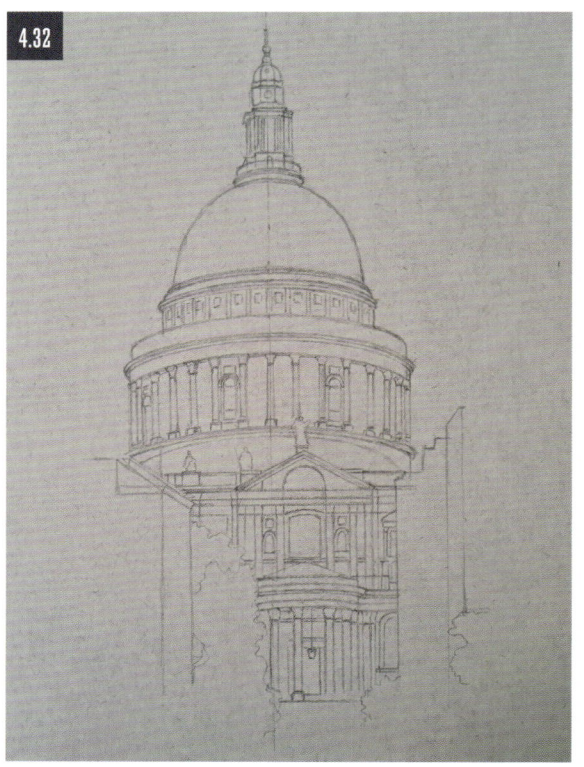

METHOD 3 Working from a Printout or Digital Screen

The basis of this method is to take accurate measurements with a ruler from a printout or digital screen, and then use those measurements as anchor points to help you get the proportions of the drawing right.

I find this method very useful for the initial pencil drawing, as it's a quick and accurate way to draw out smaller-sized pictures. It's a helpful tool for getting the initial proportions right, which is important in detailed architecture drawing like this.

The reference you have printed out will need to be the same actual size as you want the drawing to be. Alternatively, you could create a formula of, for instance, doubling the measurements to enlarge the drawing or halving the measurements to reduce the drawing. However, this can be a complicated way to do things, so in those instances I would recommend using the grid method instead.

I usually start my picture off by taking a few measurements from the printout or my Samsung tablet, and then I draw the rest freehand as my confidence grows. Feel free to experiment and see what works for you in terms of how many measurements you need to take to help you draw the building.

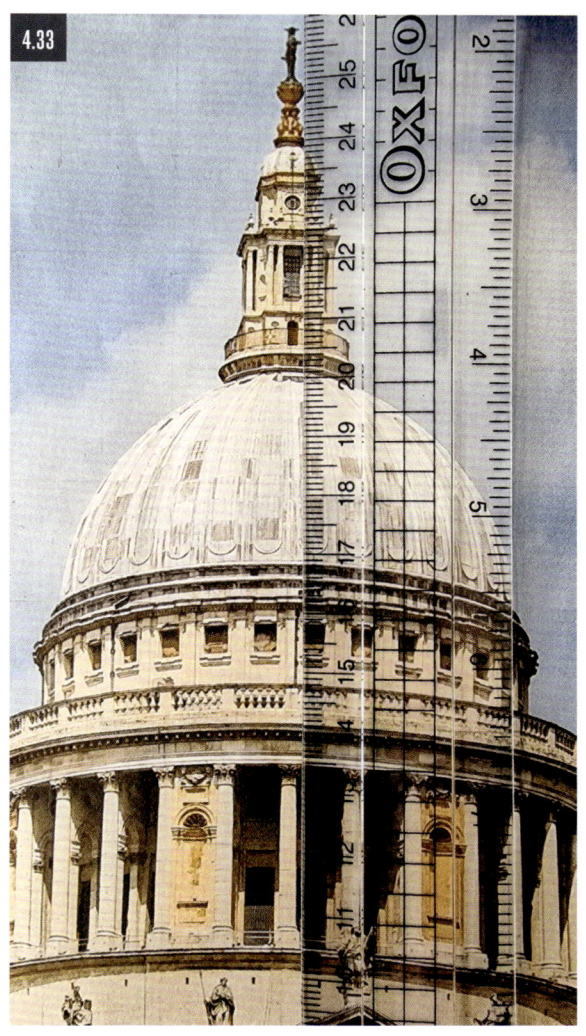

Step 1: Determine the central points

Find the centre of your paper and draw a vertical line down the centre of the page.

Now, measure the length of the whole building on your reference photo, and then use this measurement to work out where to accurately place the drawing centrally on the page (**FIGURE 4.33**).

Step 2: Create measurements and use them as guides for your drawing

On your reference photo, measure the distance from the very top of the building to the top of the dome (**FIGURE 4.34, NEXT PAGE**). Then transfer this measurement to your paper, measuring down from the top mark on your paper and making another mark where the top of the dome should be.

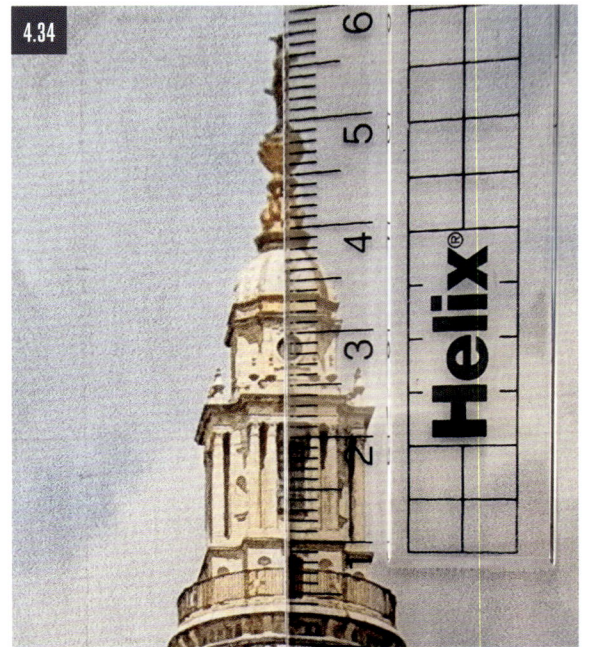

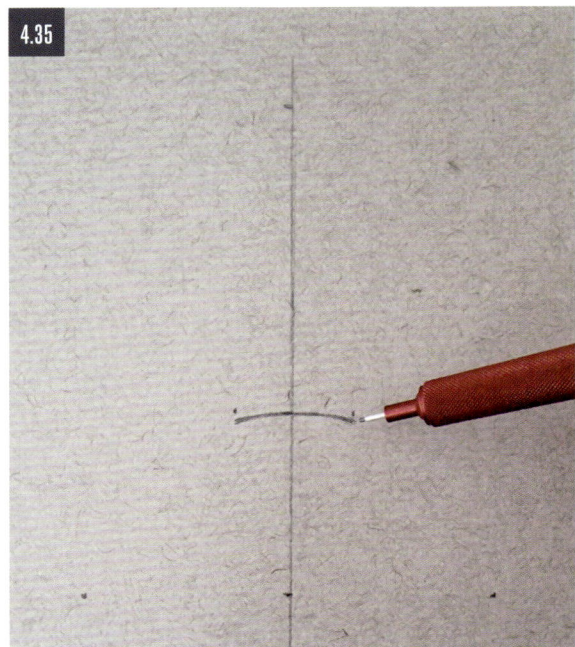

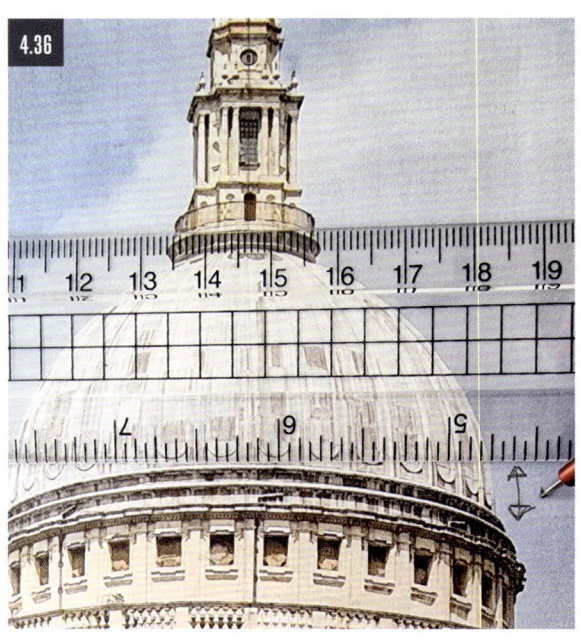

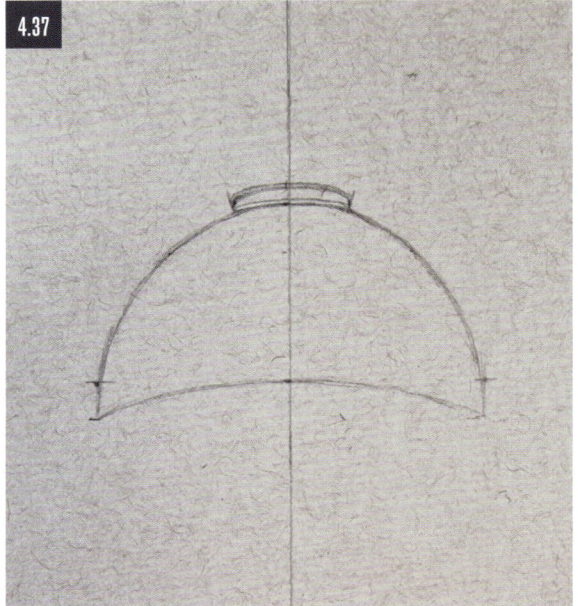

Next, measure the height of the dome and the width at the top and base. Transfer these measurements onto your paper using the central line as your guide (**FIGURE 4.35**). You are using these initial measurements as accurate guides and anchor points to start you off.

Place your ruler straight across the base of the dome to see the distance between the base and the centre point of the dome's ellipse shape (**FIGURE 4.36**). Measure this distance to help you accurately create the shape of the dome. Using the measurements as a guide, draw in the curves of the dome—a bit like a "connect the dots" drawing activity (**FIGURE 4.37**).

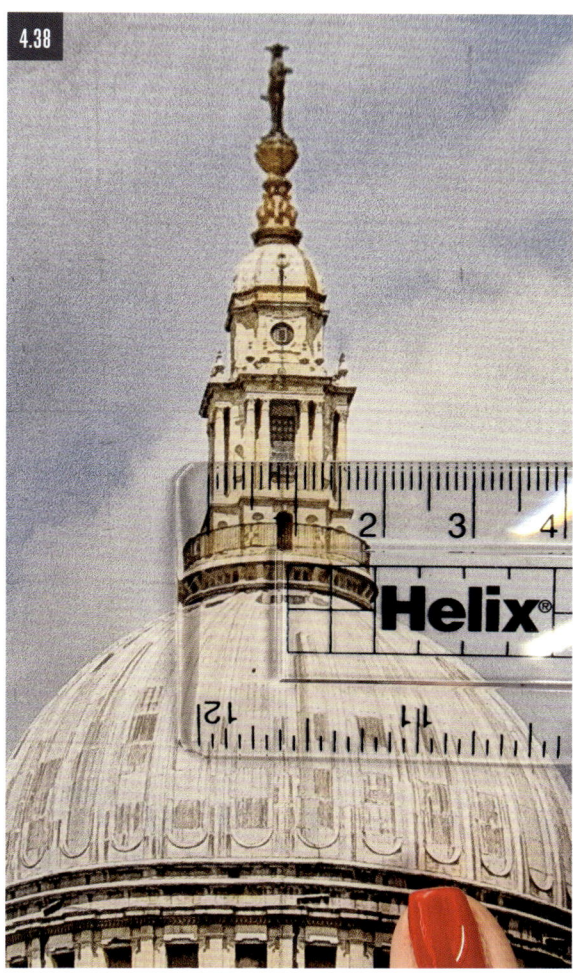

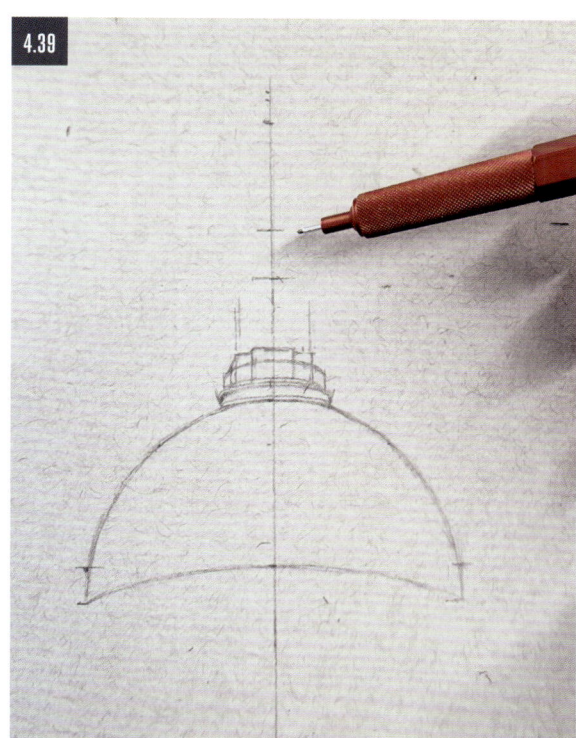

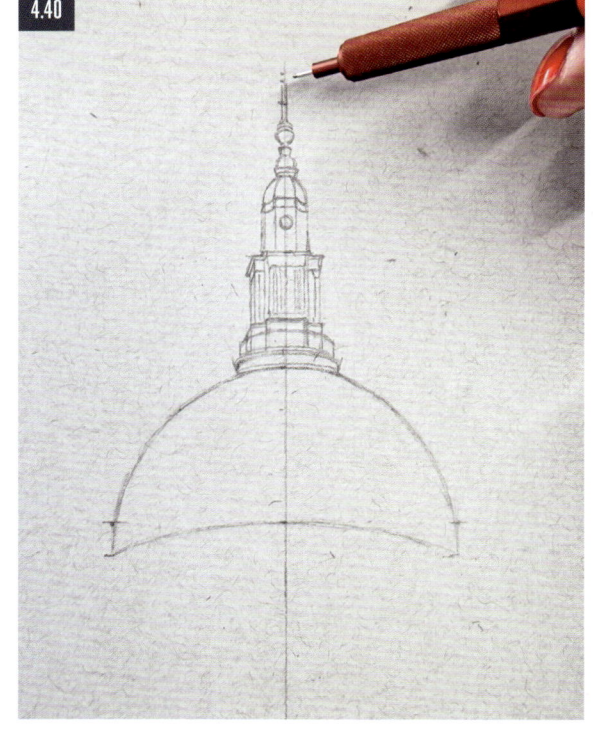

Continue in this fashion, measuring the width and height of each main shape, and use the measurements to add on the next part of the building (**FIGURE 4.38–4.40**).

Once you get started and find a rhythm of working, you may find that you are able to use a combination of accurate measurements as anchor points and your own judgement for some of the spacing.

Pay attention to where the different shapes meet and line up, and use your ruler to check that both sides of the drawing line up and are straight (**FIGURE 4.41, NEXT PAGE**). If you need to, measure the distance at the side of the building as it protrudes outward (**FIGURE 4.42, NEXT PAGE**).

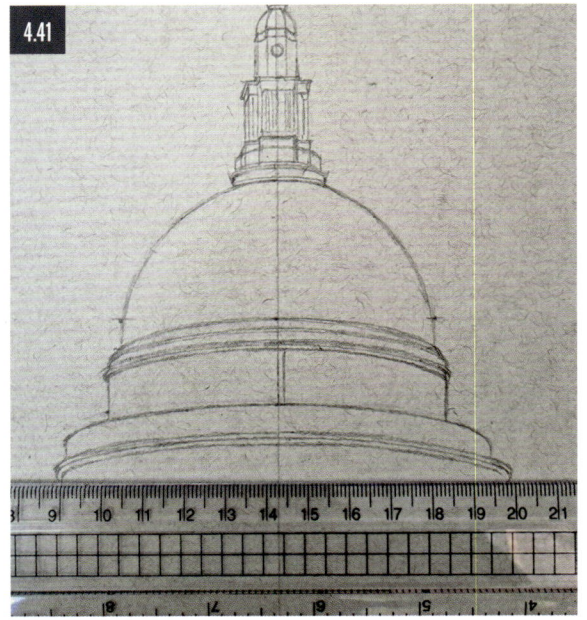

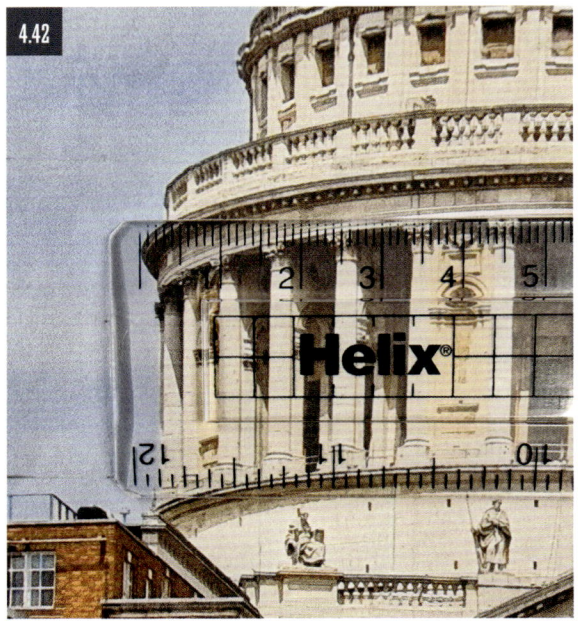

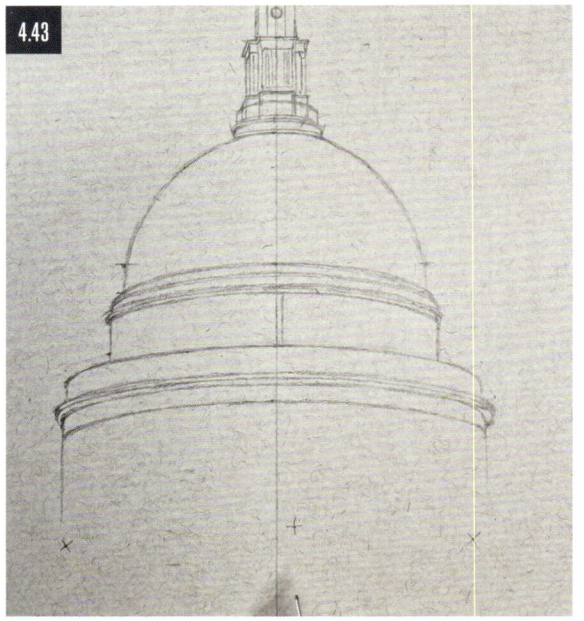

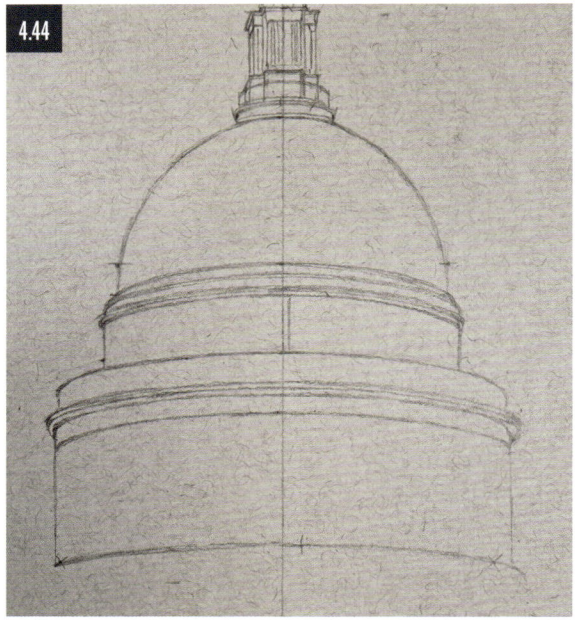

Measure just about anything that helps you get your placement of the shapes just right—for instance, the distance between the columns as well as the column heights and widths.

Continue working down the building, one section at a time, using your anchor points as your guide, but still look closely at your reference photo as well (**FIGURES 4.43** and **4.44**).

This is just like a puzzle—you are piecing each shape together until you have covered the whole page (**FIGURE 4.45**). You can add more details later with fineliner pen.

Drawing and Illustrating Architecture

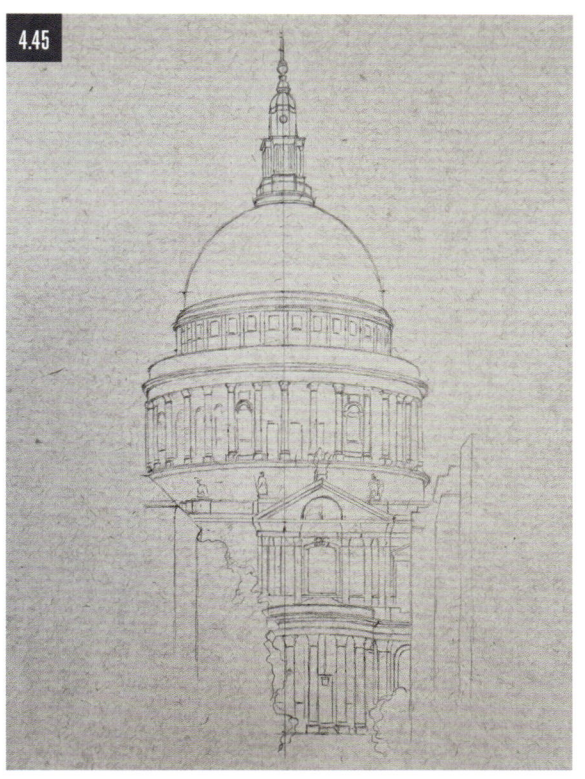

4.45

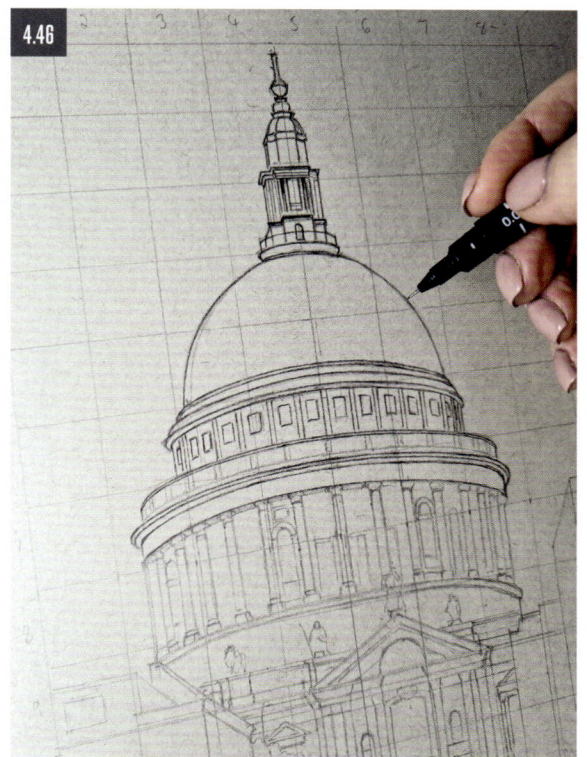

4.46

Step 2: COVERING THE PENCIL LINES WITH INK

Now that I have shown you the different ways to draw out your picture, we can move onto the next steps: covering the pencil lines with a black ink fineliner pen, adding depth and shadows, and then finally adding vibrant colour.

Once the pencil drawing is complete, you can begin to go over the lines in ink using a 0.05mm black fineliner (**FIGURE 4.46**). Start on either the left side (if you are right-handed) or at the top. Keep your sheet of paper or tracing paper under your hand to ensure you don't smudge the pencil lines (**FIGURE 4.47**). The process is much easier if your work is kept nice and clean.

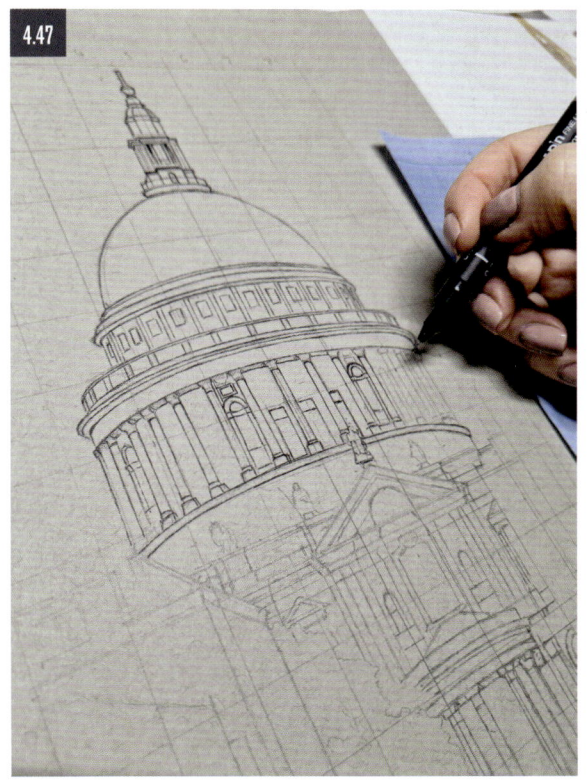

4.47

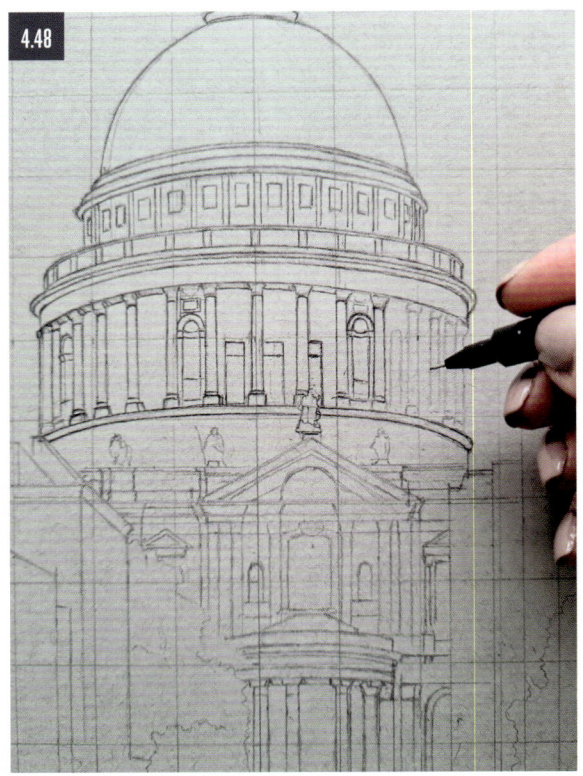

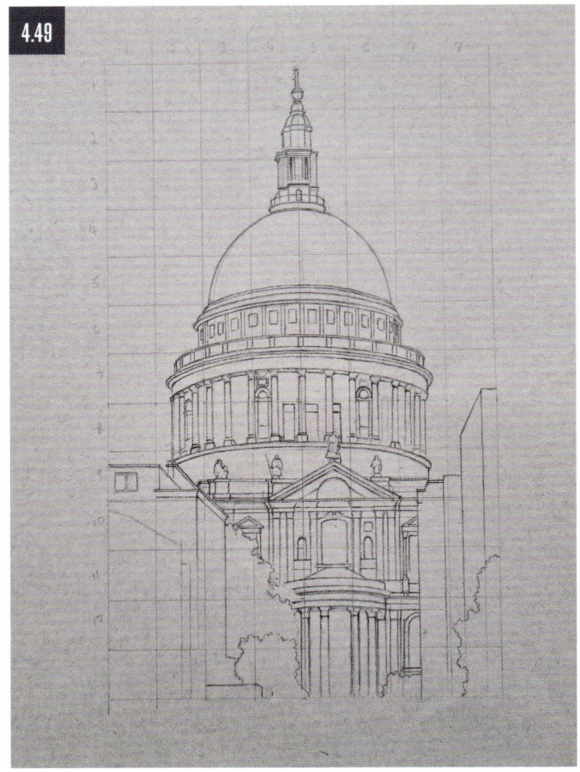

Keep working across the page until you have covered the whole pencil drawing with fine black ink lines. It's up to you if you use a ruler and set square to help you do this or do it freehand. I find it more enjoyable and freeing to do this part freehand, but do whatever feels most comfortable to you. I also like my ink lines to have a sketchy feel and not be too perfect so that the overall work is not too artificial and static (**FIGURE 4.48**).

You may find you want to adjust some of your pencil lines as you go along, as you can achieve a greater degree of accuracy with the fine nib of the ink pen compared to the pencil.

Although you can't remove permanent ink lines on the paper if you make a mistake, you can usually fade them slightly with an eraser and cover mistakes with coloured pencil or Posca pen at a later stage.

Step 3: ADDING DEPTH AND SHADOWS

The next step is to begin adding some depth to the picture. We start by adding the darkest values.

Look carefully at your photo and observe the darkest shadows. Notice the shape of any shadows and how they fall. Begin to start adding the darkest value, which is black, by slowly crosshatching these dark areas and blocking in completely dark sections like the windows (**FIGURE 4.50**). The denser you make the crosshatching, the darker the tone of the shading will be. You will immediately begin to see some depth emerge (**FIGURE 4.51**).

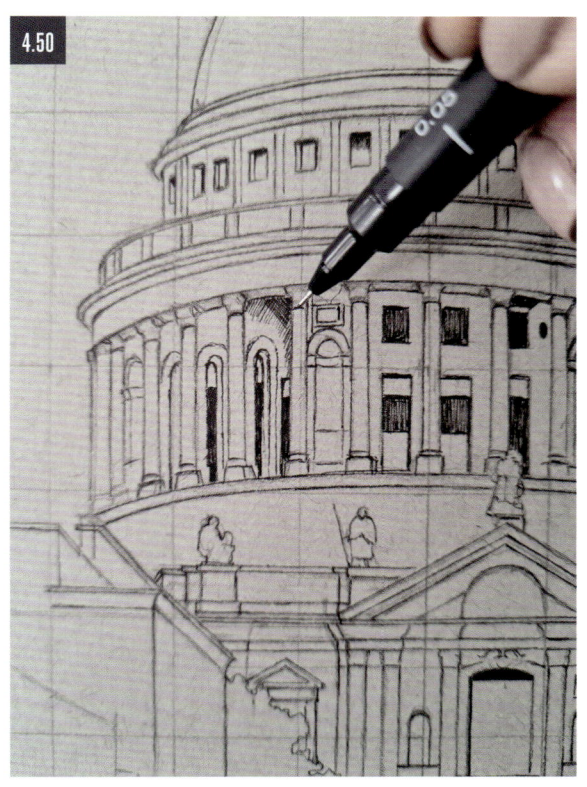

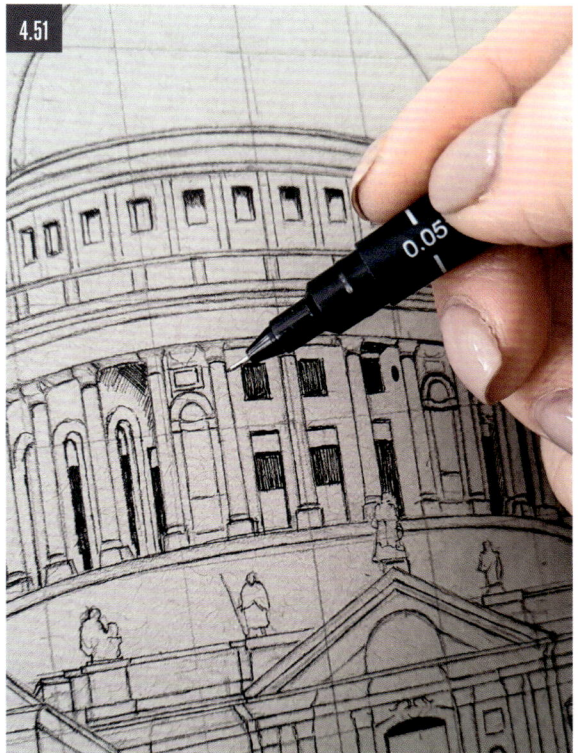

Remember that using high contrasts of dark and light tone will give the picture depth, interest, and impact, so it's an important step to focus on the darkest areas.

The aim is to create a three-dimensional-looking finished drawing.

Look for dark areas, such as where the different sections of stonework meet and the small dark regions beneath and around windows, and add these in too.

The use of crosshatching and little ink lines gives the drawing interest. As you progress with adding these in, you'll see your drawing start to come to life before your eyes. It's amazing how quickly the drawing begins to evolve as soon as you start to add depth (**FIGURE 4.52**).

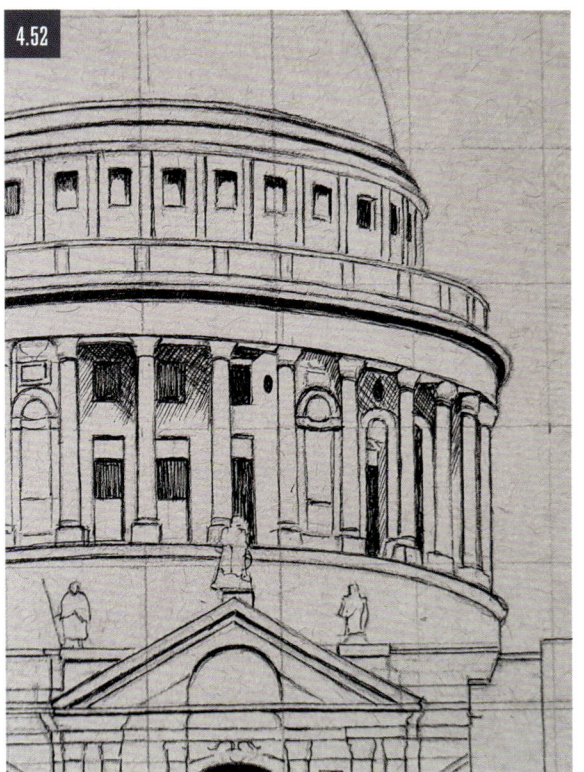

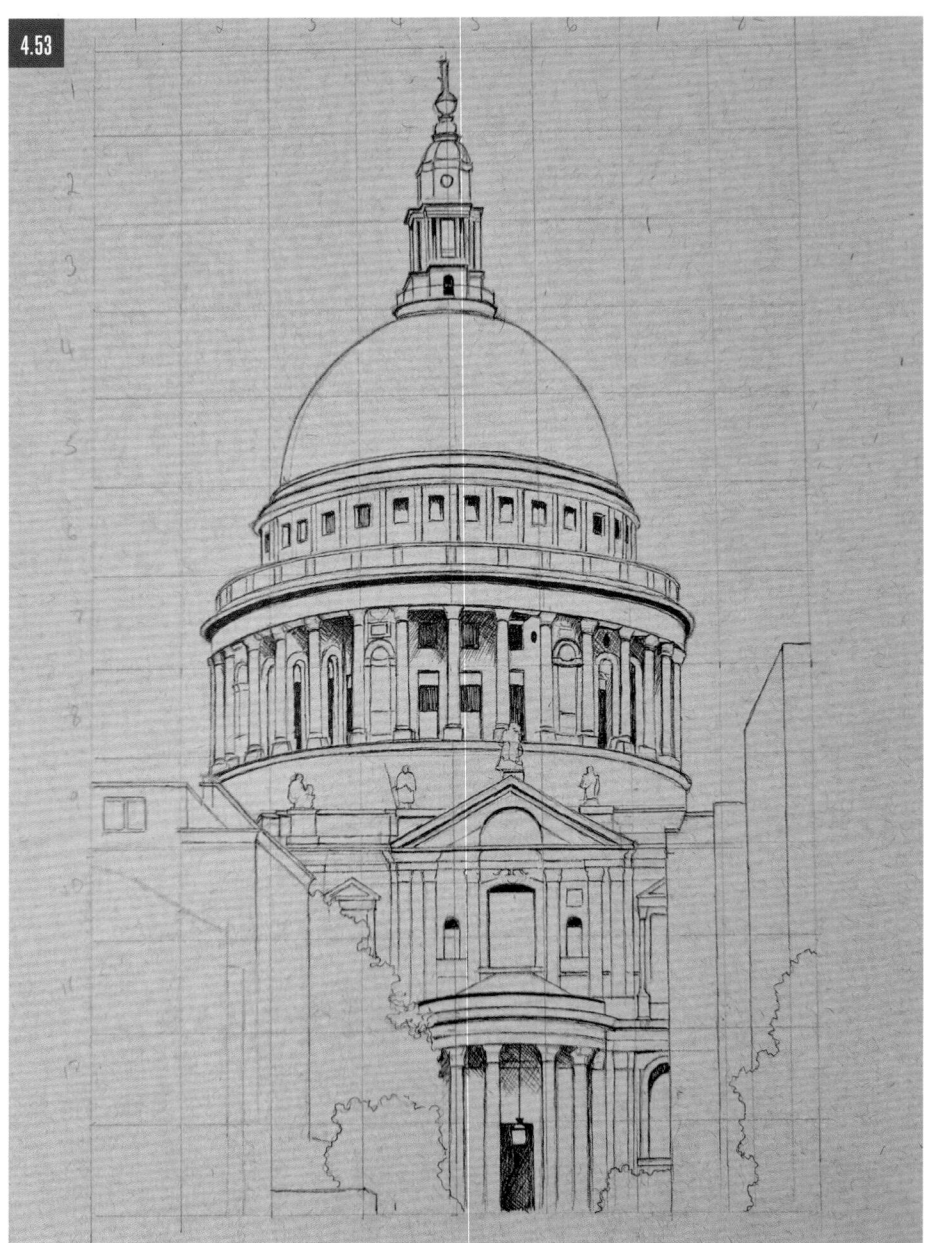

4.53

Continue working across the whole drawing until your pencil lines are completely covered in ink and any crosshatching is complete (**FIGURE 4.53**). We will go back in and touch up these areas with more ink at a later stage.

Something to note is that shadows often have a mix of colour in them and aren't usually completely black. Photographs can sometimes make them look like they are. When I start to add colour, I like to add interest by adding cool violets or a warm yellow ochre near the edges. This is particularly true of cast shadows that are projected onto the ground.

Drawing and Illustrating Architecture

Step 4: ADDING COLOUR

The next stage is to start adding layers of colour with your coloured pencils and the brightest highlights with white pencil and white gel pen or Posca pen. Before you begin, gently erase some of the graphite pencil lines. Do this gently so as not to weaken the strength of the ink lines.

For the whole of the colour work in this drawing it is a process of slowly building up the pencil layers using just a few colours, and also concentrating on mid-tones and dark tones plus adding the brightest highlights.

> ➤ White gel and Posca pens go down on the page easier when used straight on the paper. If you need to use them on top of pencil, get the ink flowing by pressing the nib down onto a separate clean sheet of paper.

The main focus in the reference photo is the dome and lantern on the top, so I'm going to start there. Note that the sun is high in the sky above the cathedral, causing all the shadows to be cast downward.

Begin by adding colour to the lightest areas using white pencil and white Posca pen (**FIGURE 4.54**). Then start applying the next lightest shade, Ivory. Layer the Ivory colour over the top of the white to achieve a bright and rich creamy colour.

Look closely at the photo and really observe the colours and the brightest and darkest areas. Keep the lightest areas crisp and clean so any white highlights you add go onto the paper easily and remain bright.

> ➤ Keep your sheet of paper or tracing paper under your hand to keep the work clean.

For the dome, apply two or more layers of crisp white pencil and blend them together (**FIGURE 4.55**). Although the dome isn't completely white, this

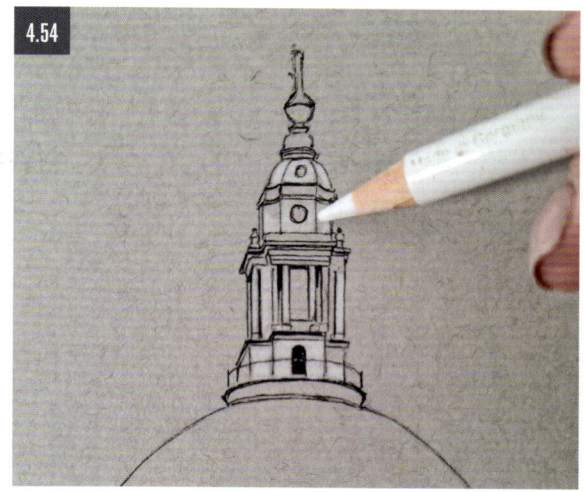

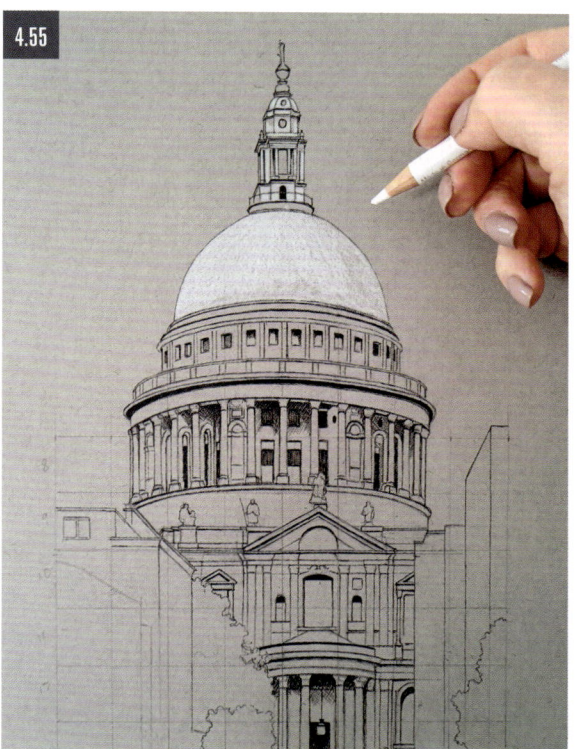

gives a nice opaque base on which to add more layers of colour. Use your white gel pen or Posca pen to add white highlights to the dome and some of the curves of the building below (**FIGURE 4.56, NEXT PAGE**), and begin to add some white pencil to the central columns as well. Next, if you haven't done so already, lightly mark in the shapes and curves on the dome with pencil (**FIGURE 4.57, NEXT PAGE**).

Further build the colour by adding some Silver Grey. Use light strokes moving in the direction of the curves of the dome. Now use Warm Grey IV and Dark Sepia to lightly shade in the grey areas on the dome (**FIGURE 4.58**). Warm Grey IV works as a great mid-tone grey, and I'm using it for all the mid-tone shadows (**FIGURE 4.59**).

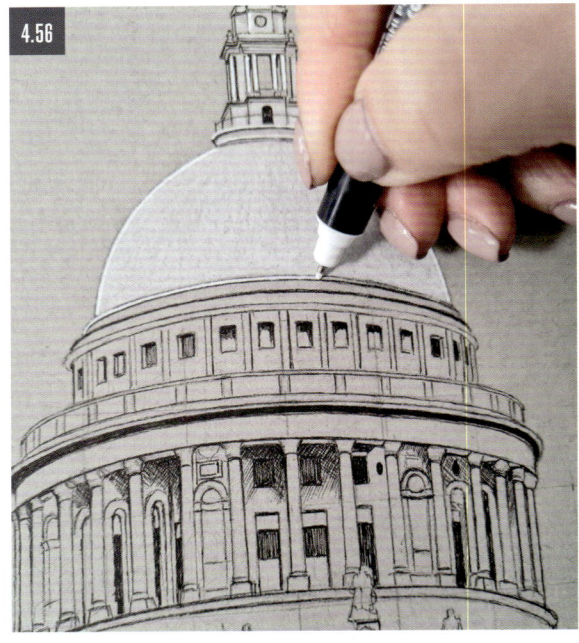

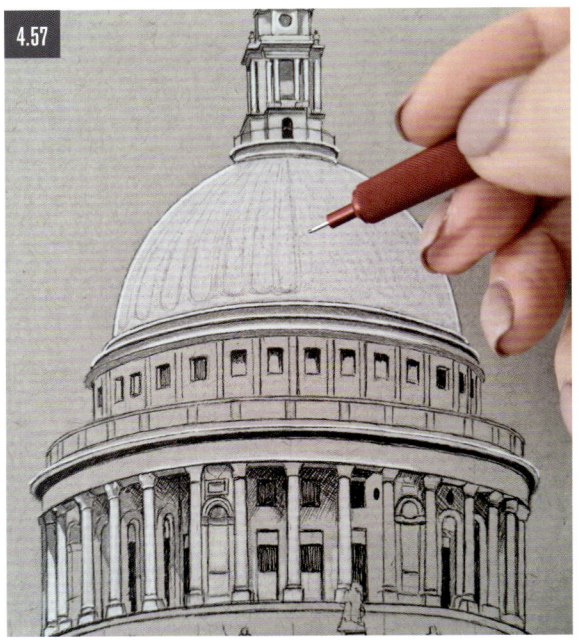

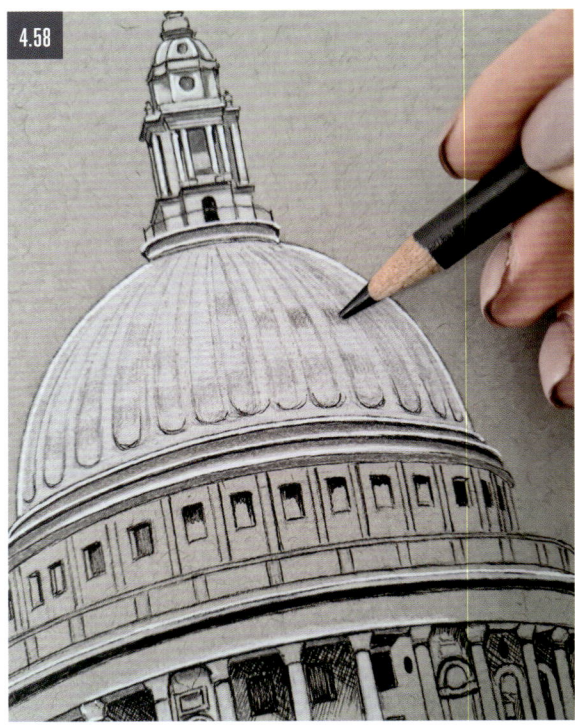

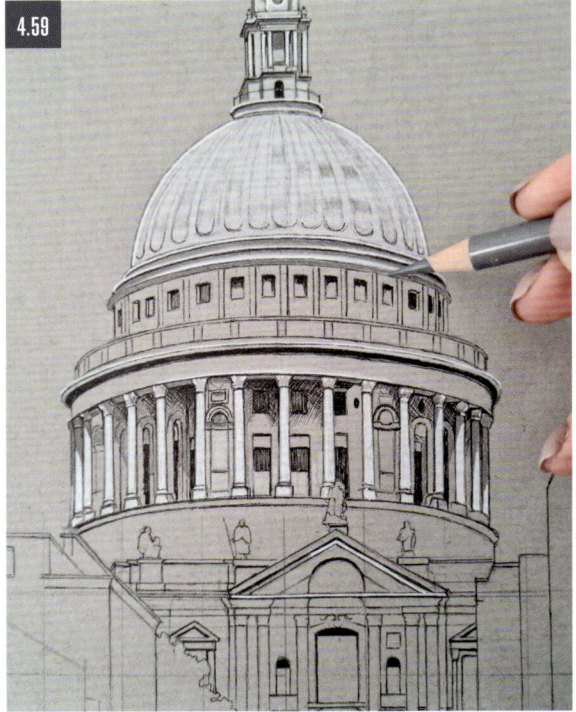

Drawing and Illustrating Architecture

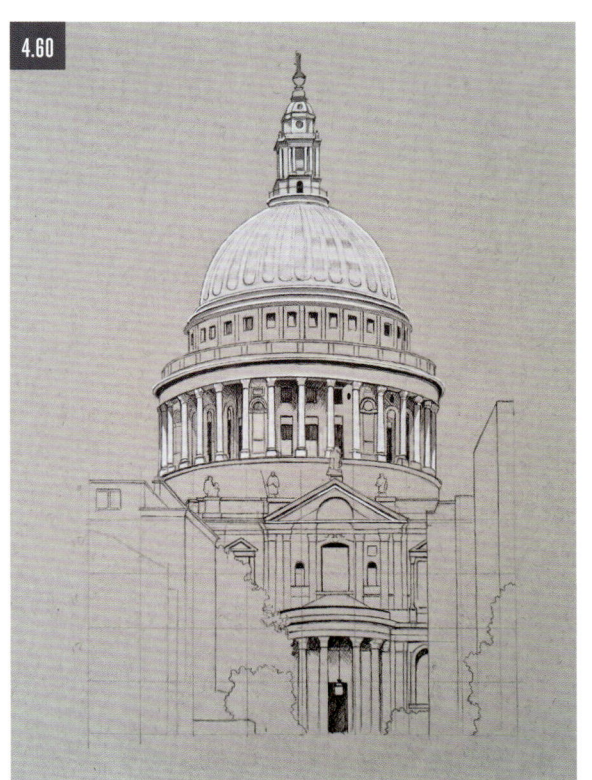

Use your white Posca or gel pen to colour the central columns. The bright white against the dark shadows will make them really stand out and create some beautiful depth (**FIGURE 4.60**). Now move on to using an Ivory pencil to begin replicating the cream-coloured stonework (**FIGURE 4.61**).

Add more depth to any darker shadows using Payne's Grey and your fineliner (**FIGURE 4.62**). As you slowly build up more contrast throughout the drawing and add more depth using the darkest darks and lightest colours, your artwork will start to pop on the page.

Use a very sharp Ivory pencil to draw in the balustrade that goes all the way around the building (**FIGURE 4.63, NEXT PAGE**). Then use Payne's Grey to add the darkness in between.

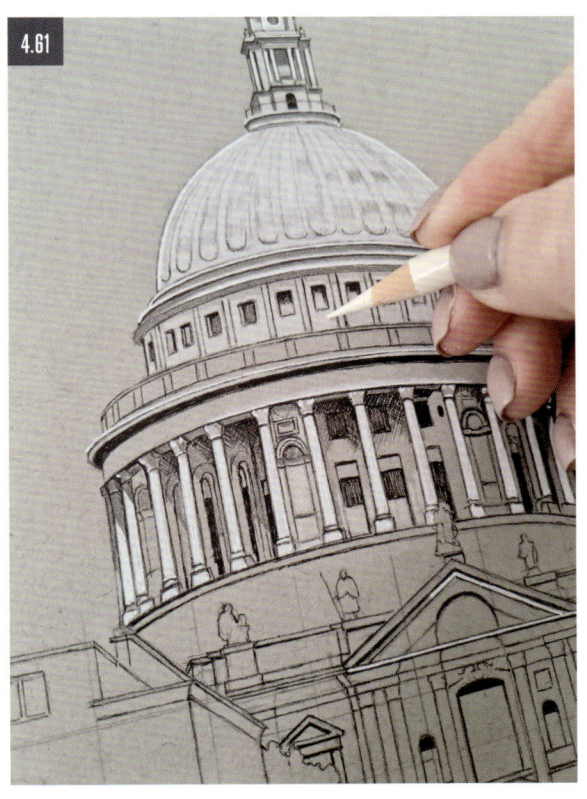

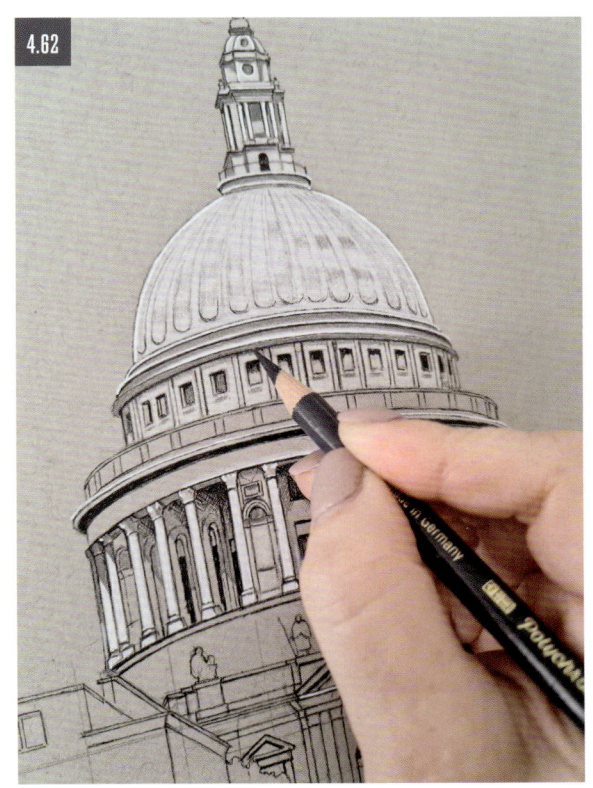

Continue to work your way all over the building layering and deepening the pencil with just these few colours. Lightly colour with the Brown Ochre pencil on top of areas of ivory where you want to create yellow tones and to slightly warm areas of shadow that have reflected sunny light (**FIGURES 4.64** and **4.65**).

Work your way down the structure with your Ivory pencil, adding colour to the lower parts of your drawing (**FIGURE 4.66**).

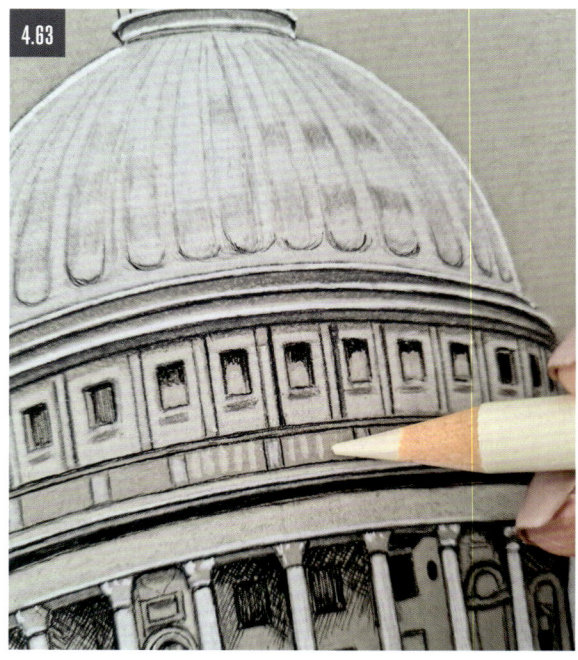

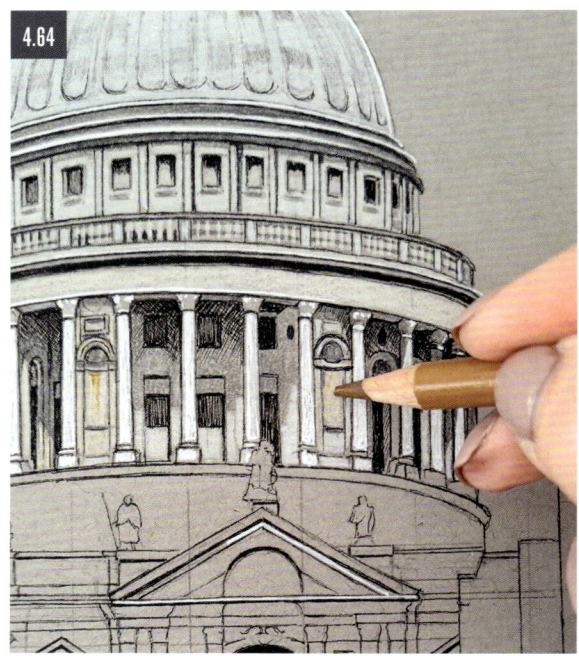

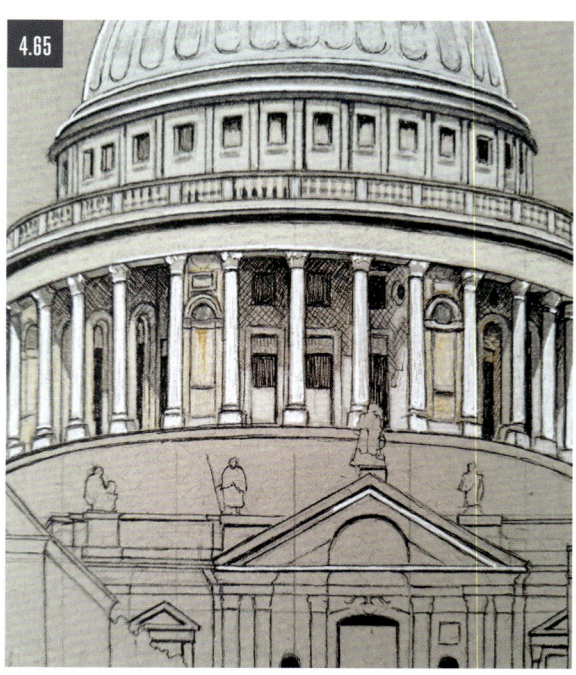

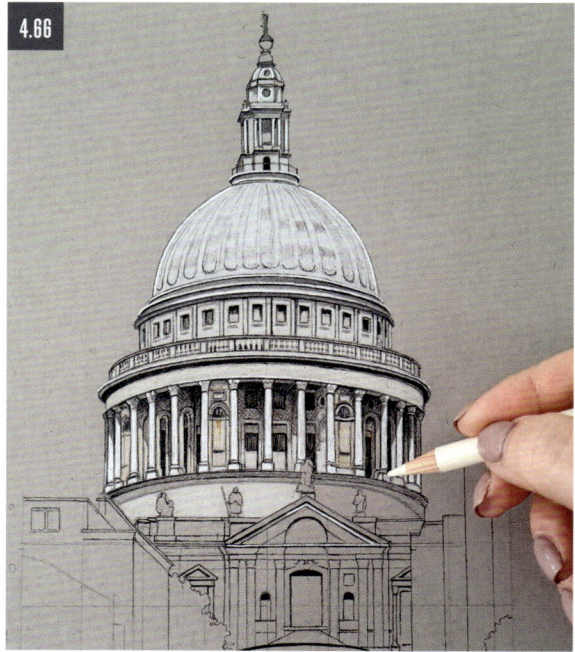

Drawing and Illustrating Architecture

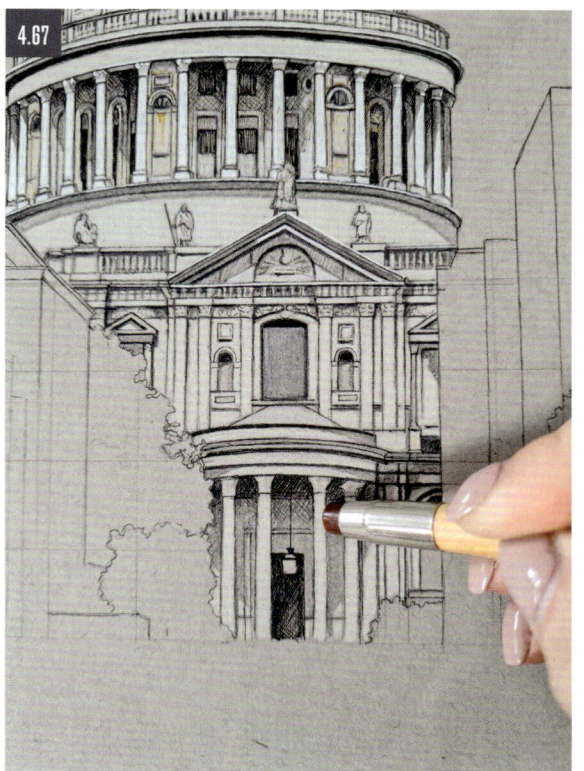

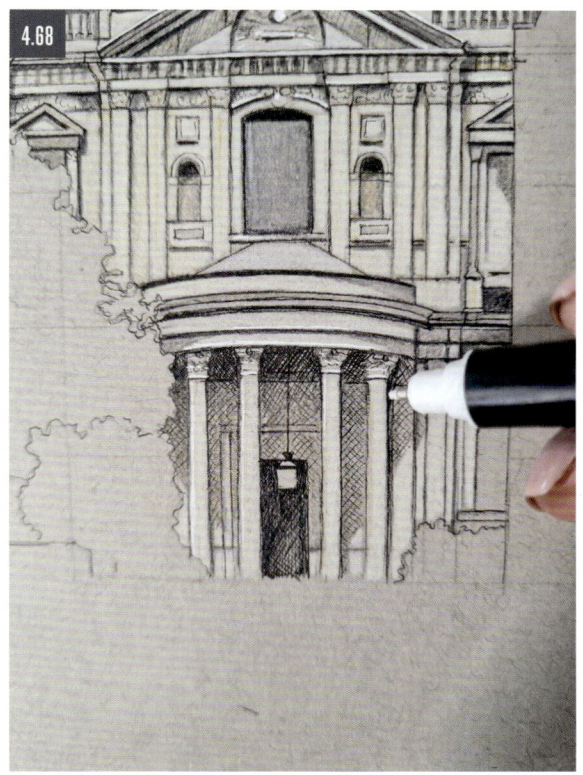

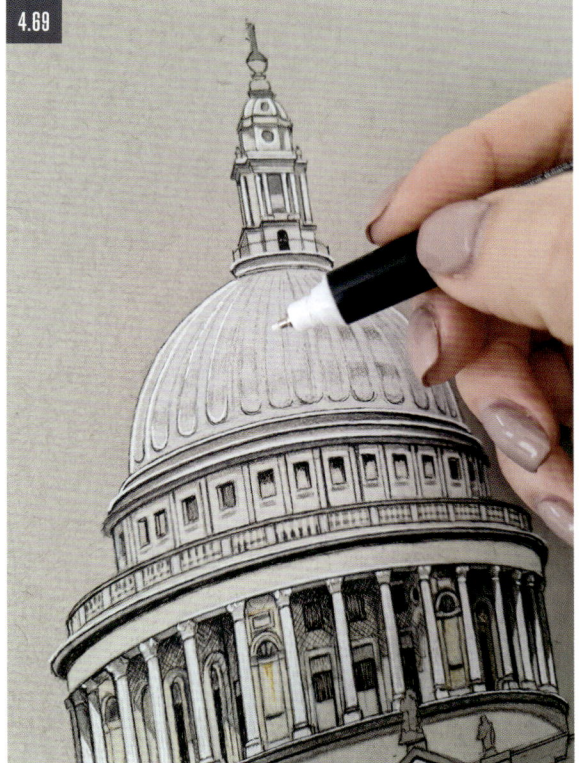

Use your blender to push the colours together (**FIGURE 4.67**). You can also add more crosshatching in the darkest areas straight on top of pencil. This adds a nice textured look and finish.

Use a white Posca or gel pen to highlight the very lightest areas like the dome, columns, and tops of the statues (**FIGURES 4.68** and **4.69**).

Step 5: BUILDING LAYERS OF RICH COLOUR

Move across your work adding more and more layers of colour. You can achieve a greater richness of colour by applying many thin layers and blending them together, rather than trying to create one thick layer.

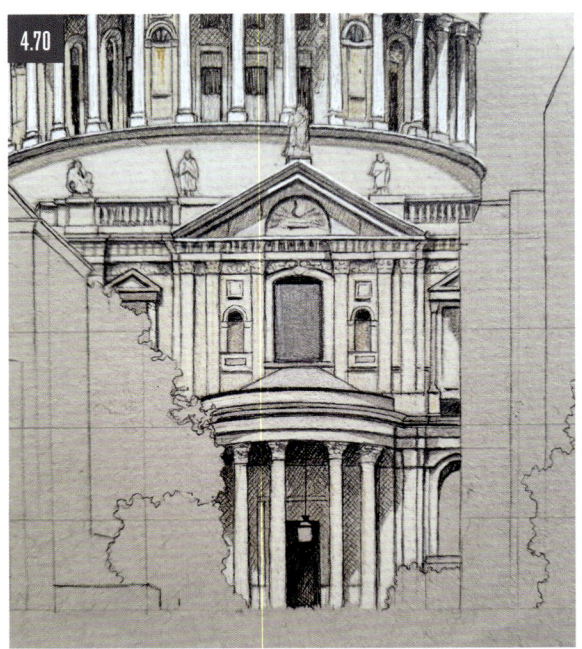

Continue to work in this way until you have filled your whole drawing with colour (**FIGURE 4.70**).

> ➤ Remember that the beauty of working in coloured pencil is that you can rub it out and start again if you aren't happy with the results. You can also rub out any ink lines that have been placed on top of pencil!

Step 6: ADDING DETAILS AND DEFINITION

Use your fineliner pen to add more tiny details and definition, like the railings going all around the bottom of the lantern (**FIGURE 4.71**). You can suggest complicated and difficult-to-see details with loose lines and small dots of colour (**FIGURE 4.72**). Add more crosshatching and lines to increase depth, if necessary. Adding crosshatching on top of pencil looks nice and adds interest. You can also add extra details with your fineliner pen on top of pencil.

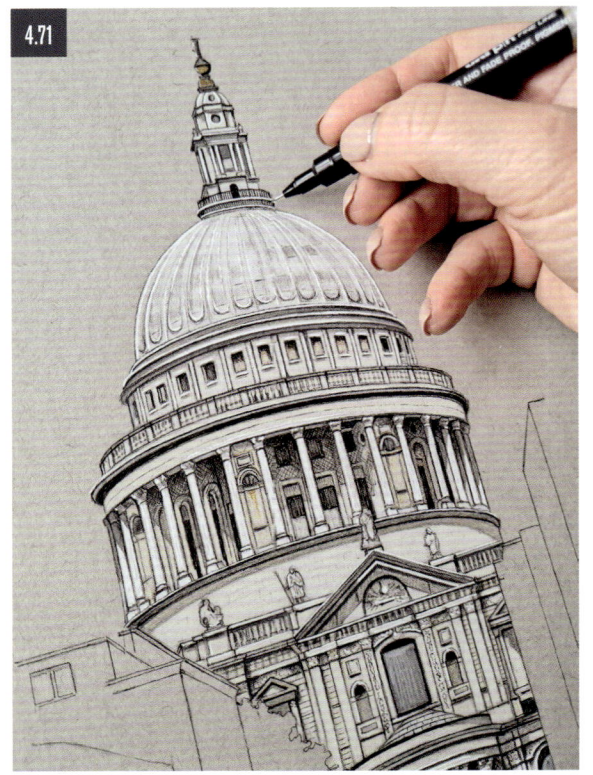

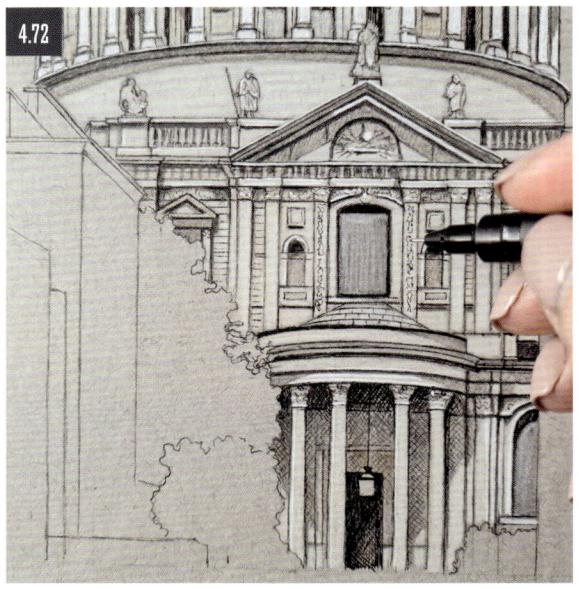

Mark in more brickwork as well. It's up to you how far you go with the details. I always take it to the max!

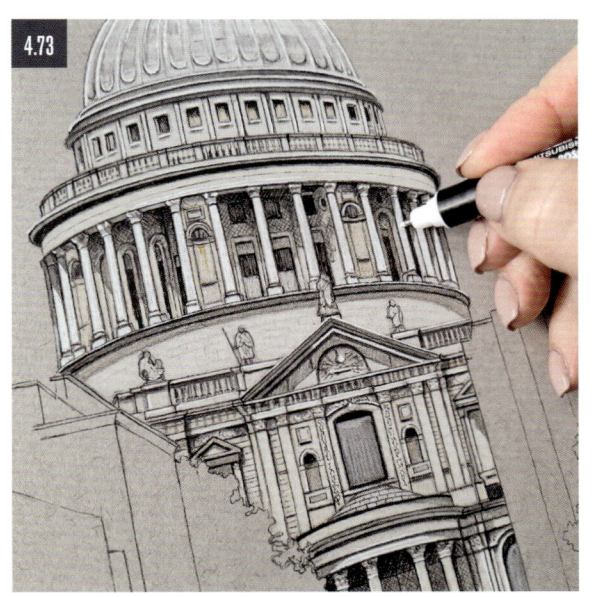

4.73

Step 7: FINISHING TOUCHES

If possible, in this last step, deepen or brighten the colours further to ramp up the contrast just a little bit more. This will further increase the three-dimensional effect.

Check to see if you can improve and brighten any highlights with white gel or posca pen (**FIGURE 4.73**).

Now sit back and admire your work, and don't forget to sign your masterpiece!

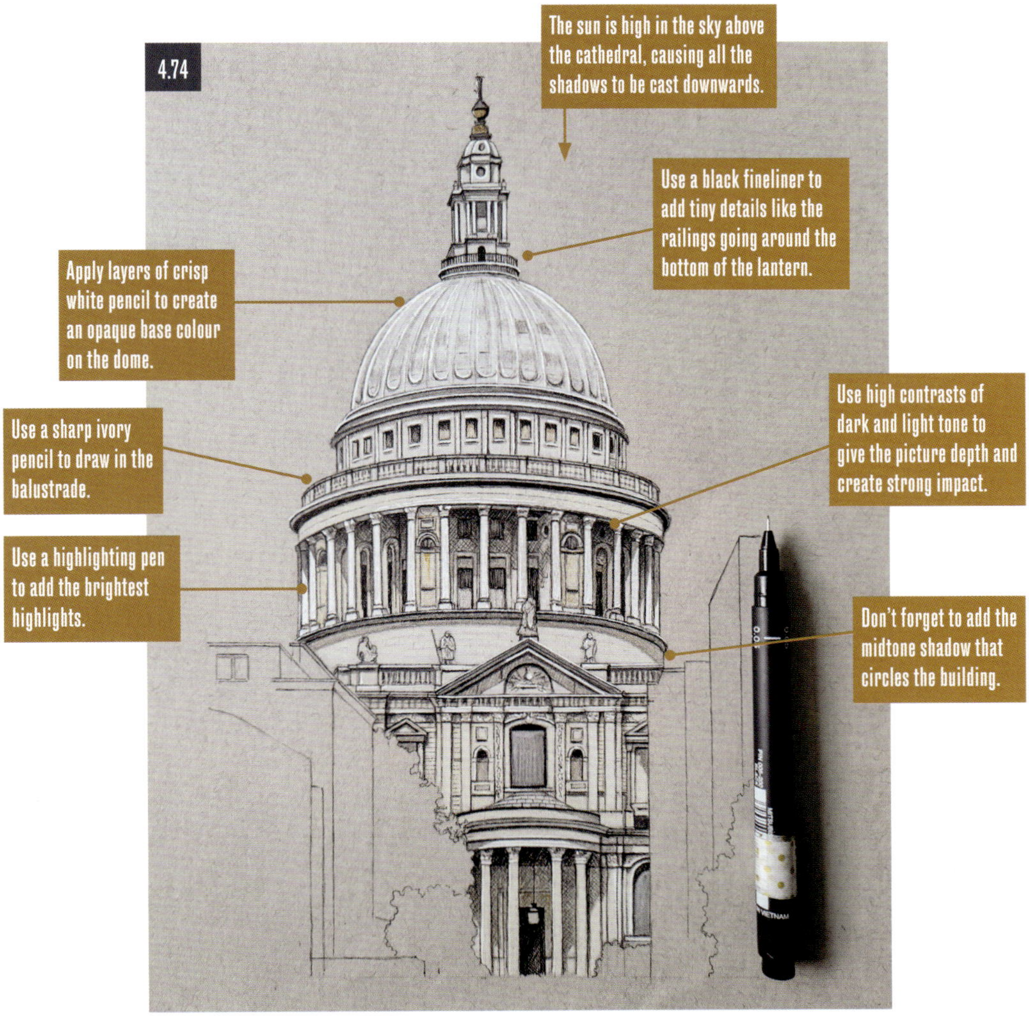

4.74

The sun is high in the sky above the cathedral, causing all the shadows to be cast downwards.

Use a black fineliner to add tiny details like the railings going around the bottom of the lantern.

Apply layers of crisp white pencil to create an opaque base colour on the dome.

Use a sharp ivory pencil to draw in the balustrade.

Use high contrasts of dark and light tone to give the picture depth and create strong impact.

Use a highlighting pen to add the brightest highlights.

Don't forget to add the midtone shadow that circles the building.

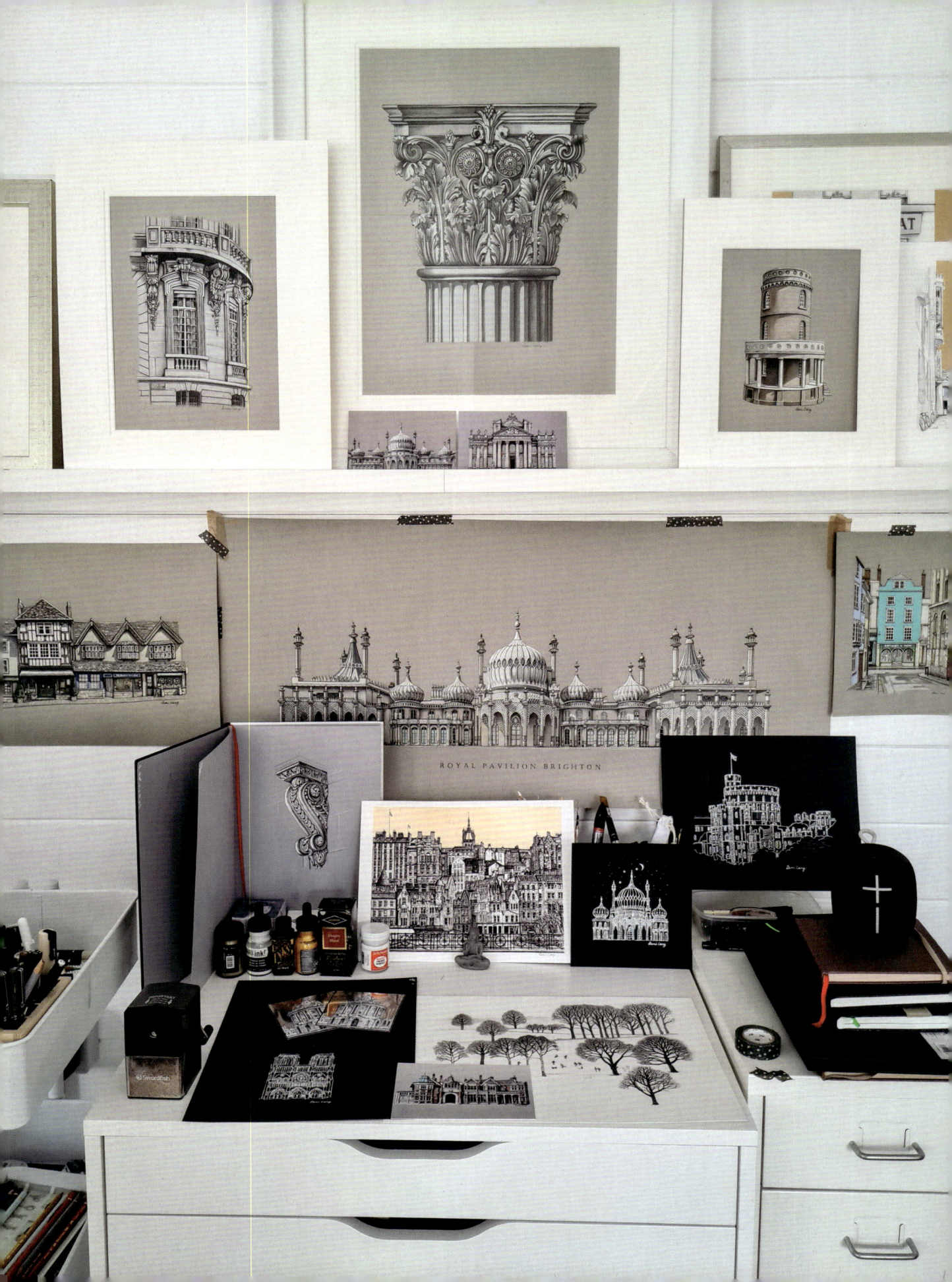

ROYAL PAVILION BRIGHTON

Projects

In Part Two of this book, there are five main projects for you to work on. Chapter 6, Architectural Details, has lots of mini projects within it that will help you with any future architecture illustration projects.

For each project I have chosen a reference photo of a beautiful building or detail. You can either choose to use this photo or use one of your own to apply the techniques described in each chapter. As mentioned before, all the project reference photos are available to download at rockynook .com/drawing-illustrating-architecture.

I have mainly used the same brand of pencils for all the projects, with a few exceptions. If you can't get one of the listed colours, use a similar colour—it will work just as well.

I hope you will learn new techniques as you follow the step-by-step pattern that I use to create this style of architecture illustration. This is my own style and is not definitive. I'm sure that with practice and time you will find your own style and methods to create your artworks. This is a springboard to get you started!

While working on the projects, remember that if you start to get tired or lose focus, it is better to take a break or start again the next day. This will prevent the quality of your work from suffering. It is much better to come back later with fresh eyes.

Enjoy the process and remember that patience and practice are key.

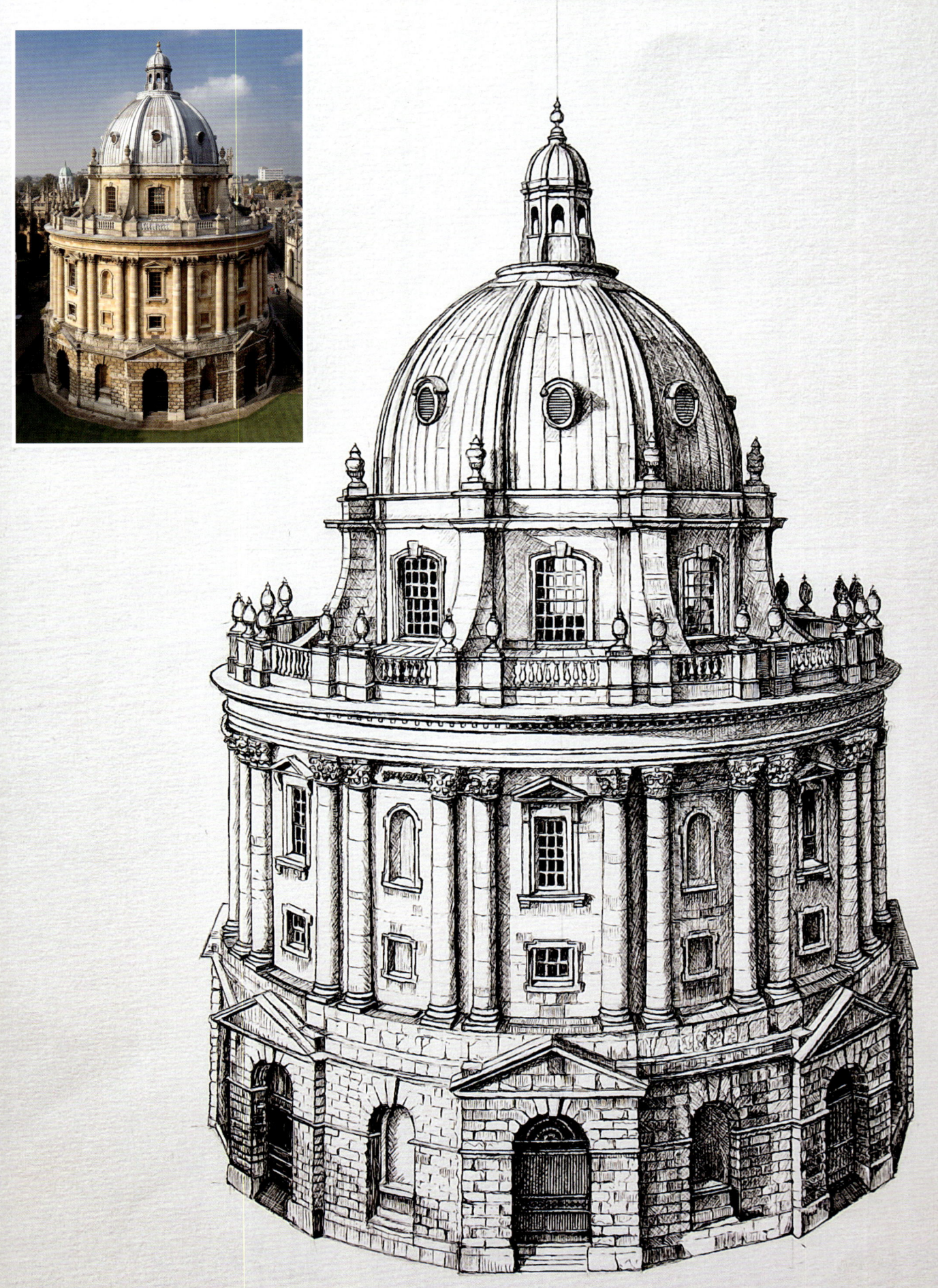

CHAPTER 5

Black-and-White Sketch

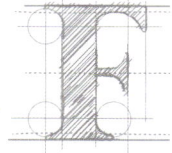or this project, we are going to create a drawing in black and white using just a black 0.05mm fineliner pen on white paper. Pure pen-and-ink drawings can look stunning left as monochrome, and they are a lot of fun to do without having to think about colour. We'll create the various tones and shadows within the subject using varying densities of cross-hatching, marks, and lines, all with black ink.

To demonstrate the process, I've chosen a photo of the Radcliffe Camera, which is a unique and iconic landmark situated in the heart of Oxford University in England (**FIGURE 5.1**). This unusual circular building is a working library used by Oxford University students that is designed in a neoclassical architecture style. It was built between 1737 and 1749.

For this project, I decided to work completely freehand because I wanted the freedom of working in pure ink on paper. You can, of course, use another method to draw the image, like taking measurements from a digital screen or using a grid. The choice is yours—any of the methods will work. It's important to do what you are most comfortable with.

At first glance, you may think, *I can't draw that, it's far too complicated!* But if you look closely over the photo, you will notice a lot of repetition. For instance, you may draw one window or column, and then notice that there are others of the same style, just at a different angle. By working on one section of the building at a time, you will be able to draw out the image with relative ease and then move on to focusing on adding depth with tone and shadows.

The most difficult part of this project is getting the curved shape of the building positioned correctly. Just know and accept that it will take time to complete the artwork, especially the pencil drawing, although you might be faster than me!

MATERIALS

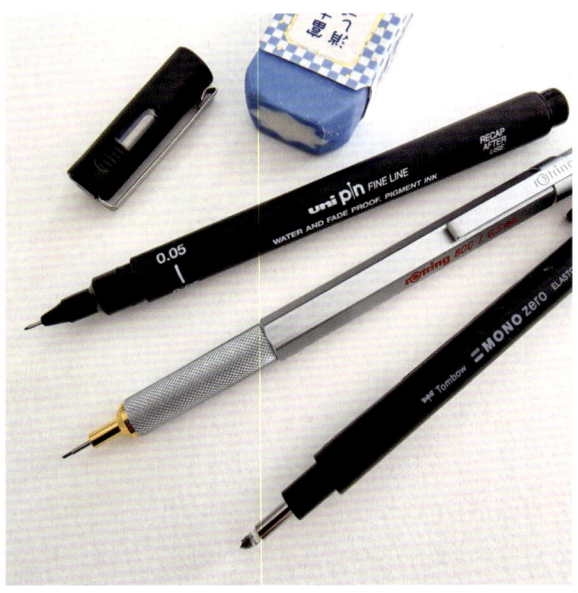

- ▶ White cartridge or watercolour paper
- ▶ Sharp pencil
- ▶ Black 0.05mm fineliner pen
- ▶ Ruler
- ▶ Set square
- ▶ Eraser

Choose a paper that is quite smooth and a good weight, such as high-quality cartridge paper or hot press watercolour paper. A smooth paper will enable you to draw precise detailed lines, and a good-weight paper will provide a robust support for your drawing that will look good in a frame when you are finished.

You can choose to use a different type of pen, like a fine-nib fountain pen, but before you start the ink work, I recommend testing it out on a separate piece of paper to make sure that the lines you create are fine enough.

Step 1: DRAW WITH PENCIL

The first thing to do is decide on the approximate size you want the drawing to be. It should be big enough to allow the beautiful architectural details to be seen relatively clearly. I would suggest printing the reference photo at A4 size, and then working on A3 size paper so that the drawing will fit nicely with some white space around it.

Once you have decided on the sizes, print out your reference photo and get ready to draw! Make sure that your ruler and set square are nice and clean so that they don't mark the white paper.

Begin by finding the centre of the page and drawing a vertical line downwards. As with all the projects, the drawing will be placed centrally, using this line as a guide to position the whole picture.

Remember, the initial sketch doesn't have to be perfect with every single detail drawn in. You also don't have to draw everything you observe. At this stage, or even later on, it is your choice how far you go with the details. More precision and details can be added later when you start introducing black fineliner pen—it is easier to draw small details with a fine pen nib.

Next, imagine how the drawing will look and fit onto the page, and determine where the small dome at the very top of the Radcliffe Camera will be placed (**FIGURE 5.1**). It will need to be positioned near the top of your paper. If your printout is the same size as the drawing will be, you can lay it on top of the paper to help visualise its placement.

Now take your pencil and start sketching the outer lines of the small dome at the very top (**FIGURE 5.2**). Notice how symmetrical it is. Once the first lines are in place, sit back and have a good look to make sure it is equal on both sides.

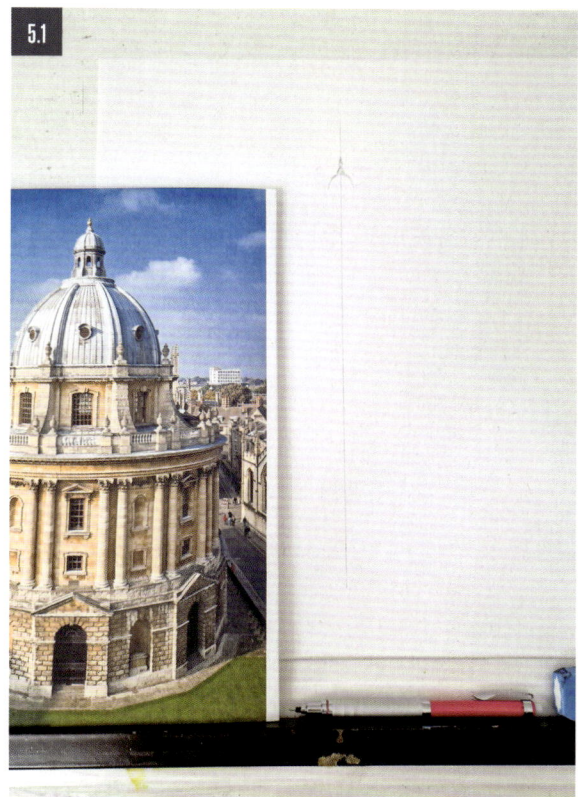

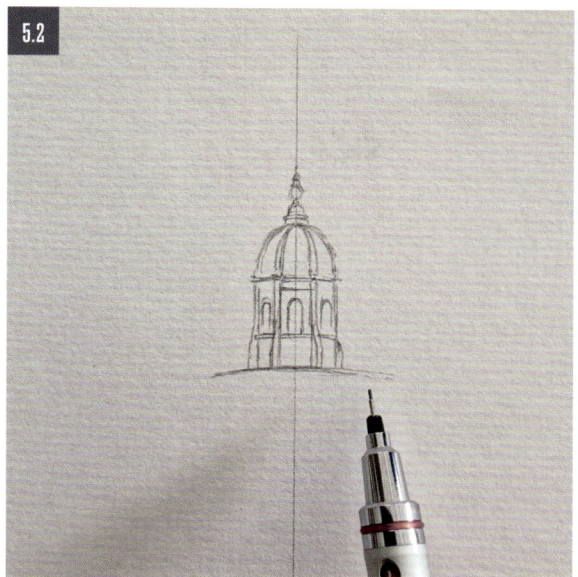

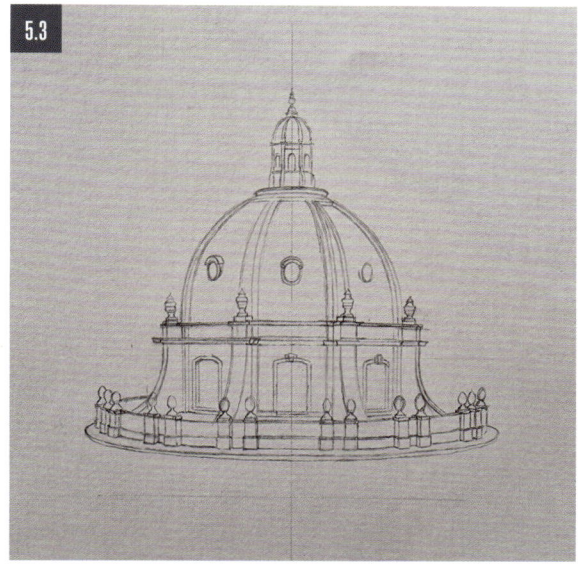

From this point onwards, start adding in more shapes, slotting them together like puzzle pieces as you move downwards towards the larger dome (**FIGURE 5.3**). Use your ruler to make sure that both sides of the drawing are straight and line up.

> ➤ Check that the different shapes that make up the building line up and slot together in the same position as in the photo.

As I've said before, drawing is like working on a puzzle. Each element of the subject matter has to be drawn in the correct shape and placed at the correct angle and distance from the next shape for everything to work and come together. By focusing on each area one at a time, slowly drawing in individual shapes and lining them up with what is above, below, and around them, you will end up with a correctly shaped building overall.

If you are drawing freehand, you may need to erase again and again until you get it right. This is a normal part of the process of drawing a complicated structure.

It will require some patience to get the curved shape of the building just right. It is worth taking the time to do this, as the rest of the drawing will then fall into place more easily. You will create the overall illusion of a three-dimensional circular building.

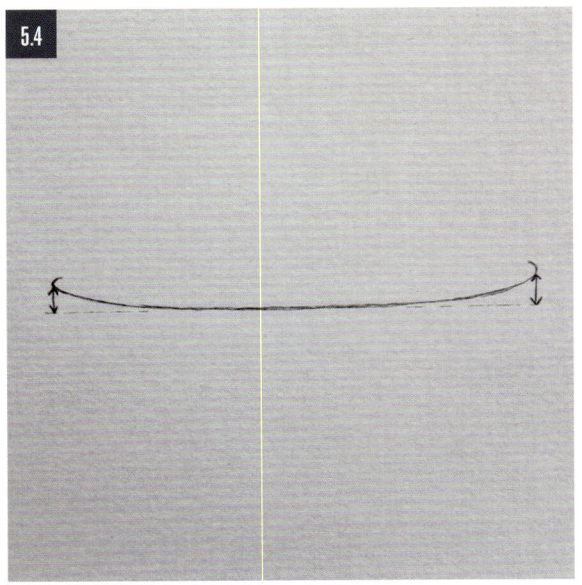

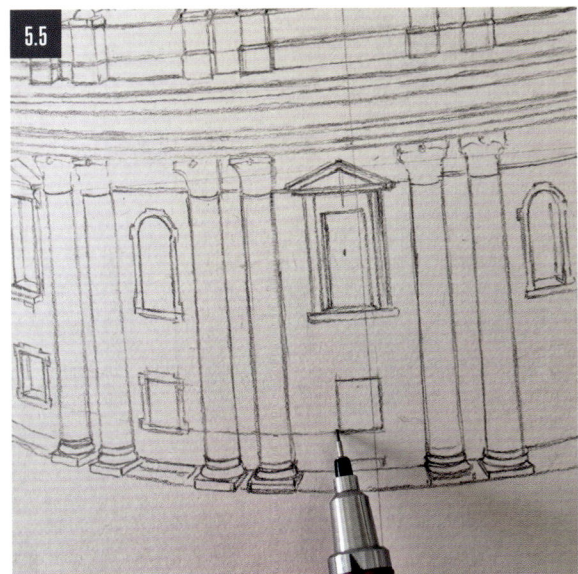

If you are drawing freehand, you will need to judge just how curved the line is that follows the contour around the building. How much does this line curve up as it nears the outer edges of the building? Use a ruler to help you gauge the distance between the base of the curve in the middle and its height at the outer edges (**FIGURE 5.4**). Remember that the building is a circular shape and the aim is to convey the curved structure and form with carefully placed lines that create a three-dimensional illusion. It may take a few attempts to get this right.

> ➤ You may want to consider using the grid method (page 55) to help you get the positioning right.

To line up the windows correctly, first sketch light guidelines following the curve of the building where the base of the windows should be (**FIGURE 5.5**). From this anchor point, you can then draw in the rest of the window.

Continue working down the building to the last section (**FIGURE 5.6**). You can use the windows and columns in the upper sections to line up the last parts (**FIGURE 5.7**).

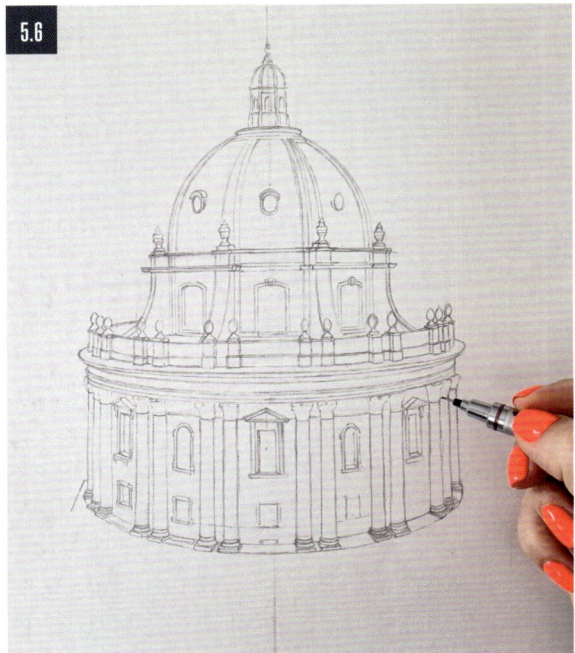

When you get to the end of the pencil drawing, breathe a deep sigh of satisfaction and relief—the hardest part is done! Now we move on to the ink work.

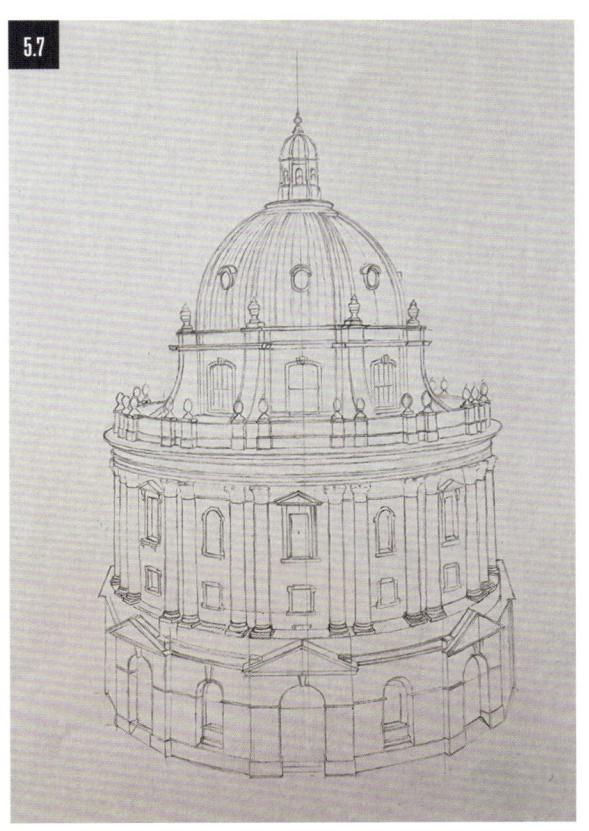

Step 2: INK WORK

For the whole of the drawing, you will need to use a variety of different pen strokes to indicate the patterns and textures you can see within the reference photo. You will also use them to convey shadows and tone in the form of shading, mainly with crosshatching and hatching.

The shading will need to vary in density depending on how dark the shadow is. To make shadows and areas of tone darker, simply add more layers of pen strokes.

By leaving areas of the paper white or reducing the number of lines, you can indicate the more highlighted side of the building where the light source hits the stonework directly from the left.

Try to keep the pen strokes of your mark-making and shading consistent across the whole picture, in relation to the tonal values you are replicating.

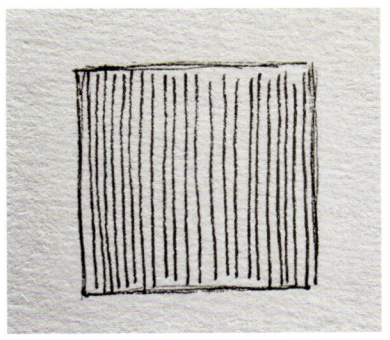

Hatching

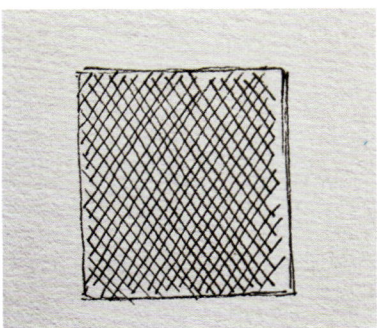

Crosshatching

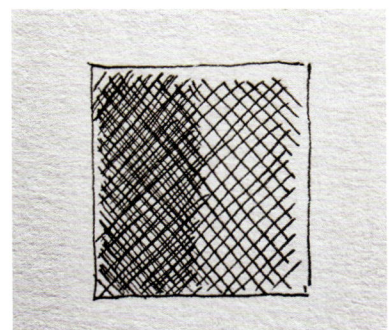

Increased density-crosshatching

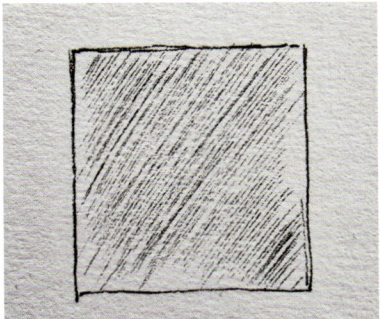

Light Shading

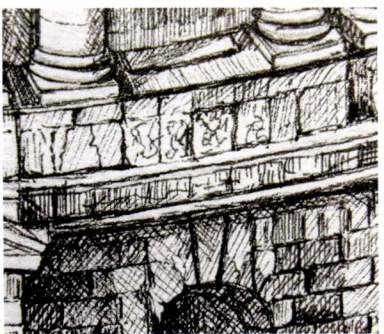

Stonework Texture

Black-and-White Sketch

Choosing the right tones and keeping them consistent and uniform across the work will help convey the overall intended effect more clearly. In this case, there are light tones on the left of the building with slightly darker mid-tones in the middle, and then finally the darkest tones for the most shadowed areas on the right of the building.

Before you start inking, have a good look at the reference photo to establish in your mind some understanding of where the light, middle, and dark values are across the image. This will enable you to anticipate where the varying tones will need to be created.

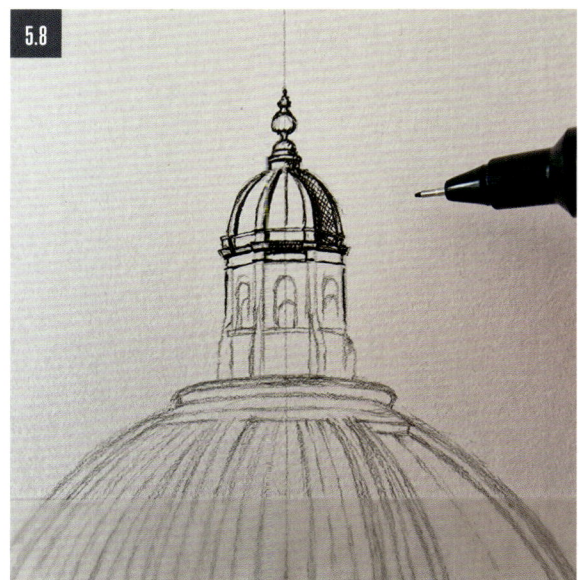

Let's get started!

Take your fineliner pen and begin inking in the small dome at the very top by going over the pencil lines (FIGURE 5.8). Keep a clean sheet of paper over the rest of the drawing to avoid smudging the delicate pencil work. You might find it useful to loosely tape it in place so it doesn't move.

Just like you did with the pencil drawing, work on one area at time, putting the outlines in first. Work lightly to begin with, and then build up the lines. You can't erase them once they are down, but you can usually cover small mistakes with crosshatching or sometimes some white ink—no one will ever know!

➤ Cover any small mistakes with random lines, shading, or white ink.

You can also add extra details that were too small and fine to draw with the pencil, as the pen nib is very fine and nimble compared to the pencil nib.

Notice that the light source comes from the left side of the building, so the main shadows are on the right side, with smaller shadows cast to the right of the individual elements like the columns.

When one area is outlined, you can begin adding some crosshatching and depth to the darkest areas. Use pure-black, dense lines for the darkest areas, like the occlusion shadows where different parts of the building meet and the dark shadows within the small dome (FIGURE 5.9). Then use different densities of shading to create the varying tones of the shadows. Again, you want to begin lightly and build up the density as necessary.

Once the mini dome at the top is complete, work your way down to the larger dome, starting on the left side. Begin by lightly drawing in the curved lines that go vertically down the dome (FIGURE 5.10). Pay attention to the spacing between these lines. The gaps are closer together on the outer edges and wider in the central area. Observing the correct spacing will contribute to the overall three-dimensional illusion.

Drawing and Illustrating Architecture

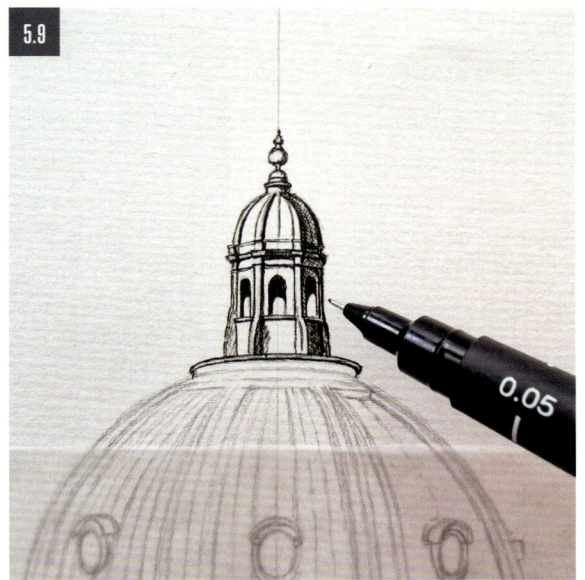

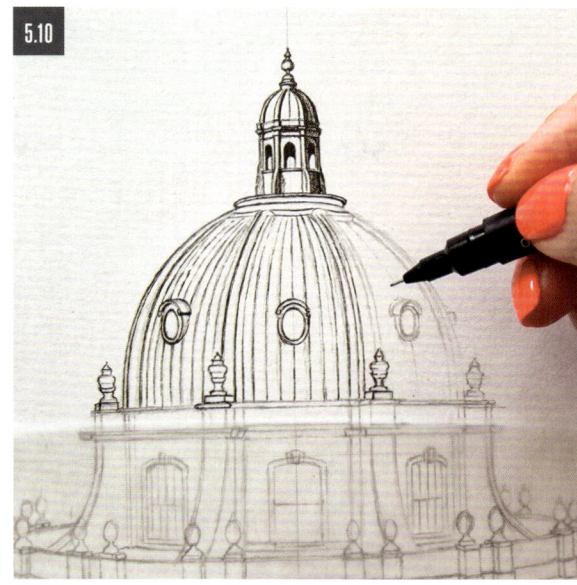

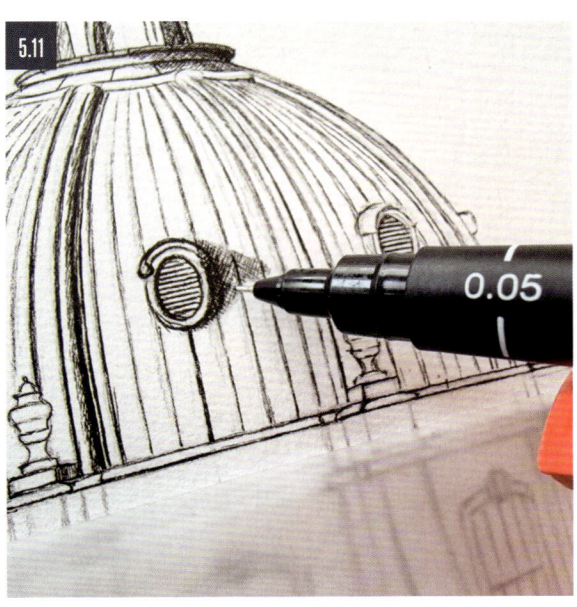

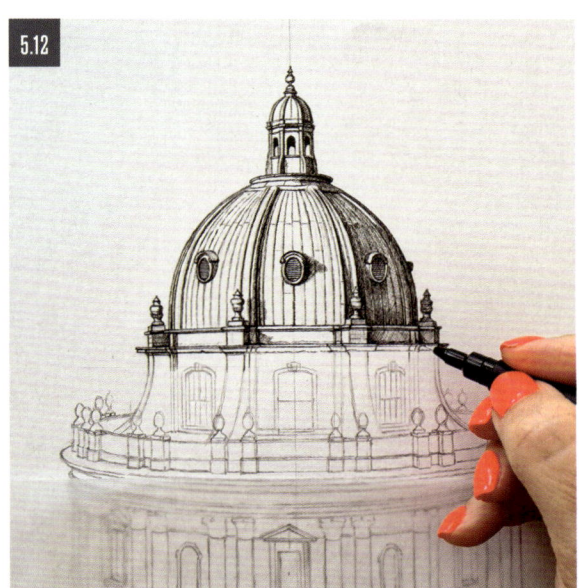

I find that a good way to place these lines is to draw the line that comes down centrally from the middle of the small porthole windows first, and then draw in the other lines on either side of it.

After you have drawn the main lines of the dome, begin working on the shadows. Lightly sketch in the shadow around the central porthole window (**FIGURE 5.11**). Use a light pencil line to define

the shadow shape first if it helps. Notice how the shadow is slightly darker as it nears the window, so you'll want to increase the density of the shadow there with crosshatching.

Vary the density of the crosshatching to match the different depths of tones within the shadows (**FIGURE 5.12**). Focus on one small area at a time and use small delicate strokes.

Where the shadows are clearly defined in the photo, follow these neat lines when you replicate them in your drawing. Clearly defined shadows really bring artwork to life!

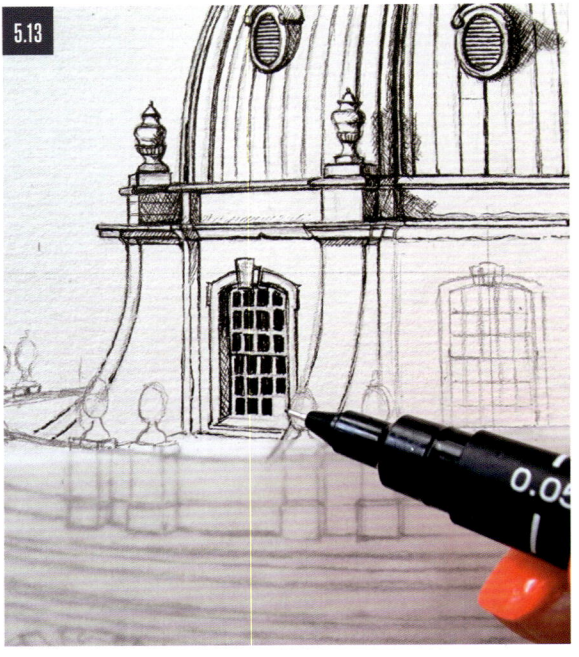

Once the dome is finished, lower your protective paper and start on the next section.

When you get to the windows, gently mark in the grid of the window frames with pencil, and then fill in the black squares (windowpanes) in between the pencil lines with ink (**FIGURE 5.13**). Leave small channels where the pencil lines are for the window frames. For the windowpanes that aren't completely black, either leave them clear or add a variety of ink lines to suggest what is there.

As mentioned before, you may find that you change some of your pencil lines with the precision of the pen nib and add in more details as you see them.

Build up the textures and shading of the stonework—it's up to you how far you go with this (**FIGURE 5.14** and **5.15**). You can always go back and add more details later if you choose to. You can also go back and increase the depth of tone within of any of the shadows.

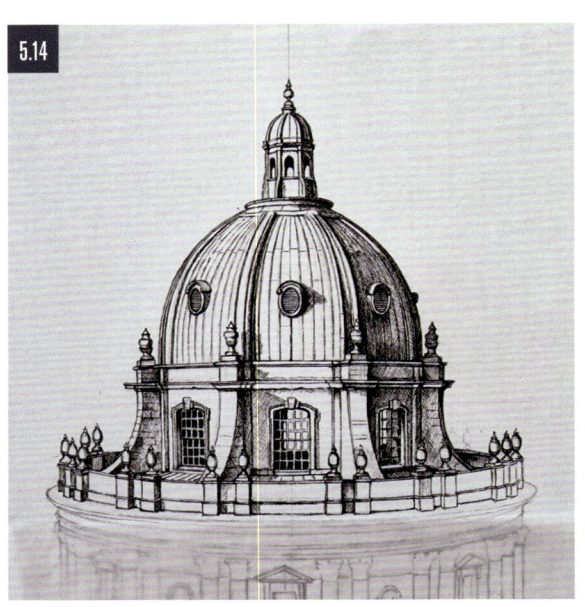

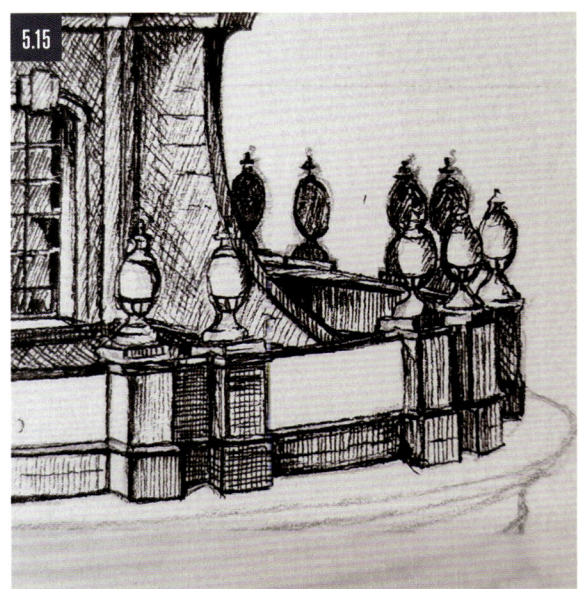

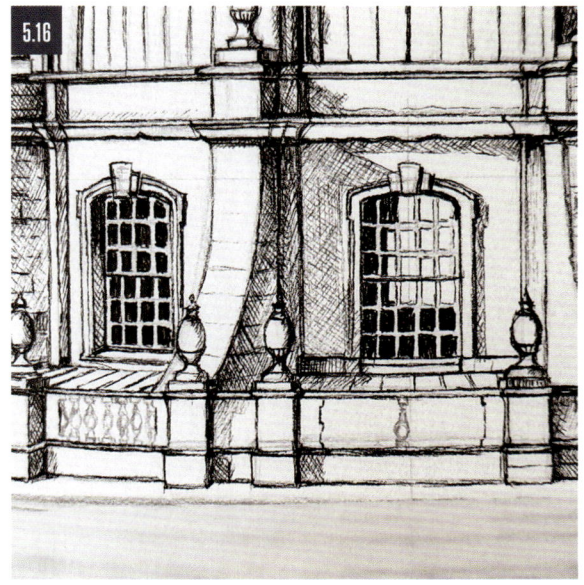

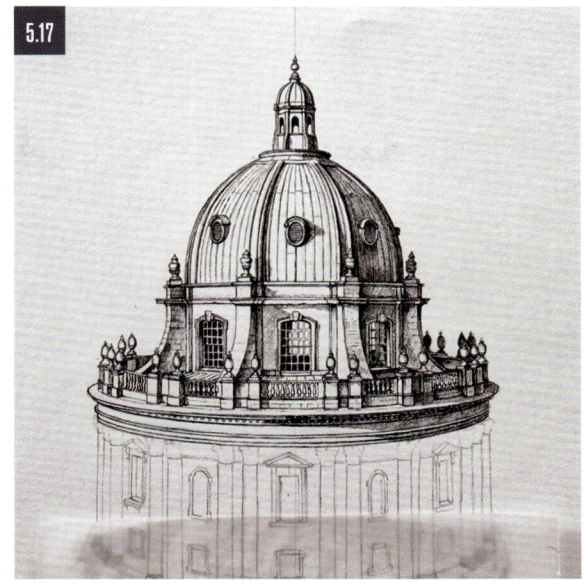

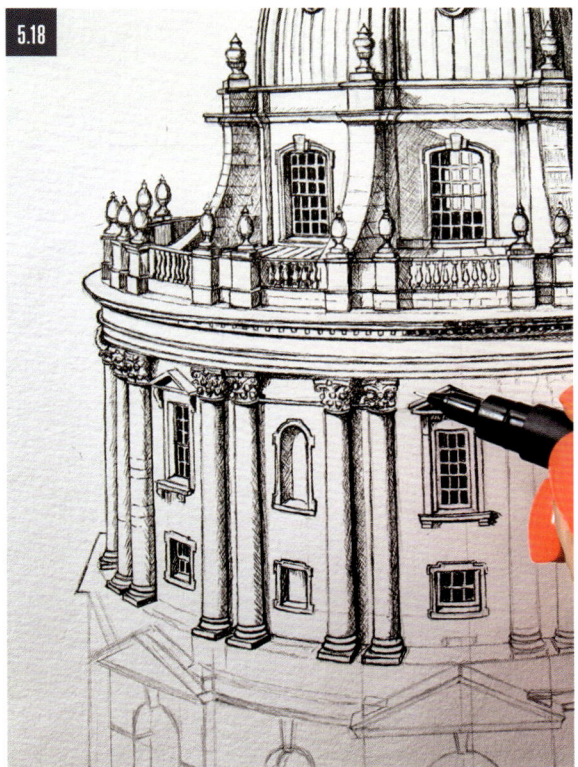

It's better to go slowly and build up the tones layer by layer. Remember that it's easy to add more and nearly impossible to take away!

If the outlines lose their clarity, redefine them as you go along.

If you haven't done so already, it's time to mark in the balustrades (**FIGURE 5.16**). I always find these forms fiddly and time-consuming to sketch. The first thing to do is count how many there are in each small section, and then mark in the central one. The others can then be placed equally on either side of it. These are small parts of the building compared to the rest of the drawing; it would be hard to draw them perfectly, so use an element of suggestion (**FIGURE 5.17**).

Next, lower your protective paper again and begin the next section. Working on the left side first, begin drawing in the columns, and then build up the shading down the right side of each one where the shadow is (**FIGURE 5.18**). Notice how dark the shadow is in the space where the column meets the wall.

It is quite hard to see the exact details of the Corinthian part of the column at the top, as not all the details are clearly defined within the photo. Draw in the basic shapes that you can see, and then suggest the rest of the details with random lines and some shading.

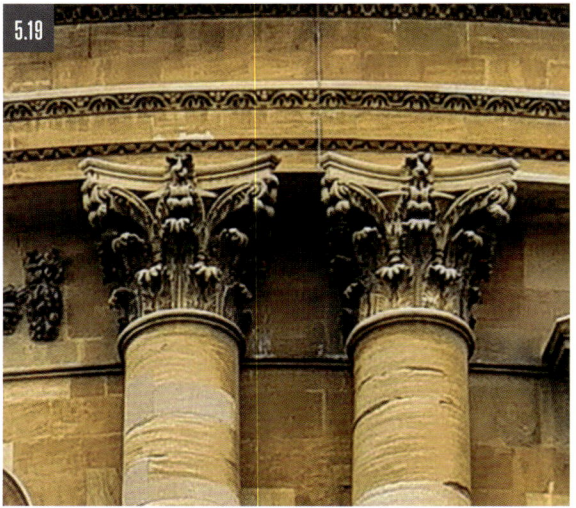

Look at the close-up photo of the Corinthian column to help you understand where the components of this ornate feature should be, like the folds of the acanthus leaves (**FIGURE 5.19**).

Continue using crosshatching or simple hatching for the shadows (**FIGURE 5.20**). Randomly mark in the blockwork on the column shafts with pen strokes that follow the contour of the rounded form of the tall pillars.

Work steadily from left to right until the whole middle section of the drawing is complete (**FIGURE 5.21**). Remember to observe that the shading is darker on the right side of the building. You can go back and adjust this later when you come to the end of the project.

When the mid-section is complete, move down to the final section at the base of the building. Start by going over the main pencil outlines with your ink pen, then begin marking in the stonework with

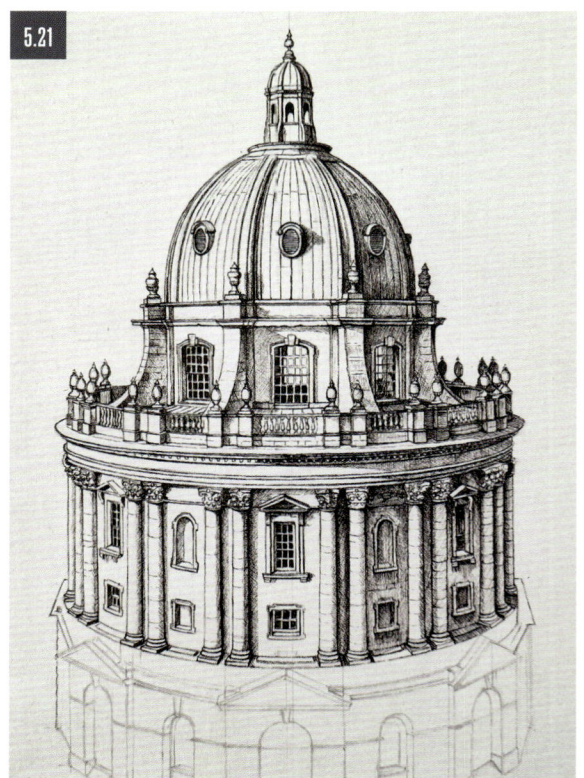

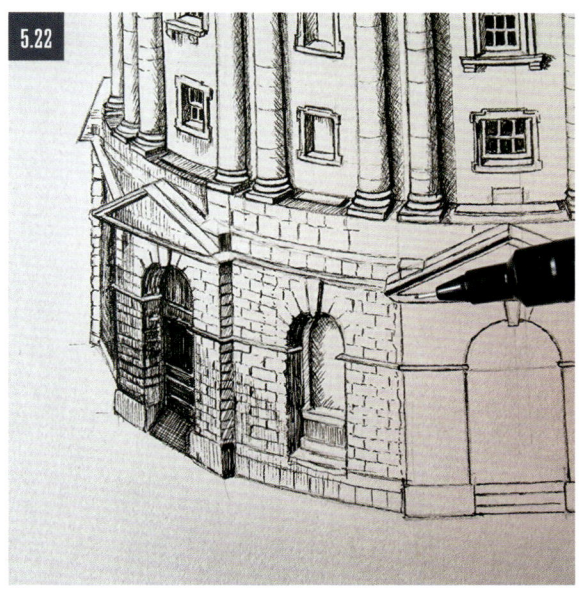

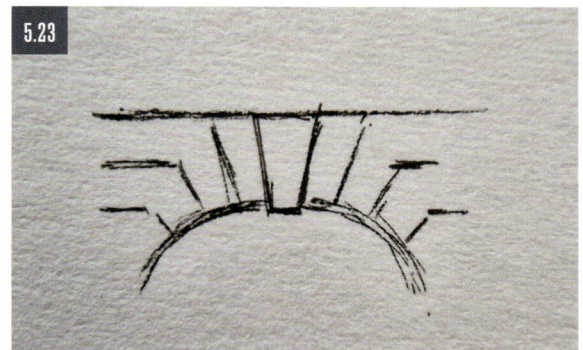

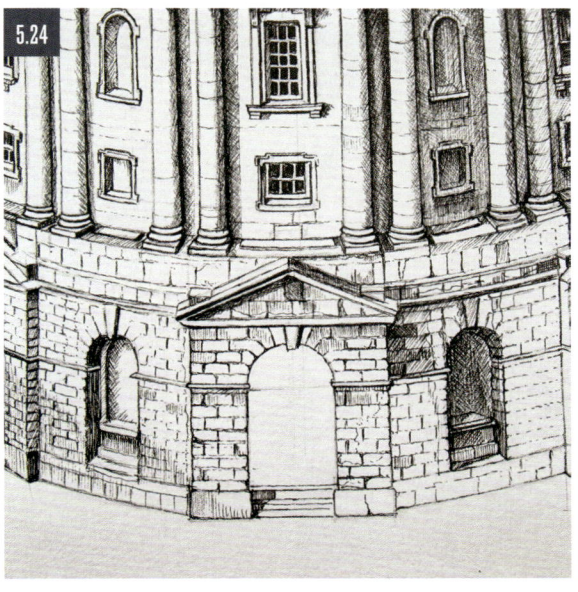

light, slightly broken lines (**FIGURE 5.22**). Use pencil to mark the stonework lines first if you need to, or if you prefer, go straight in with ink. It all depends on how confident you are feeling. Let your lines follow and accentuate the curved contours of the building.

Continue marking in the stone shapes and building up the different tones and textures of the stonework using a variety of pen strokes. Roughly replicate the patterns within the stonework and notice the different pattern at the top of the arches (**FIGURE 5.23** and **5.24**). The blocks aren't all perfect—some of their edges are quite wobbly and there are lots of marks and different shades of colour in the stonework, as it is all very old. Use random, wobbly pen lines to illustrate any cracks and marks (**FIGURE 5.25**). Where the stonework is darker and more shadowed on the right side, build layers of shading using crosshatching and hatching.

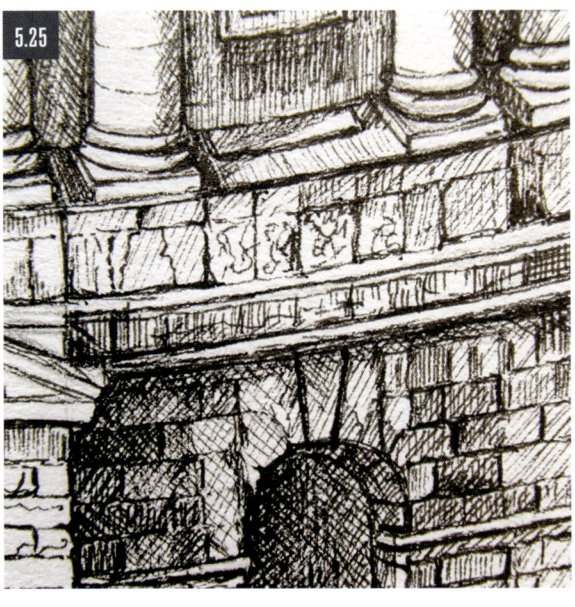

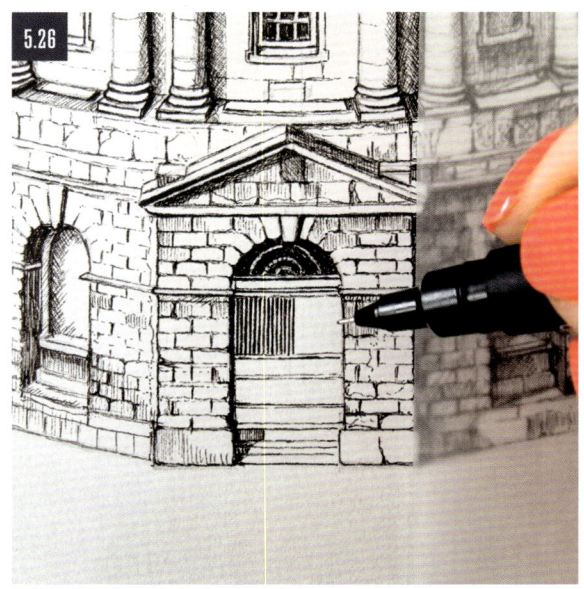

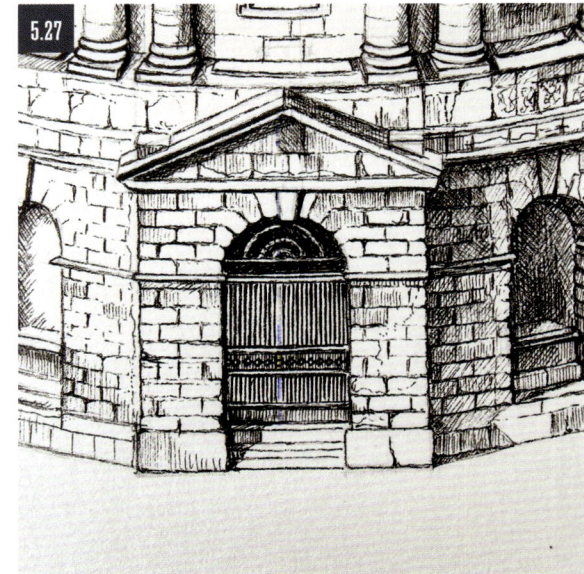

You are nearing the end of this detailed project, and hopefully you can see the fruits of your labour appearing before your eyes.

For the entrance gates, draw in black lines to simulate the darkness behind the ironwork (**FIGURES 5.26** and **5.27**). Leave gaps for the lighter areas where the ironwork is painted gold, then crosshatch over the top of the whole door, making the lines denser on the left side where the shadow is deeper (**FIGURE 5.28**).

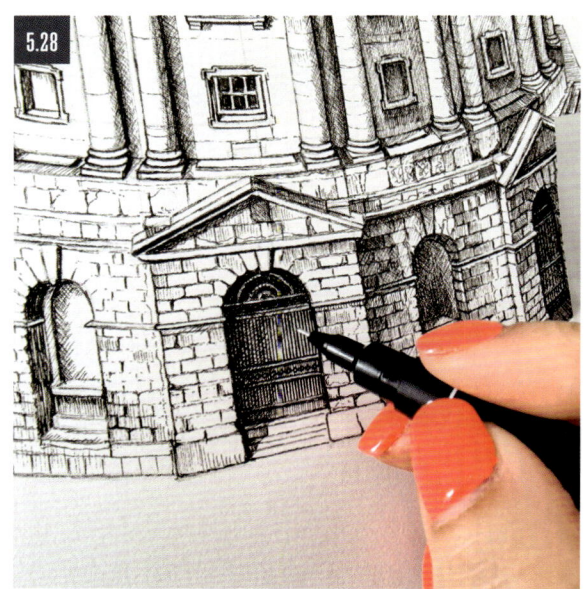

When you get to a point where you feel finished, sit back and take a good look at your drawing, paying attention to the depth of tone in the shadows (**FIGURE 5.29**). You can easily go back and add more.

Sometimes it's good to pause and leave the work for a few days, then come back with fresh eyes to evaluate everything again. You can often see adjustments that need to be made much more quickly and clearly. This will also stop you from overworking your drawing.

5.29

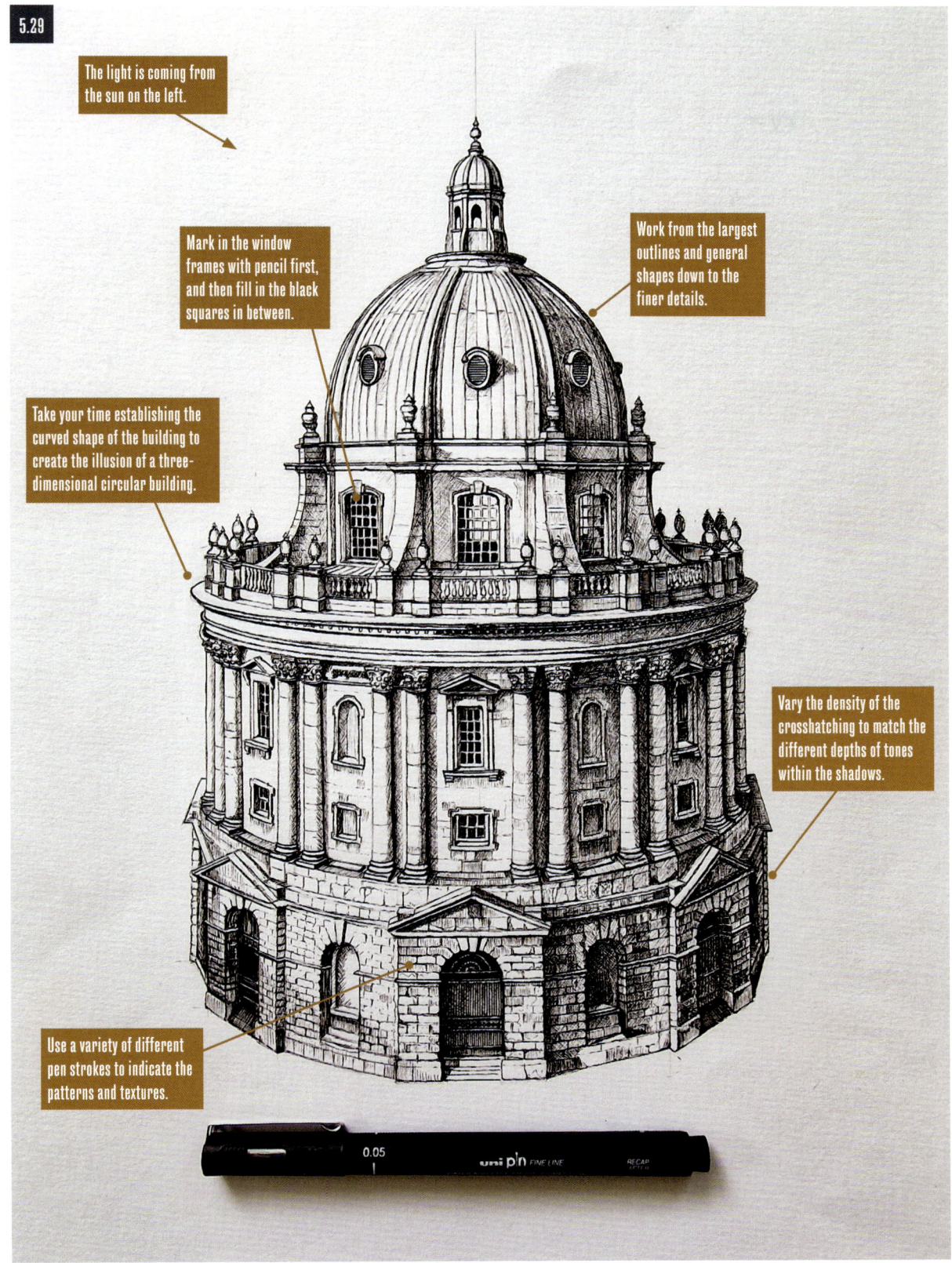

The light is coming from the sun on the left.

Mark in the window frames with pencil first, and then fill in the black squares in between.

Work from the largest outlines and general shapes down to the finer details.

Take your time establishing the curved shape of the building to create the illusion of a three-dimensional circular building.

Vary the density of the crosshatching to match the different depths of tones within the shadows.

Use a variety of different pen strokes to indicate the patterns and textures.

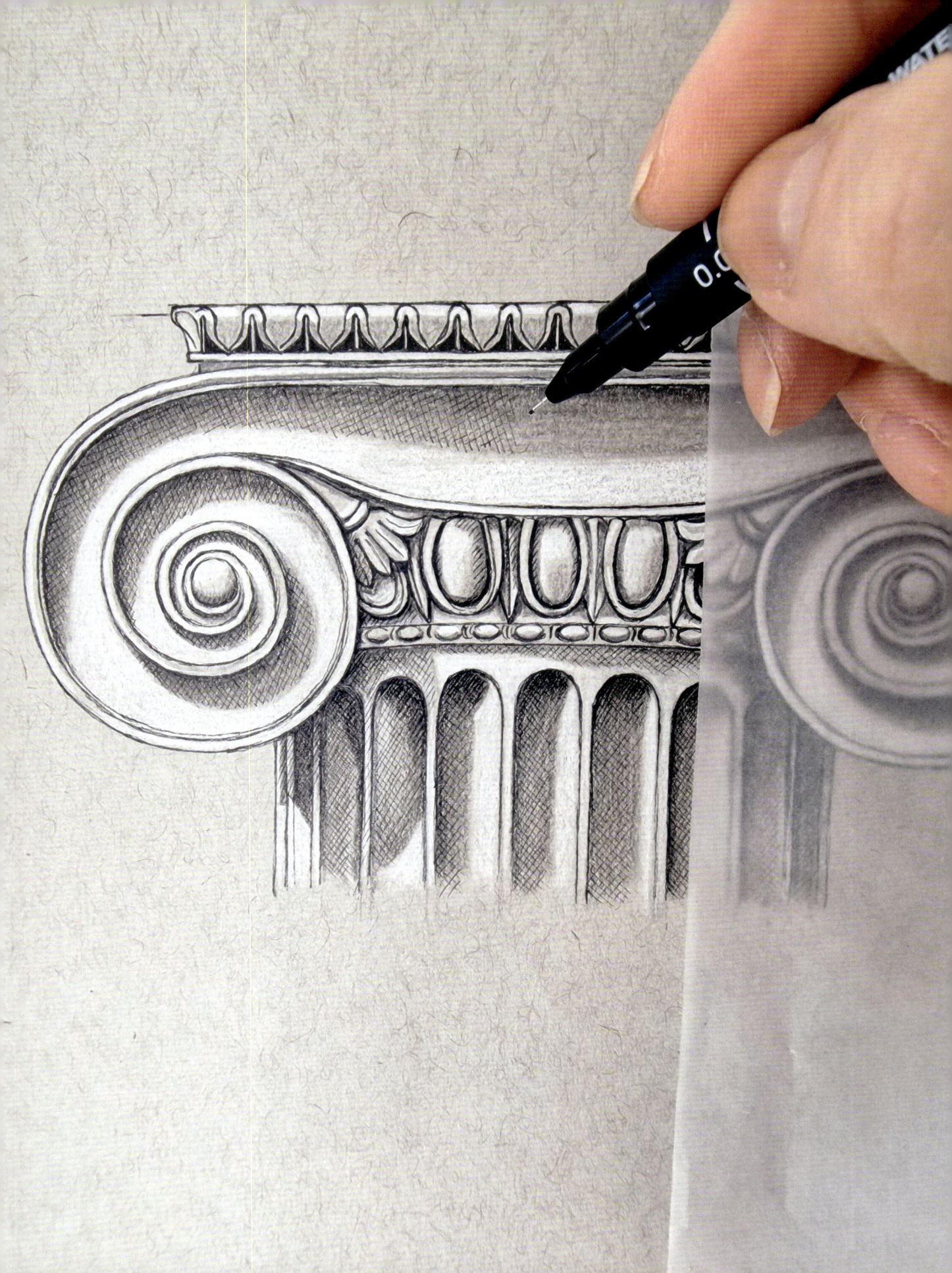

CHAPTER 6

Focusing on Architectural Details

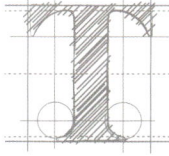

This project covers the different elements that make up a building. We don't always have time for a large project, or perhaps we just want to relax and sketch away in our sketchbooks. When I'm in this zone, I will search my photo library for a beautiful, intricately detailed photo of something like a Corinthian or Ionic column, or maybe a statue.

I'm inspired by the age-old intricate stone carvings found on old buildings like cathedrals, stately homes, and old schools and colleges, and I photograph them everywhere I go for future reference. If you take a moment to look closely at these structures, you can find acanthus leaves, angels, scrolls, kings, vases, unicorns, and so much more! For instance, if you look at the details on Notre Dame Cathedral, you will see row upon row of saints, kings, and gargoyles perched on every corner. Picking out just one element that appeals to you can make for a really interesting sketch. If you don't have your own photos for this, you can find lots of subjects to draw from on Pinterest.

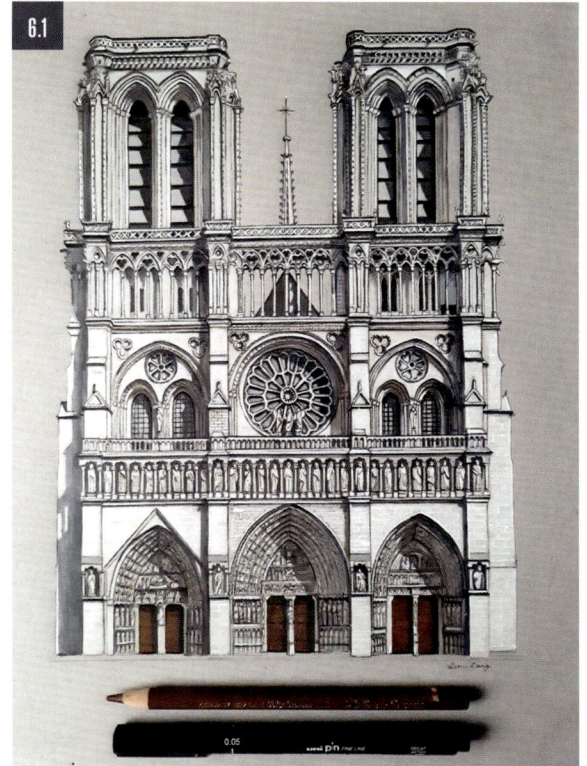

6.1

I also want to focus individually on the more essential parts that make up a building, such as brickwork, stonework, windows, doors, roof tiles, and chimneys. Learning to draw these individually will help you when you are working on a larger project like a house where all the elements will be combined.

Some of these different elements can also make for interesting and beautiful artworks on their own, and knowing how to draw them correctly will add an extra dimension to your work.

Let's start with the building blocks: bricks and stonework.

Drawing Bricks

Bricks vary in texture, tone, shapes, and sizes. They come in many different colours, from yellow hues to blue, red, and purple. Some are old and handmade whereas newer bricks are straight and made by a machine. They can also be laid in many different ways and patterns. For instance, they are often seen standing on their ends, side by side in a row above windows—this is called the soldier course. Adding details such as these will take your work to another level.

When you look closely at a brick wall you will see a variety of shades of colour, marks, and texture, as no two bricks are the same. They also crumble and become weathered, which adds even more details and interest to draw in the viewer. Taking these different elements into account will add variety and make your wall look more interesting and realistic.

I have a basic brick colour palette that I use, which I add to or take away from as needed. For this exercise, I am using a photo of an old red brick wall that I took near my home (**FIGURE 6.3**).

Materials

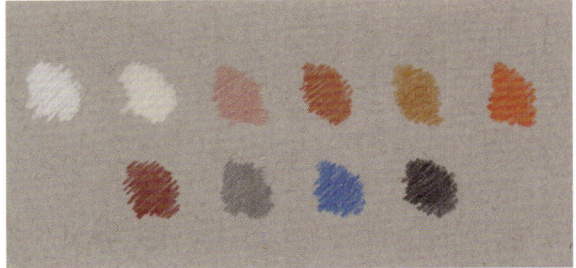

- ▶ Toned paper
- ▶ Sharp pencil
- ▶ Black 0.05mm fineliner pen
- ▶ Coloured pencils: White, Ivory, Cinnamon, Sanguine, Burnt Ochre, Orange Glaze, Indian Red, Warm Grey IV, Cobalt Blue, Payne's Gray
- ▶ Blender

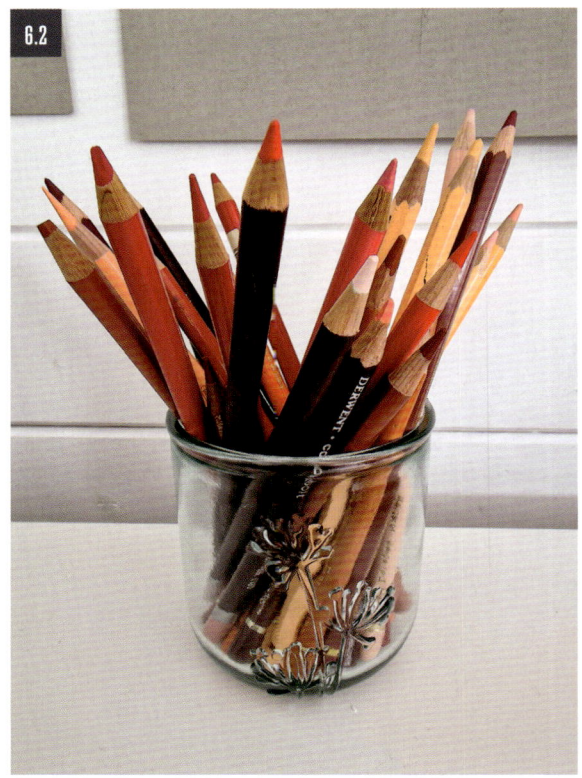

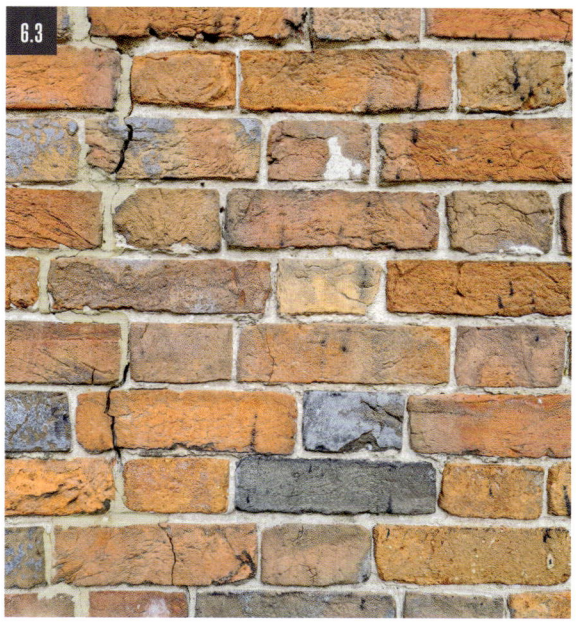

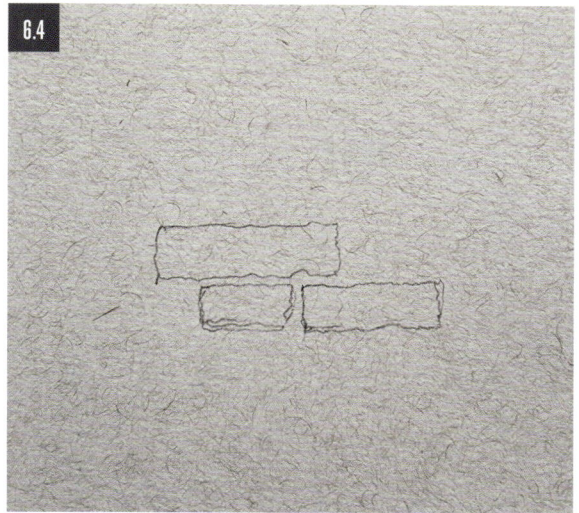

Step 1: Draw with Pencil

Start by drawing an initial pencil line to determine the outer edge of the brick shapes, leaving a channel between the bricks to show where the mortar is (**FIGURE 6.4**). I find the best way to start is to choose one brick, draw it, and then position all the others around it (**FIGURE 6.5**). You can use a ruler to lay down some equally placed horizontal lines as a guide to help you position the bricks in a straight fashion if you wish.

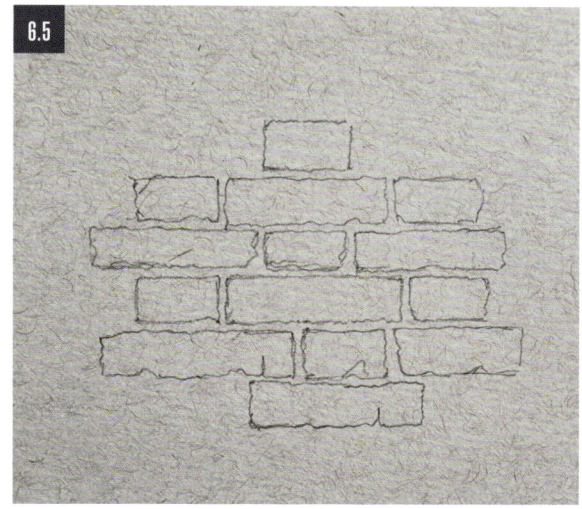

You probably won't draw bricks at this size and detail very often, but this is a good exercise to understand brick colours. If you are confident, you can skip this stage and go straight in with drawing the bricks in ink.

Step 2: Cover the Lines with Black Ink

Carefully go over your pencil lines with a black ink fineliner pen (**FIGURE 6.6**). You can also begin adding any cracks in the wall as you go around the bricks. Keep your lines quite wobbly like the uneven edges of the bricks.

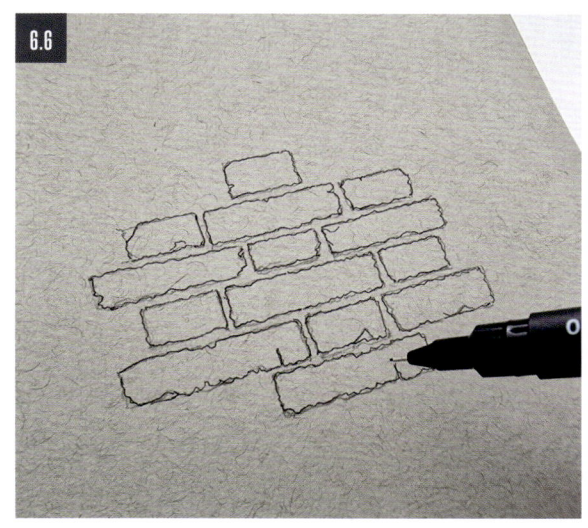

Step 3: Add Colour

Cover the bricks in a light layer of Ivory, which will serve as a base colour to lift the next layers of colour (**FIGURE 6.7**). Then begin randomly adding a variety of shades of the colours you can see across the bricks on top of the Ivory, building the layers as you go (**FIGURE 6.8**). Work from the lightest colours first, leaving the darker colours until last. As you are working, use your blender to blend and smooth out the colours where necessary.

The colour doesn't have to be solid across the entire brick. Any single brick will contain a mix of colours, especially old bricks, which are called "stocks." Use the reference photo as a rough colour guide, but you really can randomly lay the colours down and the finished result will still look like bricks (**FIGURE 6.9**)!

Payne's Grey works well for the dark greys on the surface of the bricks and for the cracks and marks in the bricks. On the grey bricks you will notice there are some blue colours. To create this effect, add layers of Cobalt Blue with Warm Grey IV and white (**FIGURE 6.10**).

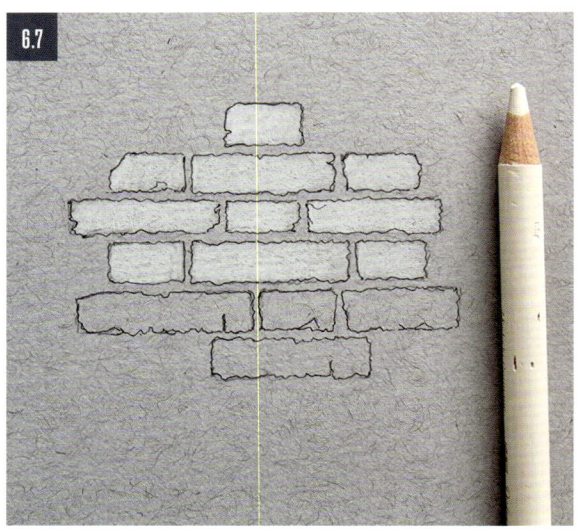

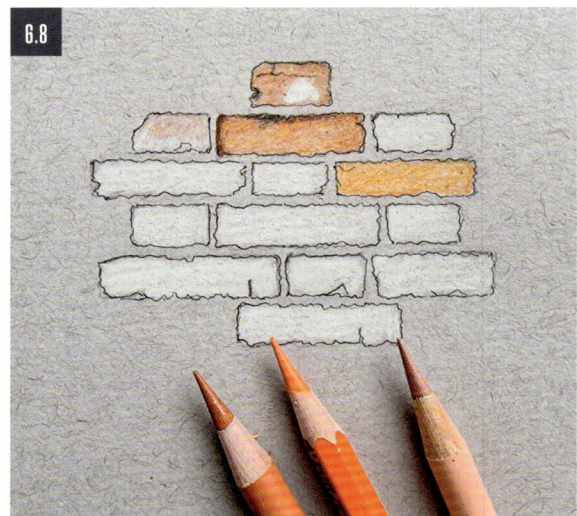

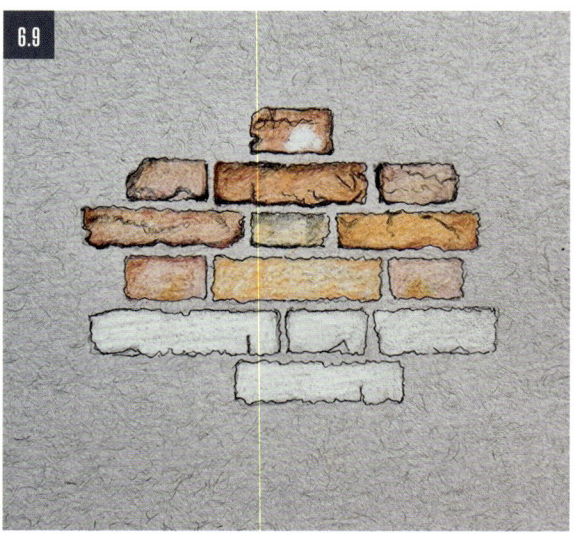

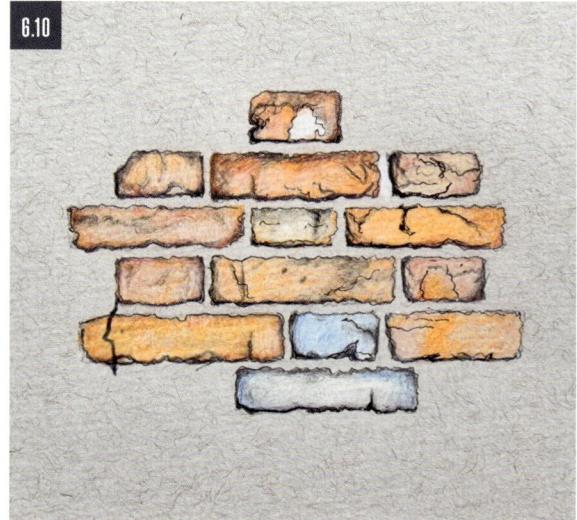

Drawing and Illustrating Architecture

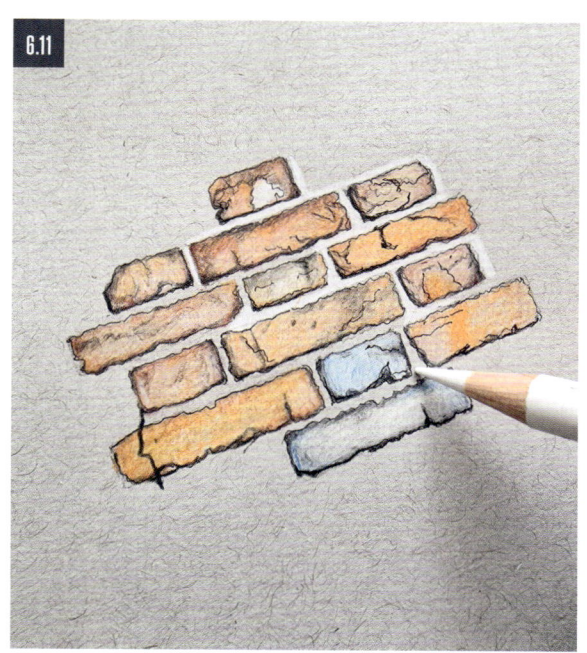

6.11

Carefully place the thin shadows along the sides and bottom of the bricks to create the illusion of the bricks protruding slightly from the wall. This step makes such a difference to the final look of the drawing and adds the realism we are after.

Now use a white pencil to colour the mortar between the bricks. This should instantly make the bricks stand out and elevate the colours (**FIGURE 6.11**).

Step 4: Add Final Details

The last step is to add more details like cracks and marks and redefine the darkest lines and shadows with your fineliner (**FIGURE 6.12**). You can also use the white pencil as a final pencil layer to lift and brighten the colours, if required.

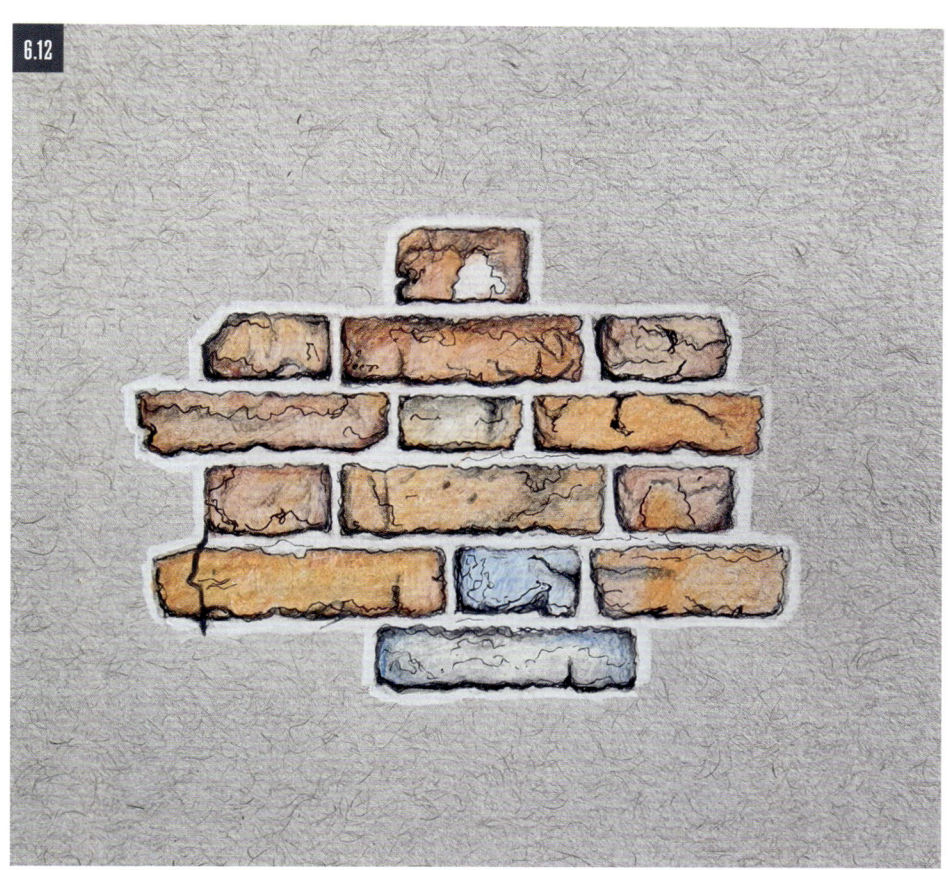

6.12

Drawing Stonework

Buildings made from stone tend to be older than those made with bricks. The stonework is usually laid in a very random manor with not as much of a repetitive pattern as brickwork. I find this makes it easier to suggest random stone shapes and draw them in loosely. Stonework is usually a pale sandy beige or grey in colour.

Many of the world's most ancient longstanding buildings were built of stone. The impact of the passage of time makes for all sorts of interesting details like cracks, crumbling stone, and water-marks on the weathered old buildings. You can have a lot of fun freestyling this look using pens, pencils, and white opaque pen.

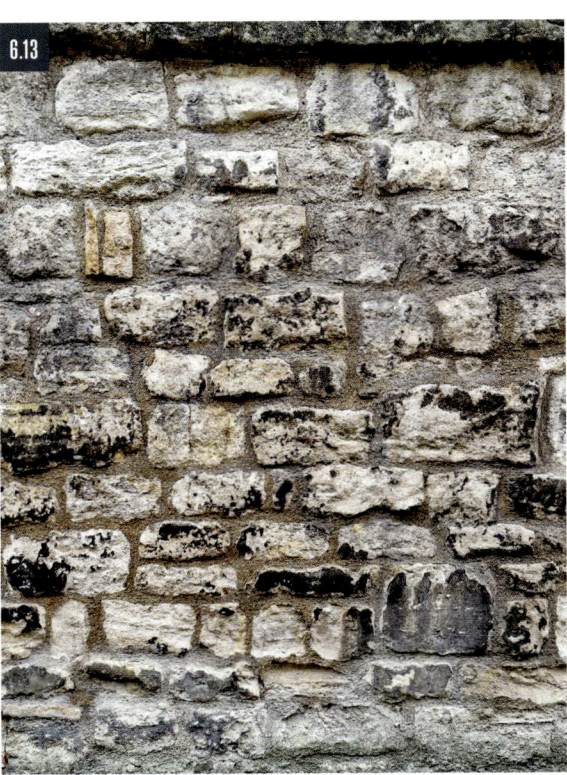

Drawing stonework is much the same as drawing bricks but with a lighter colour palette and a more random style.

Materials

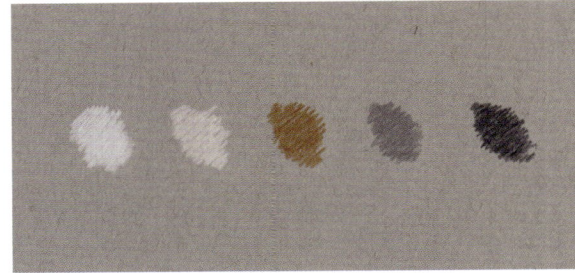

- Toned paper
- Sharp pencil
- Black 0.05mm fineliner pen
- Coloured pencils: White, Ivory, Brown Ochre, Warm Grey IV, Payne's Gray
- White gel pen

Step 1: Draw with Pencil

In the same way as for the bricks project, begin by drawing in the random shapes of the stones using the reference photo as a guide. Notice how uneven the shapes are and that no two are the same.

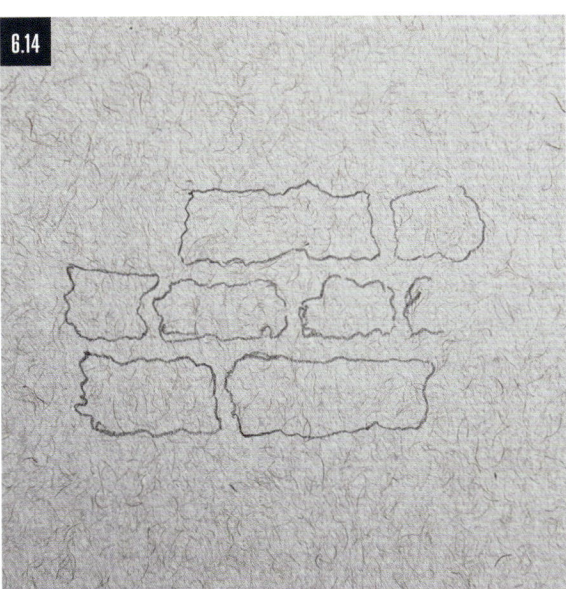

Step 2: Cover the Lines with Black Ink

Now cover the lines with ink using your 0.05mm fineliner pen, keeping everything uneven, random, and wobbly. Then add in the darkest areas that line the edges of the individual stones.

Step 3: Add Colour

The next step is to begin adding some colour, starting with the lightest colours, white and Ivory. I haven't used a blender in this project because I want to create the texture of the stones and not smooth everything out.

Use the sharp point of your white pencil to define the edges of the stones in the lightest areas (**FIGURE 6.16**). Use a firm pressure to create a good, opaque layer of white. We will accentuate this with white gel pen in the last stage.

Next, cover all the stones in a light layer of Ivory to create a base layer.

Now add the darkest marks you can see on the stones using the darkest pencil, Payne's Grey (**FIGURE 6.17**). Move the pencil in small circular motions, applying a firm pressure to create the dark marks and speckles on the stones. By varying the pressure you apply on the pencil, you can vary the depth of the grey tones (**FIGURE 6.18**). Use Warm Grey IV for the softest pale greys.

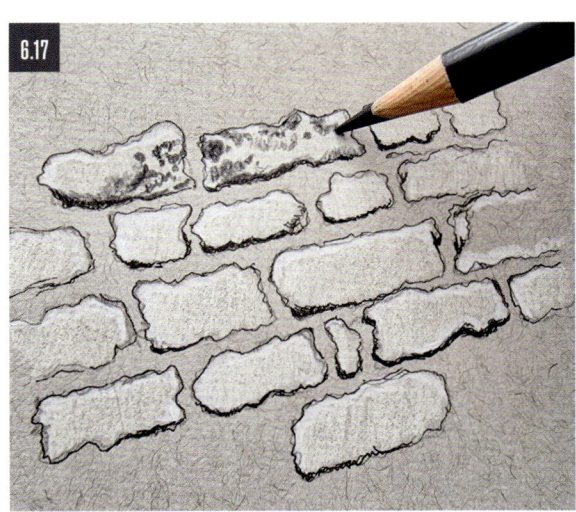

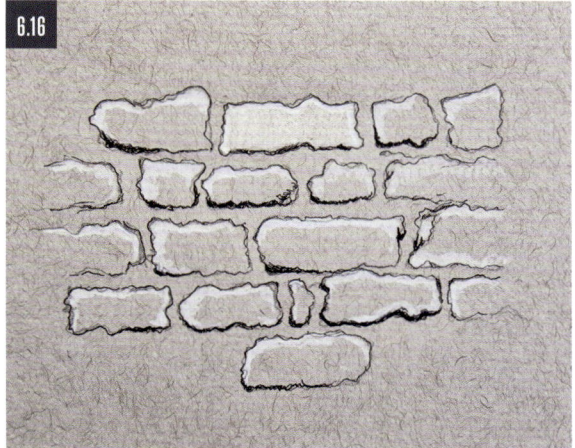

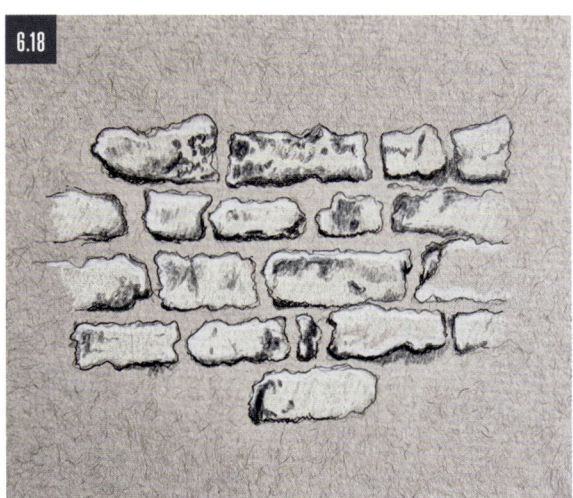

Next, use Brown Ochre over the areas that have a yellow tone to them (**FIGURE 6.19**). This is a colour that I use regularly for stonework. It warms the stone and is a good colour match for sand-coloured stones.

Brighten the lightest areas with more layers of white and Ivory, avoiding the dark marks and speckles already there (**FIGURE 6.20**). Use a firm pressure to create a strong colour.

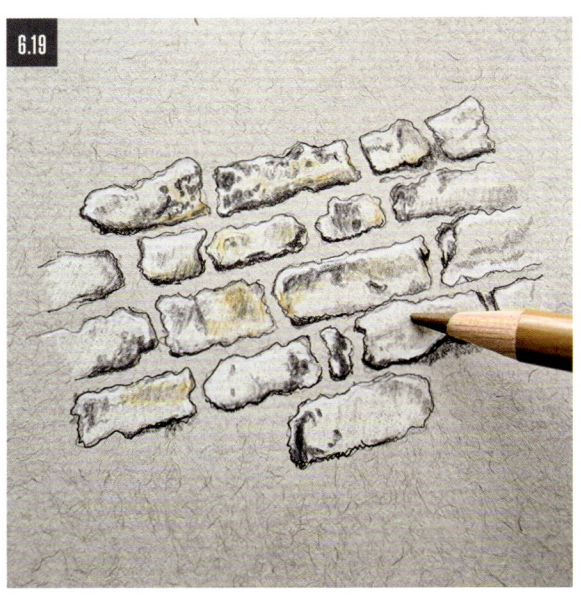

Move on to colouring in the mortar between the stones by first applying a layer of Warm Grey IV. Then use Payne's Grey to darken the edges of the stones and any other areas that are darker (**FIGURE 6.21**). Follow this with layers of brown ochre to create the sandy colour of the mortar.

Step 4: Add Final Details

In this final step, redefine the outlines of the stones with your fineliner and darken the darkest areas. Draw cracks and dots randomly across the stones and mortar (**FIGURE 6.22**). This will help to create an old textured finish to the wall.

Lighten any areas of the mortar that are too dark with a little Ivory pencil.

Lastly, use a white gel pen to highlight the lightest areas along the edges of the stones (**FIGURE 6.23**). This final step is what lifts the colours and helps create a 3D effect. If you use the white gel pen lightly, it is less likely to clog. If it does clog, run the nib back and forth on clean paper to get the ink moving again.

There you have your completed stone wall study (**FIGURE 6.24**). You can use this technique for any stonework you draw on future projects.

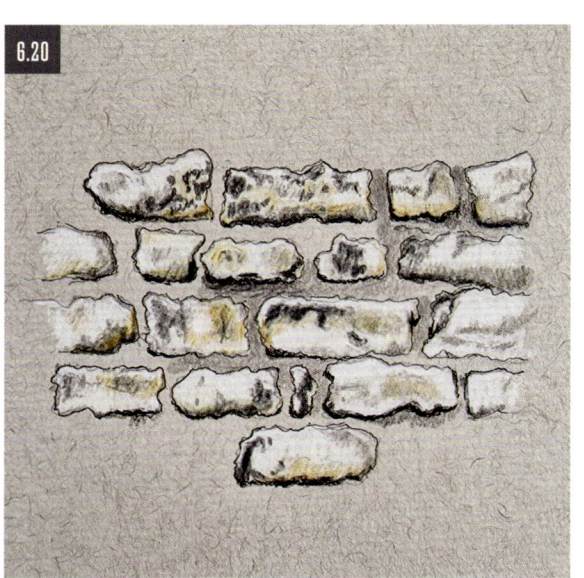

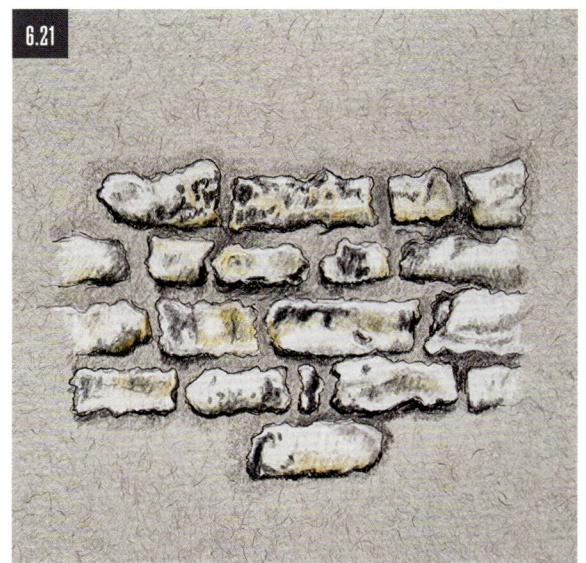

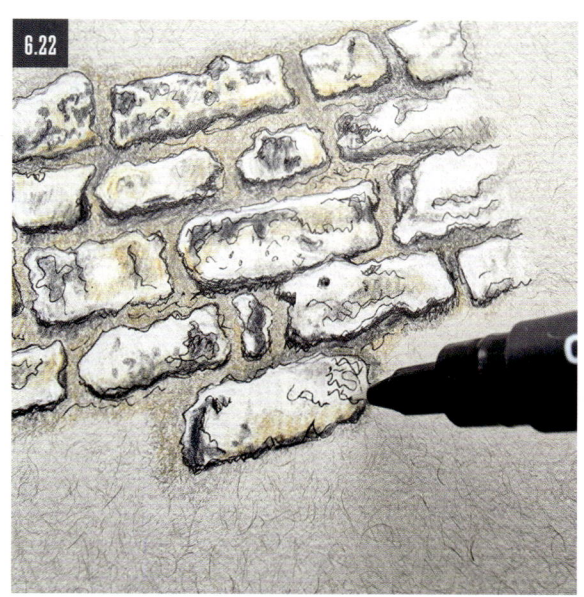

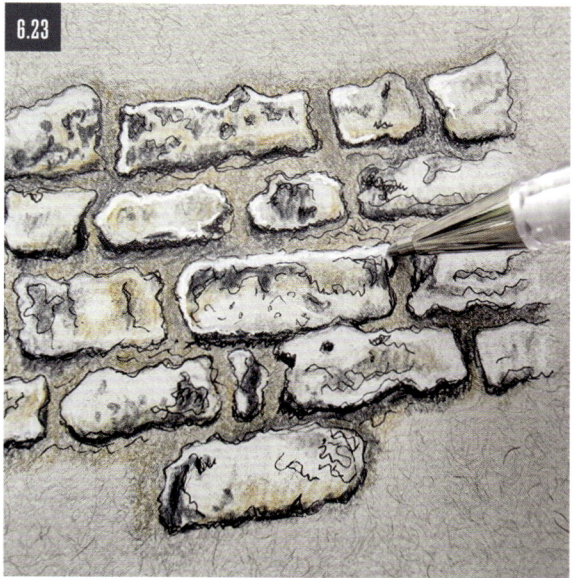

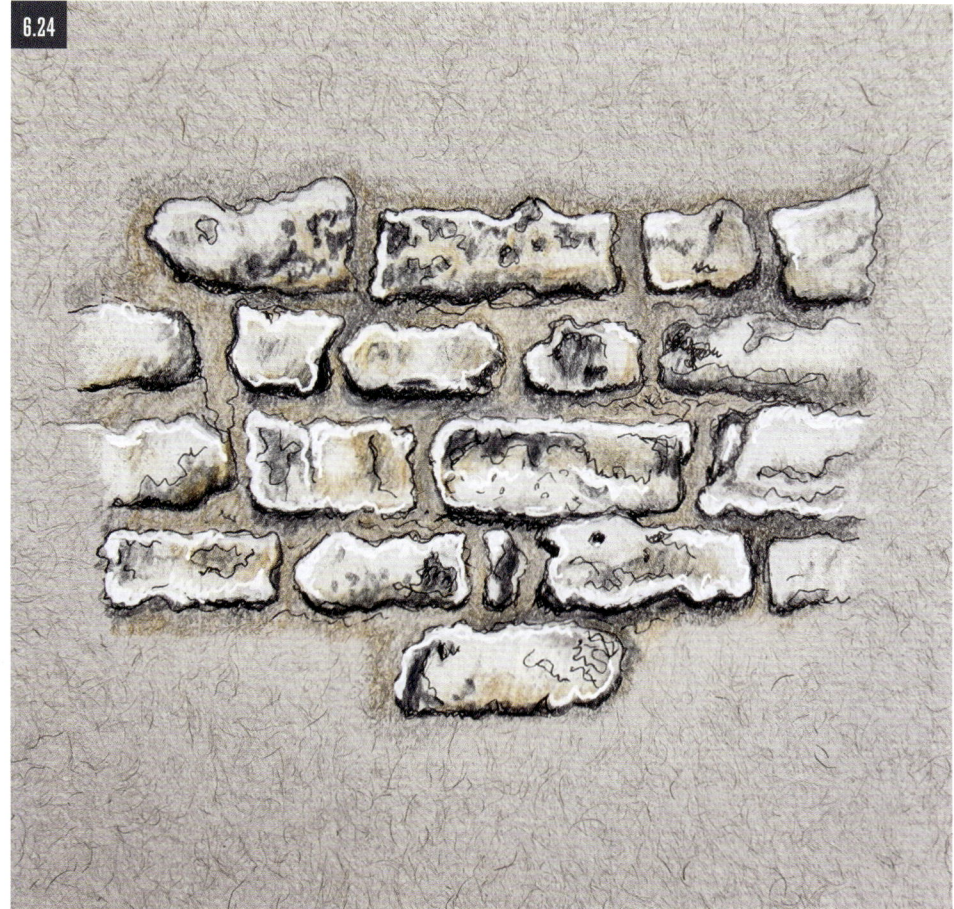

Roof Tiles

Roof tiles shouldn't be overlooked in a drawing. Although drawing them can sometimes feel repetitive and somewhat mundane, their colours can be quite beautiful, especially when they are enriched by bright sunlight. My favourites are the deep orange and terracotta rooftop tiles found across cities like Venice (**FIGURE 6.26**). If the tiles are drawn in a realistic way with the right shading, they can add extra depth to your picture.

Materials

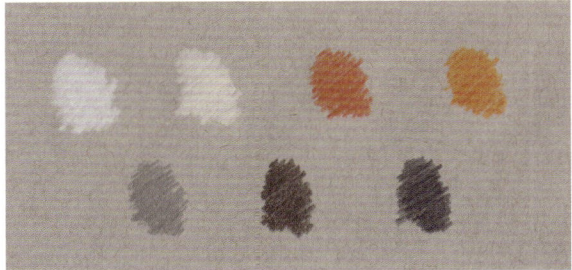

- ▶ Toned paper
- ▶ Sharp pencil
- ▶ Black 0.05mm fineliner pen
- ▶ Coloured pencils: White, Ivory, Sanguine, Terracotta, Warm Grey IV, Sepia, Payne's Grey

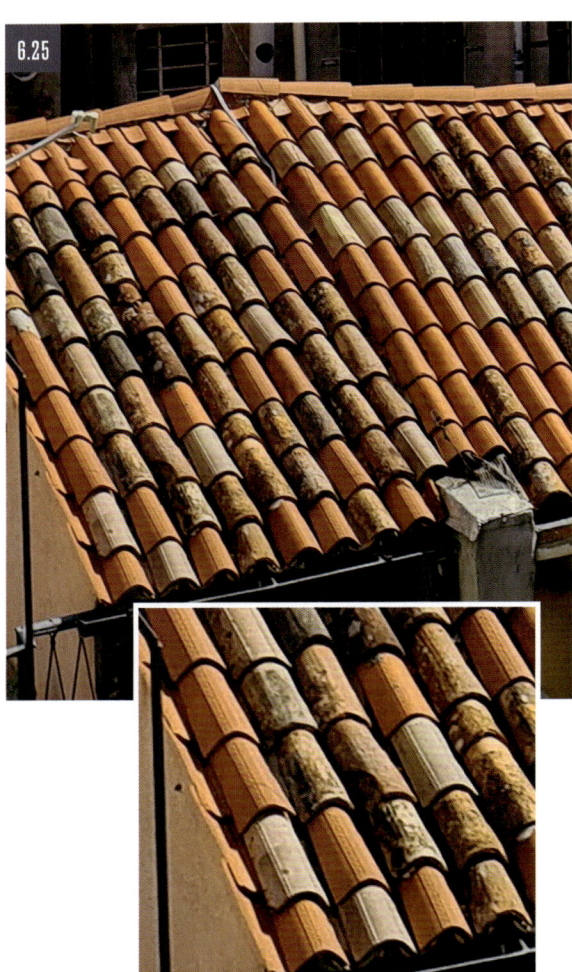

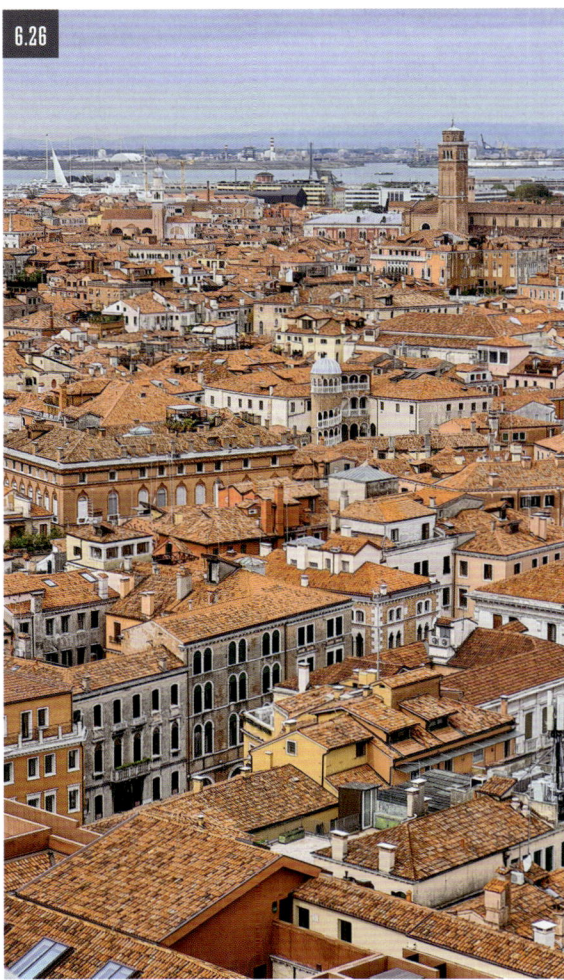

Step 1: Draw with Pencil

Begin by sketching in a few rows of the tiles (**FIGURES 6.27** and **6.28**). You don't need too many, as this is just an exercise to look at where the shading and shadows are. Pay attention to where the tiles line up, where they meet, and to the arched shape of them.

Step 2: Cover the Lines with Black Ink

Go over the pencil lines with your black fineliner (**FIGURE 6.29**), then draw in and darken the shadows between the tiles and the curved dark ends of each tile (**FIGURE 6.30**). You can also add in any obvious lines running through the tiles.

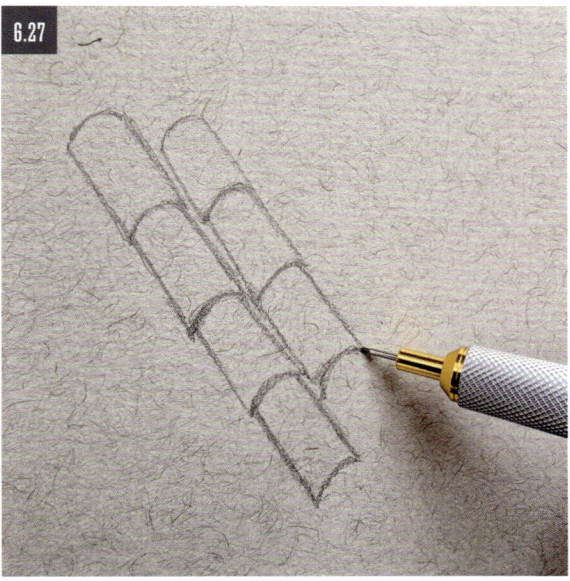

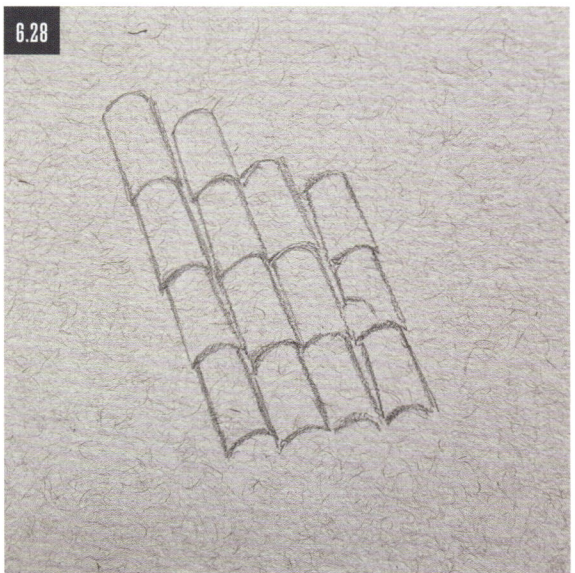

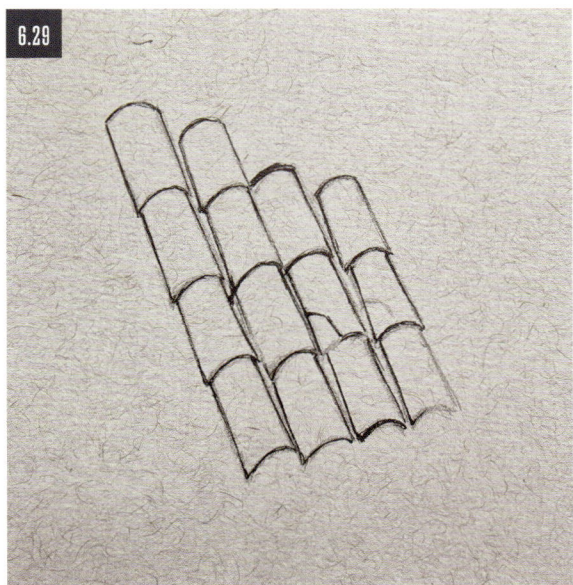

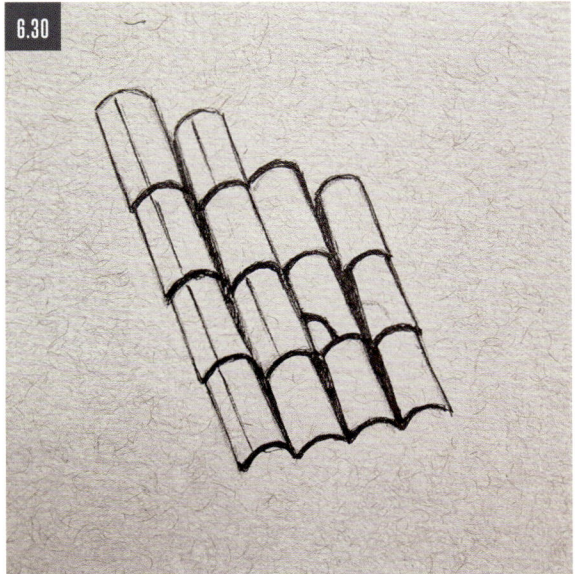

Step 3: Add Colour

Begin by adding two layers of white to the side of the tiles where the sunlight hits. In this case, it is the right side (**FIGURE 6.31**).

Also add some Ivory colour to the left side of the lighter beige-coloured tiles. The colours you add don't have to be placed exactly as you see them in the reference photo—the thing to focus on is creating a strong shadow on the left side of the tile and keeping the right side in the light. This is what will make them look three-dimensional and create the illusion of the sun beating down on the tiles.

Next, add a layer of Sanguine pencil to the left side of the terracotta-coloured tiles where they are in shadow (**FIGURE 6.32**). Use Warm Grey IV on the left side of the beige-coloured tiles to add shadow and to create the marks on the tiles (**FIGURE 6.33**).

Now use a Terracotta pencil to add a layer on top of the Sanguine-coloured areas, and extend the colour over the top of the tile to the light side (**FIGURE 6.34**). Move the pencil lightly over the white to create a terracotta-coloured glaze.

Darken the marks on the tiles with a Sepia pencil, and then, finally, use Payne's Grey to go in and darken any shadows, especially the dark crevices deep between the tiles (**FIGURE 6.35**). Also add in the shadow along the bottom of the tiles (**FIGURE 6.36**).

And that's it! It's unlikely you'll have to draw tiles this big, but it's good to understand how to shade them, as this attention to detail will always shine through.

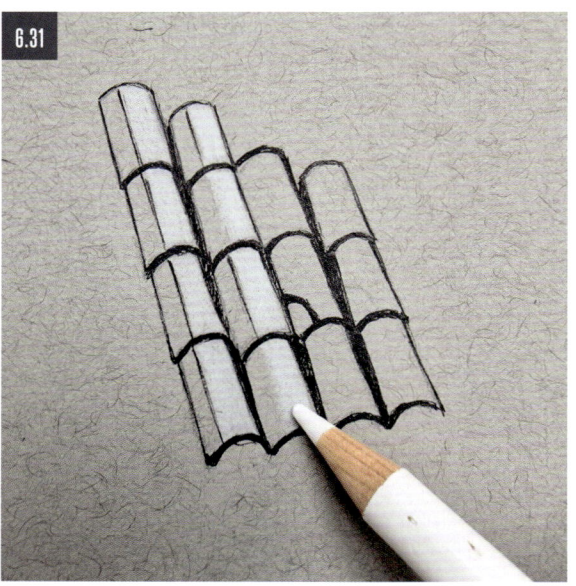

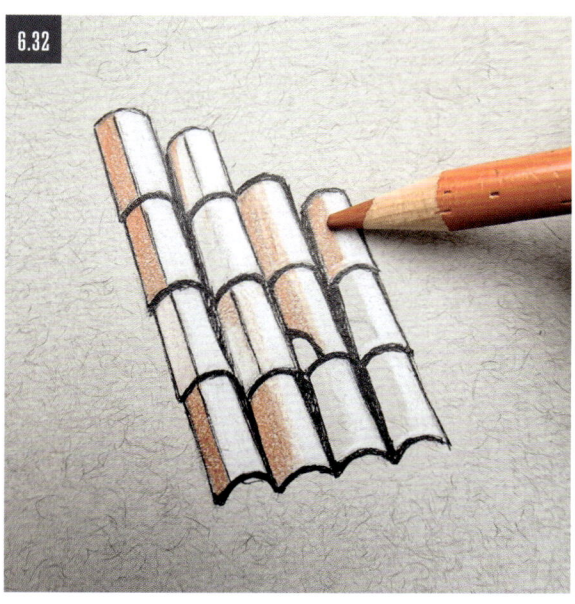

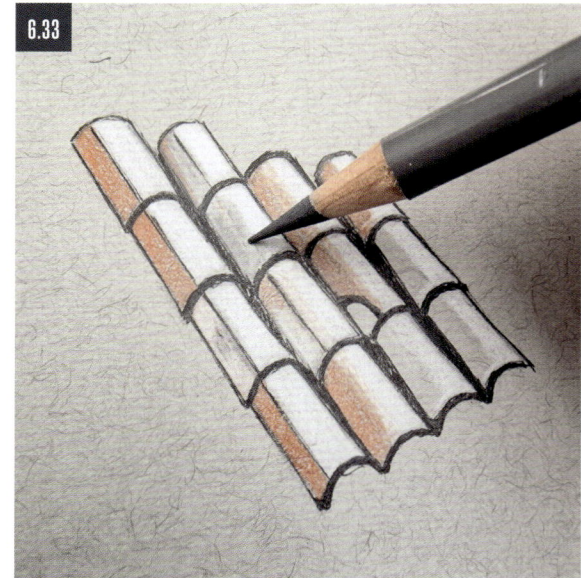

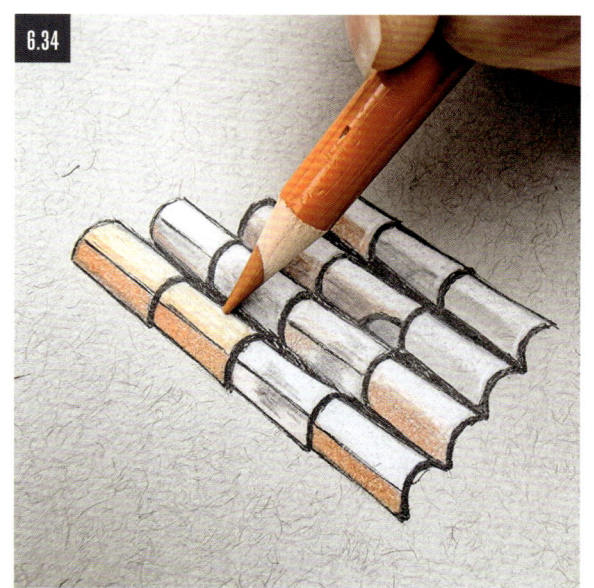

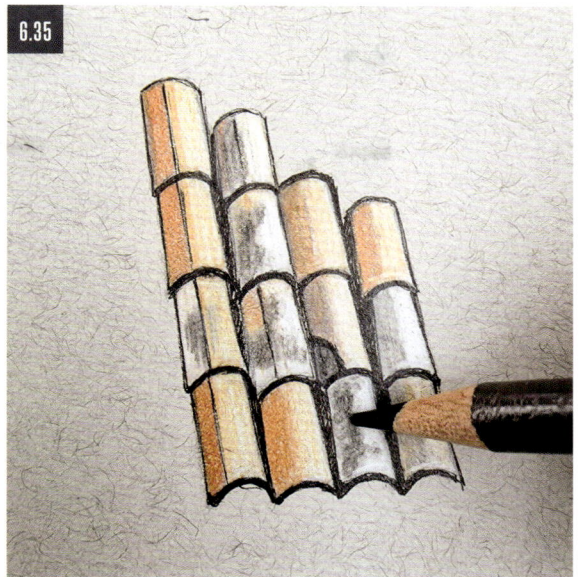

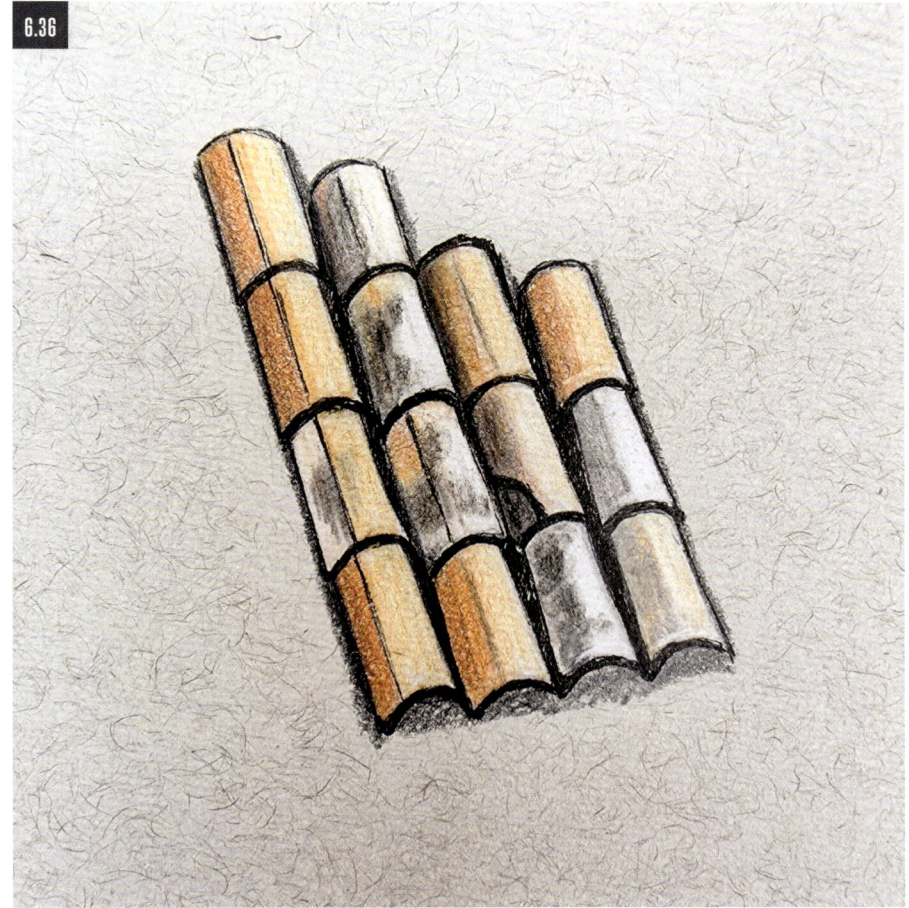

Chimney Pots

Chimneys are a lot of fun to draw and it's quick and easy to make them look three-dimensional. They also add interest and character to drawings. In this exercise, you will draw them at a larger size than you probably would in a regular size artwork, but it will help you gain an understanding of their shape and how the light source hits them on one side and a shadow is created on the other side. Making use of this contrast between light and dark in your drawing will instantly create a three-dimensional illusion.

Think of the endless rows of chimneys across the rooftops of Paris!

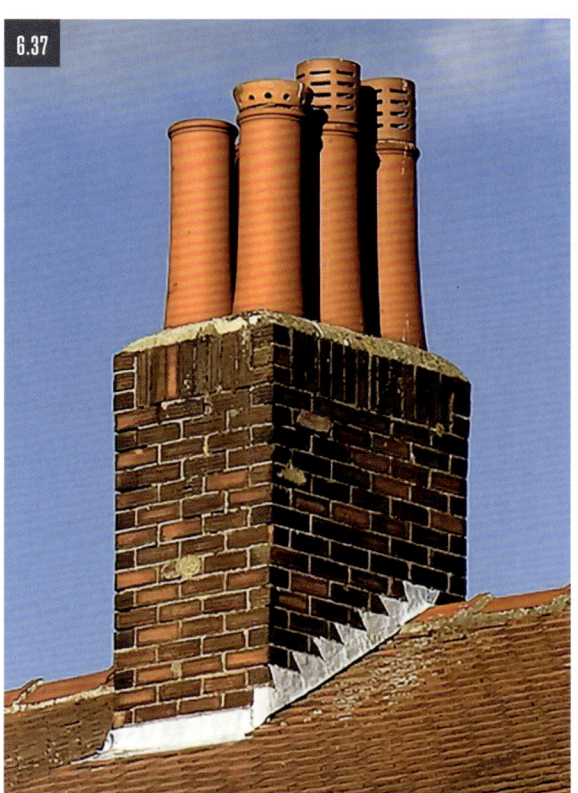

Materials

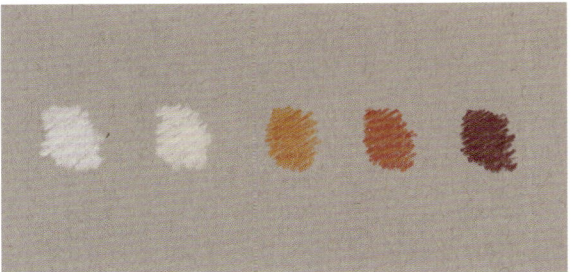

▶ Toned paper
▶ Sharp pencil
▶ Black 0.05mm fineliner pen
▶ Coloured pencils: White, Ivory, Terracotta, Sanguine, Caput Mortuum Violet
▶ White gel pen or white Posca pen
▶ Blender

Step 1: Draw with Pencil

Begin by making a pencil sketch of the chimney pots (**FIGURE 6.38**). This is, again, just an exercise, so the drawing doesn't need to be very big. You can use a small grid if it helps you, or you could take the height and width measurements of the first chimney pot to use as a guide for the others.

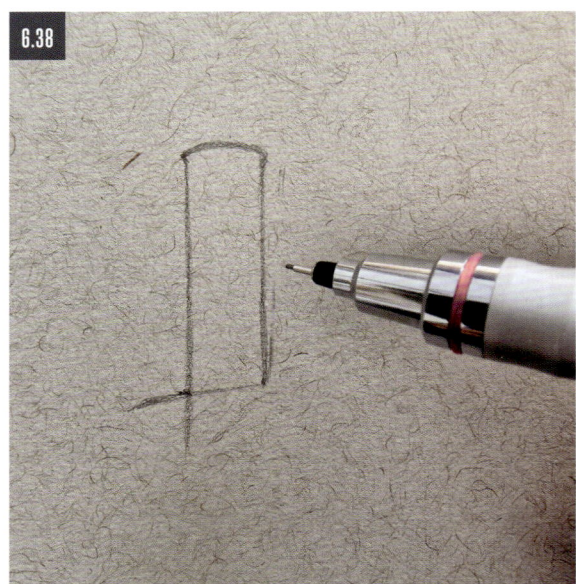

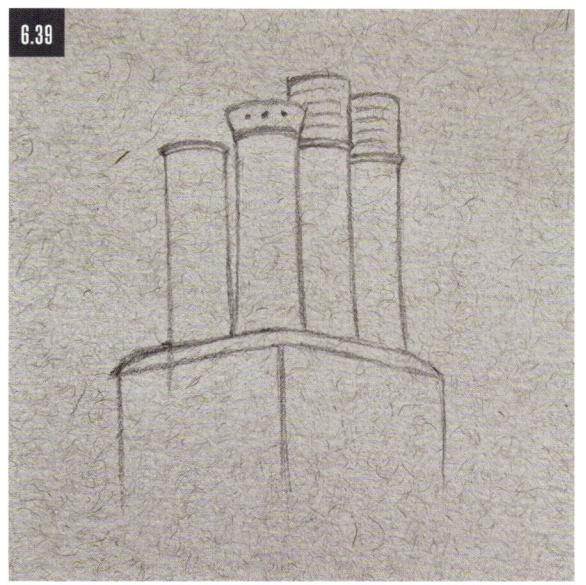

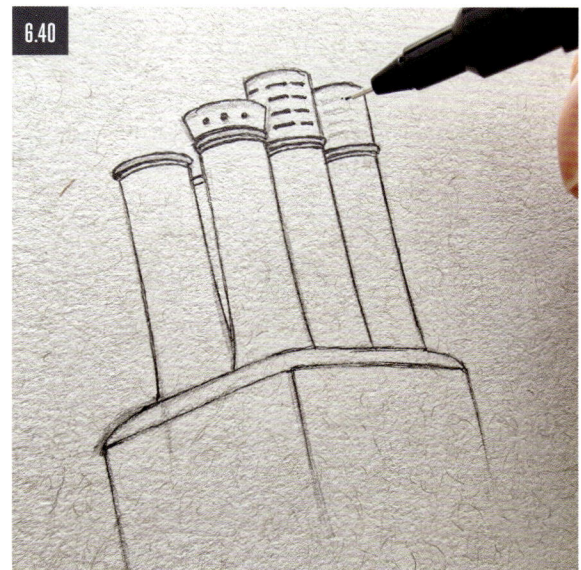

Notice how the pots flare out slightly at their base; they are not perfectly straight.

When all the pots are in place, draw in some curved lines on the top of the two rear pots, which you can then use as a guide to draw in the four rows of small slats with ink in the next step (**FIGURE 6.39**).

Step 2: Cover the Lines with Black Ink

Now go over the pencil lines in ink. Don't be afraid to alter your lines slightly, as you can achieve better precision with the fineliner than with a pencil. Mark in the little slats and circles at the top of the pots (**FIGURE 6.40**).

Begin adding the dark shadows on the left side of each pot with crosshatching (**FIGURE 6.41**). I find it easiest to work all the way down in one direction, then cross over those lines with lines in the other direction. Darken the outer edge of the cross-hatching by drawing vertically downwards.

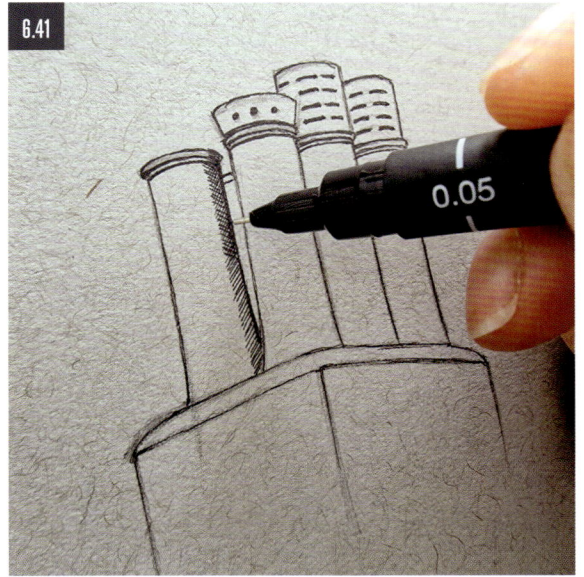

Finally, draw in some random brick shapes if you want to (**FIGURE 6.42, NEXT PAGE**). I am going to add some random colour to these in the next step, but I want to leave them unfinished.

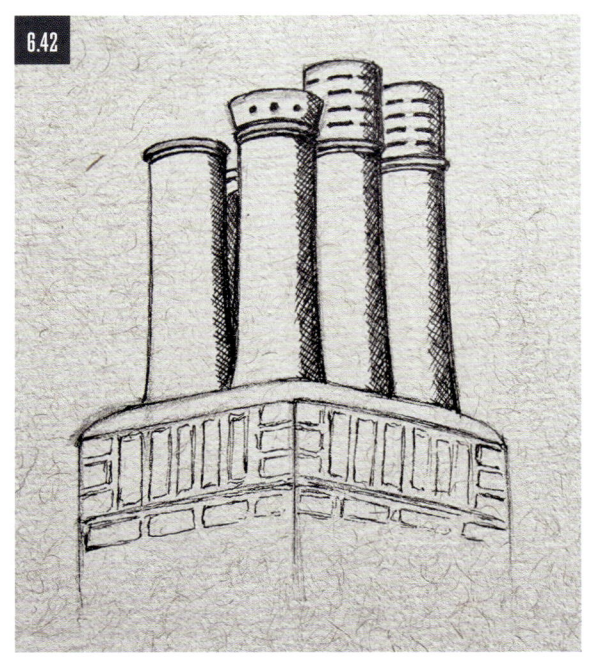

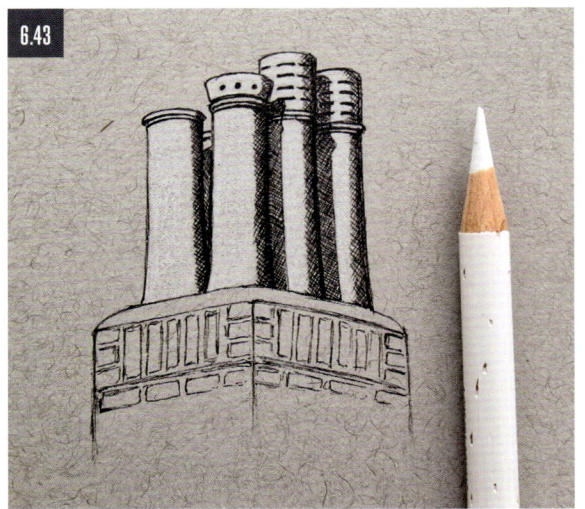

Step 3: Add Colour

Now it's time to add some vibrant colour to make the pots glow!

As with previous projects, we'll begin with adding a layer of white all over the pots to lift the next layers of colours (**FIGURE 6.43**). Make the white more opaque in the centre of the pots where the highlights are.

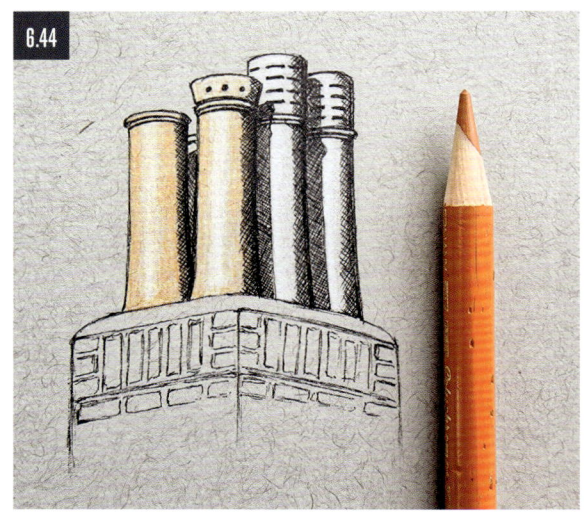

Next, take your Terracotta coloured pencil and add some layers of colour across each pot, including lightly over the crosshatching (**FIGURE 6.44**). Slowly build up this colour, beginning with light stokes and then progressing into small circular movements (scumbling) on the top layers (**FIGURE 6.45**). Use your blender occasionally to push the colours together.

Now introduce some Sanguine coloured pencil, focusing on the darkest areas (**FIGURE 6.46**). As with the Terracotta, build the colour up until it is nice and rich.

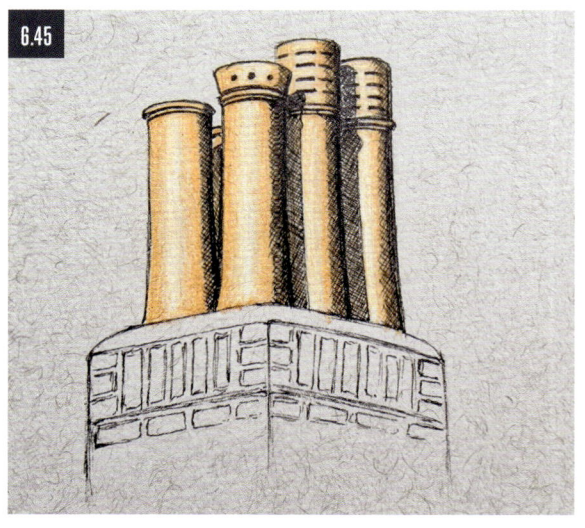

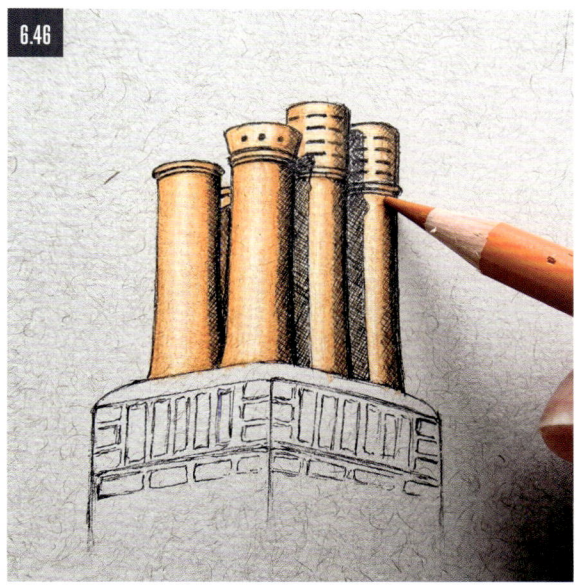

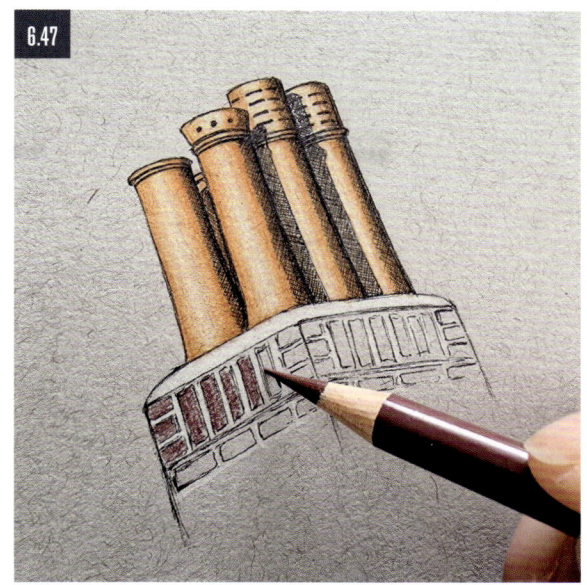

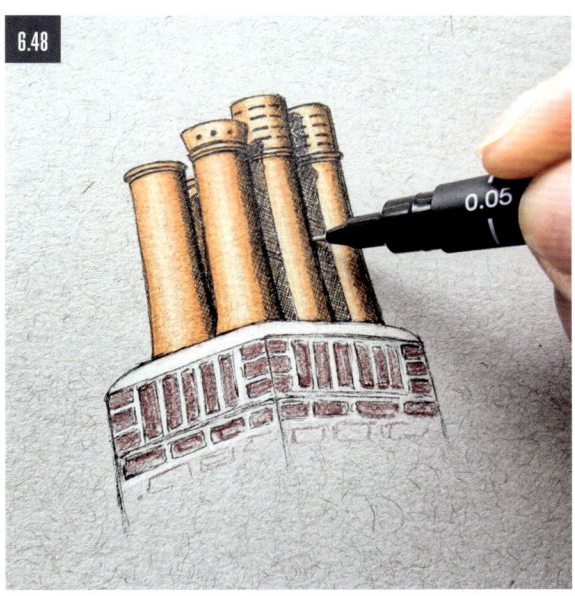

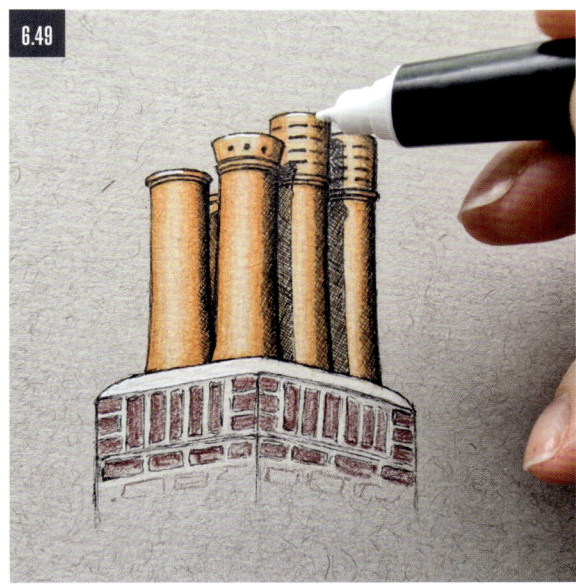

Finally, use Ivory to gently go over the vertical highlight running down the pots, and then to colour the top of the chimney stack and the cement between the bricks. Next, use Caput Mortuum Violet to quickly and lightly colour the bricks, fading the colours near the bottom to create a loose and unfinished look (**FIGURE 6.47**).

Step 4: Add Final Details

The last step is to use your fineliner to go over the dark edges of the shadows and the spot where the bases of the pots meet the top of the chimney stack to add some extra definition (**FIGURE 6.48**).

Finally, use a white highlighting pen to run along the top of each pot at its lightest point and on the top of the chimney stack on the side that faces the light source (**FIGURE 6.49**).

White highlighting pens work well for adding that extra dimension to chimney pots, a useful thing to remember if you are ever working on larger building projects.

The more you work on illustrating architecture, the more familiar you will become with the colours of the different elements of buildings. The same types of building materials tend to be used again and again across the different styles and periods of architecture.

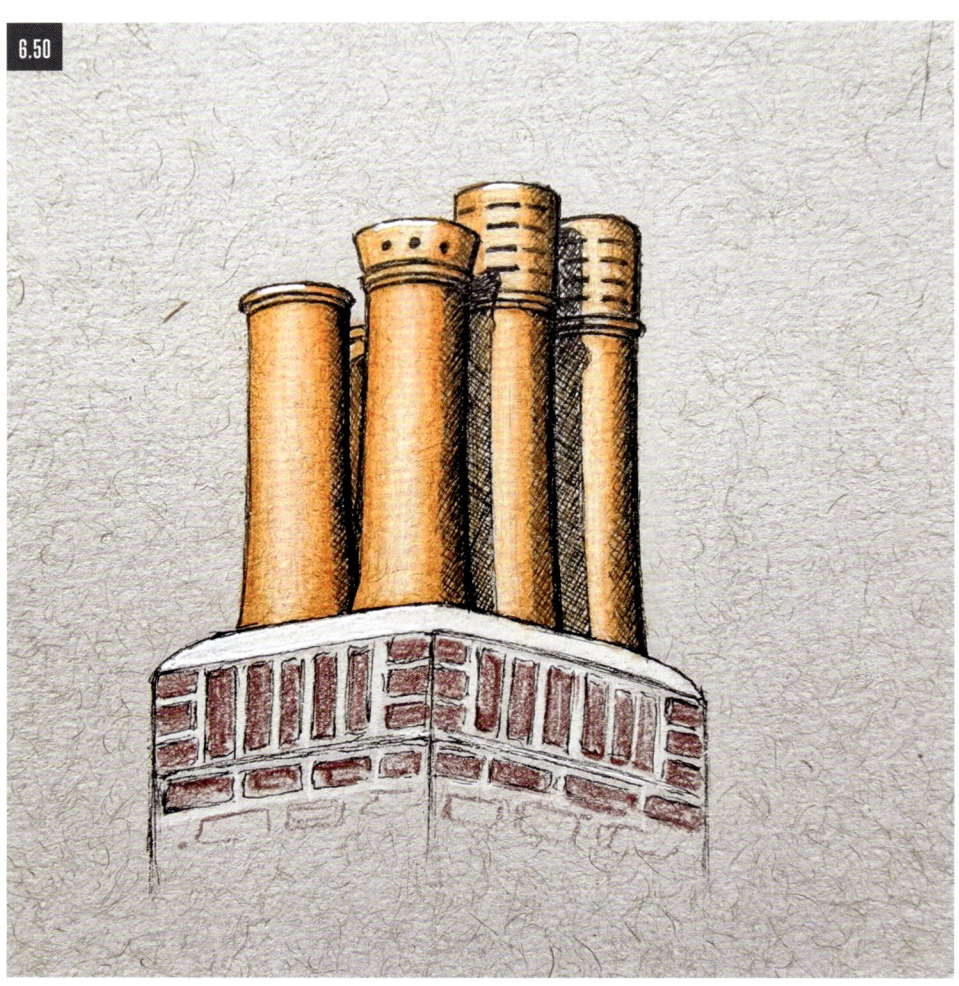

6.50

Windows

Windows can be very interesting to draw and are an attractive feature of buildings. Plus, there is so much variety among them. Think church windows, windows with shutters, windows with curtains and plants...the list is endless. You are sure to be able to find an interesting window to draw no matter where you are in the world!

For this exercise I have chosen an old, slightly ornate window from an old English college. I like how the curtains inside the window drape, and we'll look at how to create the folds of the fabric with pencil.

The white woodwork of the frame contrasts greatly with the darkness of the room within and

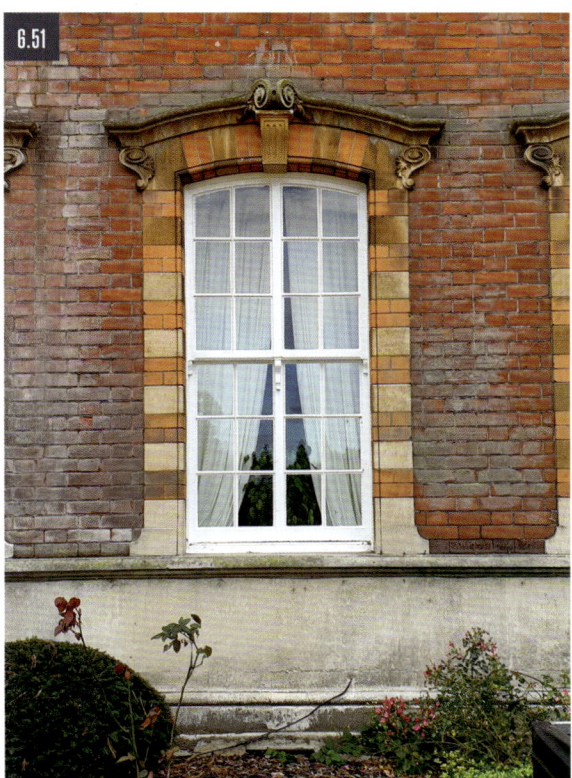

makes a good frame for the colourful shapes and patterns of the surrounding bricks.

The slightly curved top of the window plus the scrolls and serifs are an intricate part of the building and add a lot of interest, in addition to making the window stand out more.

Materials

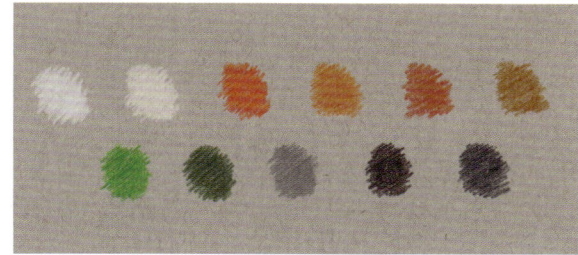

▶ Toned paper
▶ Sharp pencil
▶ Black 0.05mm fineliner pen
▶ Coloured pencils: White, Ivory, Orange Glaze, Terracotta, Sanguine, Brown Ochre, Permanent Green, Chrome Oxide Green, Warm Grey IV, Sepia, Payne's Grey
▶ Blender
▶ Eraser

Step 1: Draw with Pencil

I find that the easiest way to draw a window is to start with the basic rectangle of the outer part of the white window frame. Once these proportions are correct, you can build outwards and inwards, slotting everything together. Remember to keep a clean sheet of paper under your hand to prevent your pencil work from smudging.

For this exercise, I took the measurements of the outer part of the white frame from my digital screen, having first decided what size I want the whole picture to be. Notice that the top of the rectangle is slightly arched and draw this in **(FIGURE 6.52, NEXT PAGE)**.

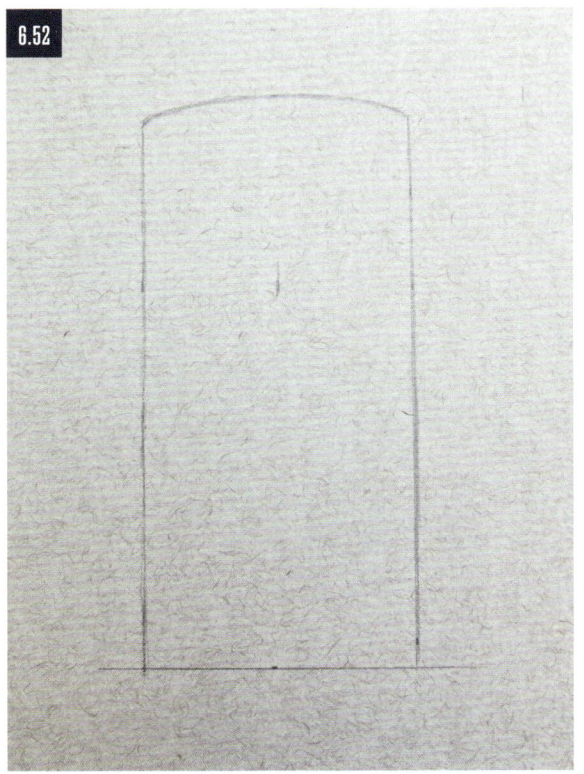

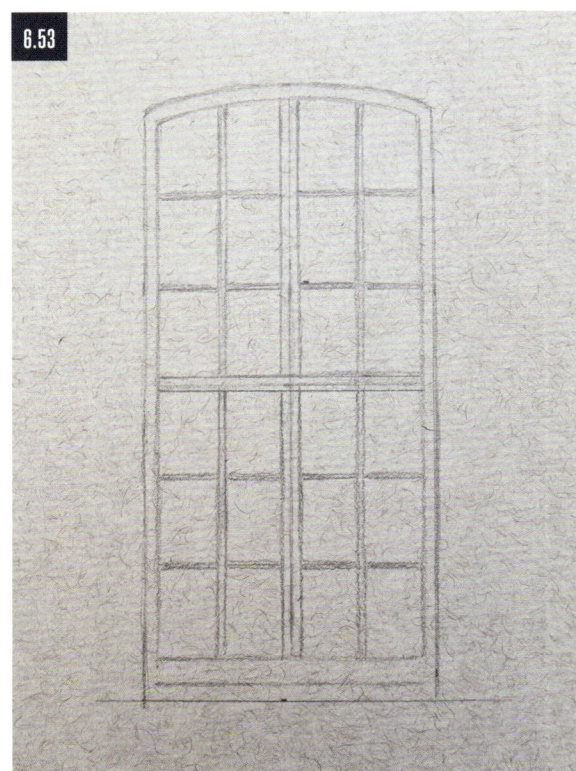

Next, add in the basic lines of the white frames around the windowpanes (**FIGURE 6.53**). For now, you just need to divide spaces between each windowpane evenly. You can add more details with greater precision using your fineliner in the next step.

Gently mark in where the curtains (drapes) will be. I have used artistic licence and positioned them more equally than they appear in the photo. You can draw in the folds in the fabric later. I do this later because it's best to keep the areas that are to be covered in the white pen as clean as possible because the ink goes down better on clean paper.

Now start building your drawing outwards. You can take measurements from your screen or printout if it helps you. I am using the windowpanes as markers to line up the positions of the bricks (**FIGURE 6.54**).

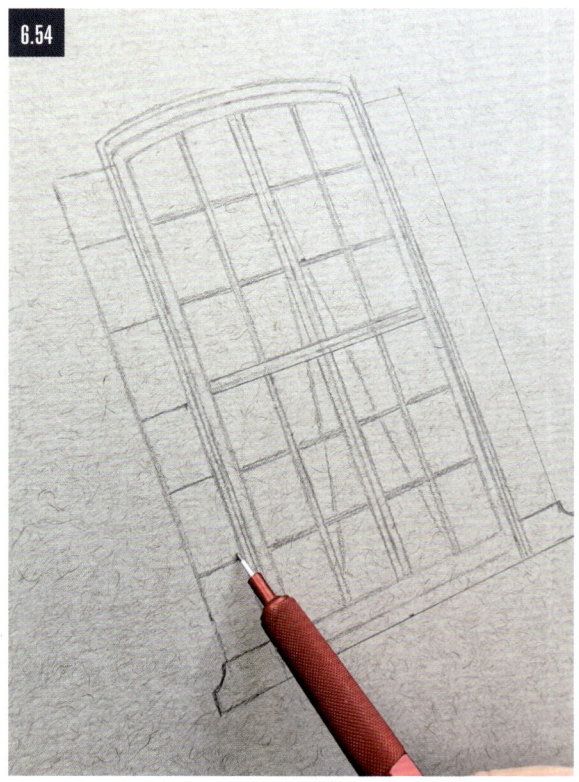

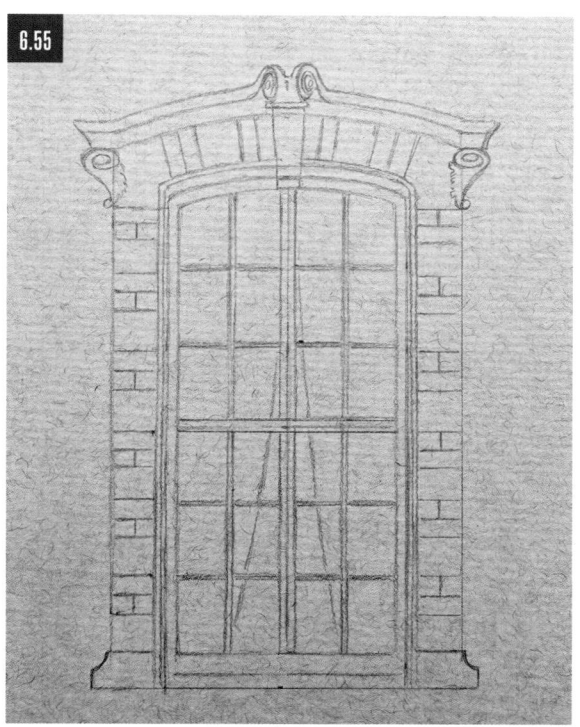

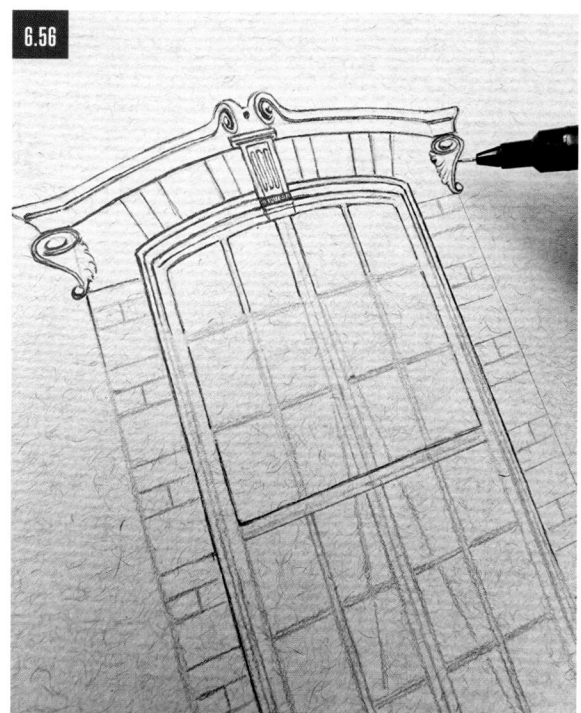

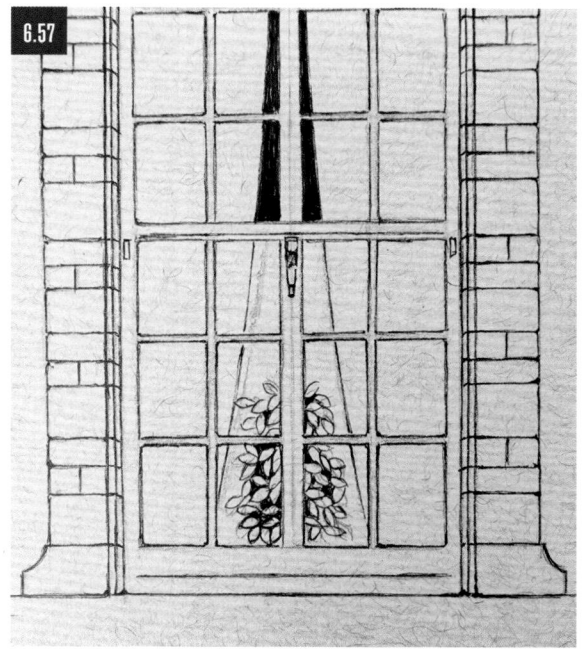

Continue in this way, piecing everything together. Notice how the brick pattern is slightly different on each side of the window. Apart from that, everything should be symmetrical.

The final things to sketch in are the serif-like shapes on both sides of the window and the scrolls right in the centre at the top (**FIGURE 6.55**). Again, it will be easier to draw with greater precision in the next step with the fineliner pen.

Step 2: Cover the Lines with Black Ink

Now that the pencil drawing is complete, go over everything with black ink (**FIGURE 6.56**). Be careful when you are drawing the channels around the windowpanes because we will be filling these in with opaque white pen and it's important that they stand out.

Darken the very darkest lines and sketch in the shadows around the scroll and serifs.

As an added detail, add in the plant at the base of the window if you want to, or leave it out if you prefer. If you decide to add it in, sketch the leaves loosely; they don't need to be perfect (**FIGURE 6.57**).

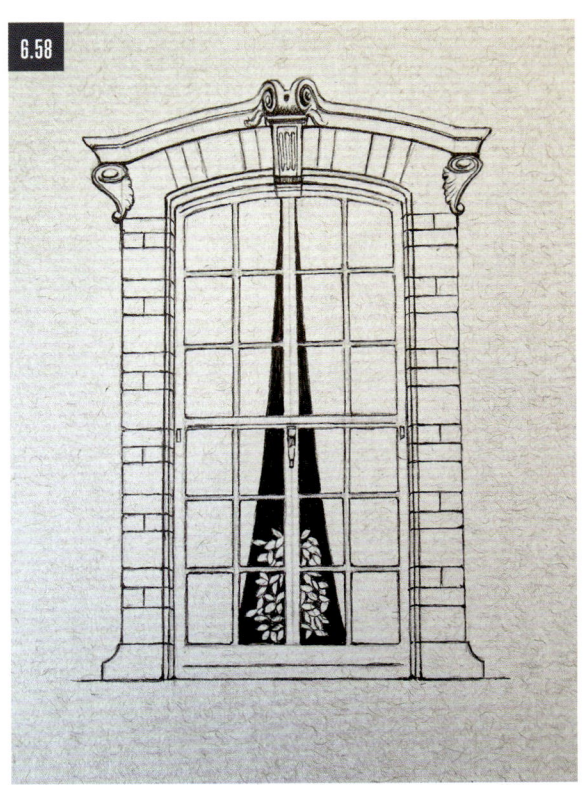

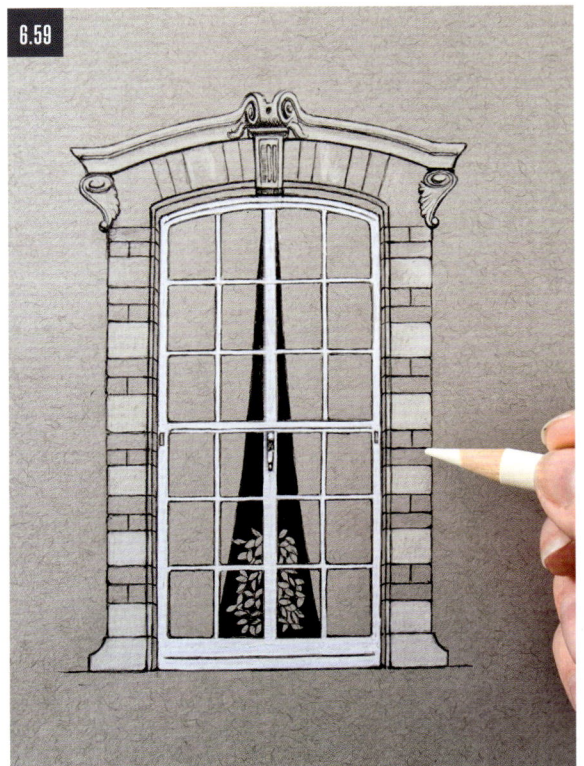

Next, black out the area behind the curtains. This is the area that is inside the room beyond the window. If you have a larger black fineliner, use it to speed up the process. If you drew the plant, draw carefully around it and randomly darken small areas around the leaves to create depth (**FIGURE 6.58**).

If you make any mistakes with your ink lines, they can usually be covered with coloured pencil and/or opaque white ink pen in the next step.

Step 3: Add Colour

Before you begin adding colour, carefully rub out any remaining pencil lines with an eraser.

Next, completely cover the white of the frame with your opaque white pen.

Now use a layer of white and then Ivory pencil to colour the lightest areas of the picture, including the scrolls, serifs, and lightest bricks (**FIGURE 6.59**). These base colours will lift the next layer of colours.

Use the Brown Ochre pencil to colour the ochre-coloured bricks and stonework. Notice how when this is applied on top of the Ivory pencil, it recreates the marbled effect seen in some of the stones (**FIGURE 6.60**). When the colour is applied directly onto the paper with no base layer underneath, it is much darker, so you can create varying tones.

For the lightest, creamy-coloured stones, use varying degrees of layers of the Brown Ochre. The bricks further down the window are pale and will only need a thin layer to warm them slightly, compared to those further up (**FIGURE 6.61**).

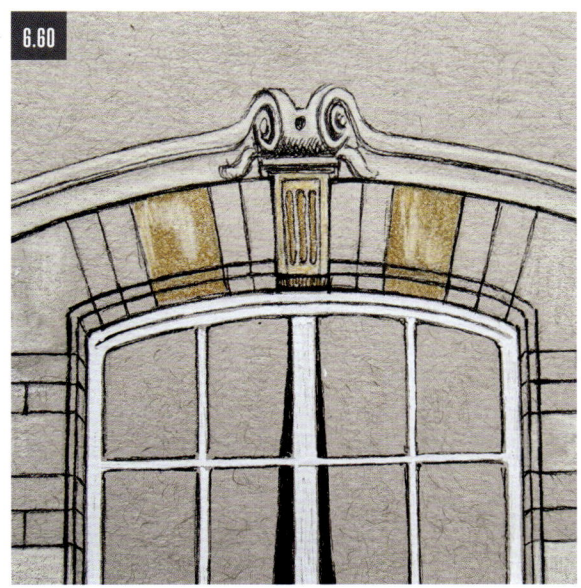

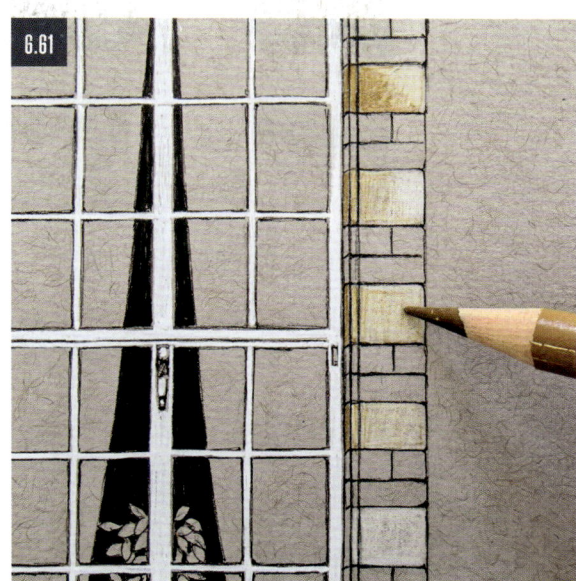

Now we will move on to the terracotta-coloured bricks. Begin by applying a light layer of Ivory to all the remaining uncoloured bricks, and then make this Ivory colour thicker with more layers applied to the bricks where the Terracotta colour is the brightest. Making the Ivory base layers more opaque will make any subsequent Terracotta colour brighter. The lighter colour shines through from underneath.

Next, use an Orange Glaze coloured pencil to cover all the terracotta-coloured bricks (**FIGURE 6.62**).

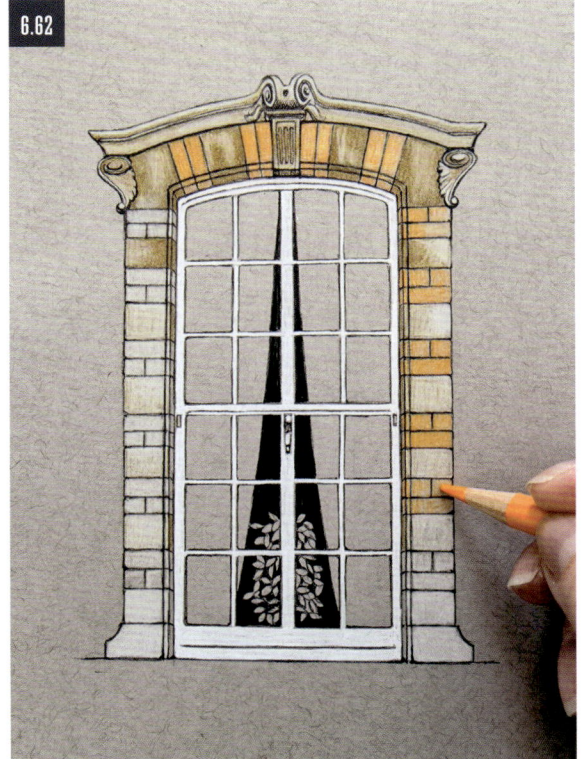

Make the layers of Orange Glaze lighter where the colour is darker. Regularly smooth out the colour with your blender, making sure the tip is clean before you do this. Then introduce some Terracotta pencil on top of the Orange Glaze colour where the colour is slightly darker.

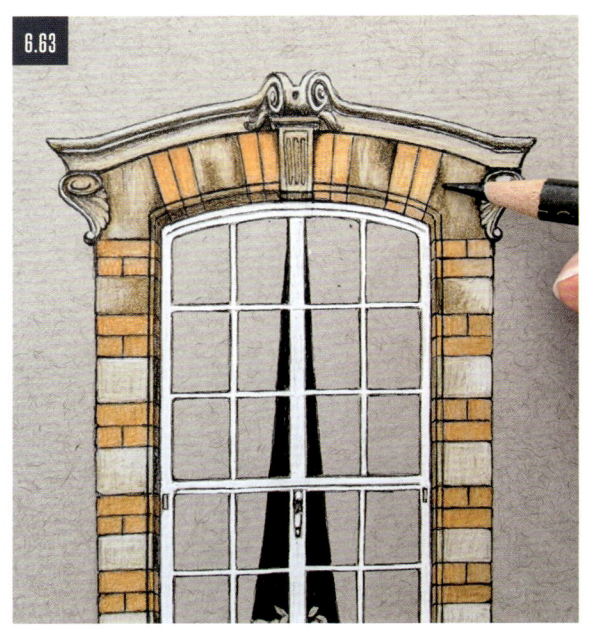

The next stage is to begin adding the darker tones of colour, starting with Dark Sepia. Use it in any crevices and to shade around the ornate top part of the window as well as on the darkest areas of the bricks (**FIGURE 6.63**).

Now take a Payne's Grey pencil and darken the shadows in the crevices still further. Run it over the horizontal shadow in the central part of the window frame as well.

Now that we've finished with the bricks, we'll colour the curtains and create the folds in the fabric.

Begin by loosely sketching in the folds in the material of the curtains (**FIGURE 6.65**). You can do this with pencil first, or if you're feeling confident, go straight in with ink like I did. The lines don't need to be identical to the photo unless you want to spend time carefully copying them over.

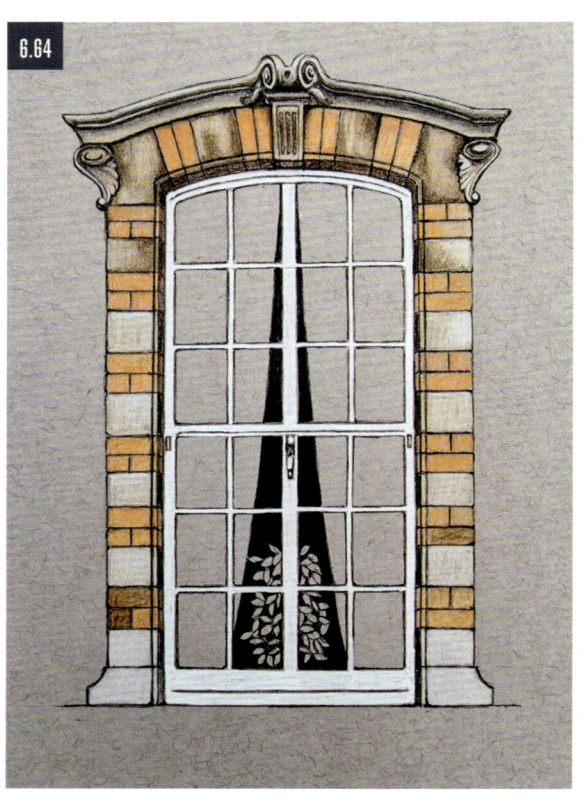

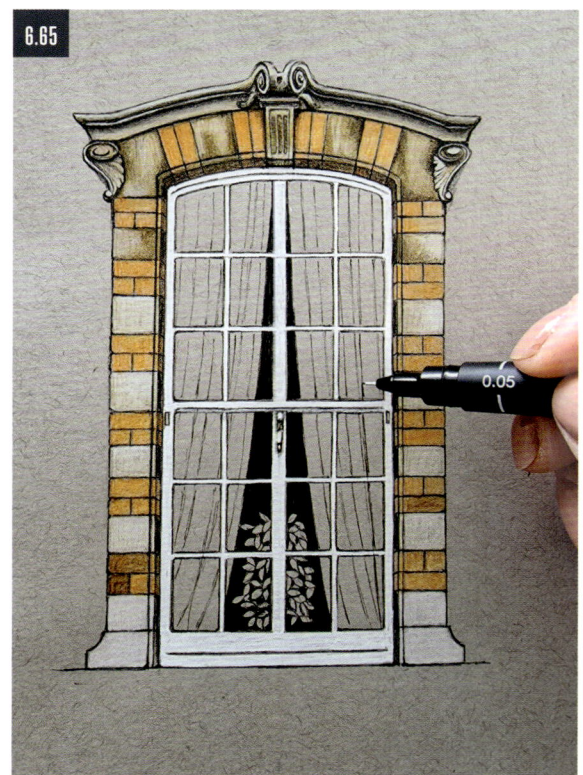

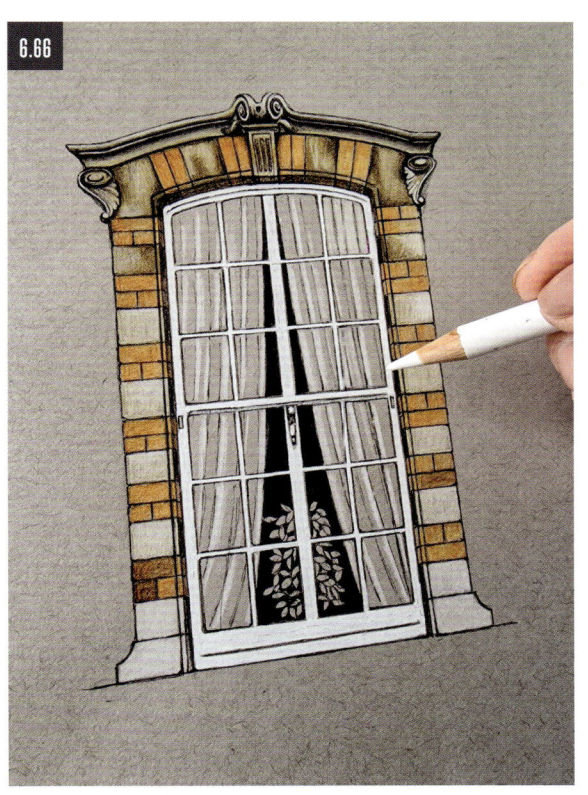

Next, use a white pencil to colour the lightest areas of the fabric, which are next to the dark lines of the folds (**FIGURE 6.66**).

Then use Warm Grey IV to add in the mid-tone shadowed areas created by the folds (**FIGURE 6.67**). Notice that the area at the top of the glass panes is darker, as it is shadowed by the top of the window.

Now go over any areas of the fabric that are still pencil-free with a layer of Ivory. The next step is to use the darker-toned Payne's Grey to accentuate the darkest folds (**FIGURE 6.68**). Then darken the area at the top of the window as well, and carefully blend the colours.

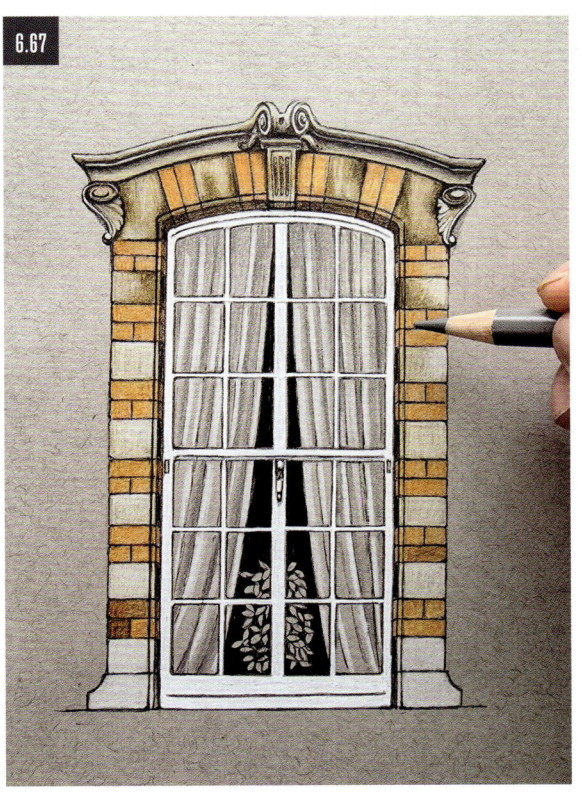

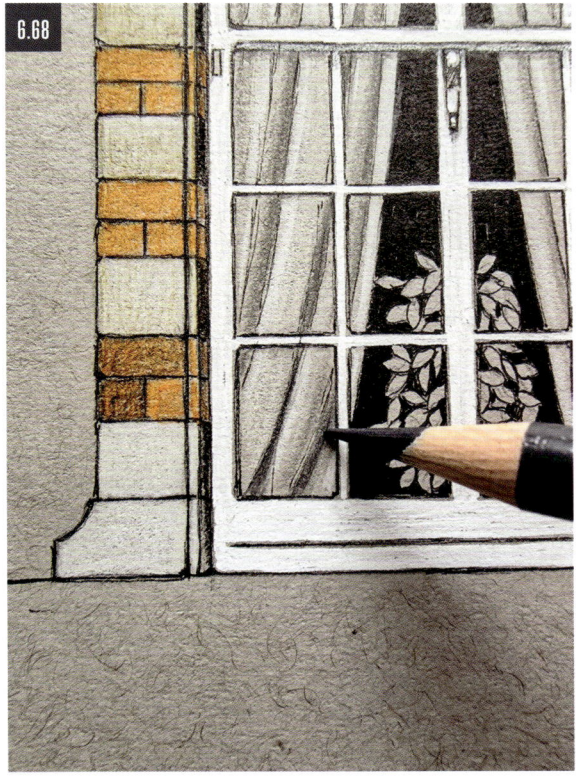

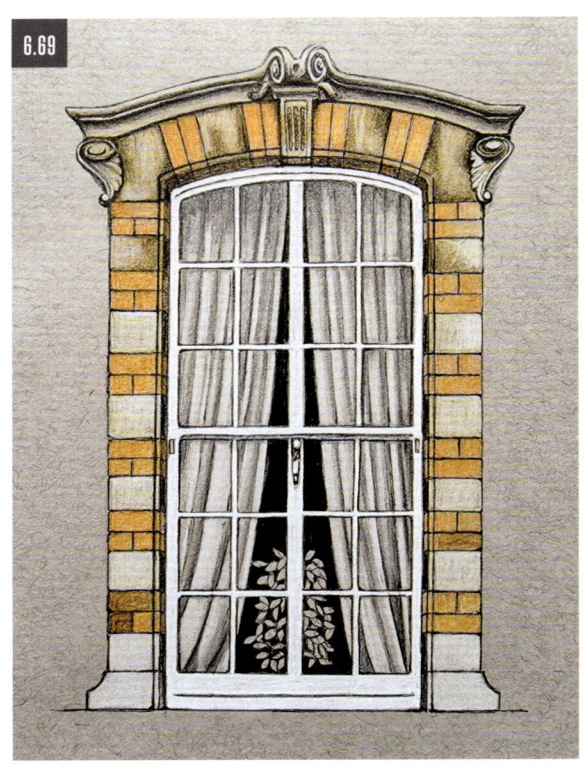

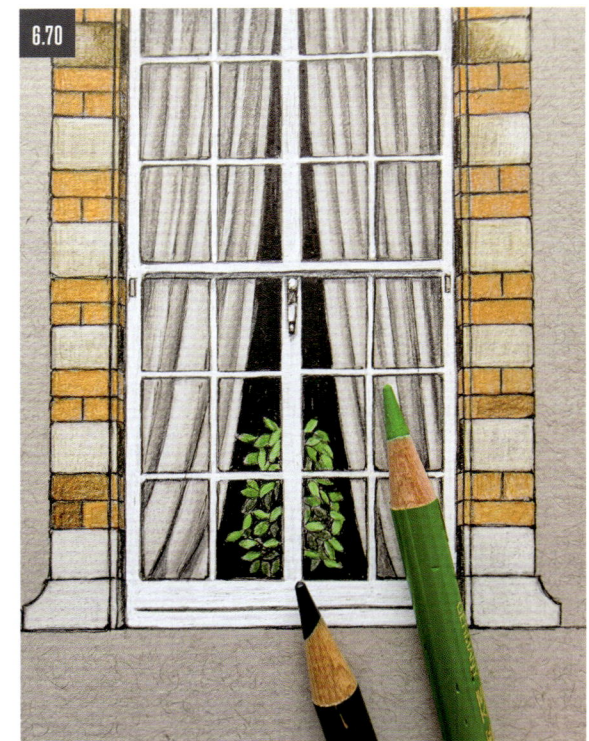

Next, redefine the windowpanes and the darkest folds of the fabric with your fineliner (**FIGURE 6.69**).

Now it's time to colour the plant. Take a dark-green pencil (I used Chrome Oxide Green) and randomly colour some of the leaves. Then use a lighter green (I used Permanent Green) to colour the remaining leaves (**FIGURE 6.70**). Finally, use white to highlight a few of the leaves to make them stand out.

Step 4: Add Final Details

In this final step, I like to loosely add some of the bricks around the outside of the window and fade the drawing out towards the edges. I like to leave this part to the very end so I can relax in this final step, forgetting all the precision and using artistic licence to create the faded outer edges.

First, draw in some random brick shapes in pencil around the outside of the window, and then cover the pencil lines in ink, leaving a few in pencil (**FIGURE 6.71**).

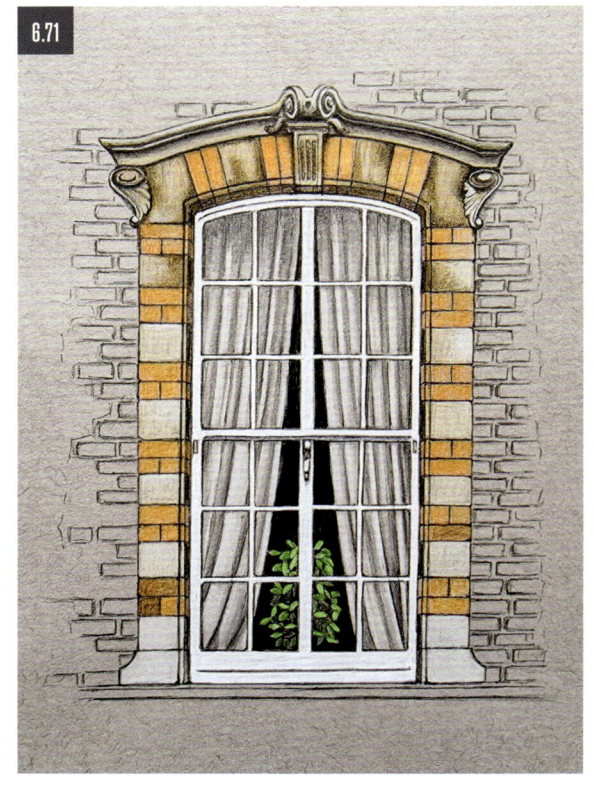

Use varying layers of Terracotta, white, and Warm Grey IV to loosely colour the bricks all over, leaving a few undone.

Do this all the way around, and then use Payne's Grey to define the line that borders the outer edge of the window and the random bricks (**FIGURE 6.72**).

You can really have fun with this and add other light lines to suggest lines and marks on the surface of the wall. I have made a few random marks with white pencil and fineliner.

Finally, check and redefine the whole picture with your fineliner pen, and then using a white ink pen to draw in the highlights on the scrolls, serifs, and along the top edges of the cream-coloured bricks (**FIGURE 6.73**).

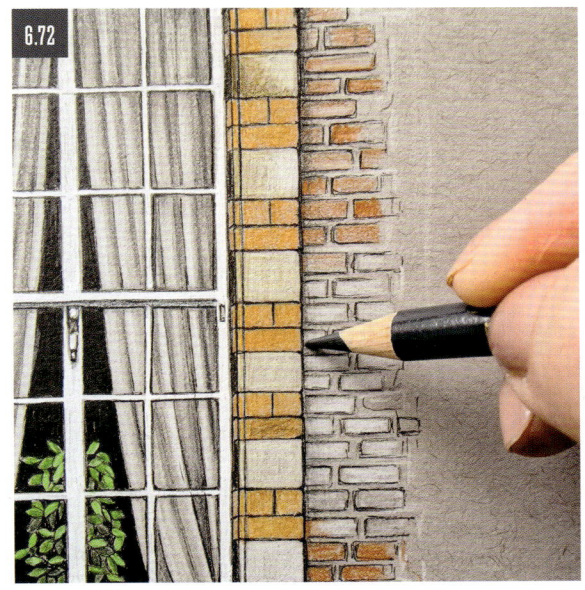

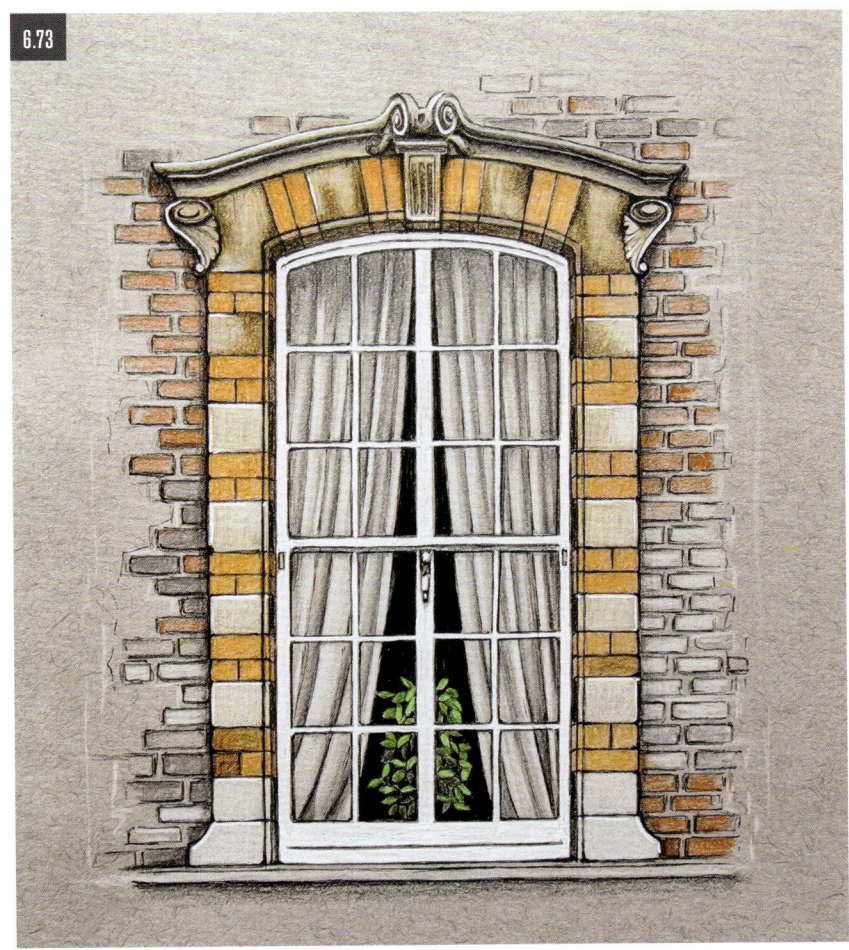

Doors

We use doors every day without really thinking about them, and yet they are often very interesting and beautiful. They can have lots of ornate, detailed hardware such as knobs, knockers, bolts, locks, name signs, and hinges. That's before you even look at their surrounds, which sometimes have decorative stone or wooden carvings. You will also often find ornate lanterns hanging above or next to a door, and sometimes little windows and boot scrapers!

There is something very intriguing about doors. If they are closed, you wonder what is on the other side, and if they are open, you may see a glimpse of what lies beyond.

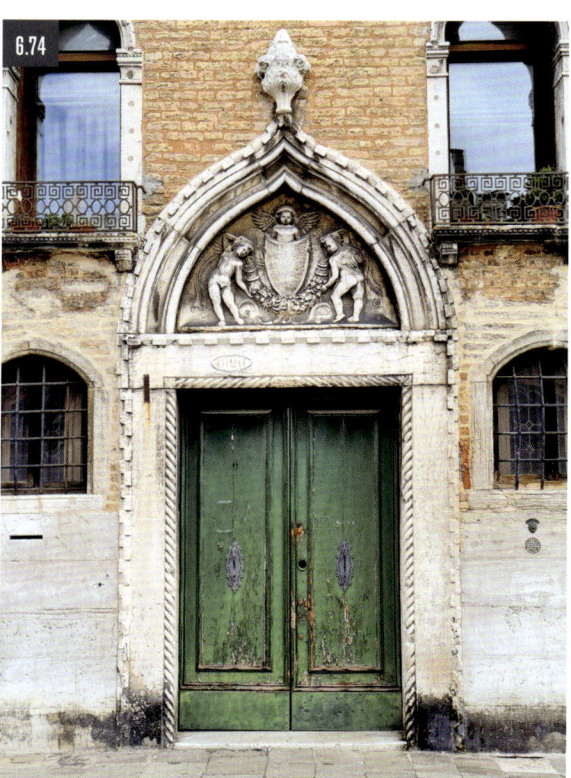

Doors make for great art subject matter and can be found worldwide in all shapes and sizes!

For this project, I have chosen a beautiful Venetian Gothic door I stumbled across in the back streets of Venice, Italy. This style is very typical of Venetian Gothic architecture. It will make for a great project, and we can focus on the carved stone cherubs within the pointed arch above the door. We can add further interest by creating the effect of the old, worn wooden door and paving stones in the foreground (**FIGURE 6.74**).

Materials

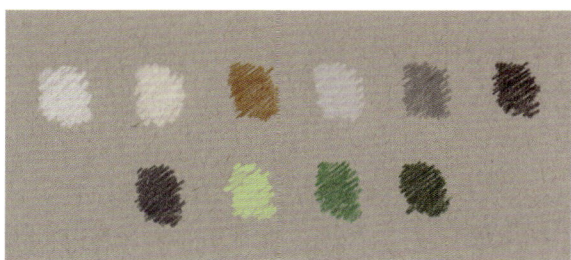

- ▶ Toned grey paper
- ▶ Sharp pencil
- ▶ Black 0.05mm fineliner pen
- ▶ Coloured pencils: White, Ivory, Brown Ochre, Cold Grey I, Warm Grey IV, Payne's Grey, Light Green (Pablo), Hooker's Green, Chrome Oxide Green
- ▶ White 0.7mm Posca pen
- ▶ Eraser
- ▶ Set square
- ▶ Ruler
- ▶ Blender

Step 1: Draw with Pencil

First, you must decide what size you would like your drawing to be and what drawing method you would prefer to use. I am going to take the main measurements from my tablet and then draw the rest freehand. Remember, you can also take the measurements from a printout or hard copy of your photograph.

If you feel more confident using the grid method, be sure to make the grid squares fairly small so that each square has enough detail in it to make the process worthwhile. You may, of course, wish to draw the whole thing out freehand!

The central green wooden doors and angel carvings above it are going to be the main focus of the drawing. They should be placed centrally on the page, leaving plenty of room around them to fade out the surrounding details.

Let's get started! Begin by finding the centre of the page and draw a vertical line down the page. Measure and draw a horizontal line where the base of the door is. As with other projects, we will use these lines as the central anchor point for the whole composition. Use your set square and ruler to help you do this (**FIGURE 6.75**).

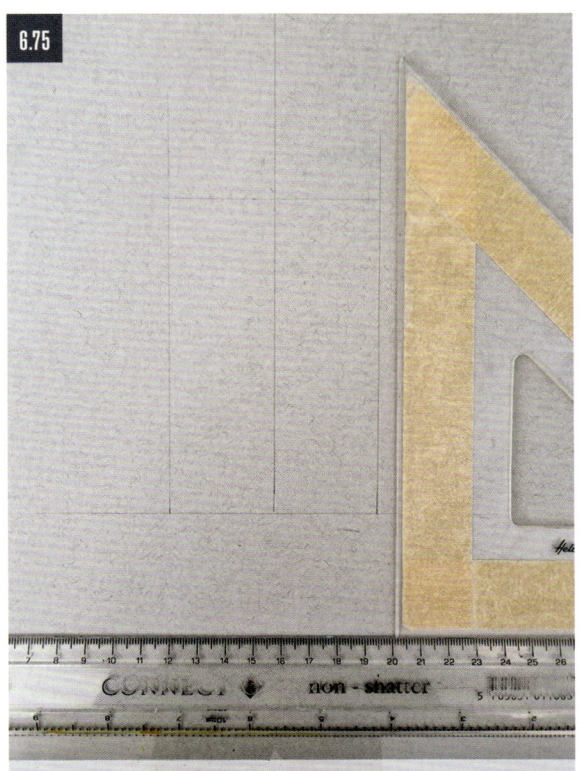

To figure out where to place the baseline of the door, measure the distance between the base of the door and the very top of the pointed arch on your reference photo. You can then use these measurements as a guide to position the drawing on the page, leaving enough room at the bottom of the page for the paving stones and enough room at the top for the ornate detail above the pointed arch.

> ➤ This is a very old door that is a little worn in places. The measurements may be a bit off in places where some of the stonework is worn or crumbling. Just use the measurements as a guide.

Next, measure and draw in the main parts surrounding the door. Measure upwards to find the distance between the top of the door and the top of the inner pointed arch, and the distance to the top of the pointed arch (**FIGURE 6.76**).

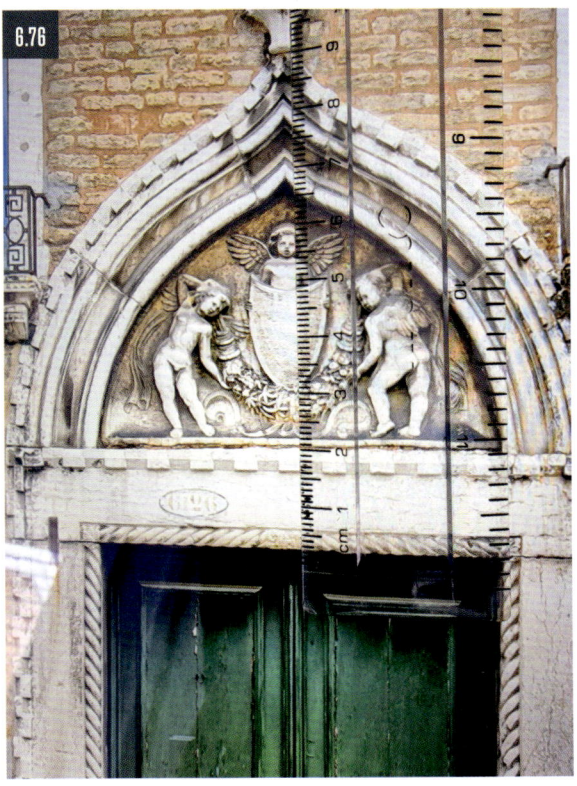

From this point onwards, I am going to draw the rest freehand using the main structure of lines as my guide. It helps that the door is very symmetrical. You can still check any measurements as you go along if you need to.

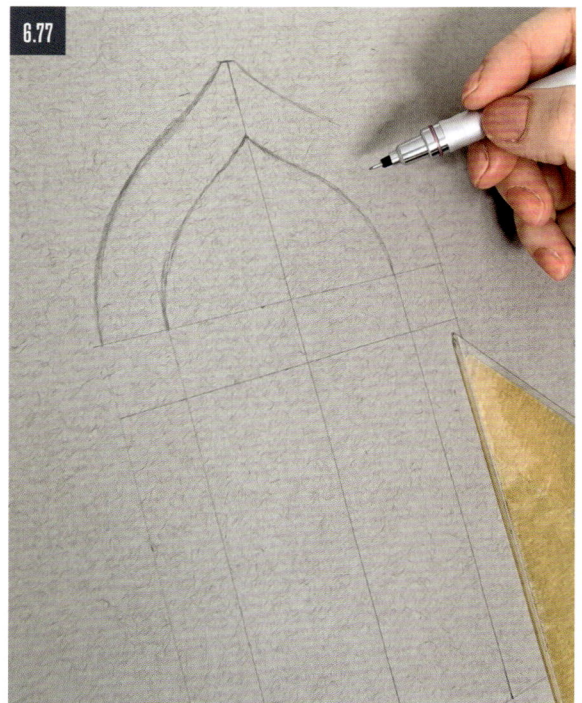

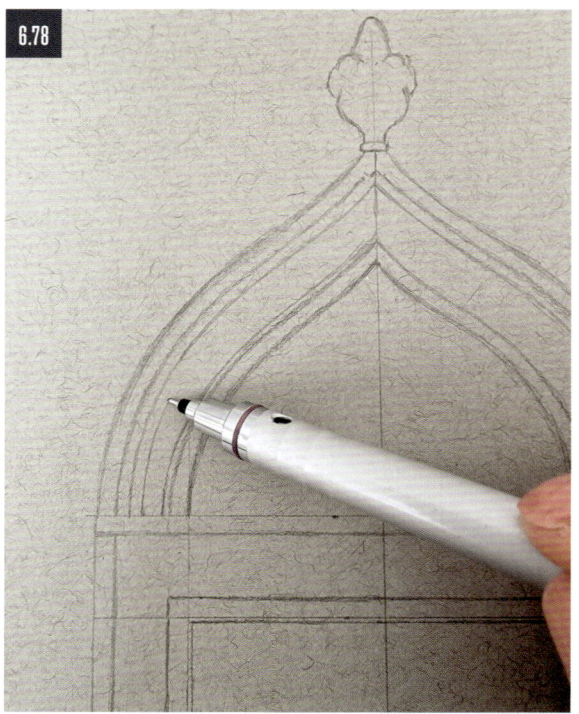

Now draw in the inner and outer curves of the pointed arch using the anchor points you have already measured (**FIGURE 6.77**). As you are sketching these in, cast your eyes to both sides of the arch to make sure they are symmetrical.

Once the two main arched lines are in place, you can slot in the other arched lines in between using the first two as your guide (**FIGURE 6.78**).

Now that the main structure is in place, sketch in the rest of the main elements of the drawing, remembering to keep a sheet of clean paper under your hand to prevent any smudging.

Take your time and be aware that details like this are quite time-consuming to work on. Start with the shield in the centre above the door, then slot in the angels and decorative details around it.

Also draw in the lines within the doors and twisted border that goes around them (**FIGURE 6.79**). This will look amazing when ink and colour are added to it!

Leave the pencil work at this point (**FIGURE 6.80**). We will go back and add the surrounding brickwork and details in the last stages of the drawing.

Step 2: Cover the Lines with Black Ink

Once the pencil work is finished, it's time to go over everything in ink.

Begin covering the pencil lines with ink, working from left to right with paper under your hand at all times (**FIGURE 6.81**). The surface of the drawing is very delicate at this stage!

The pencil lines are only an initial guide. It is possible to be more accurate with your ink fineliner and add in smaller lines as you go along. Begin drawing in any dark shadows as well, no matter how small. Keep your reference photo next to you the whole time so you can look at it continually.

I have left the angels' faces blank for the moment because it will be easier to suggest their soft features with coloured pencil in the next stage (**FIGURE 6.82**).

Drawing and Illustrating Architecture

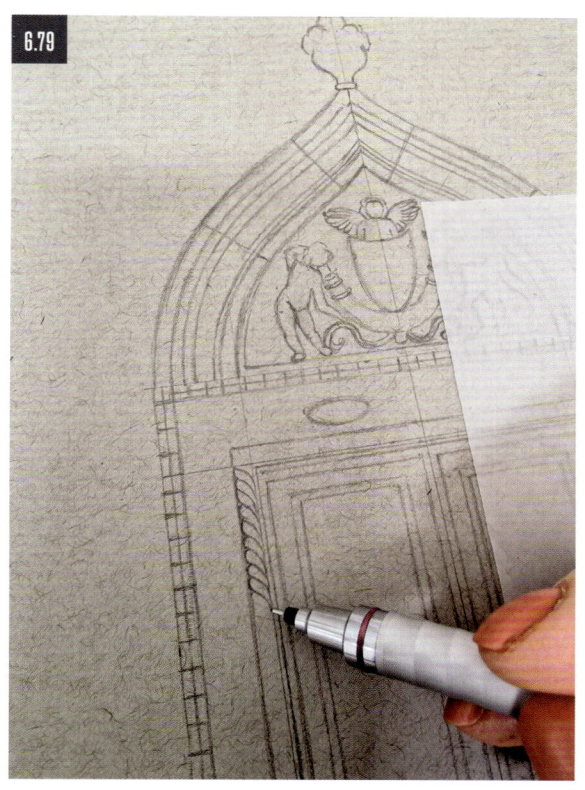

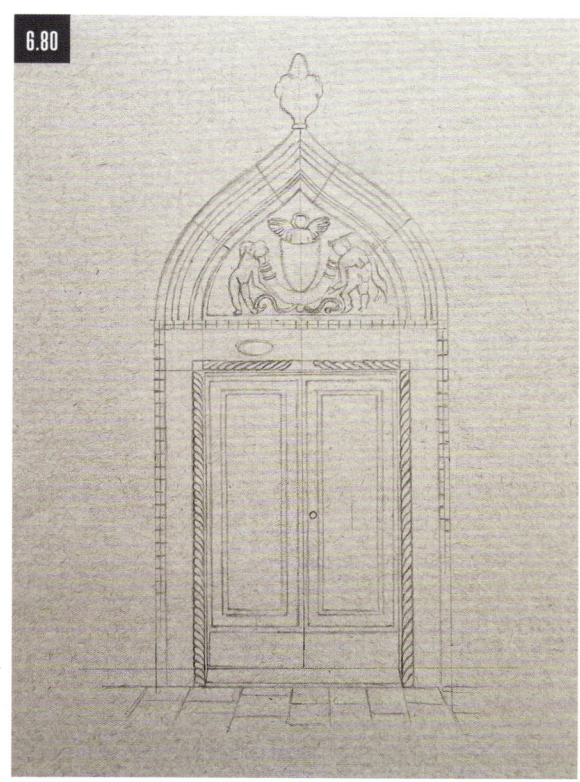

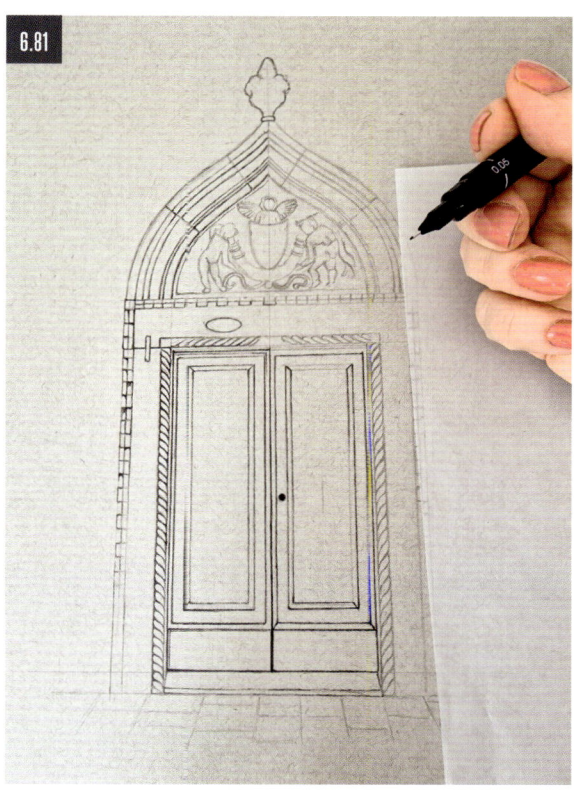

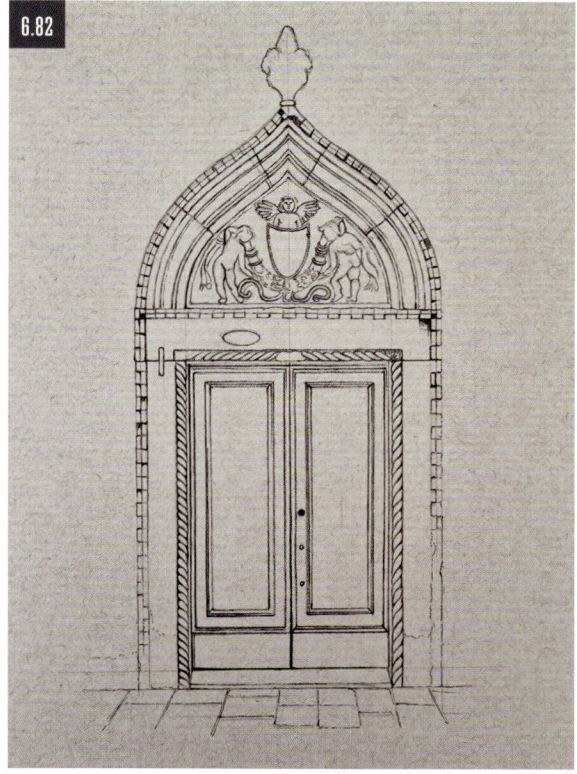

Step 3: Add Colour

Now it's time to start adding colour! First, we'll work on the arch and the door surround in sections, and then we'll move on to colouring the door itself.

For each section we work on, start with white pencil first, then work down through the tonal value scale to the darkest colours.

With a white pencil, colour the lightest parts of the decoration attached to the top of the pointed arch. Then use Warm Grey IV to define the slightly darker areas of the carved swirls within. The colours are very soft here with no dark tones, so you can just deepen the colours by adding more layers of white and Warm Grey IV.

Next, colour the lightest areas on the left side of the arch, starting with white and then Ivory where the tones are slightly lighter (**FIGURES 6.83** and **6.84**). The difference in these tones is very subtle, but observing small differences such as these will greatly improve the look of the overall piece.

Now introduce Warm Grey IV for the middle tones you can see on the arch, and then introduce Sepia for the darker patches and the marbled look on the stone arch (**FIGURE 6.85**).

Remember that each line and colour mark doesn't have to be exactly the same as the reference photo; the photo is simply a guide. If you look closely at my drawing, you will see that it is not identical to the photo.

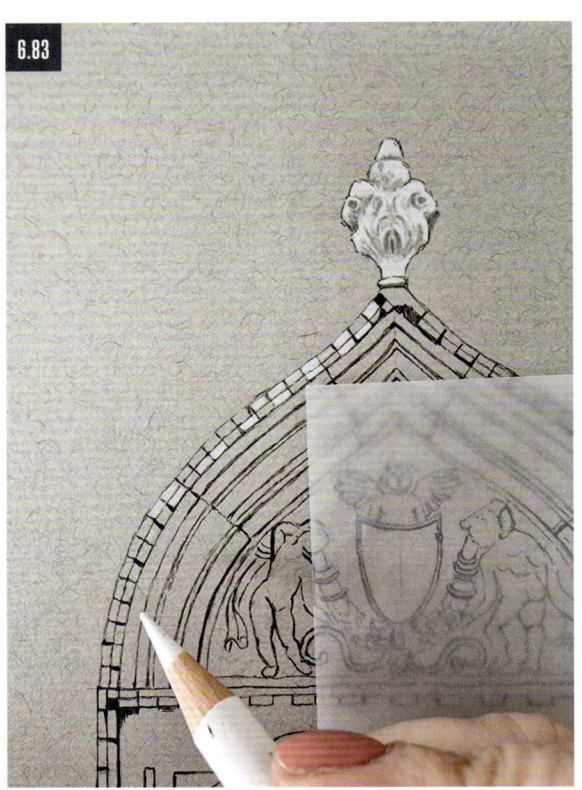

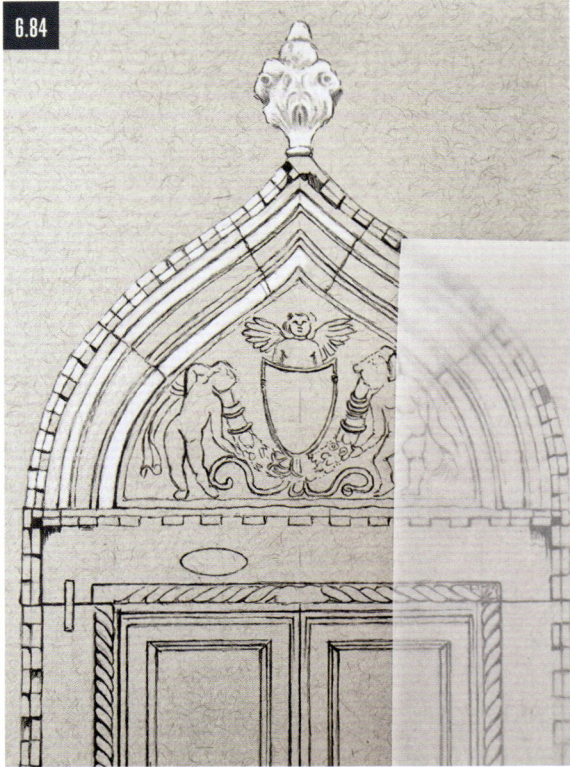

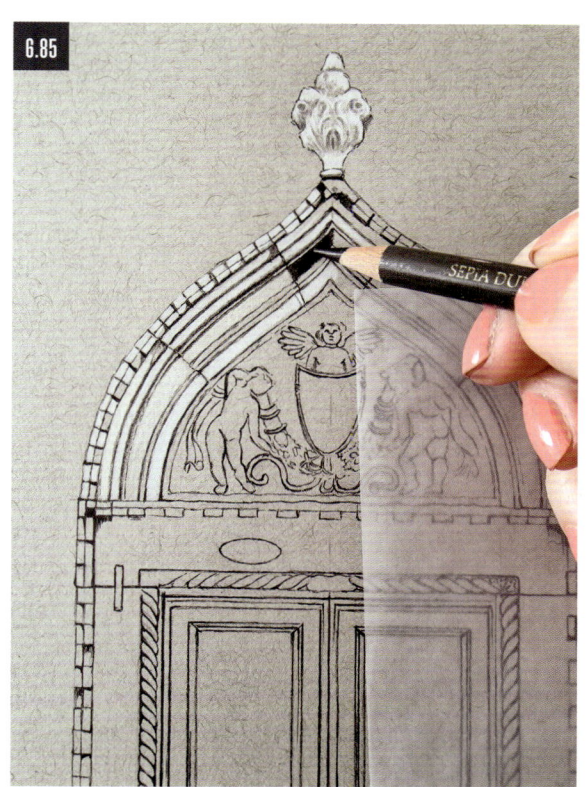
6.85

Blend any graininess in the colours with your blending tool, and then reapply more layers of colour to deepen and enrich them as necessary.

Finally, redefine the black lines with your black fineliner to neaten this section up (**FIGURE 6.86**).

You can now move on and repeat this process on the right side of the arch. Keep your pencil point nice and sharp so the colours and lines are precise and remember to blend. If you need to rub back the colour if it gets too dark, use a fine-tipped eraser for precision.

Once you have finished both sides of the arch, use a Brown Ochre pencil to gently add in the warm yellow tones (**FIGURE 6.87**).

Now move on to the central part of the arch and colour the angels and their surrounding decoration. Use small circular movements to add the colour precisely and evenly.

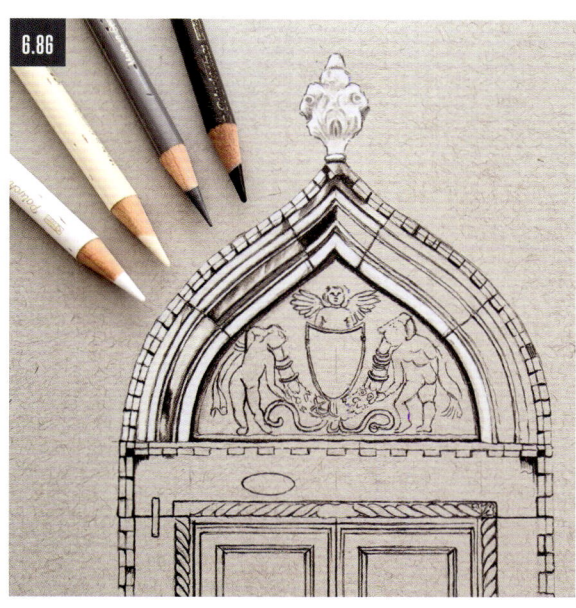
6.86

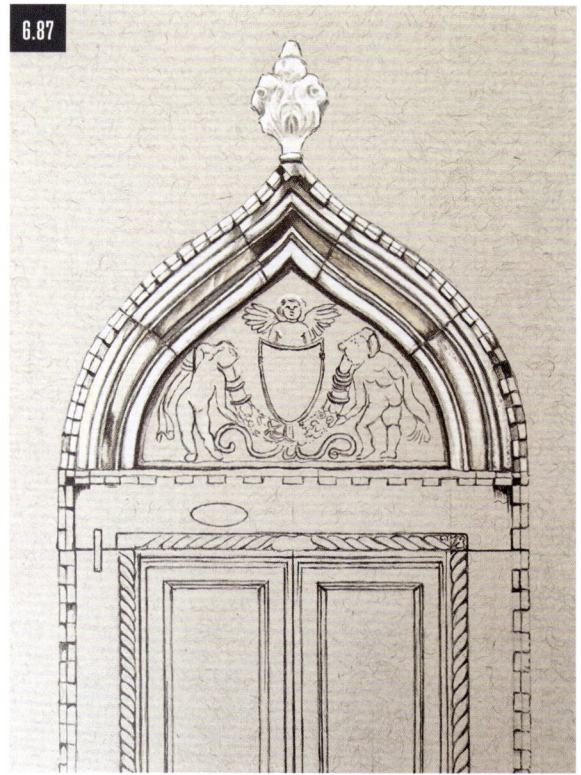
6.87

Begin by using a white pencil to colour the lightest areas. Increase the density of the colour with more layers where the colour is more opaque, as it is on the angels' legs, arms, and faces, and on the central part of the shield.

Now use the next lightest colour, Ivory, to lightly go over the white, softening it slightly, and to apply the next lightest tones. Some of the Ivory will then be covered with Warm Grey IV and Sepia, but the base layers of white and Ivory will lift any subsequent colours, making them brighter.

The central garland that the angels are holding is very detailed, so suggest the lightest details with small random marks in Ivory. When all the other colours are added and defined with fineliner, it will all come together and look just right (**FIGURE 6.88**).

Now move on to applying the mid-tone greys using Warm Grey IV. Again, vary the thickness of the colour depending on how deep the grey tone is. With a very sharp pencil point, carefully define the facial features of the angels (**FIGURE 6.89**).

The next stage is to add the Sepia colour to the darkest areas. As you apply this colour, you will see the three-dimensional illusion start to appear! Sepia and Warm Grey IV both appear quite grainy on the page, so be sure to carefully smooth the colour out as you add layers and get right into the crevices where the colour is at its darkest to create definition (**FIGURE 6.90**).

Now take your Brown Ochre pencil and apply it over the top of the other colours where you can see the yellowy tones in the reference photo (**FIGURE 6.91**). This colour always warms everything

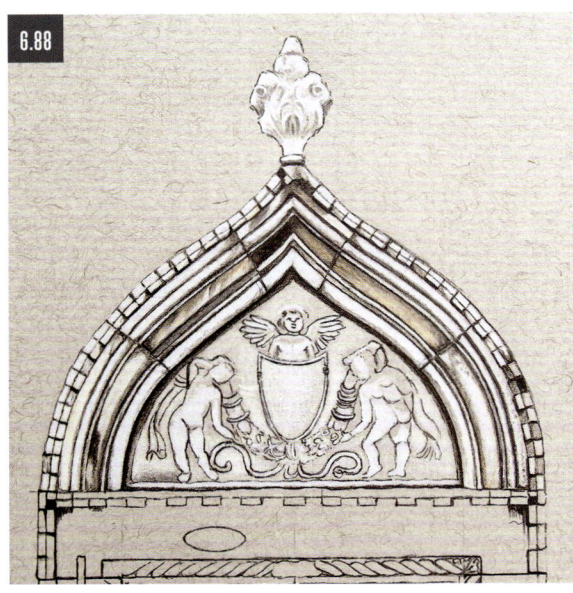

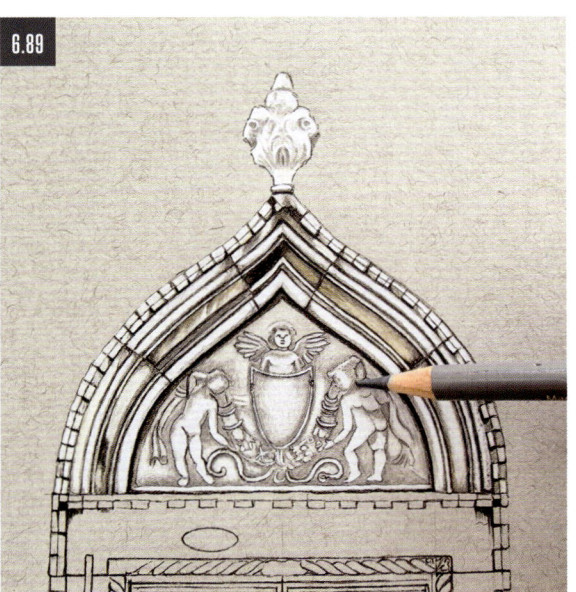

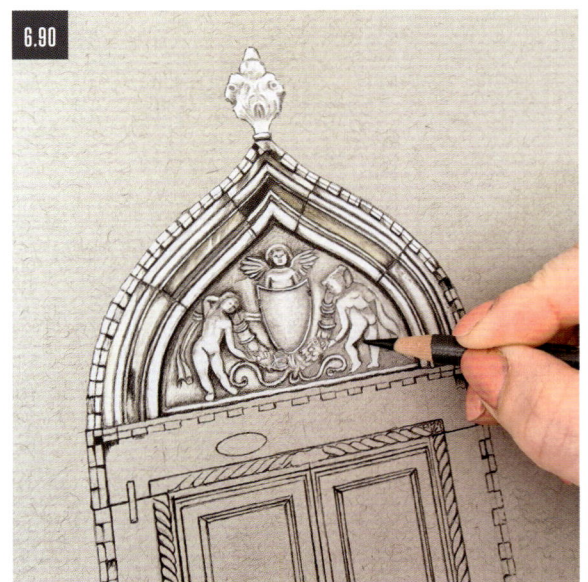

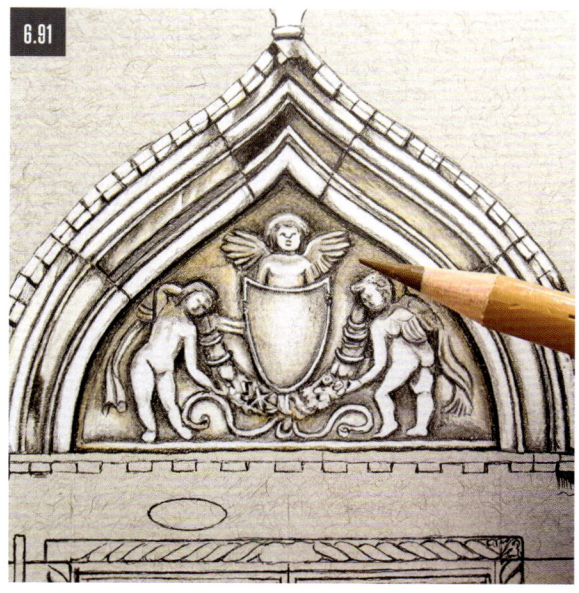

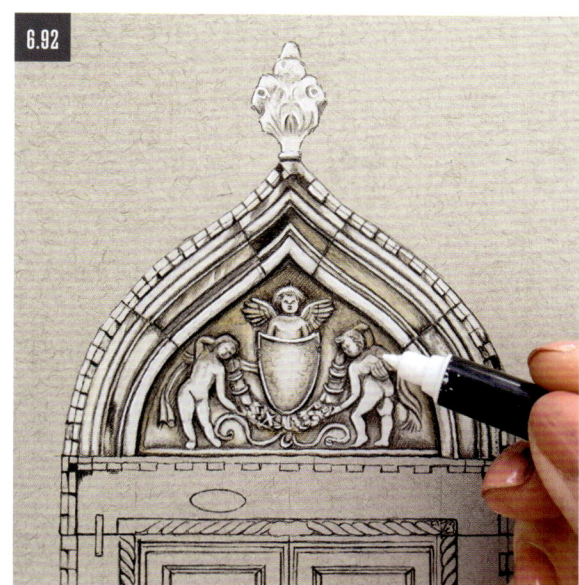

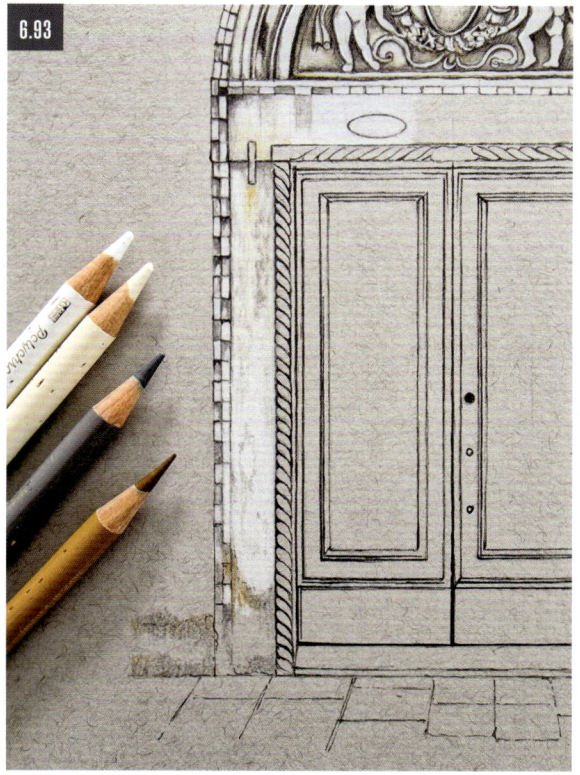

up nicely, and once blended, brings everything together.

To finish up this top part of the drawing, redefine lines that have become softened with your black fineliner pen and draw in extra details like the feathers on the wings. Some of these details are so small that they are hardly visible, but I do like to try and draw in every detail I can see.

Finally, use your white highlighting pen to define and highlight the lightest areas (**FIGURE 6.92**).

Now that the most detailed part of the drawing is finished, we'll work on the door surround with the colours we have already used, and then move on to the green door.

Begin colouring the left side of the door surround, first with a layer of white, then with Ivory, leaving the rough dark area at the base untouched by these light colours. Build the colour so it is nice and opaque. Then use Warm Grey IV to randomly colour the darker weathered and worn patches and the details around the very edge of the surround. After this, use some Brown Ochre to colour the yellowy parts (**FIGURE 6.93**).

At the base of the door surround where it is dark and weathered, start building the colours up with Warm Grey IV and some Brown Ochre, followed by Payne's Grey to draw in the darkest colour (**FIGURE 6.94**). Use small circular movements to create the weathered effect, using the photo as an approximate guide for colours and the textures.

Once this is done, colour the twisted border. Use white pencil first, colouring all over, and then use Warm Grey IV for the mid-tone around the edges, which will give the twists some dimension. Use your black fineliner to refocus any ink lines that have been lost in the pencil process.

Now move on and work your way across the top of the door border and down the right side until the surround is complete. Use the sharp point of the Warm Grey IV pencil to draw in the cracks in the stone with thin wiggly lines (**FIGURE 6.95**).

Now we'll move on to the door, working from the lightest colour to the darkest.

The door is very weathered and the marks and textures are quite complex, so the aim is to recreate this in a suggestive and loose way rather than copy each mark exactly.

Sketch in the ornate grey door knockers in the middle of the doors if you haven't already.

Begin with a light layer of Ivory where the lightest greens are. Then use a pale green pencil on top of this. I'm using a Pablo pencil in Light Green. Next, use your Ivory pencil to mark in the areas of peeling paint and outline them with a fineliner.

Now use a combination of Hooker's Green and Chrome Oxide Green to create the weathered look on the bottom two door panels. Use circular movements and blend the colours together. Then use the light green again on top to create areas of contrasting colour (**FIGURE 6.96**).

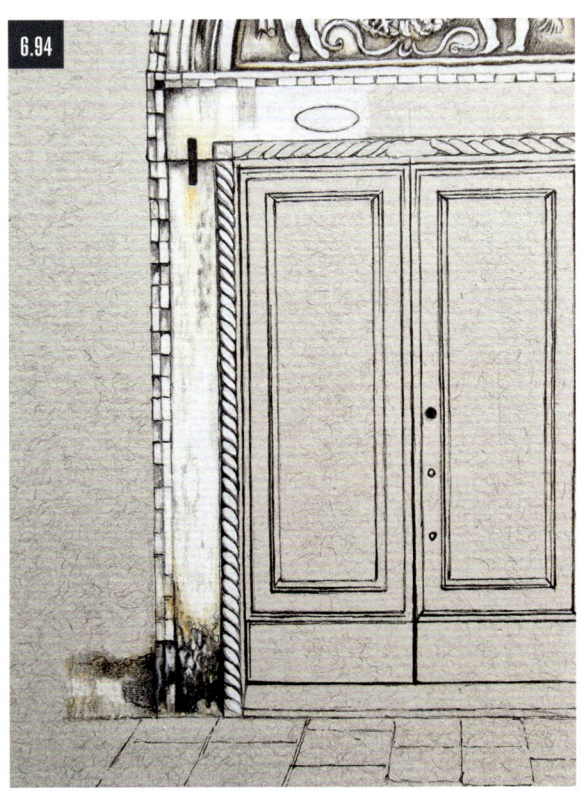

6.94

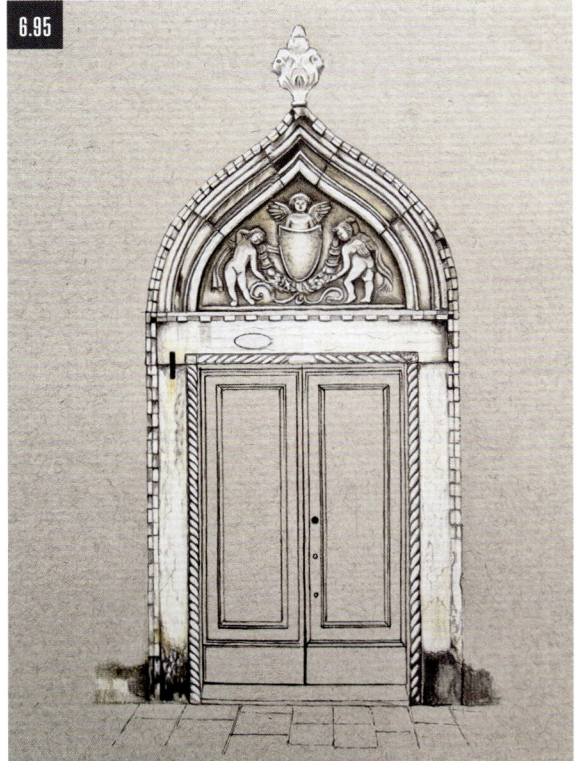

6.95

Drawing and Illustrating Architecture

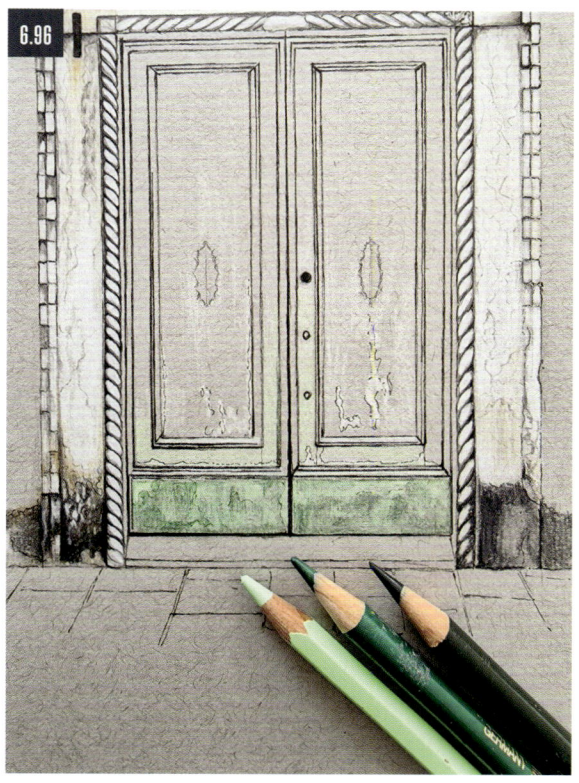

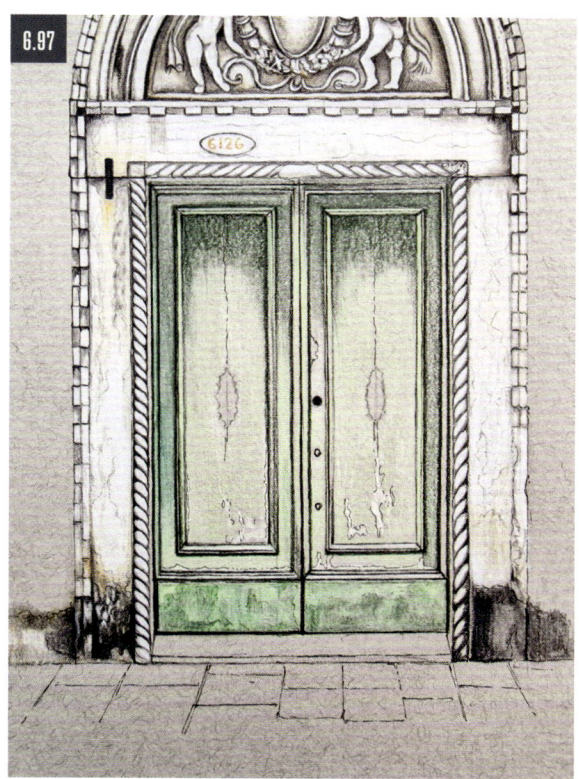

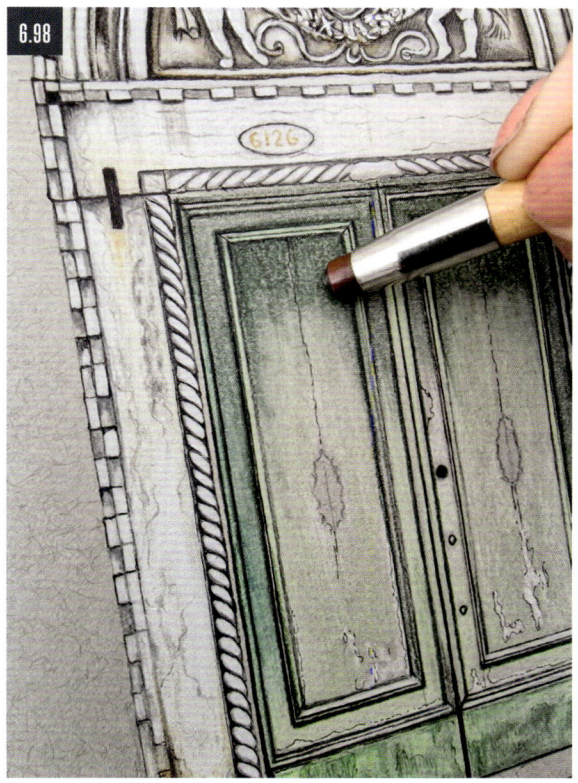

Now use the darkest green, Chrome Oxide Green, to colour the darkest parts of the whole door. Focus on the area at the top of the door where it is the darkest. Line the edges of the decorative beading at the darkest parts as well.

Add more light green on the lower part of the door, bringing the colour upwards to meet the darker green at the top. Use the light green to define the lightest parts of the moulding as well (**FIGURE 6.97**).

Blend the two colours together by dragging the darker colour downwards into the lighter green with your blender (**FIGURE 6.98**).

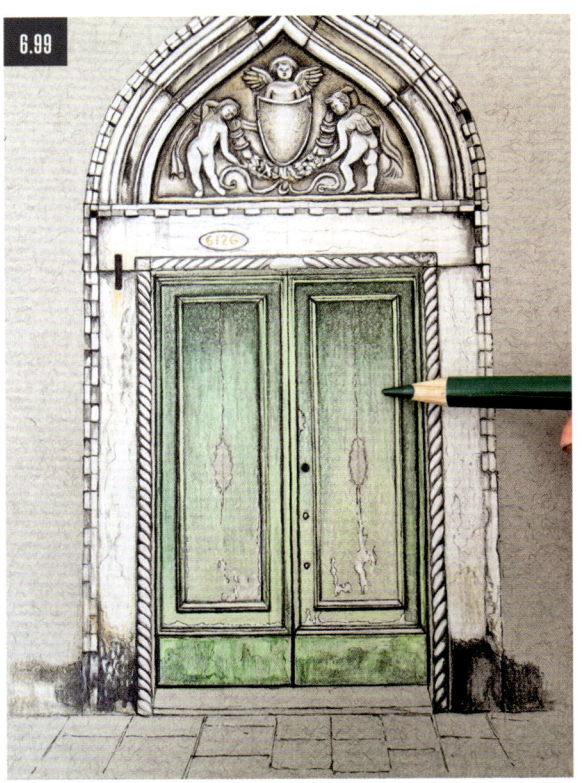

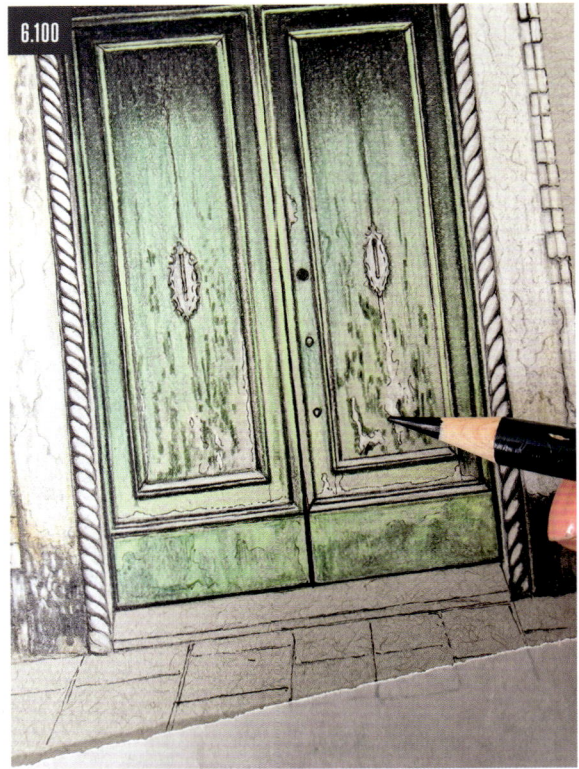

Now use the middle green, Hooker's Green, in downward strokes from the dark green at the top, all the way across the midsection of the door, to the light green to the bottom (**FIGURE 6.99**). Build the depth of colour and blend everything together.

Use Payne's Grey to darken the shadowed area at the top of the door. Again, use downward strokes and then blend. You will need to use quite a few layers to make the colour intensely dark.

Once this is done, use your fineliner to define the door knockers, and then colour them with a layer of white and grey.

Next, create the look of the peeling paint by using the darkest green, Chrome Oxide Green, to make random marks where the paint is peeling on the door. Then intensify the colour of the marks with Payne's Grey (**FIGURE 6.100**).

Now move on to colouring the step. Use a layer of white first, and then a layer of Cold Grey I.

Use the same pale grey to roughly colour the paving slabs. I like to do this loosely, showing the random pencil marks, and after all the slow precision work, this part takes just minutes! You can vary the paving slab colour by also introducing some Warm Grey IV (**FIGURE 6.101**).

In the same loose style, use a combination of white and Warm Grey IV to roughly draw in the area surrounding everything you have drawn before. Only draw and suggest the parts you want to, leaving out the rest. Choose the more dominant shapes to sketch in, and use a lighter pressure on your pencil, until it barely touches the paper, to create soft marks.

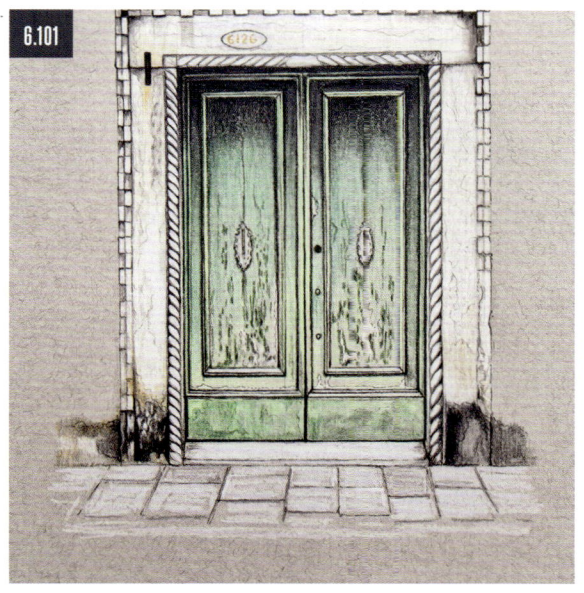

You will notice that I have completely left out the windows on either side of the arch. Roughly draw in some bricks using the same colours and randomly colour a few of them (**FIGURES 6.102** and **6.103**). You can play around with this loose style of drawing and the effects it creates. You can also erase any parts that you don't like.

Of course, if you want to, you can complete the surround in a more precise way, but this is how I like to do it.

Add some depth to the decoration on top of the pointed arch by using Payne's Grey around it. You will notice how it instantly pops out!

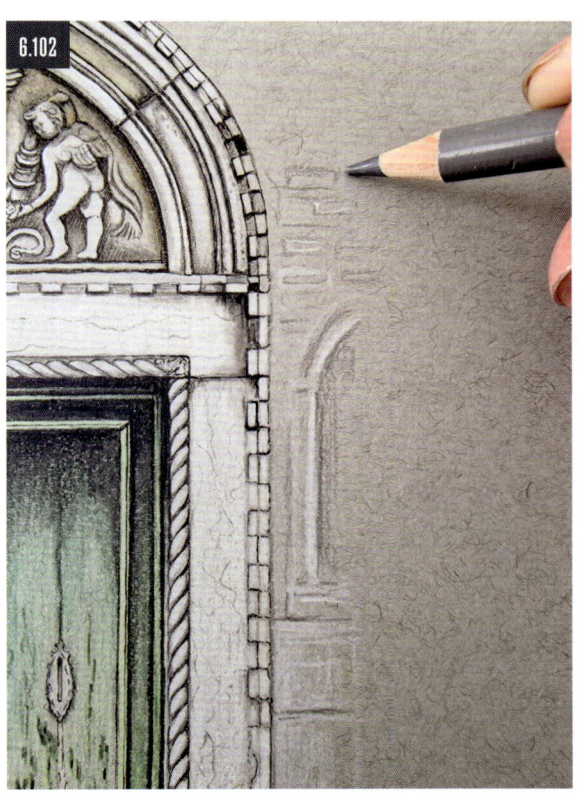

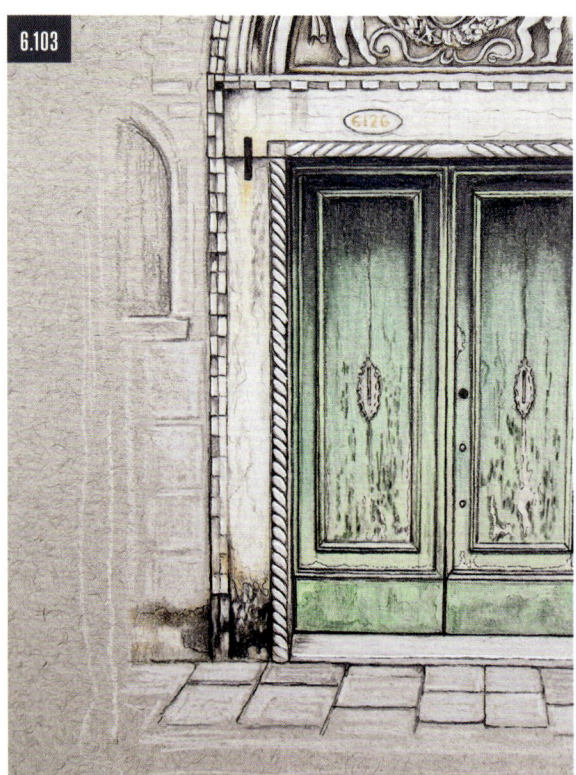

Step 4: Add Final Details

In the very last step, as always, go back over everything and redefine any ink lines that have become undefined and out of focus. Pay particular attention to the dividing line between the top of the door and the white twisted border, as the contrast between the light and the dark here add impact to the whole work.

Add touches of white highlights with your highlighter where necessary. Notice the bold highlight along the central line of the grey step, and highlight the top of each twist shape on the twisted border (**FIGURE 6.104**).

Finally, check everything over and make sure you are happy with it. This is a complicated door to work on—well done for getting to the end!

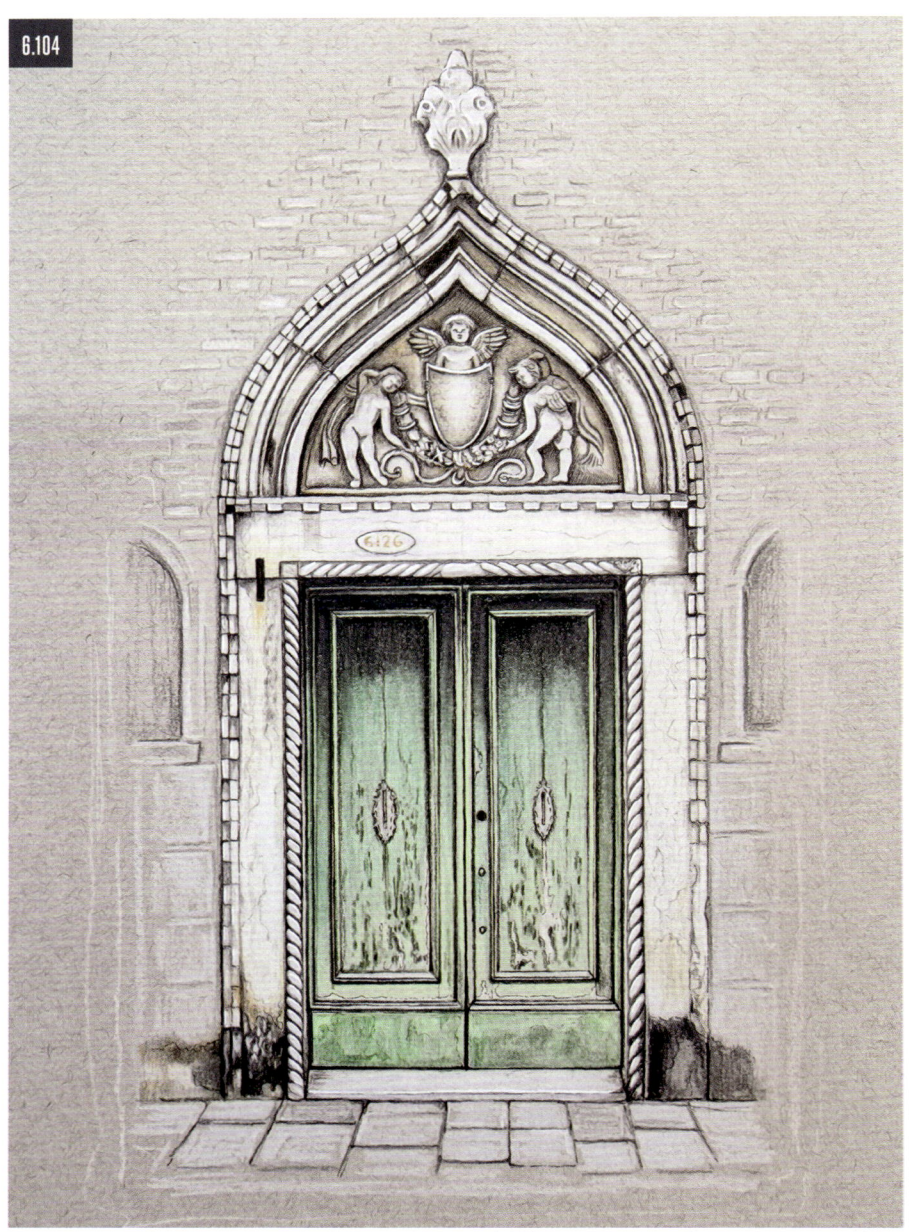

6.104

Ornate Details

In this section we are going to explore some of the ornate details that can be found on a lot of old buildings if you take the time to look closely. Even the simplest detail from a stone carving or column can be a great reference for a beautiful picture or little sketch.

The projects in this section are "mini projects" meant to be done in a faster, more relaxed way. You can finish them completely or leave them partly unfinished to create a nice undone look.

I hope they inspire you to find architectural details of your own choosing when you are out and about and that they give you ideas for your own mini projects.

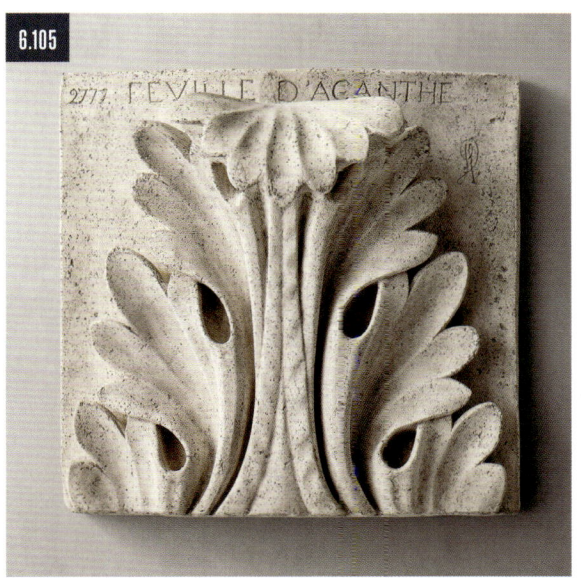

6.105

ACANTHUS LEAF

A simple detail like an acanthus leaf is perfect for a small sketch. Their swirling shapes and folds lend themselves well to drawing.

The acanthus leaf has been used as decoration in architecture for thousands of years. It was first used by the Greeks in the fifth century BC on temple roof ornaments, wall friezes, and Corinthian columns. Acanthus leaves are symbols of immortality and resurrection.

For this sketch I have chosen a photo of an acanthus leaf on a modern-day moulding because the photo is clear and will be easy to work from. It's actually quite hard to find and take a photo of acanthus leaves on a Corinthian column, for instance, because they are always so high up at the top of the column!

Materials

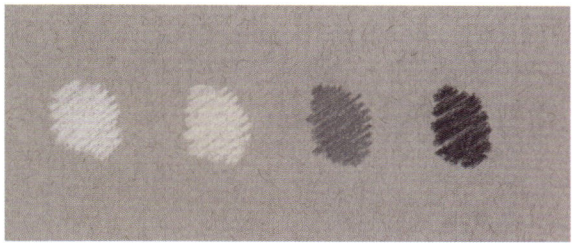

- ▶ Toned grey paper
- ▶ Sharp pencil
- ▶ Black 0.05mm fineliner pen
- ▶ Coloured pencils: White, Ivory, Warm Grey IV, Payne's Grey
- ▶ White highlighting pen
- ▶ Eraser

Step 1: Draw with Pencil

Sketch out the design quickly and loosely with pencil (**FIGURE 6.106**). The design is fairly symmetrical, so use a ruler to check that both sides of the leaf line up.

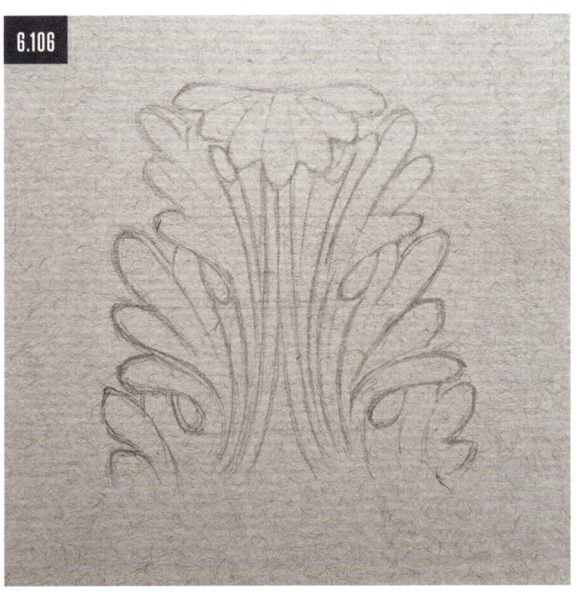

Step 2: Cover the Lines with Black Ink

Lightly go over the pencil lines in ink, and then rub out any remaining pencil lines (**FIGURE 6.107**).

Step 3: Adding Colour

You need just four colours for this drawing, beginning with white. Create the brightest highlights first by applying two to three layers in these areas first. Then use thinner layers of white as the colour where the white is not so bright (**FIGURE 6.108**).

Next, add a layer of Ivory where the next lightest colour is and as a base colour for the mid-tone greys (**FIGURE 6.109**). Use Warm Grey IV for the varying grey shadows.

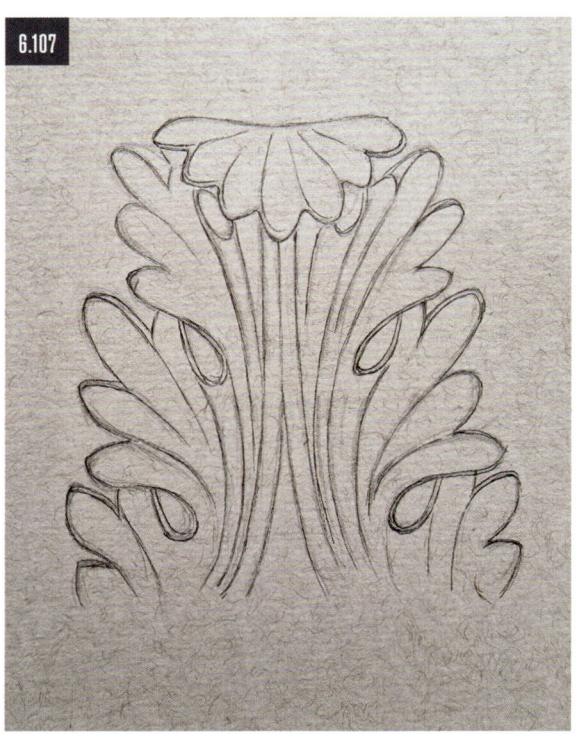

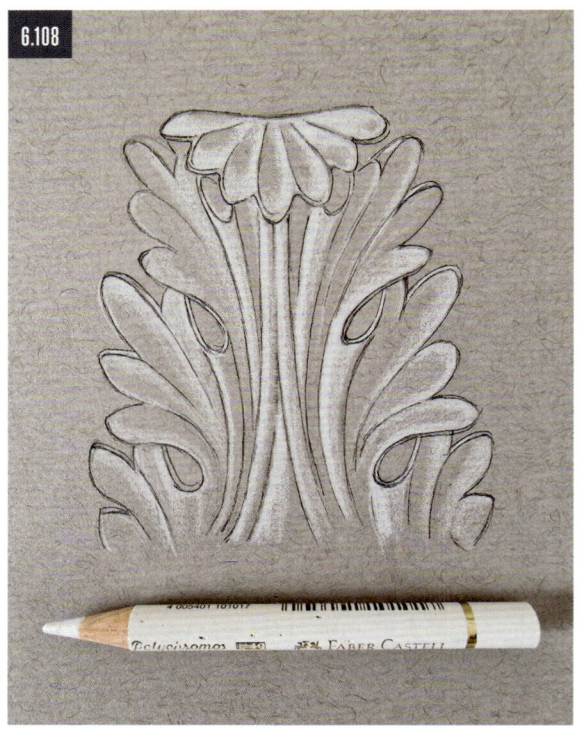

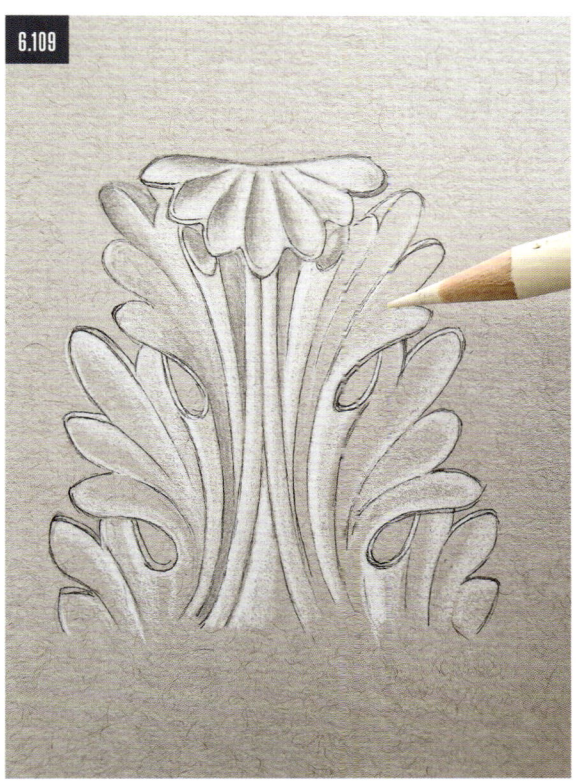

6.109

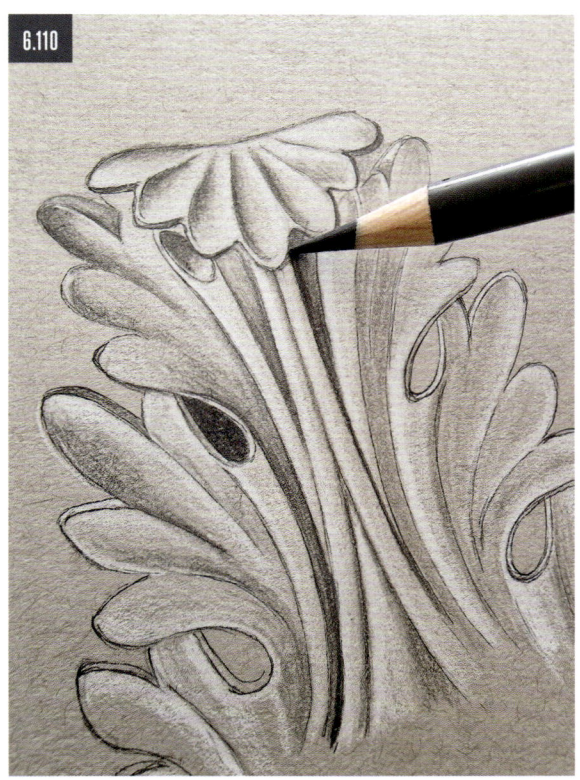

6.110

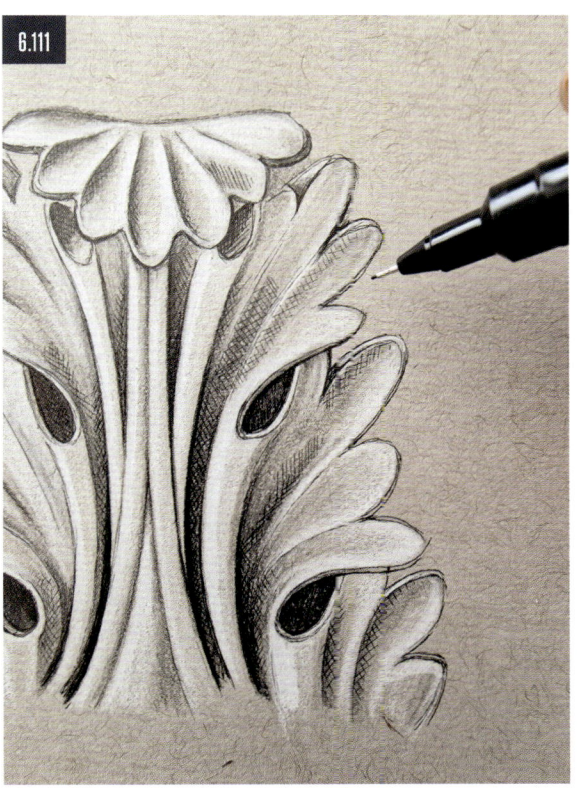

6.111

Once the mid-tones are in place, use a Payne's Grey pencil to add in the very darkest shadows. (**FIGURE 6.110**).

Strengthen the brightest whites by making the colour thicker and more opaque with more layers.

Next, redefine and strengthen the black ink lines with a fineliner pen, and darken the darkest darks with some crosshatching. Crosshatch over some of the Warm Grey IV as well (**FIGURE 6.111**). This creates a nice "sketchy" effect.

Finally, add a few highlights at the very brightest points with a highlighting pen (**FIGURE 6.112, NEXT PAGE**). All done!

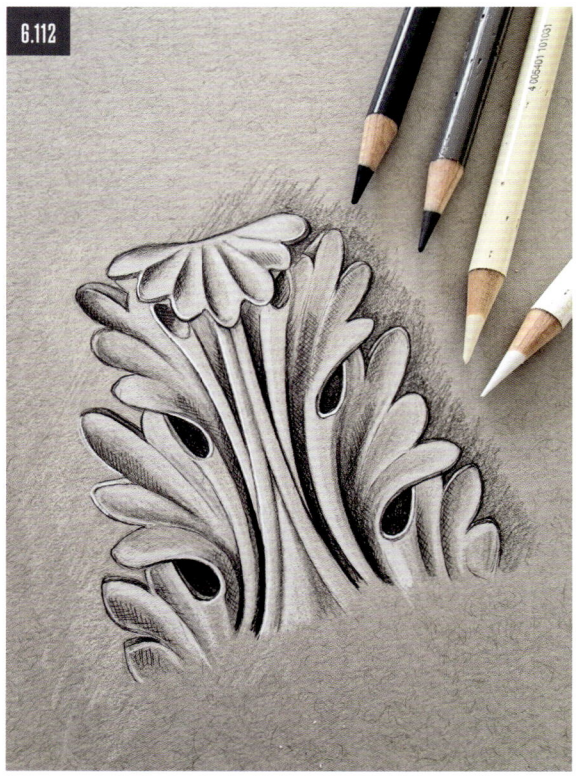

6.112

IONIC COLUMN

Next, we'll look at an Ionic column. These columns come from the Ionic order in Classical architecture. You will often find them at the tops of columns on Classical buildings where they hold the mighty weight of the building above.

This one is from the Great Court in the British Museum in London. The swirling shapes of the

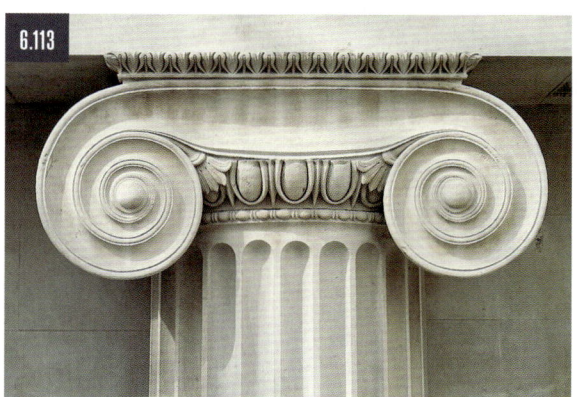

6.113

volutes and intricate details will make a great monochrome drawing. The volutes are the spiral, scroll-like ornaments that sit on top of the columns and are the major feature of columns in the Ionic order.

Materials

▶ Toned grey paper
▶ Sharp pencil
▶ Black 0.05mm fineliner pen
▶ Coloured pencils: White, Warm Grey IV, Payne's Grey
▶ White highlighting pen
▶ Eraser
▶ Blender

Step 1: Draw with Pencil

The swirling shape of the volute looks complicated to replicate, but it's a lovely shape to draw and when it is done, you'll be so pleased with yourself!

You might like to have a go at drawing this out freehand, or to help you along, take measurements from a printout or digital screen. You can also use a combination of the two methods.

Start on the outer edge of the circle on the left side and slowly draw the spiral in (**FIGURE 6.114**). Use the space between each circle as a gauge for where the next line should start. I erased parts of the circular shapes about five times before I got the shape right!

Continue drawing toward the right. Notice how each "egg" of the egg and dart pattern lines up with the arched lines on the column below.

Drawing the volute on the right side and getting it to line up and look symmetrical with the one on the left side is quite tricky. To help you, use a ruler to line up the base of each circular shape and measure the diameter across each volute to make sure they are the same (**FIGURE 6.115**).

The small pattern that runs along the very top of the column is repetitive. If you look closely, you will see that the pattern lines up centrally, so begin drawing it in the middle and work outwards (**FIGURE 6.116**).

Step 2: Cover the Lines with Black Ink

Carefully go over the pencil lines with ink, and then rub out any remaining pencil lines. Keep some paper under your hand so you don't ruin the delicate pencil work.

Black in the dark area around the eggs and in the pattern at the top (**FIGURE 6.117**).

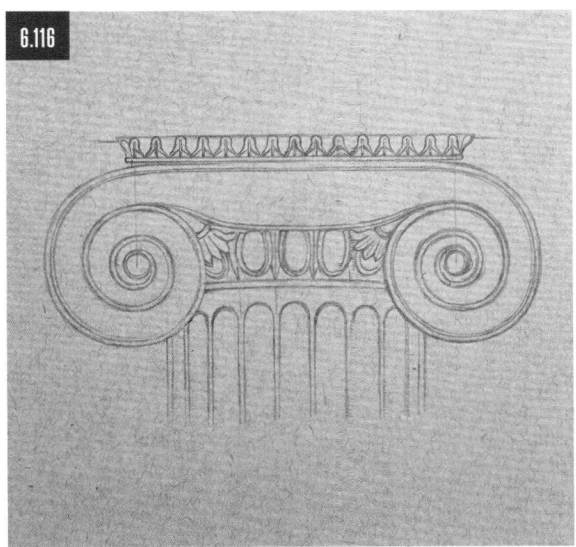

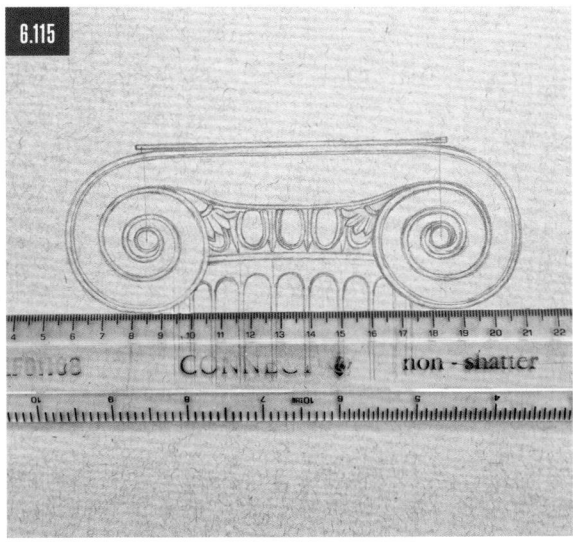

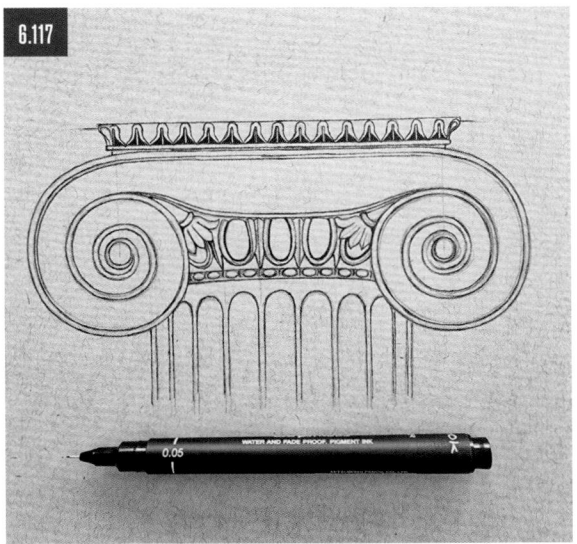

Step 3: Add Colour

We'll again keep the colour palette to a minimum in this little drawing. You need just three colours.

Start by adding the highlights first with a white pencil (**FIGURE 6.118**). Cover the whole drawing in any highlighted areas you can see. Observe where the shadowed areas are and carefully draw in the highlights up to the shadowed lines.

We are going to slightly overaccentuate the shadows in the piece to make the drawing really stand out.

Begin by colouring all the mid-tone shadowed areas with Warm Grey VI (**FIGURE 6.119**). Keep the shadows well-defined. There are some nice crisp shadow lines that can be played up, especially on the spiralled volutes. Blend the grey to smooth out any graininess.

Next, use the next darkest tone, Payne's Grey, to darken the shadows. Focus on the shadowed area on the edge of each spiral, making the shadow slightly darker where it is at the top and graduating it into the Warm Grey IV (**FIGURE 6.120**).

Blend the two greys together with a blender (**FIGURE 6.121**).

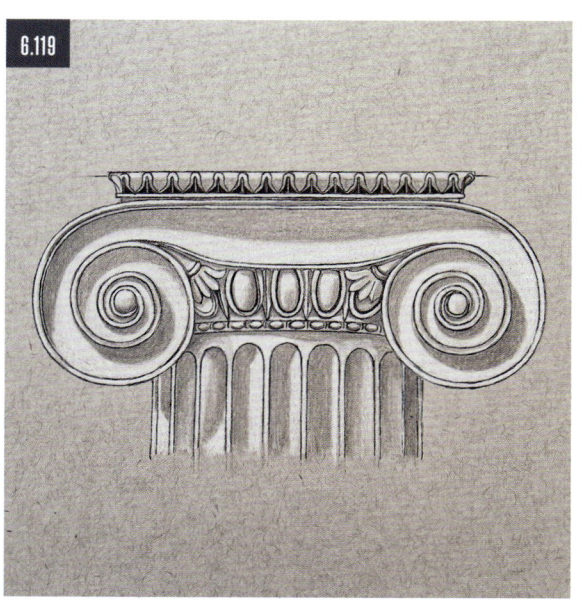

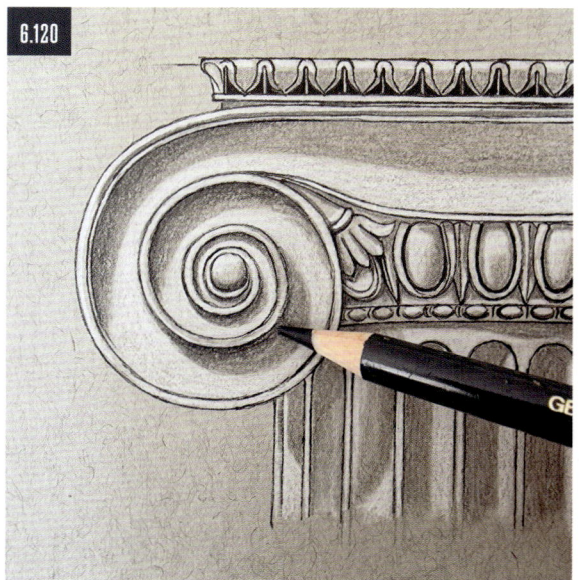

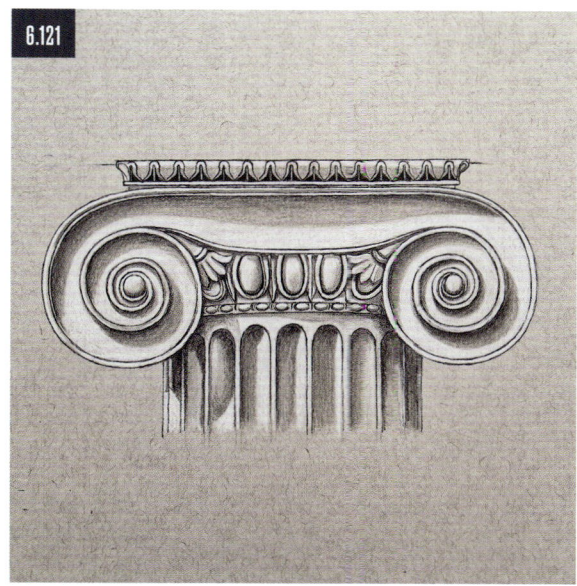

6.121

Now take your black fineliner and crosshatch across the shadows on top of the pencil (**FIGURE 6.122**). Try to keep the crosshatch lines facing in the same direction across the entire column so it all looks consistent. Make the crosshatch lines closer together and denser where the shadows are darker.

Use the fineliner to redefine the original black outlines and darken any tiny areas of shadow, especially in the crevices of the stonework (**FIGURE 6.123**).

Next, add some highlights with your highlighting pen where the colour is the lightest, and if you want to, add in some sketchy crosshatching around the outside of the volutes (**FIGURE 6.124, NEXT PAGE**). This creates a nice effect, and the added dark crosshatching makes the brighter colour of the swirling volutes appear more three-dimensional (**FIGURE 6.125, NEXT PAGE**).

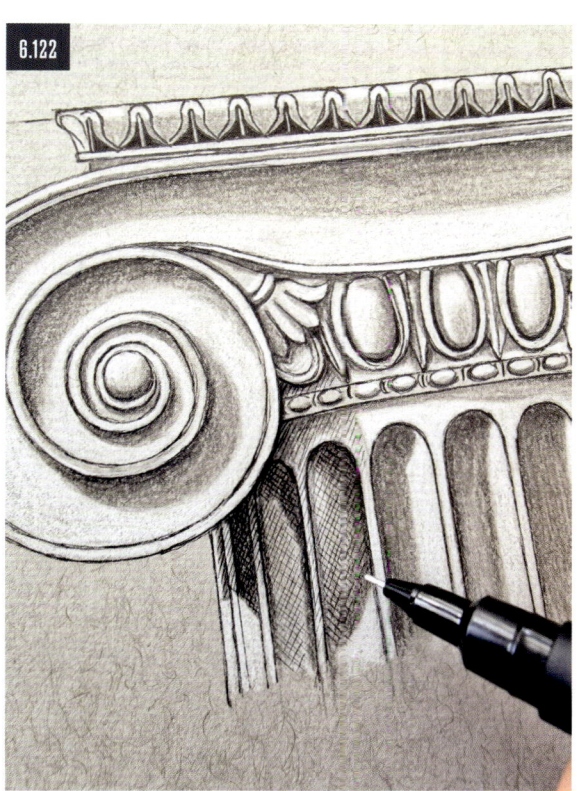

6.122

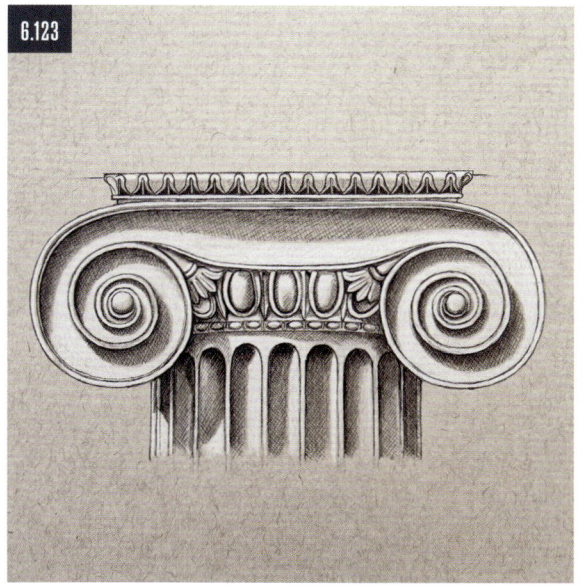

6.123

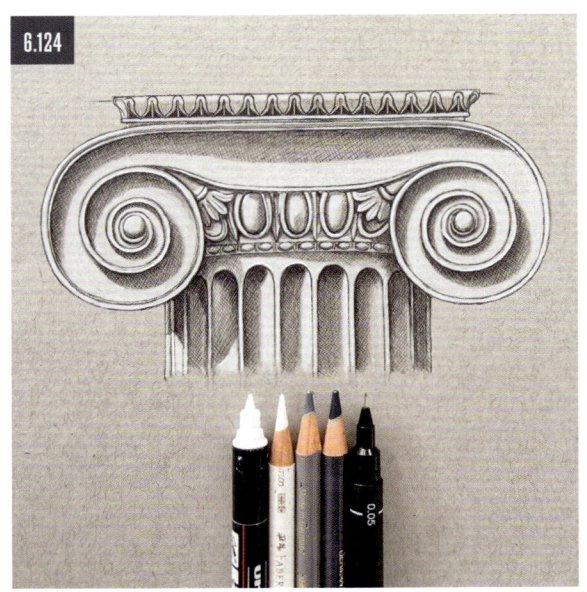

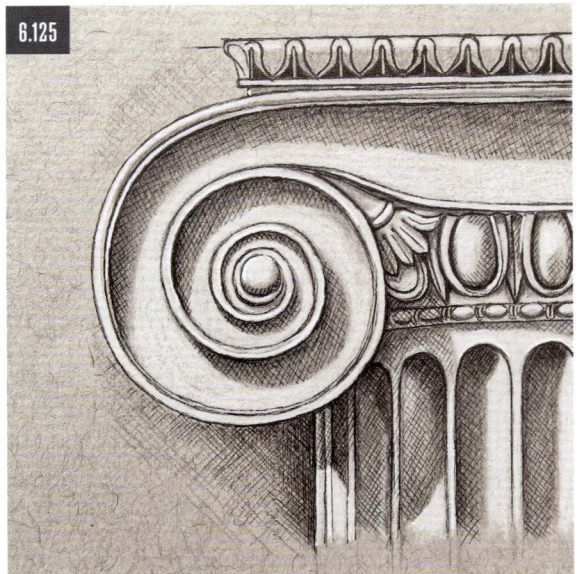

ADDITIONAL SKETCHING EXAMPLES

Here are some more examples of small quick sketches of ornate architectural details that can be easily created using just a few colours. I like to use toned grey paper, but you can experiment on different papers like, for instance, toned tan or use just white or Ivory to see what you can create!

Greek God Stone Carving

This is a drawing I did of a stone carving I found above an archway in central London. I'm guessing he is a Greek God!

I used just four colours to colour my initial line drawing, with some crosshatching on top.

The appeal for me here was the accurate and clean stone carving. I enjoyed capturing his swirling beard with minimal use of colours and lines, and with just a small amount of crosshatching on top, which I think creates an old-world look.

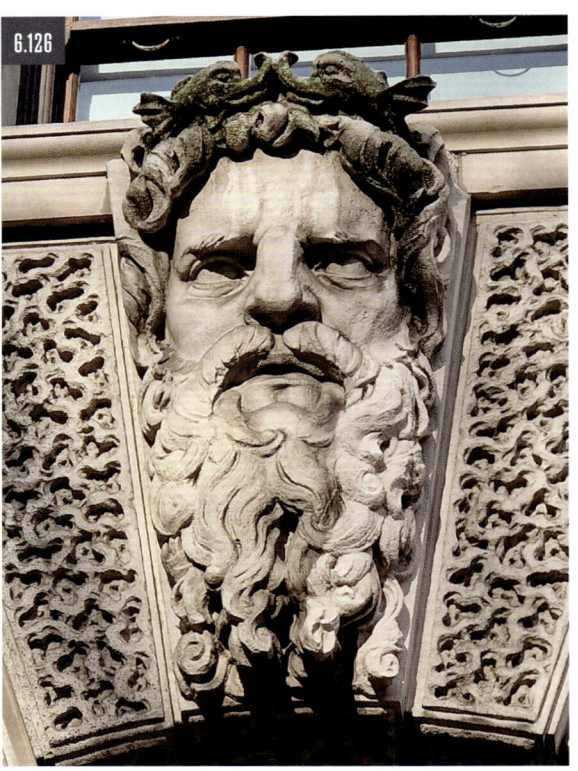

I focused on making the eyes very precise, with everything else being looser and freer in drawing style.

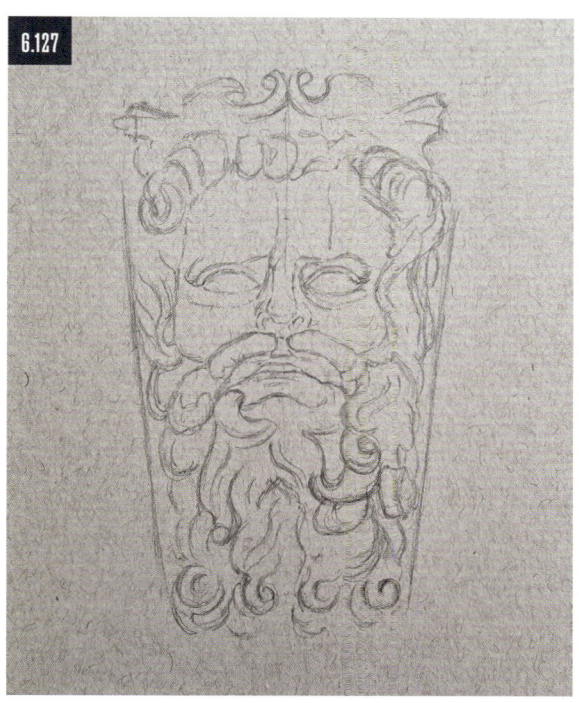

6.127

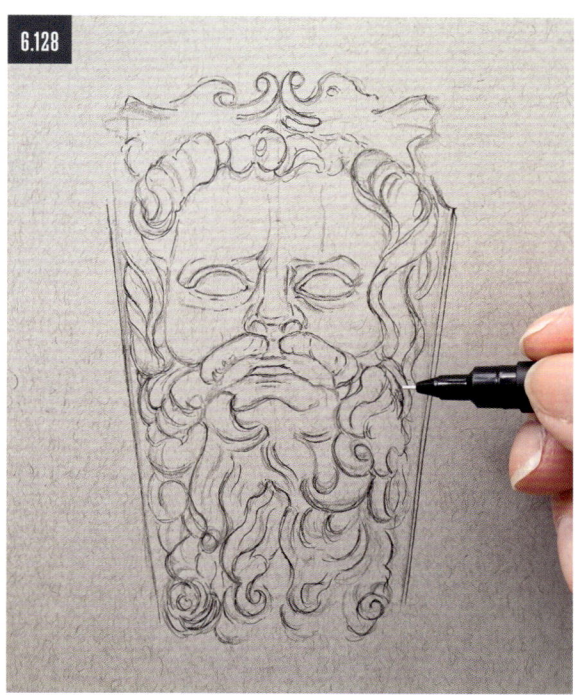

6.128

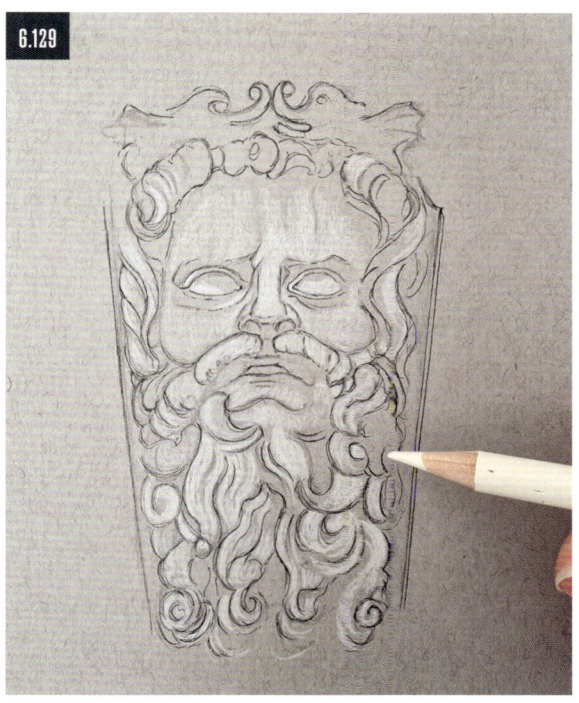

6.129

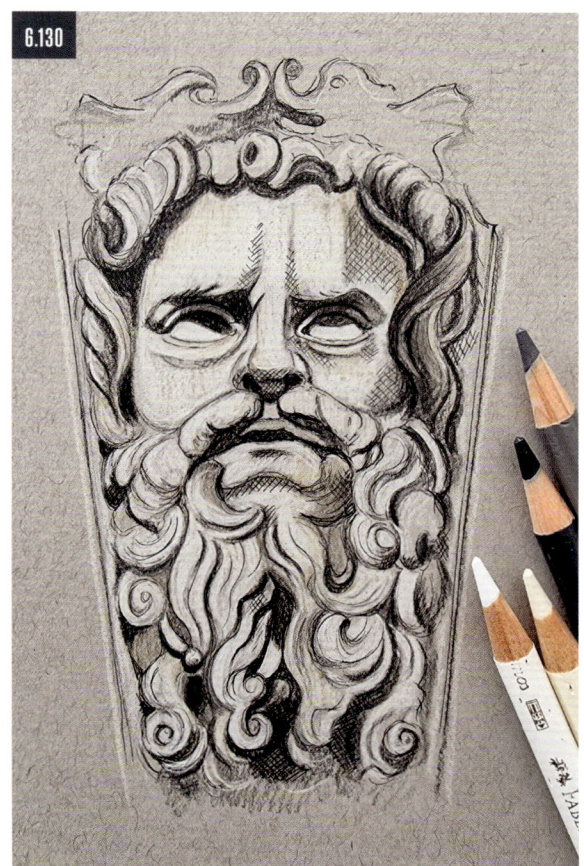

6.130

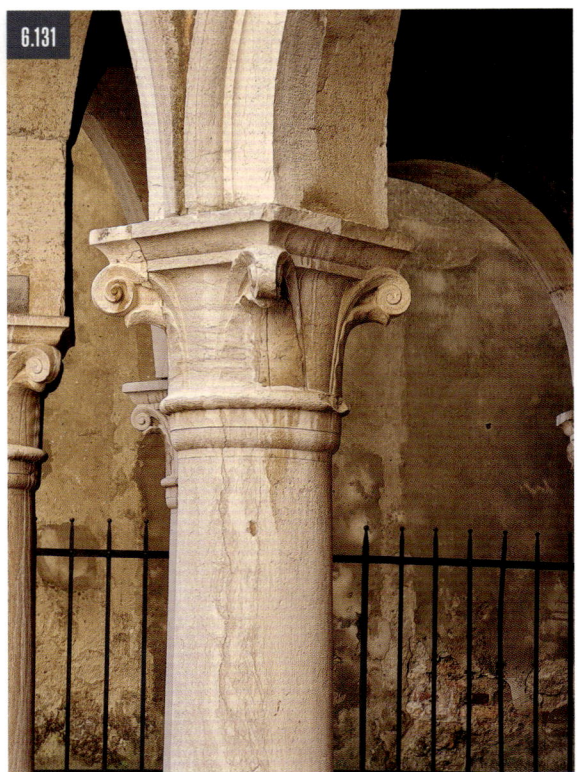

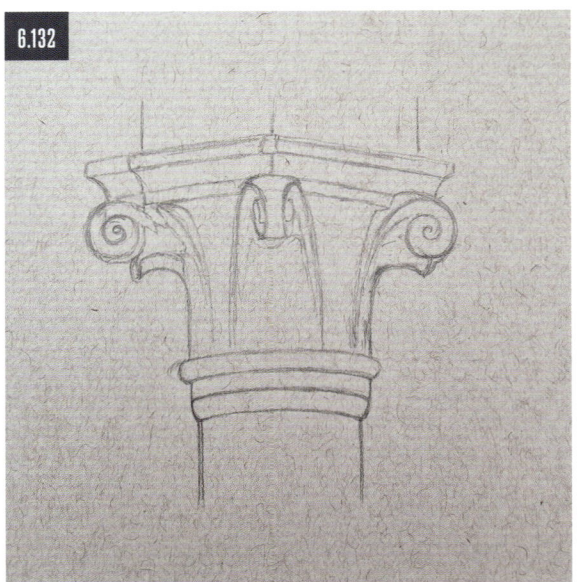

Venetian Column

This is a column from the base of a famous building in Venice called the Scala Contarini del Bovolo. The building is a tall, twisting structure with many of these columns supporting its winding staircases.

I chose one column to draw and although it wasn't a very bright day, I made use of the simple and clean lines and the natural shadow on the right side of the column to bring it to life.

It is a fairly quick sketch that I used just five colours to create. As always, I worked from light to dark, and then finished up with a fineliner pen to add details such as the cracks and some cross-hatching. I didn't use highlighter pen on this one at all. The results are very effective with minimum effort!

Hopefully you are learning the simple pattern of how I create these small architecture drawings using a minimum number of pencil colours, a black fineliner, and a sometimes a highlighting pen.

The pattern is always in this order:

1. Pencil drawing
2. Ink
3. Coloured pencil
4. Ink and highlighter

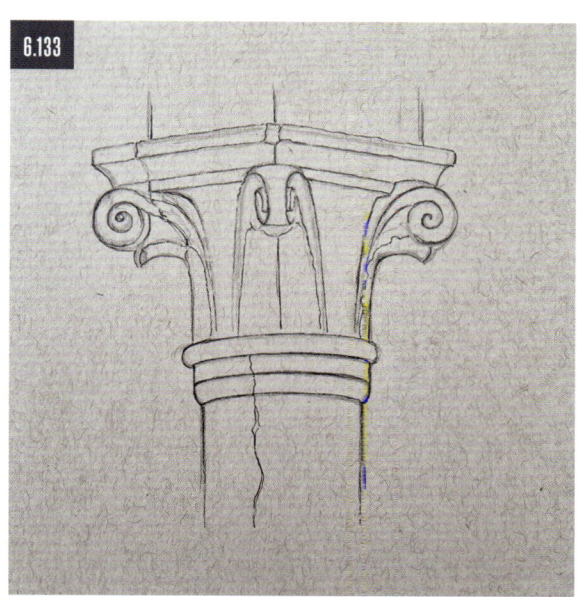

6.133

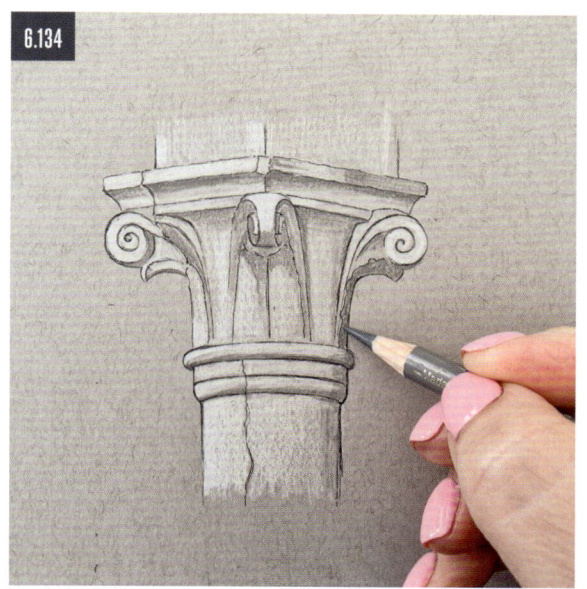

6.134

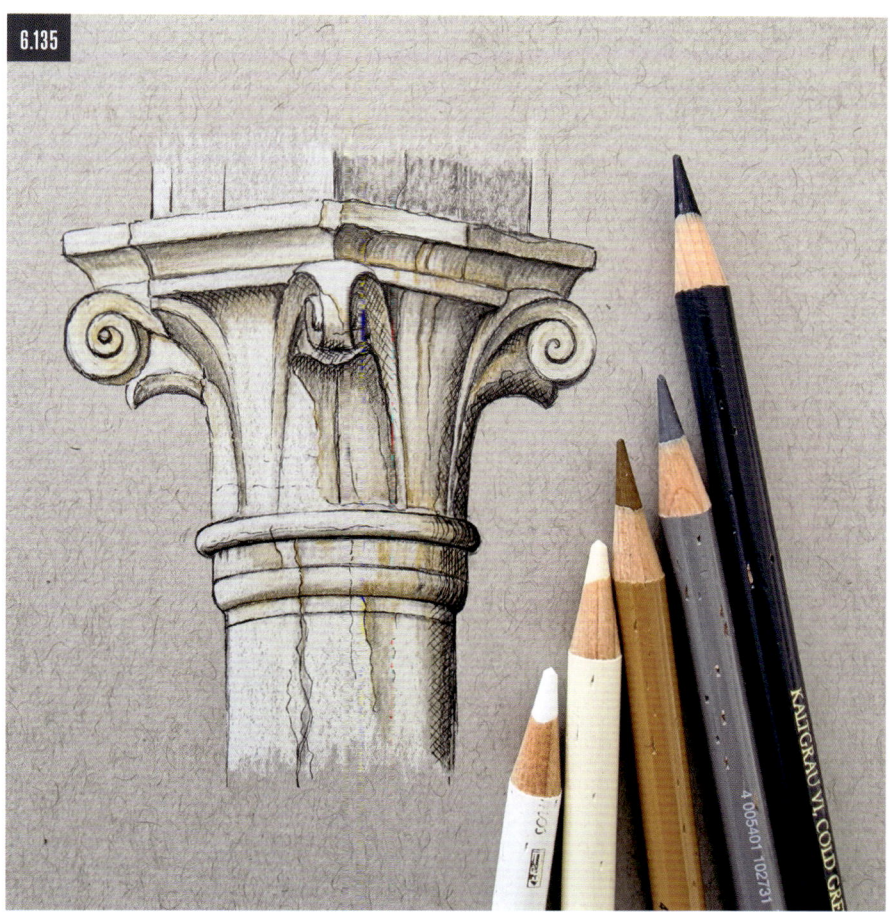

6.135

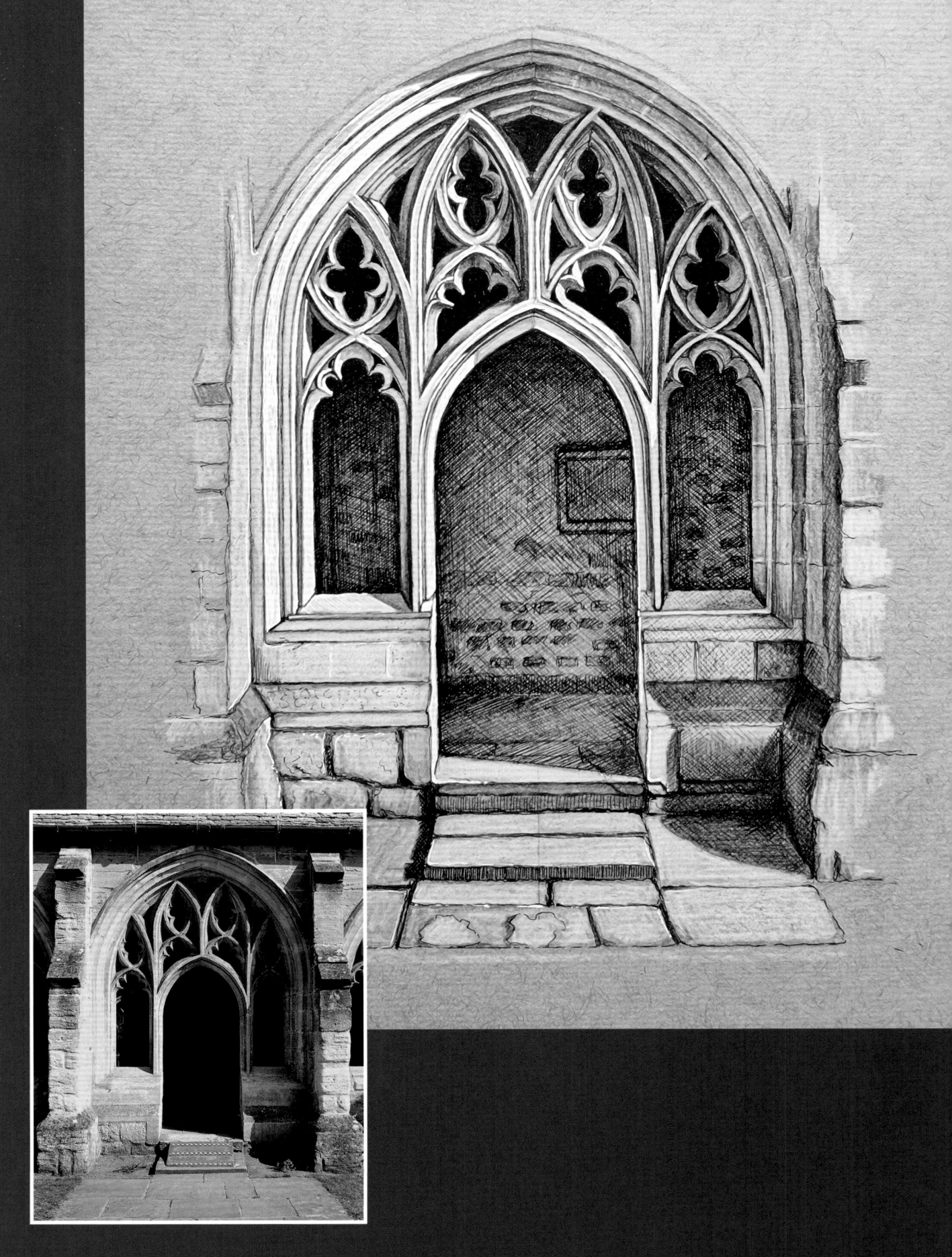

CHAPTER 7

Monochrome

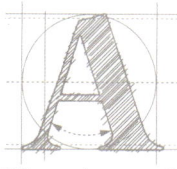

Art is a continuous, ever-changing process of learning new skills and exploring how you see things. There is a saying, "It takes twenty years to learn how to paint, and twenty years to learn what not to paint!"

No matter how good you are and how long you have been practicing art, it's always good to mix things up a bit and experiment. So, in this chapter, we are going to create a drawing using a monochrome palette. No other colours!

Working in monochrome can be very evocative and create a mood and feeling of "old-world" art.

I love the monochrome look. It's a useful and enjoyable way to look at tonal values and train your eye to see the lightest and darkest areas in a subject.

I took this photo of a cloister in New College, Oxford, UK (**FIGURE 7.1**), and converted it to black and white on my computer (opposite page). The cloister is very old and was built from Wheatley stone during the years of 1395 to 1400. Working in monochrome will create an old-world vibe that suits the subject.

This image appealed to me not only because of the beautiful shapes carved into the stone, but also because of the bright sunlight shining down onto the structure, creating perfect shadows and extremes in contrast. You can use this photo to work from or choose your own.

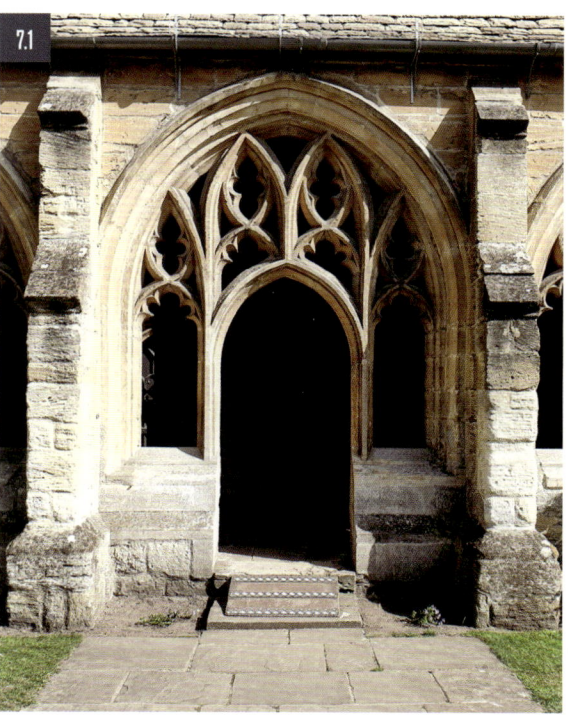

7.1

Fun fact: Scenes from the Harry Potter film *The Philosopher's Stone* were filmed at this cloister!

Gather everything you need from the materials list and let's get started!

MATERIALS

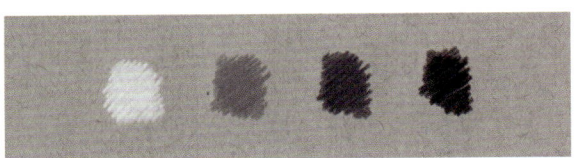

- ▶ Toned grey paper
- ▶ Sharp pencil or mechanical pencil
- ▶ Black 0.05mm fineliner pen
- ▶ Coloured pencils: White, Warm Grey IV, Payne's Grey, Black
- ▶ Extra-fine-nib white Posca pen or white gel pen
- ▶ Eraser
- ▶ Blender

Step 1: DRAW WITH PENCIL

Decide what size you want your drawing to be. For this project, I have chosen to use method 3 (refer back to chapter 4, page 65) for drawing out the initial pencil drawing. I will take precise measurements from my tablet to use as anchor points combined with freehand drawing where I feel confident.

You may prefer to use the grid method (method 1, page 55) to help you. Do what feels most comfortable for you.

I know that at first glance the photograph of the cloister looks quite complicated, but look again more closely. The basic lines of the stonework, without the complications of the highlights and shadows, are much simpler. The image is more or less symmetrical and there are patterns there to be repeated.

This will be another central composition, so find the centre of the page and draw in a vertical line.

Start with the most central archway (**FIGURES 7.2** and **7.3**).

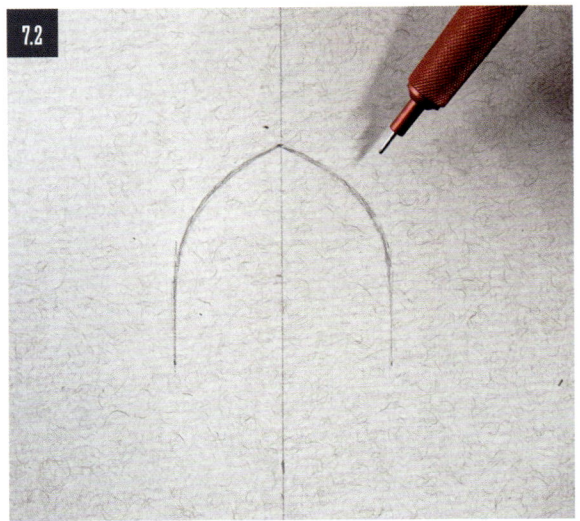

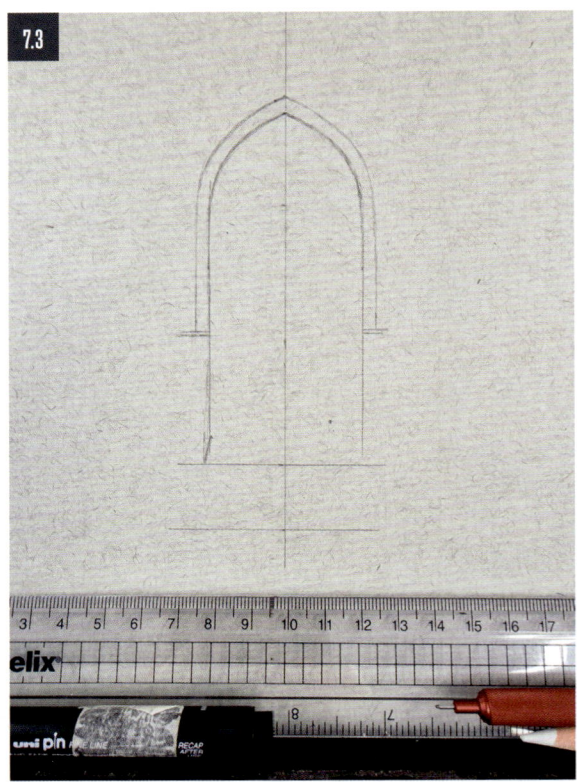

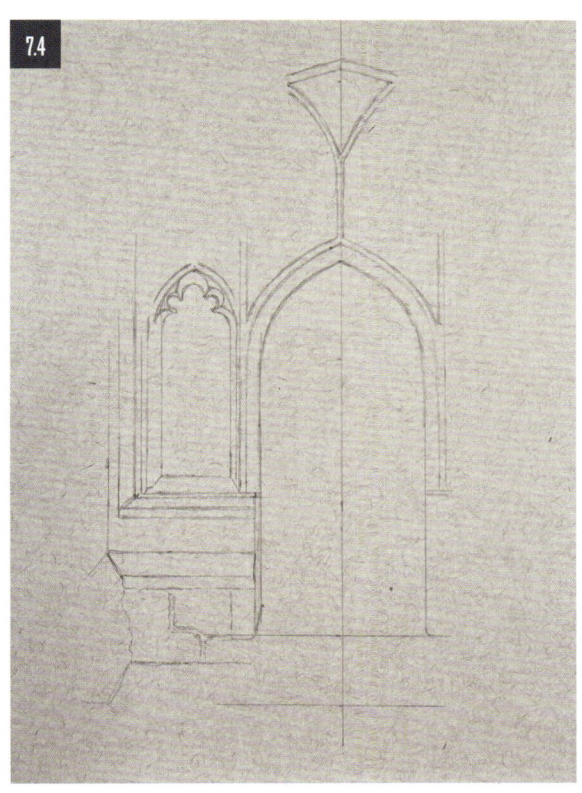

You can build your drawing from this central point, taking measurements as you move outwards until the outline pencil drawing is complete (**FIGURES 7.4–7.6**).

Remember to keep a clean sheet of paper or tracing paper under your hand to keep your work clean (**FIGURE 7.7, NEXT PAGE**).

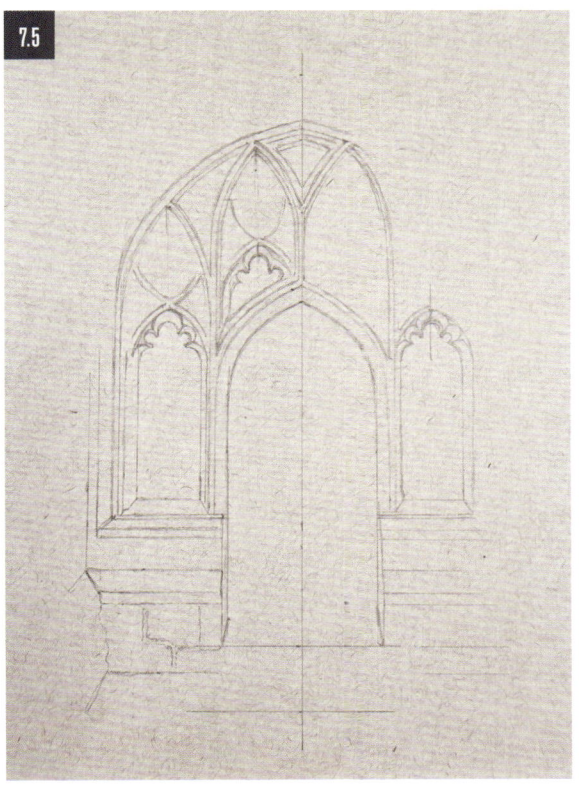

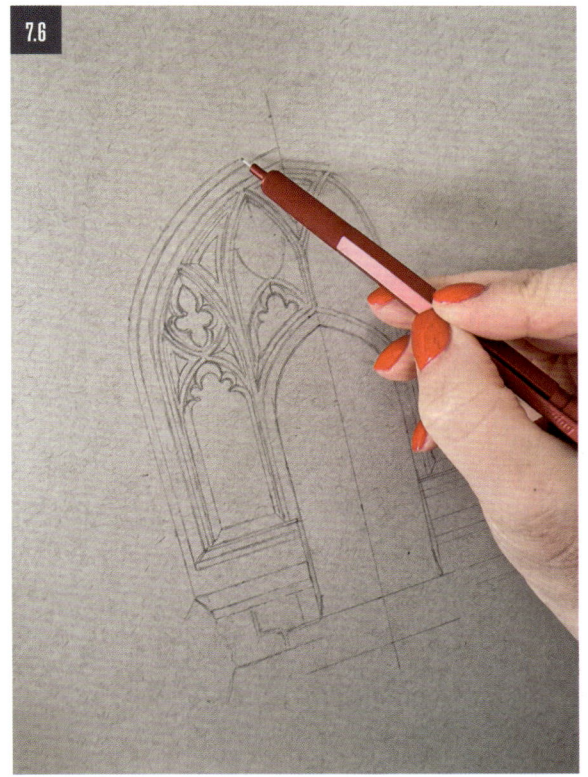

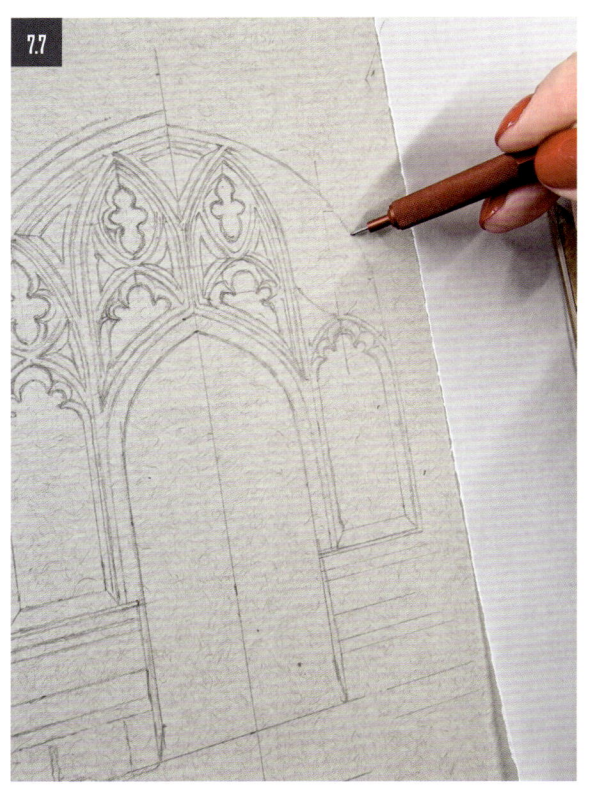

Take a good look at the stonework of the cloister and you will see that not all the lines are straight; in fact, they are quite wobbly in places, especially on the edges of the big blocks of stone. The stone is rough, very old, and worn away in many places. Replicating the wobbly lines in your drawing will add character and interest to your work and will also help create an overall realistic effect (**FIGURE 7.8**).

Keep going until you have finished the main pencil drawing. I decided to keep my outer lines very loose, as I want the finished piece to look slightly unfinished (**FIGURE 7.9**).

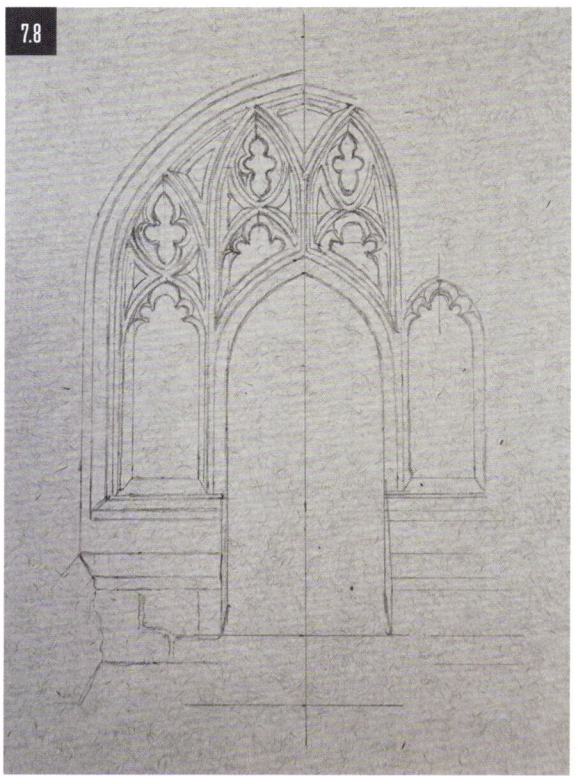

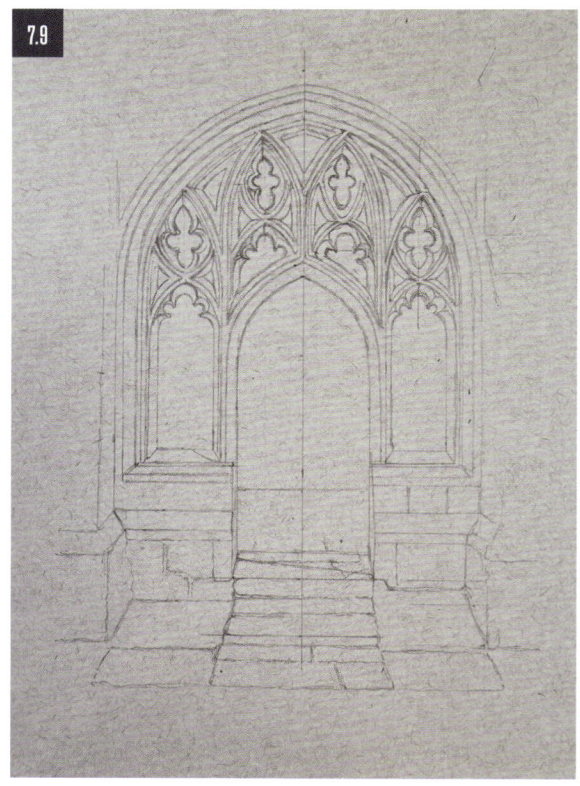

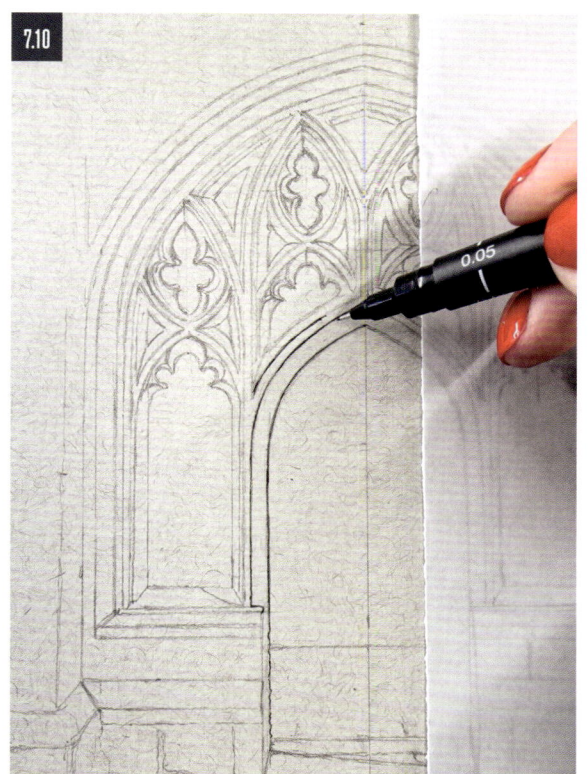
7.10

Step 2: COVER THE LINES WITH BLACK INK AND ADD SHADING

Now it's time to cover your pencil lines with black ink. Using a black 0.05mm fineliner pen, begin covering the pencil lines, paying special attention to the lines that surround the most highlighted areas and keeping them nice and clean (**FIGURE 7.10**).

It's okay if not every line is perfect. There are lots of tiny lines and no one except you, the artist, knows what should and shouldn't be there. Wiggle your pen as you move it along to create the wobbly and uneven lines of the stonework (**FIGURE 7.11**). Keep referring back to your reference photo to observe where these areas are.

Continue this process, working from left to right, until you have covered the whole drawing in ink (**FIGURE 7.12**).

Once this is done, gently rub away the remaining pencil lines with an eraser.

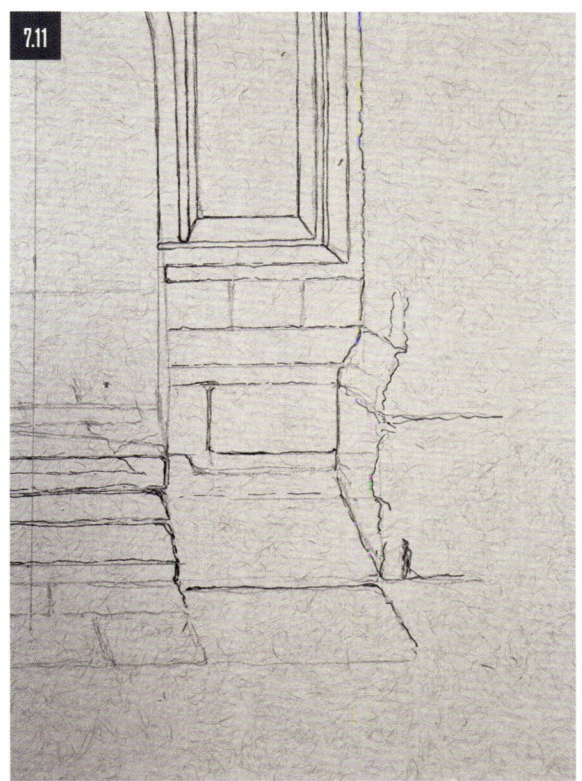
7.11

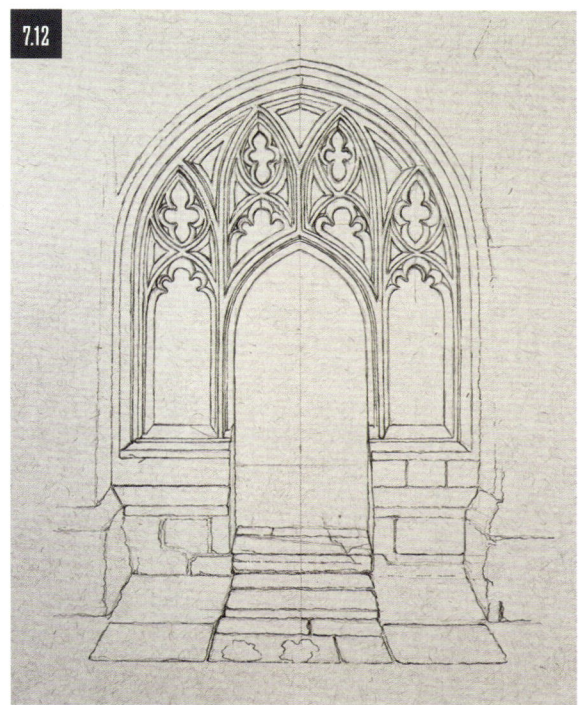
7.12

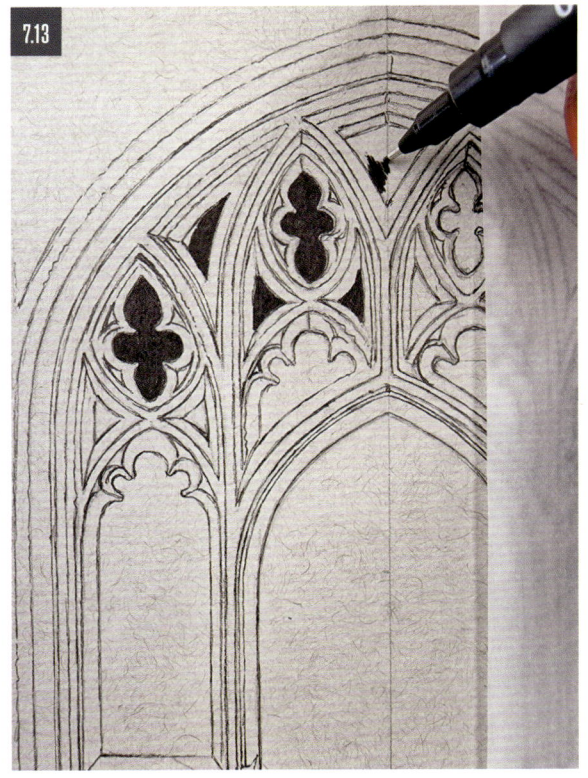

7.13

Next, you can begin to add in the very darkest areas of shadow (**FIGURES 7.13** and **7.14**). You can use a pen with a slightly larger nib if you have one to cover ground quicker and speed up the process of blocking these areas in. I used a 0.4mm Unipin black fineliner.

The shadows in the lower windows and doorway aren't completely black, so use crosshatching all over, then use downward vertical strokes to create a graded shadow that gets lighter near the bottom (**FIGURES 7.15** and **7.16**).

Continue to do this across both windows and the door, building up the layers of shading (**FIGURE 7.17**). Keep your crosshatching lines going in the same direction across all three areas to achieve a consistent look.

Begin to randomly mark in some of the shapes you can see in the shadows, like the stonework and the sign (**FIGURE 7.18**). This helps add to the illusion of depth. Continue to build up the depth of the shadows with more and more crosshatching (**FIGURE 7.19**). You can also go back and add to this later if required.

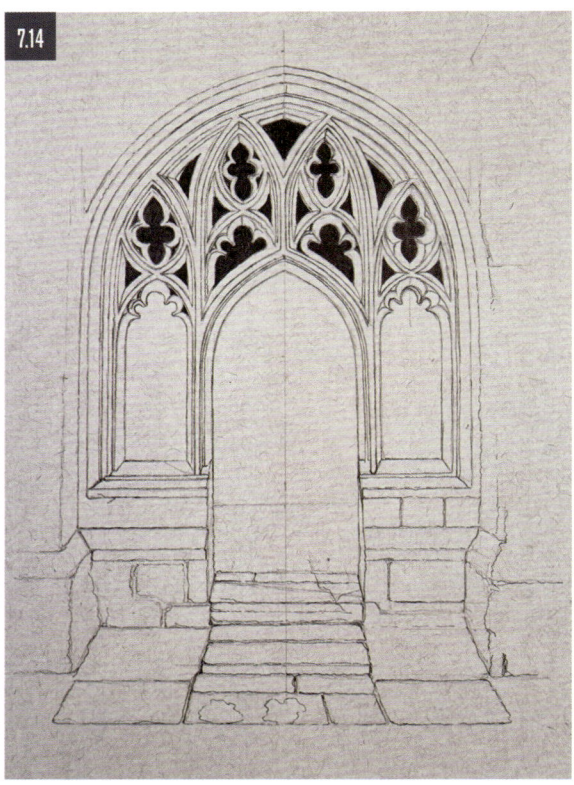

7.14

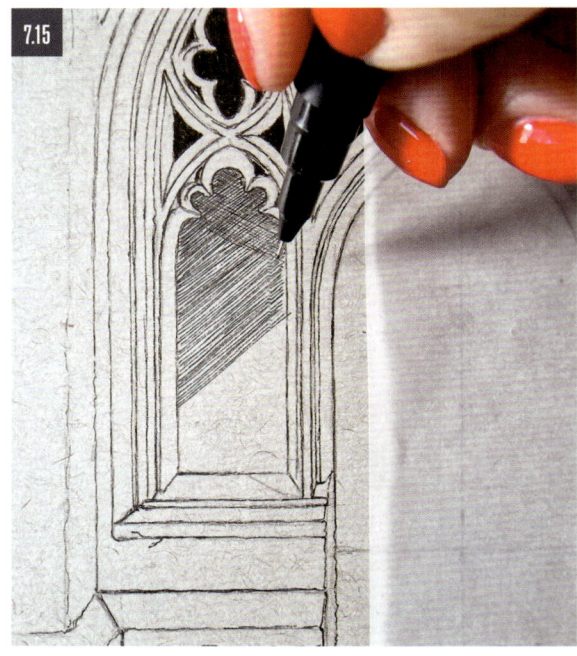

7.15

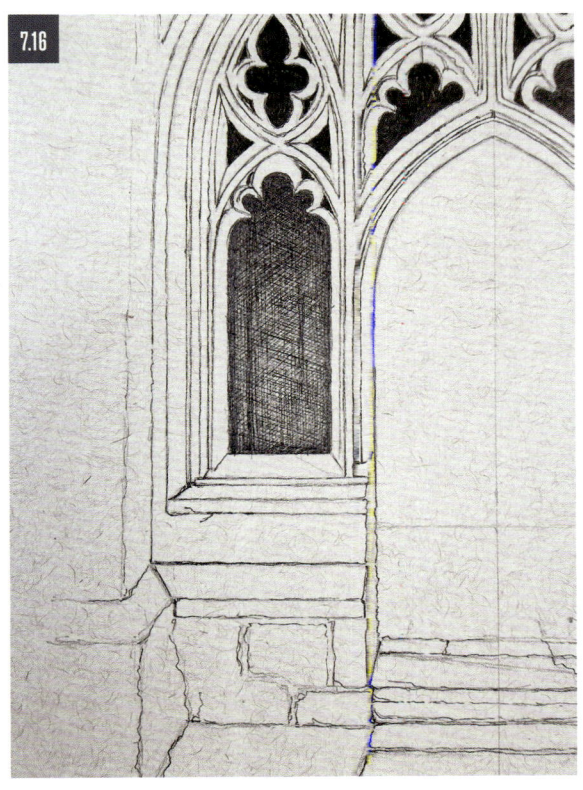

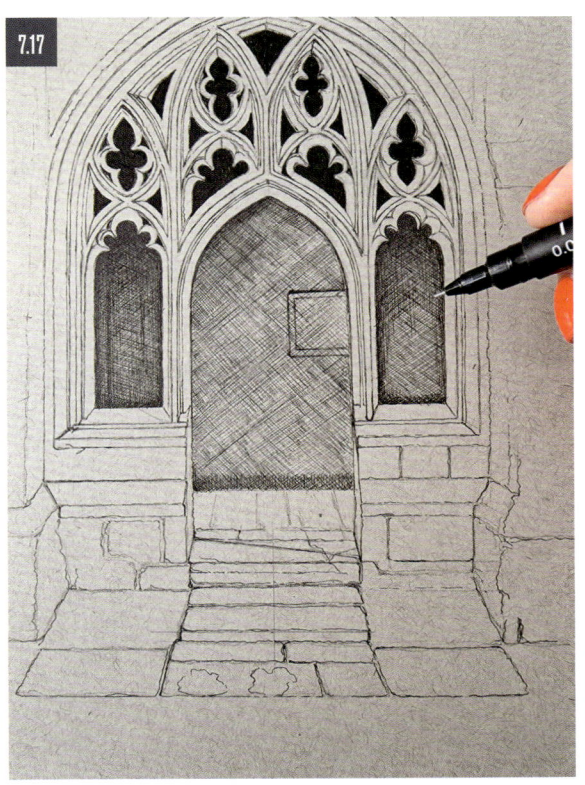

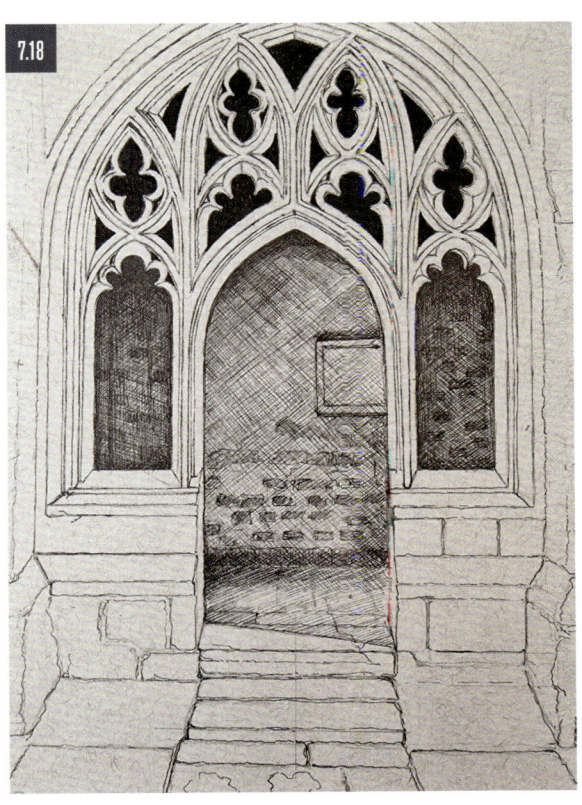

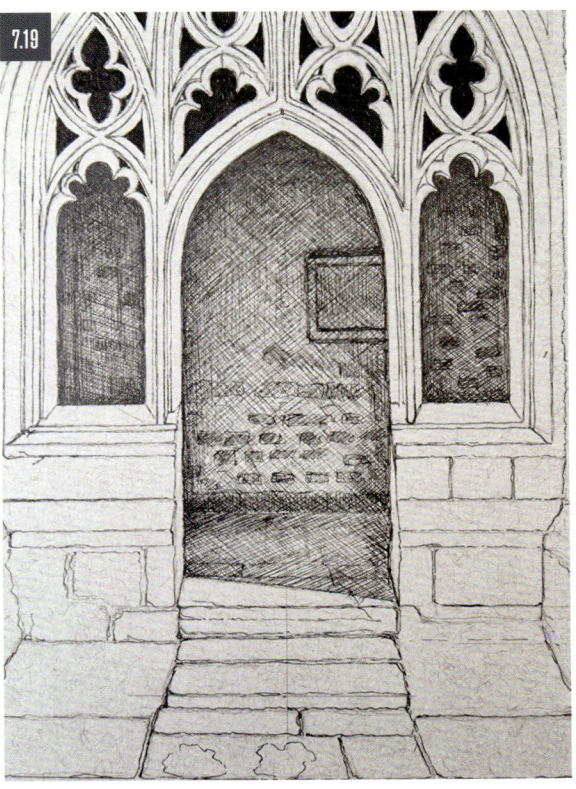

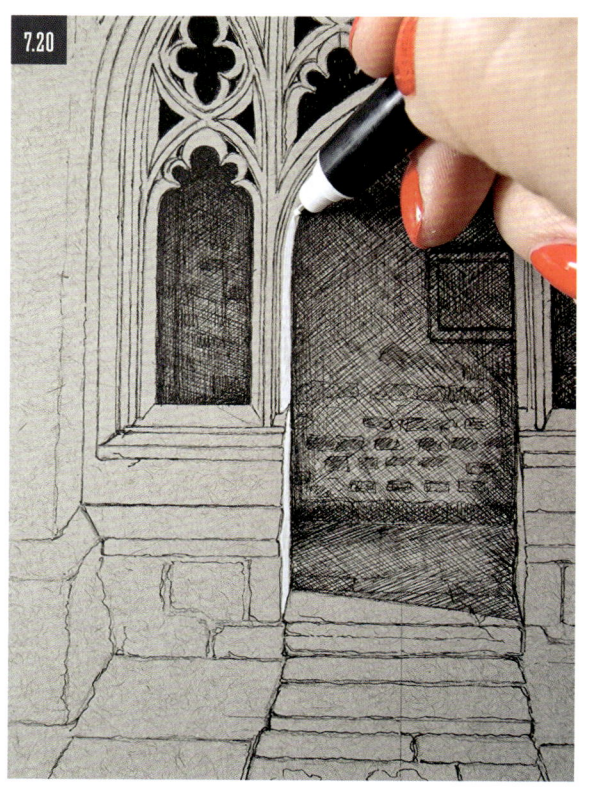

Step 3: ADD LIGHT, MEDIUM, AND DARK TONES

The next step is to start adding the brightest highlights. Look closely at the reference photo and pick out the most obvious highlights, then draw them in with your highlighting pen (**FIGURES 7.20** and **7.21**). It's a good idea to do this first, as the highlighting pens go down best on clean paper.

> ➤ If the white ink in your highlighting pen is clogging, push the nib down on a separate piece of paper to get the ink flowing.

Now begin adding white pencil, which is the next tone down, to the areas you can see that are not quite as bright as the very brightest highlight (**FIGURE 7.22**). This is detailed and fine work, so it helps to keep your pencils nice and sharp!

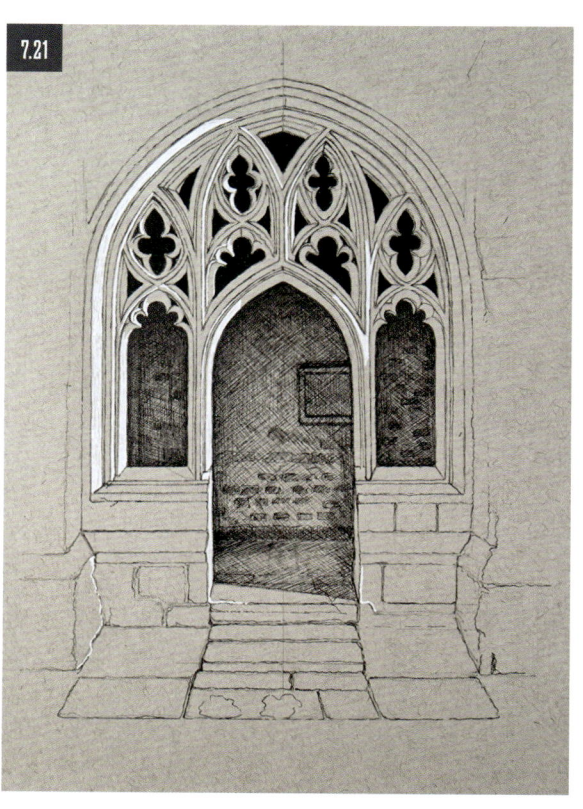

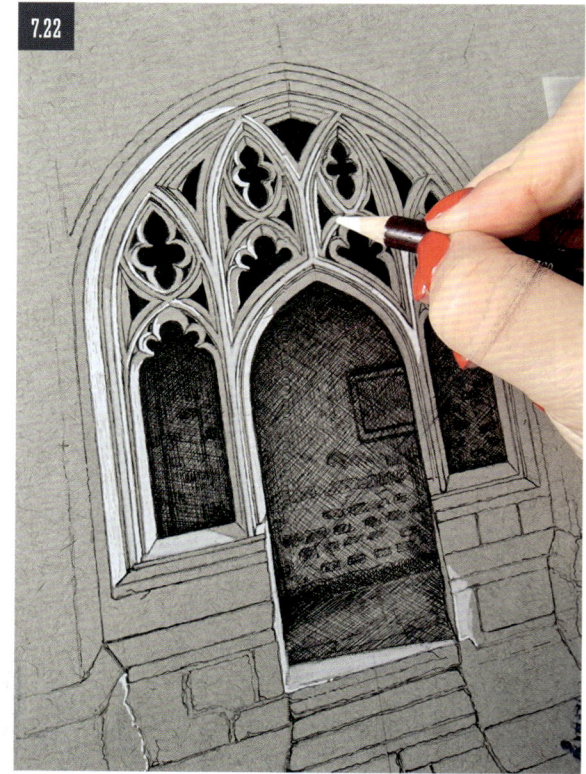

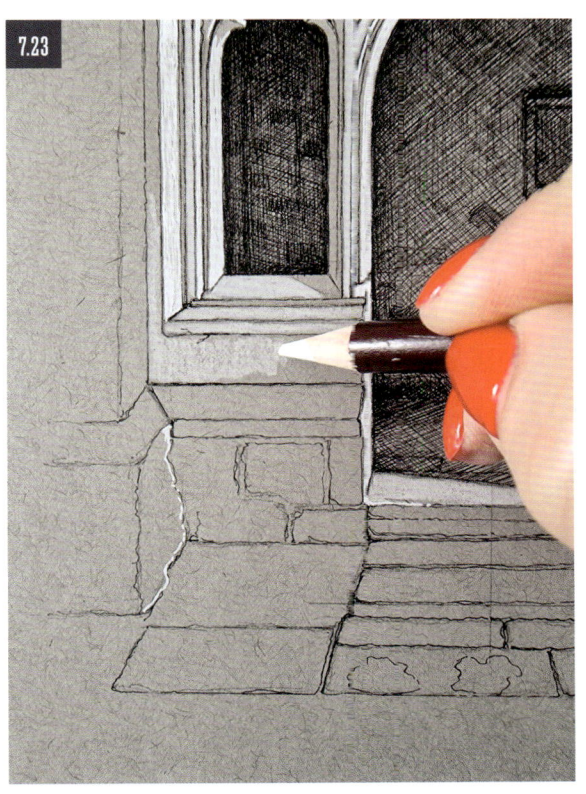

You can continually adjust the tones as you go along. You can also use a light layer of white pencil to create a softer tone of white (**FIGURE 7.23**), and then build on top of this with other darker or lighter tones later if necessary.

The next stage is to begin adding the mid-tones with Warm Grey IV and the dark tones with Payne's Grey (**FIGURES 7.24** and **7.25**). Move around the drawing, adding each tone that you see. Alternatively, you can complete one area before you move onto the next. This is the exciting part, as your drawing will start to come to life.

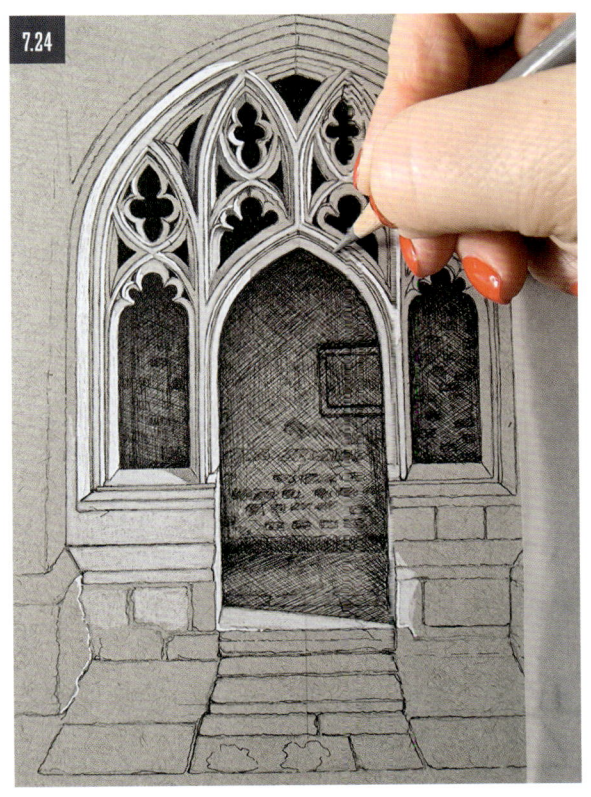

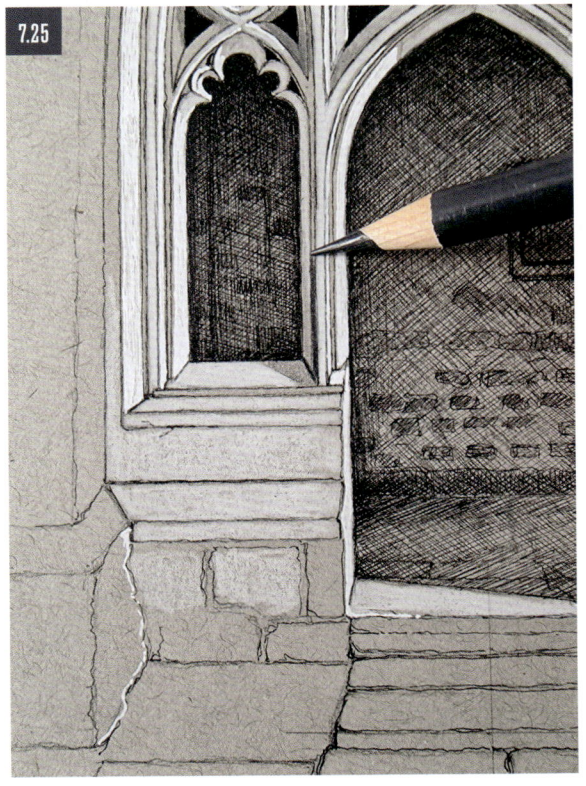

Continue to build layers of colour across the drawing using a combination of white, mid-tone grey, and dark grey (**FIGURE 7.26**). On the right side where there are more areas of shadow, use more mid-grey and dark grey (**FIGURE 7.27**).

Blend the colours together with a pastel blender if you have one (**FIGURE 7.28**). This smooths out the colour and removes any graininess. Redefine the ink lines as well, and crosshatch over the pencil in the very darkest areas (**FIGURE 7.29**).

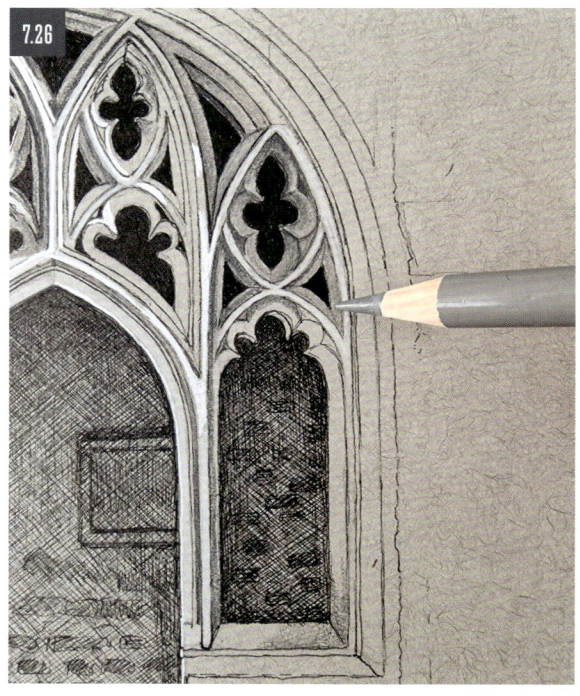

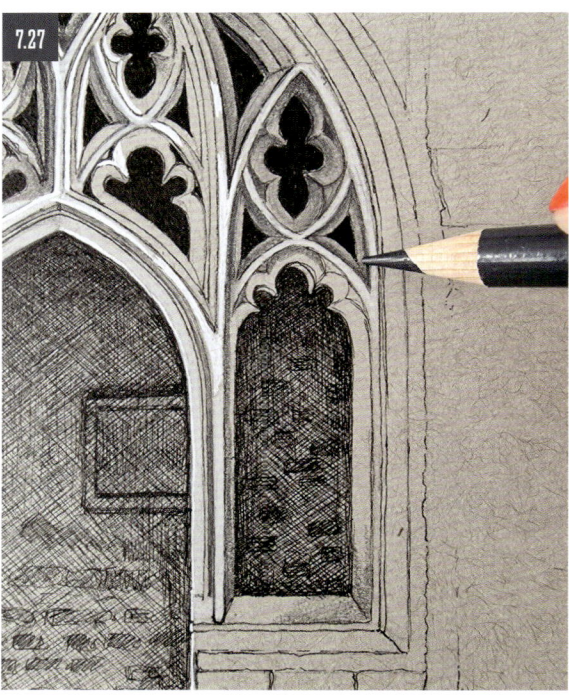

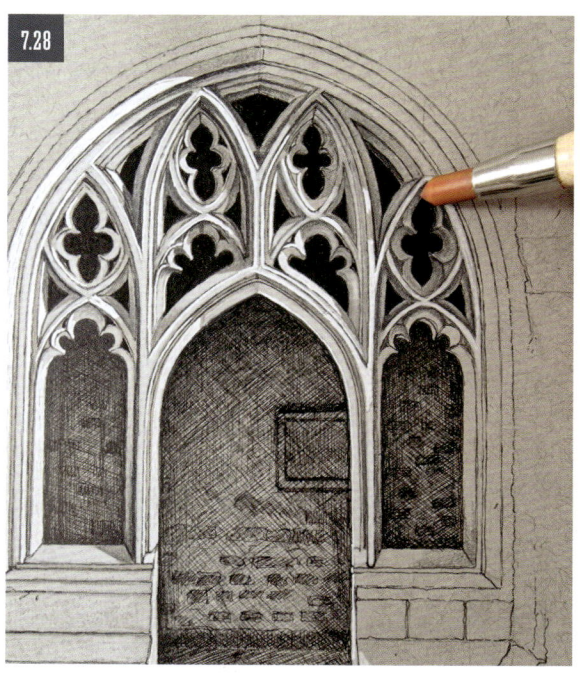

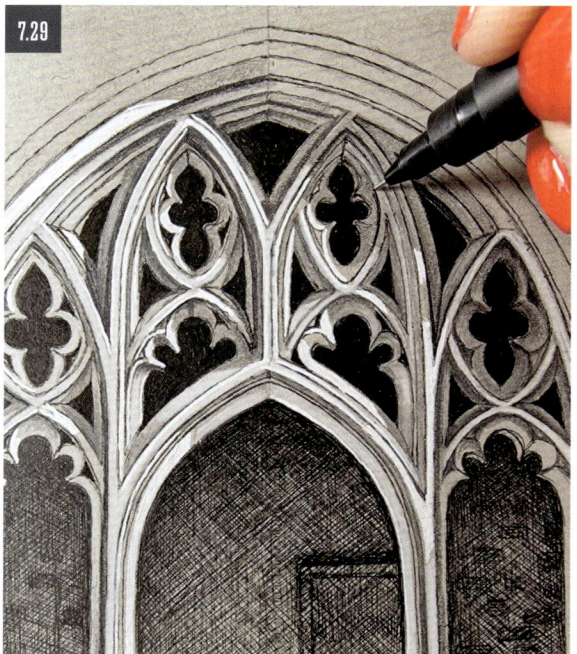

Drawing and Illustrating Architecture

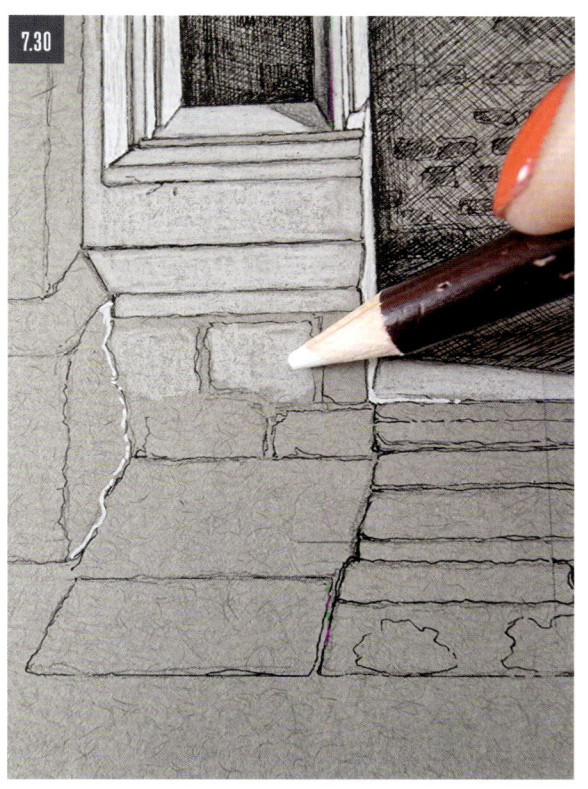

For the large stone bricks and outer areas of the drawing, use soft, random shading to gently phase out the drawing to achieve an unfinished look (**FIGURES 7.30** and **7.31**).

Step 4: ADD FINAL DETAILS

Strengthen the darkest shadows using a combination of black pencil with fineliner crosshatching on top (**FIGURE 7.32**).

Fill in the paving stones with soft white shading, adding more layers where necessary to brighten the white colour. Now use the black pencil to define the lines in between the paving stones (**FIGURE 7.33, NEXT PAGE**).

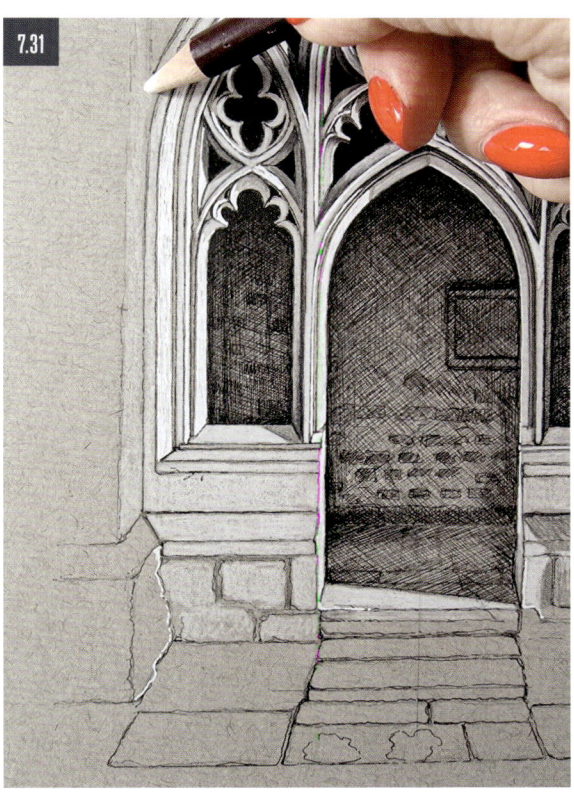

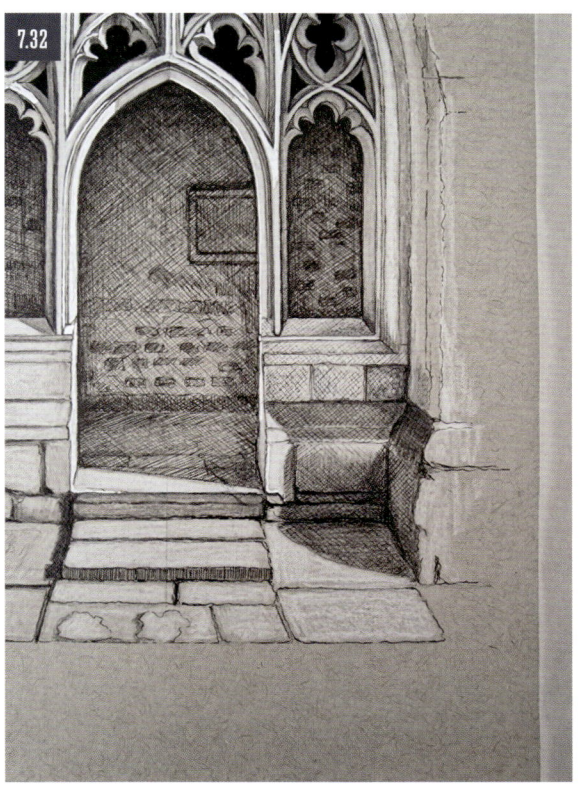

Add more random shading and black ink lines to loosely define the stonework around the edges of the cloister. Next, use dots and random lines to replicate texture on the stonework (**FIGURE 7.34**).

Finally, check everything over and maximise any highlights and shadows, and then sit back and admire your achievement!

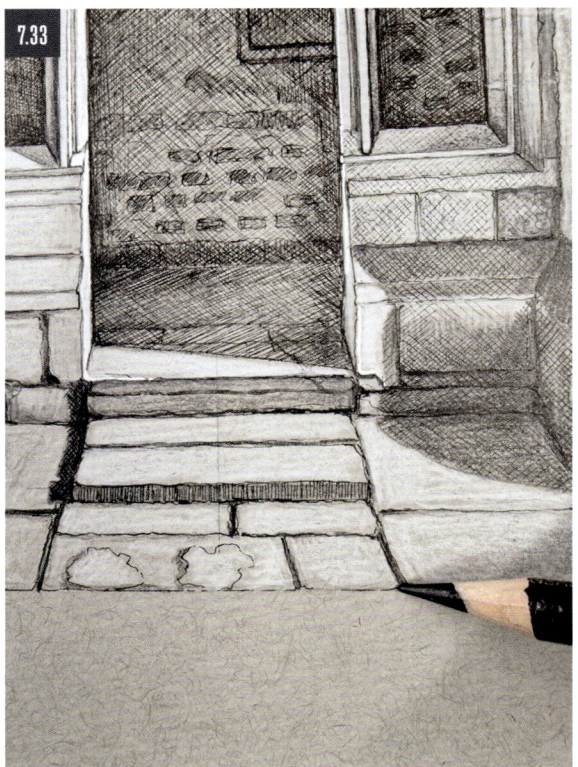

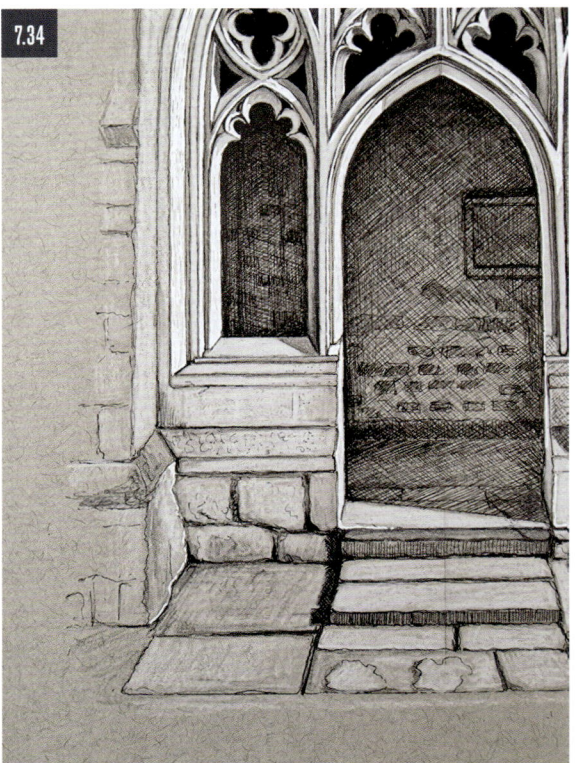

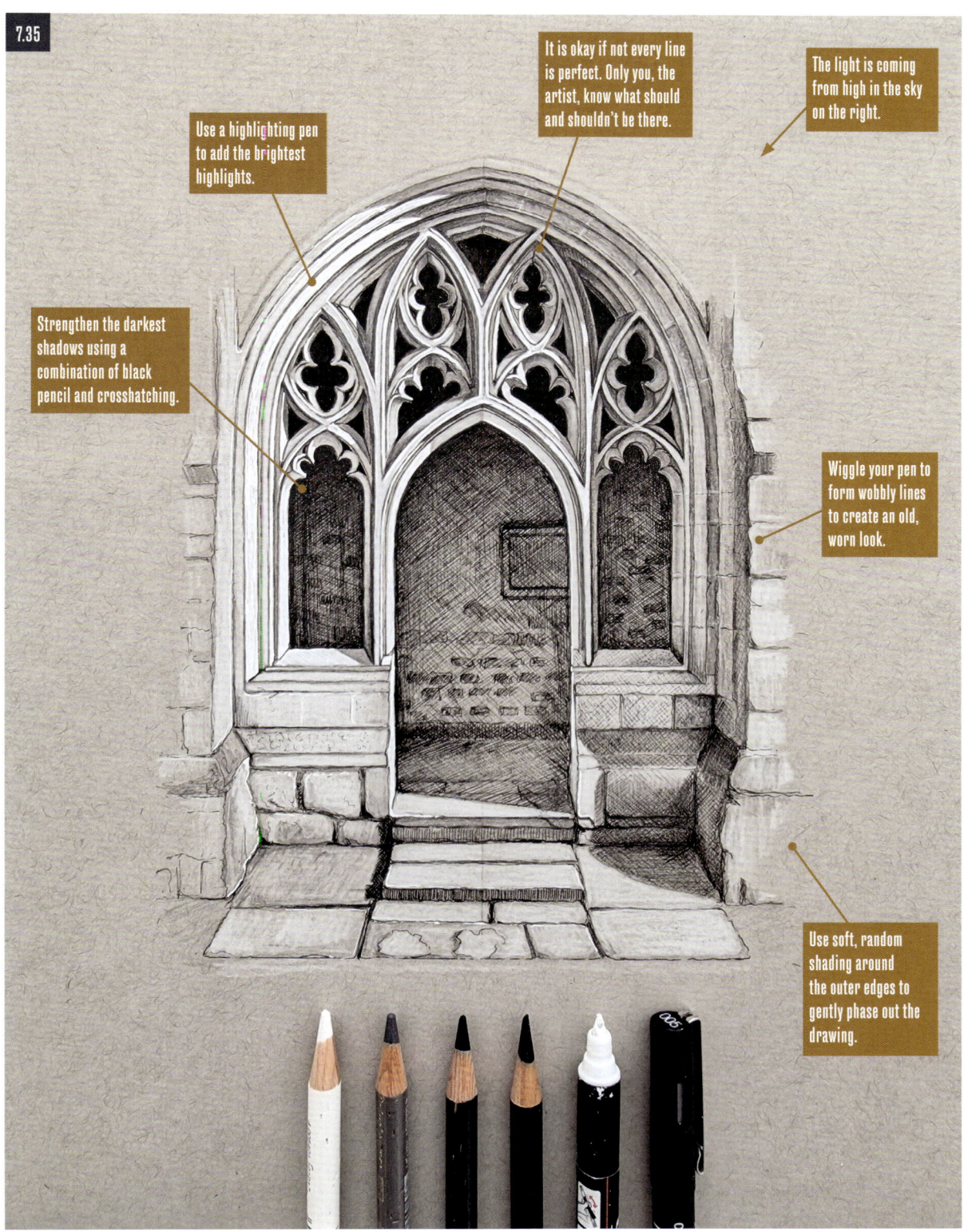

Use a highlighting pen to add the brightest highlights.

It is okay if not every line is perfect. Only you, the artist, know what should and shouldn't be there.

The light is coming from high in the sky on the right.

Strengthen the darkest shadows using a combination of black pencil and crosshatching.

Wiggle your pen to form wobbly lines to create an old, worn look.

Use soft, random shading around the outer edges to gently phase out the drawing.

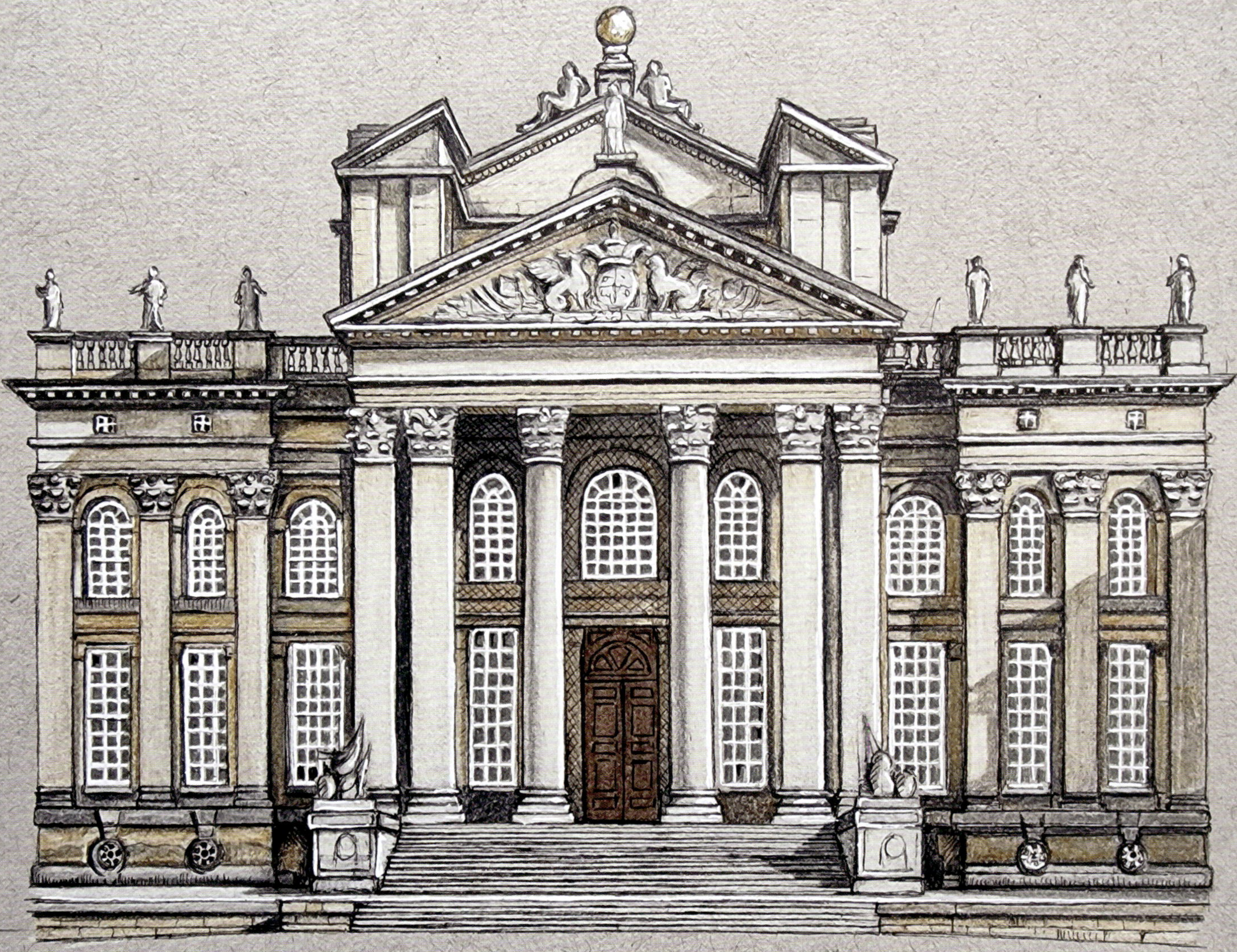

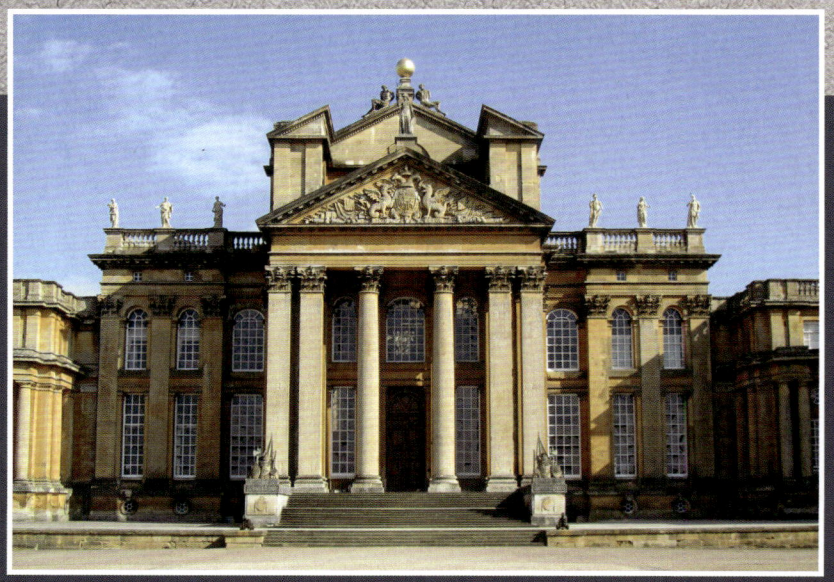

CHAPTER 8

Full-Colour Drawing

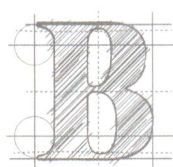

Blenheim Palace is a country house in Oxfordshire. It is one of England's largest houses and was built between 1705 and 1722. It is designed in the English baroque style and is the home of the Duke of Marlborough.

I am fortunate to live not too far from this stunning building and have drawn it many times, which is why I thought it would make a great project for you to work on too.

I chose this reference photo because there are some nice shadows to work with and the photo captures the symmetrical elements of the building perfectly.

MATERIALS

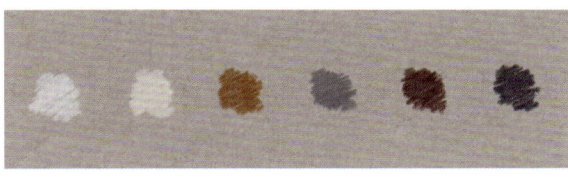

- ▶ Toned paper
- ▶ Sharp pencil or mechanical pencil
- ▶ Black 0.05mm fineliner pen
- ▶ Coloured Pencils: White, Ivory, Brown Ochre, Warm Grey IV, Burnt Umber, Payne's Grey
- ▶ Ruler
- ▶ Set Square
- ▶ Dark-grey fineliner pen (optional)

Step 1: DRAW WITH PENCIL

Let's get started! I am using method 3 (page 65) for the initial drawing and am taking measurements from my digital screen. I chose this method because I want the drawing to be precise and accurate, as befits the beautiful architecture of Blenheim Palace.

As with the previous artworks, begin by drawing a vertical line in the centre of the page, followed by a horizontal line approximately two-thirds of the way down the page. You will use the horizontal line as the base line for the whole drawing and the very bottom of the steps.

Begin taking measurements from between the columns and build outwards like a puzzle, slotting the shapes together (**FIGURE 8.1**). This building is actually quite easy to draw from this angle because it is so symmetrical and everything lines up.

Note that the two central columns are different widths at the top and bottom, although at first glance, they look the same width all the way up.

Some of the details are difficult to see clearly—for instance, the details of the statues and the columns. You can suggest these with loose lines (**FIGURE 8.2**).

Once the columns are in place, you can use them as markers to line up other parts of the building. It's the same for the windows—most of them line up, so once you have one in the correct place, you can use it to line up the others (**FIGURE 8.3**).

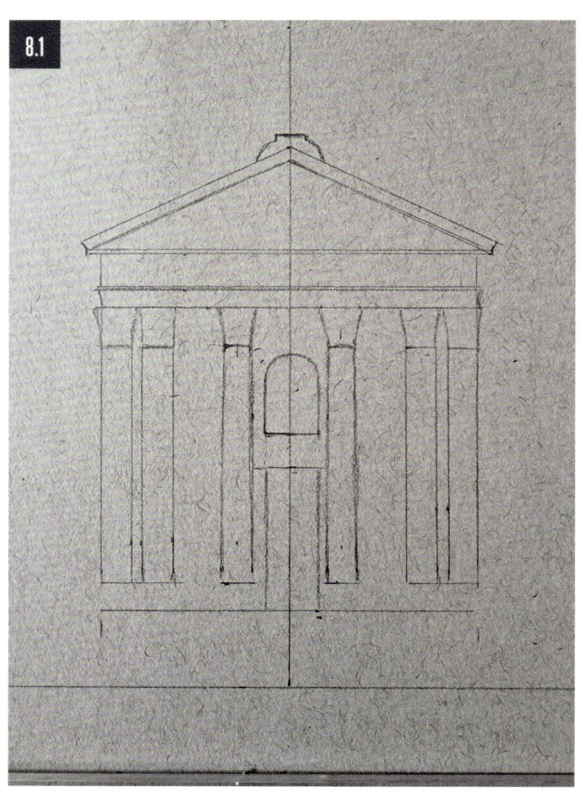

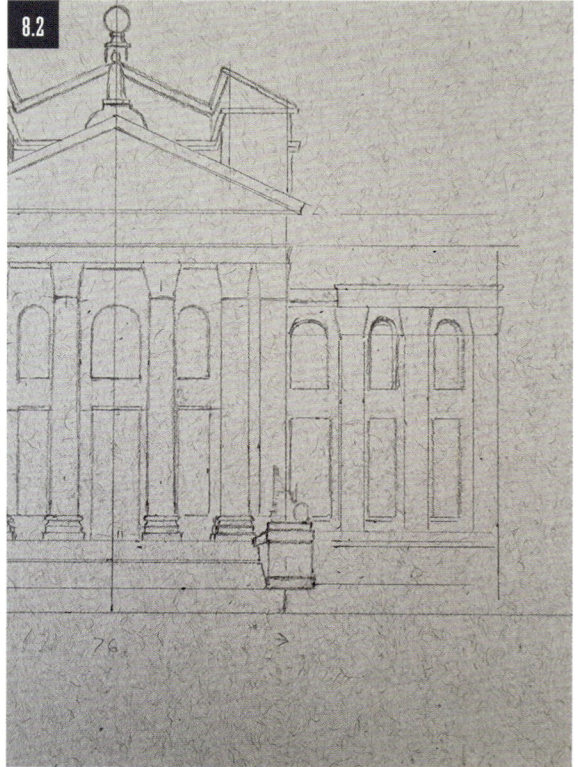

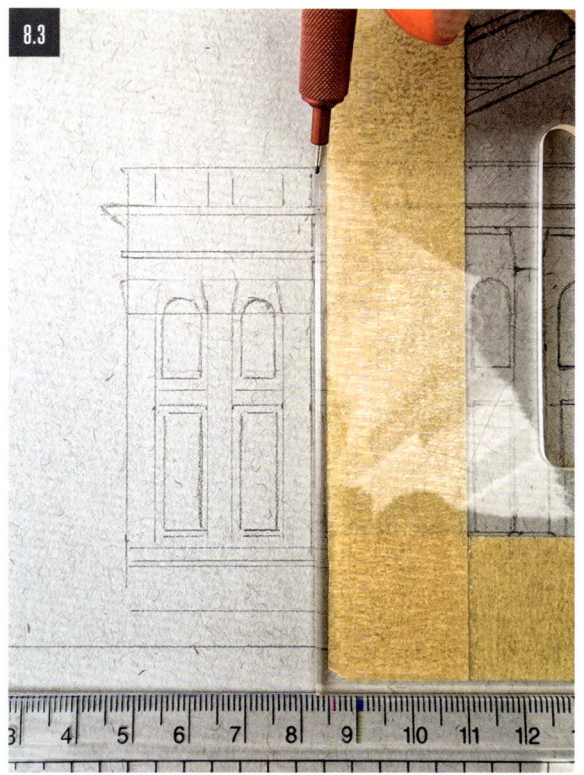

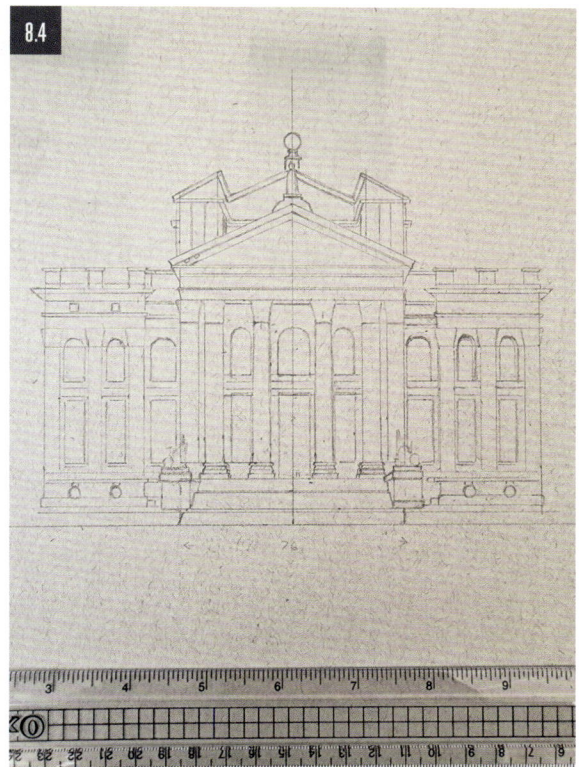

When you are finished, check everything over and make sure both sides are symmetrical (**FIGURE 8.4**). You can go back in and add more details later with a fineliner. It's important to get the basic structure of the drawing down on the paper and covered with ink so there is less risk of smudging and making the work messy.

Step 2: COVER THE LINES WITH BLACK INK

You should be starting to get the hang of this. The next step is to add ink and create a skeleton-like structure of black lines. Start at the top with paper under your hand so you don't smudge the delicate pencil work (**FIGURE 8.5**).

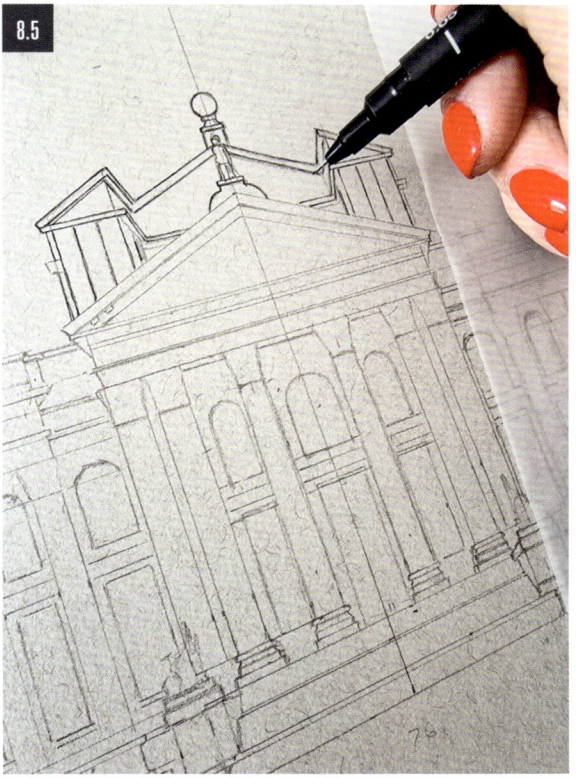

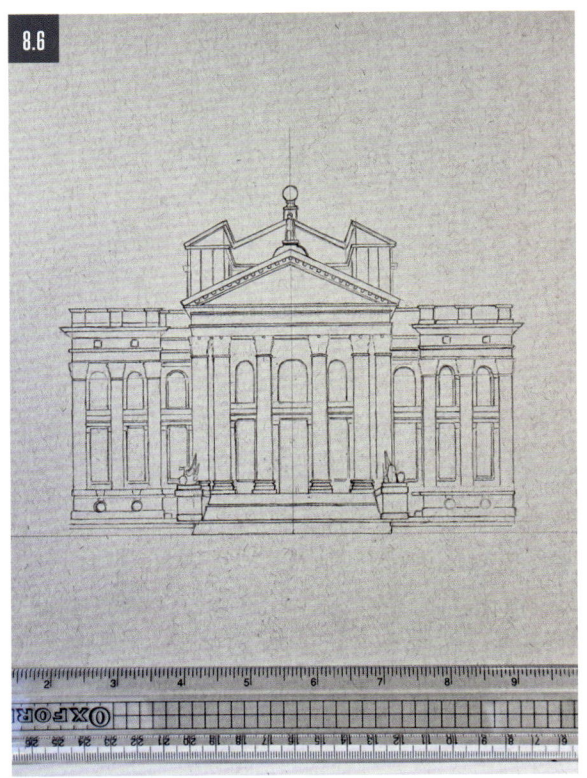

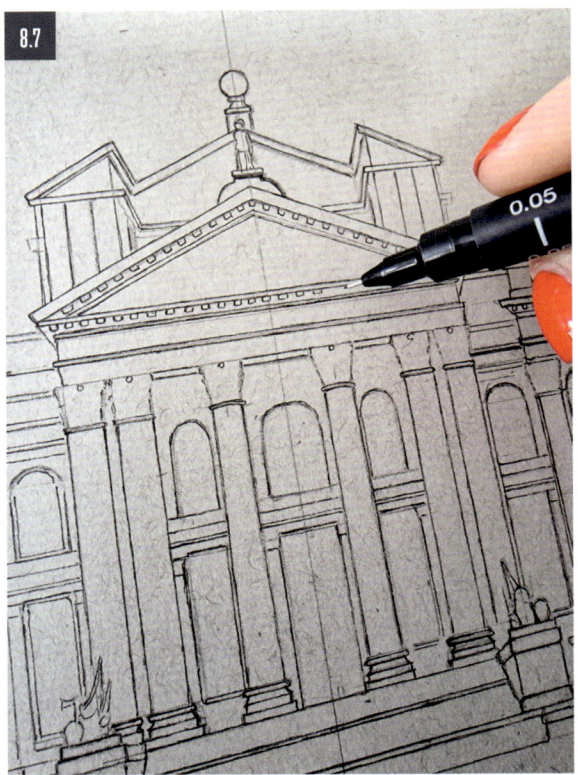

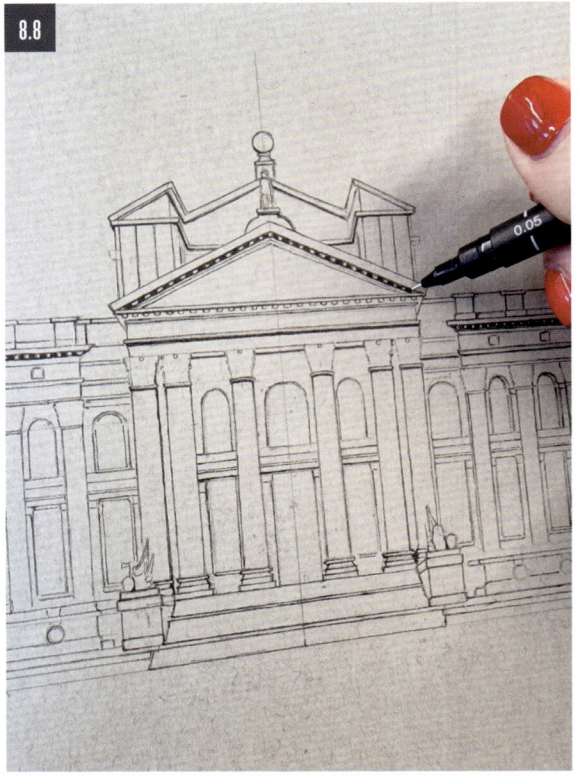

Move from the left of the drawing across to the right side until the whole drawing is covered in black lines (**FIGURE 8.6**). I like to do this part freehand with the occasional use of a ruler if I absolutely need it. This keeps the lines slightly looser, and I find it more enjoyable to draw freehand. If you prefer to use a ruler, feel free to do so.

Also add in any obvious dark lines and use your fineliner to add in the dark shadows around the details (**FIGURES 8.7** and **8.8**). It's easier to do this with the precision point of a fineliner rather than pencil.

Leave the details of the Corinthian columns and the design on the pediment until later.

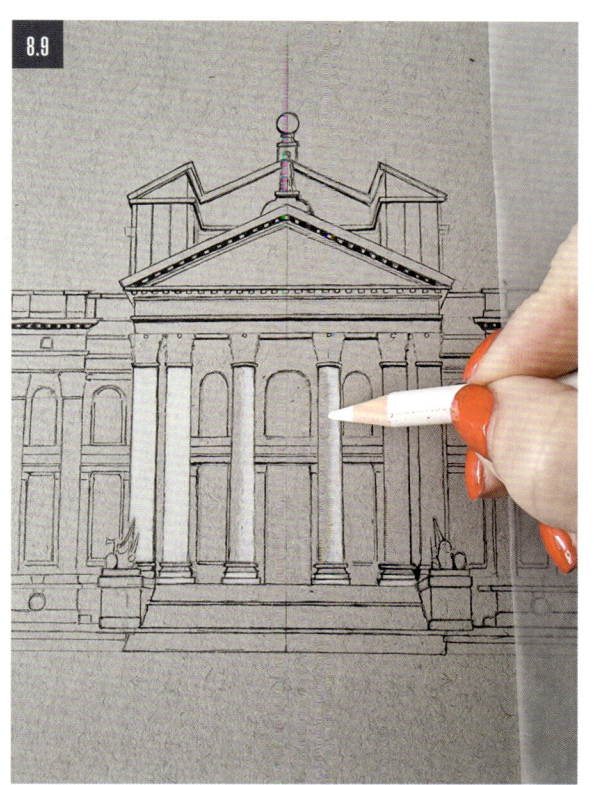

Step 3: ADD COLOUR

Now it's time to start the process of adding some colour to your work.

Begin by adding a layer of white to the central columns (**FIGURE 8.9**). Placing the lightest colour down first will make the next layer stand out more. I am starting in the middle because the brightest highlights are here and it's the focal point of the drawing. Getting the colours right here will set the tonal values for the whole piece.

Now add a layer of Ivory on top of the white. Then gently shade down the left side of the two most central columns with Warm Grey IV (**FIGURE 8.10**).

Gently blend the colours with a blender and apply additional layers of Ivory on the right and Warm Grey IV on the left until the depth of the colours is bright and even. Slightly deepen the shadows on the left with Payne's Grey (**FIGURE 8.11**).

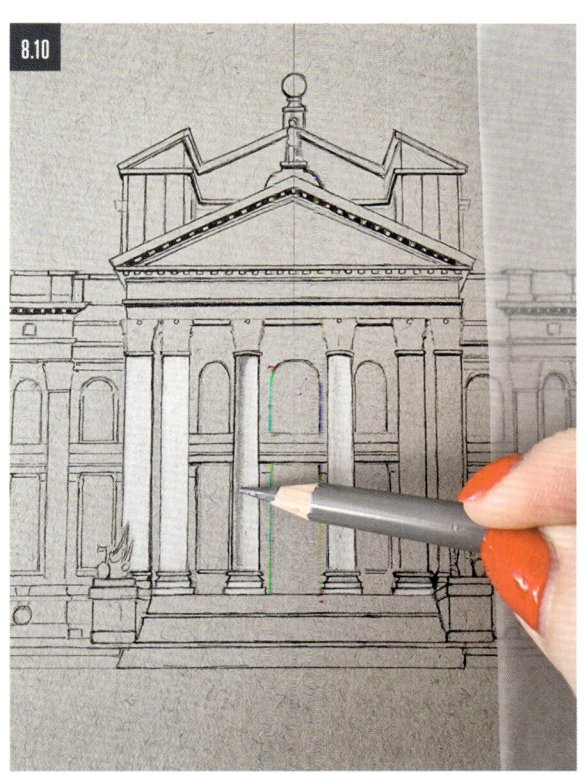

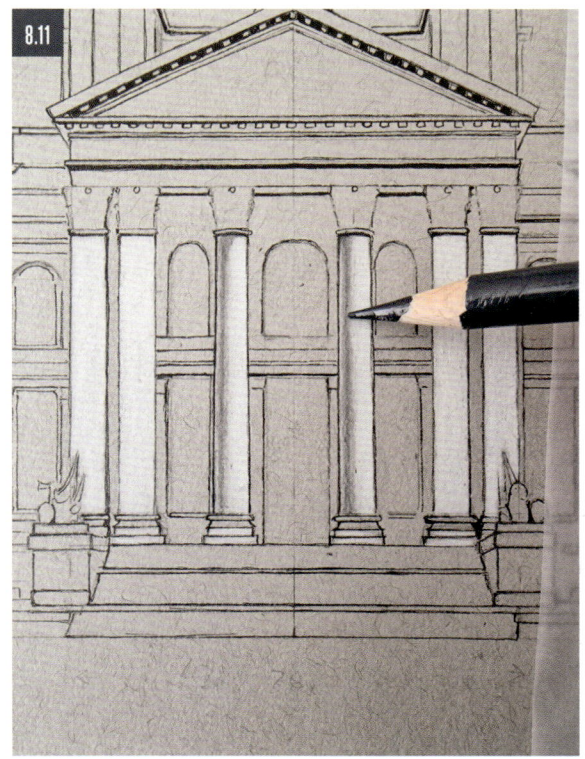

Add a very fine layer of Brown Ochre on top of the Ivory to warm the stone colour, and use Payne's Grey to define the darkest areas of the column bases (**FIGURES 8.12** and **8.13**).

Next, add a base layer of Warm Grey IV to the shadows between the columns (**FIGURE 8.14**), then add layers of Payne's Grey and Brown Ochre on top of this to create a warm, dark shadow (**FIGURE 8.15**). Be aware of the strips of light peeping through the columns and avoid making these areas dark. Instead, colour these light areas with Ivory followed by a layer of Brown Ochre.

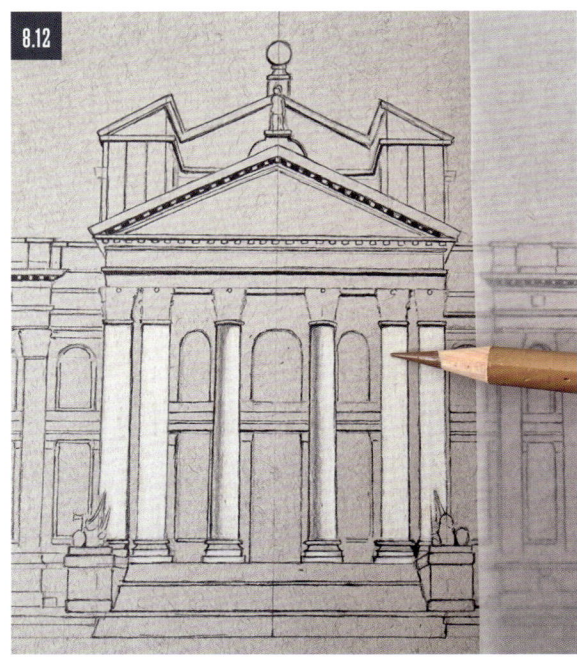

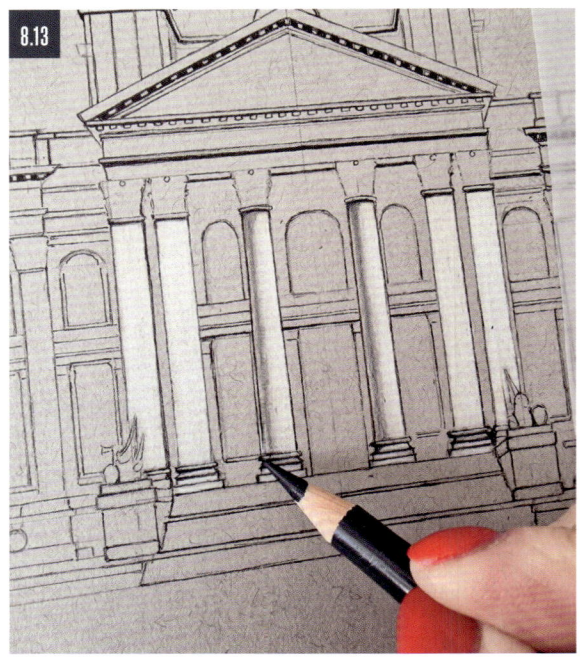

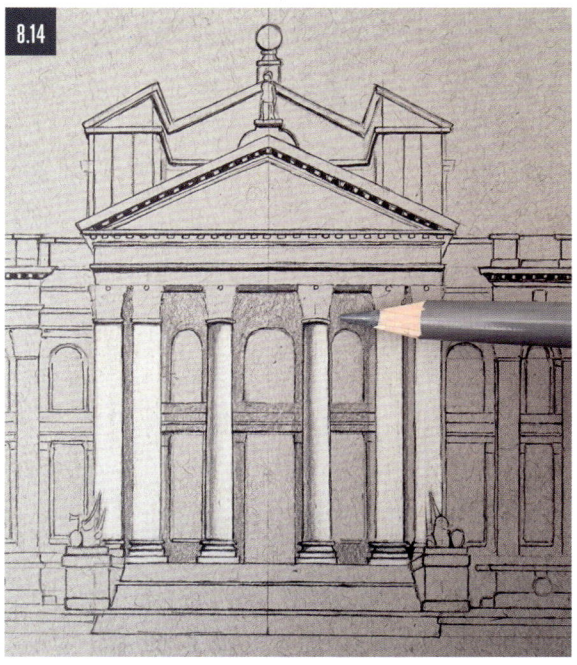

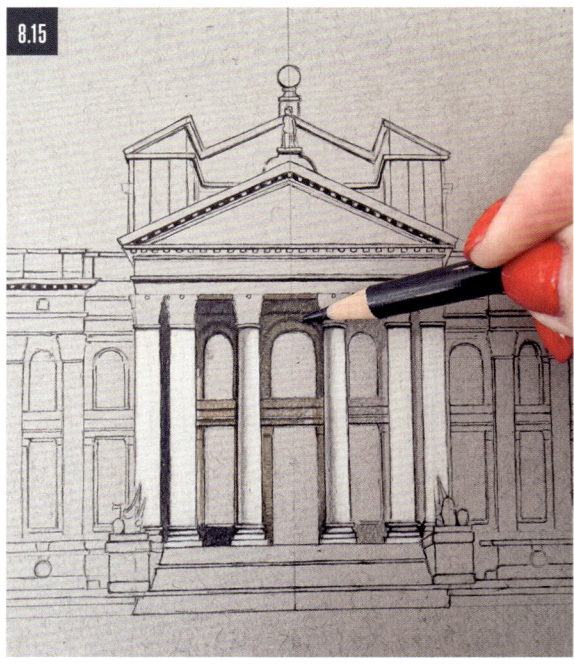

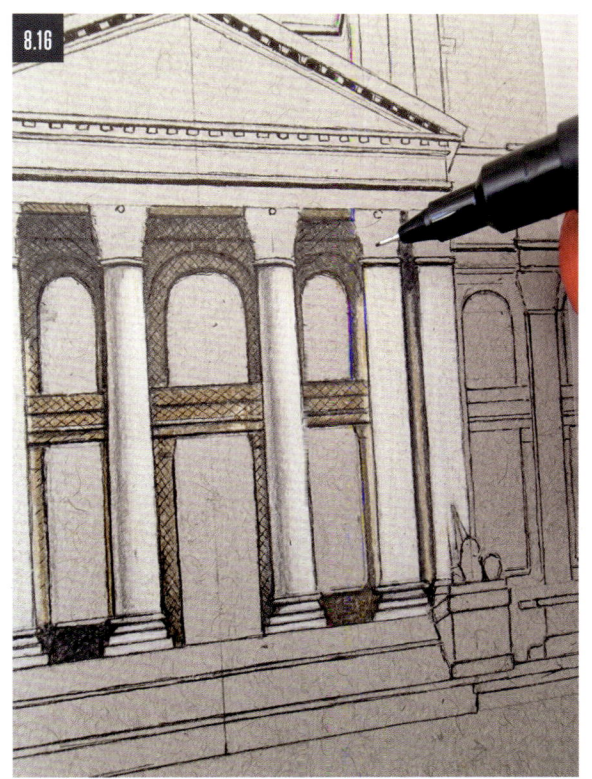

Mark in any dark lines you can see in the shadows, such as the arches over the windows.

Now, lightly crosshatch over the top of the shadows and redefine your ink lines where necessary (**FIGURE 8.16**).

Using a white Posca pen, carefully draw in the window frames (**FIGURE 8.17**). It's easier to do this directly on the clean paper rather than on top of pencil lines, as it is less likely to clog up the nib. We will lightly go over the bright white lines later with pencil to darken them slightly, as they are in shadow, but I find using these pens is the best way to get precise white window frames.

Now use either a dark-grey fineliner (if you have it) or a black fineliner to add in the windowpanes (**FIGURE 8.18**). This can be quite tricky and time-consuming, but it looks good when it's done!

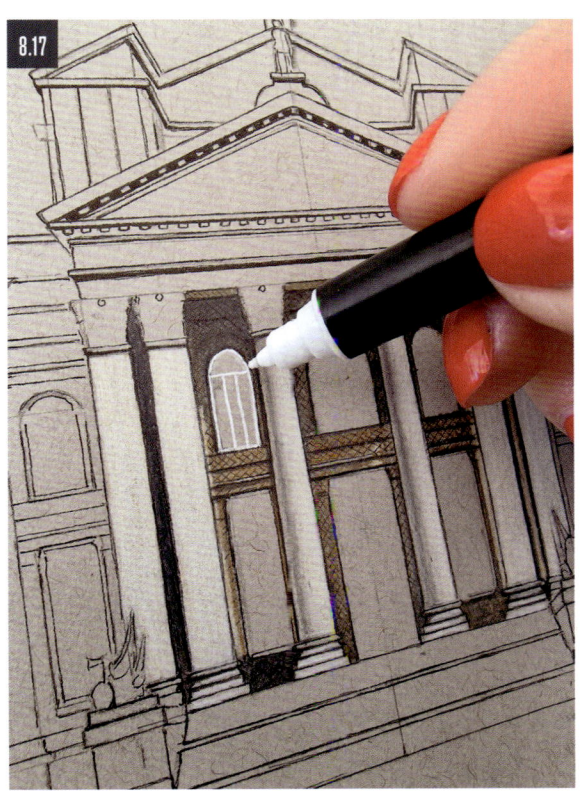

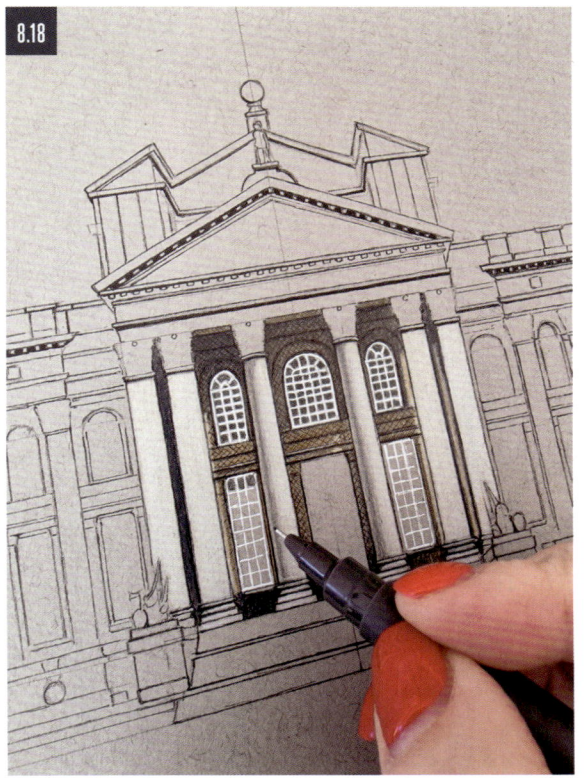

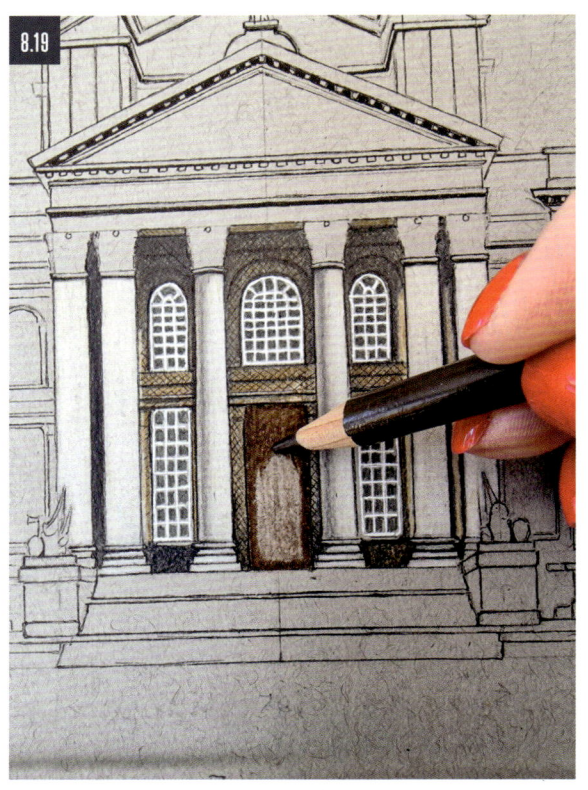

For the main entrance door, first add a light layer of Ivory, followed by two to three layers of Burnt Umber (**FIGURE 8.19**). Blend these layers together until you have a rich dense colour. Add the details of the panelling on top of this with a fineliner (**FIGURE 8.20**).

> ➤ Ink lines that are drawn on top of pencil can easily be erased off.

Now let's take a look at the ornate top part of the Corinthian columns. The details are quite hard to see closely, so loosely sketch what you can see with a fineliner, and then use a combination of Payne's Grey, Warm Grey IV, and Ivory to colour them (**FIGURE 8.21**).

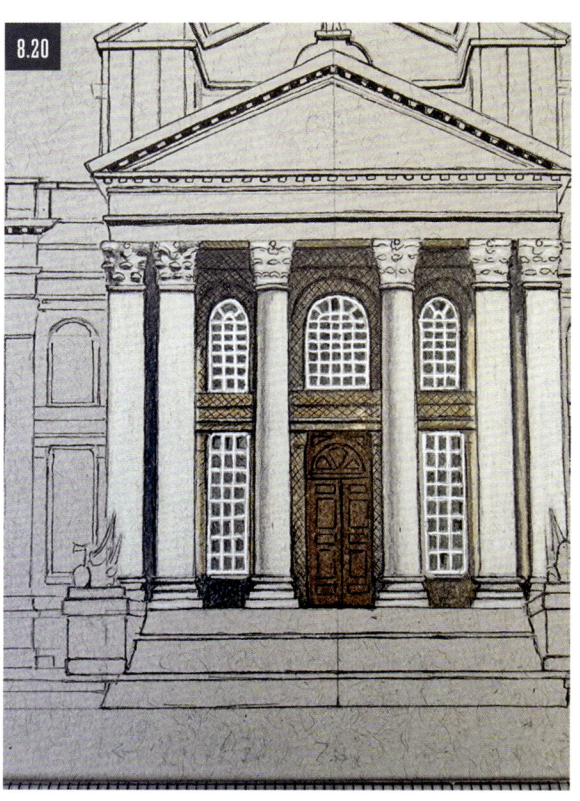

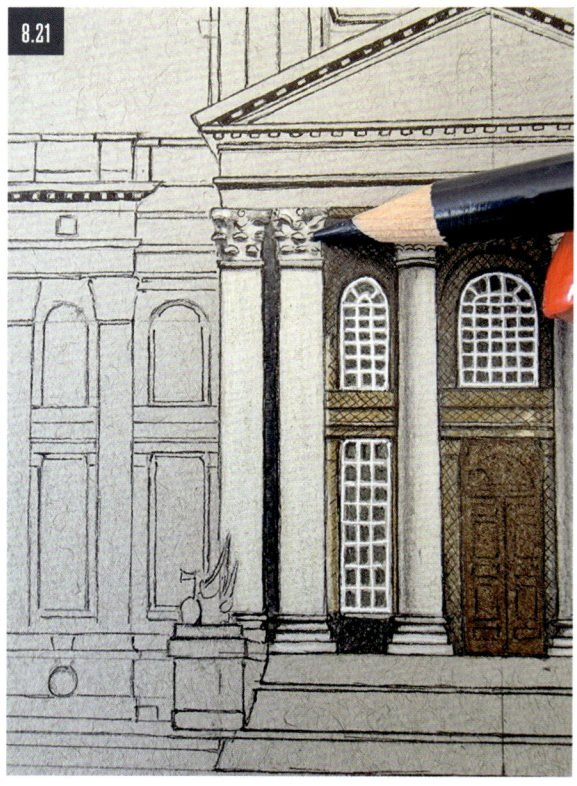

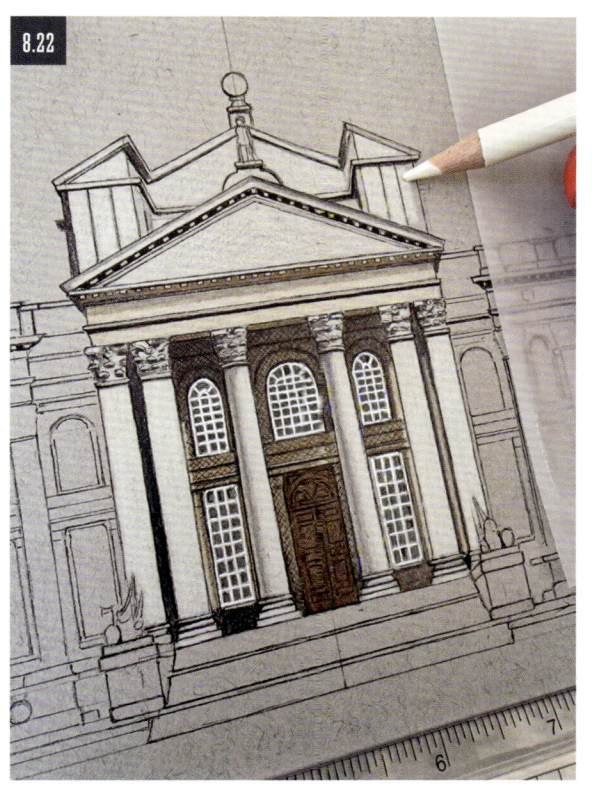

Continue building layers of colour upwards using the same combination of colours, starting with a base layer of Ivory (**FIGURE 8.22**). Use Warm Grey IV to gently mark in the clearly defined shadows in the photograph (**FIGURE 8.23**), and add a layer of Brown Ochre to warm everything up and replicate the ochre colour of the stone.

Use a fineliner to add in some of the tiny details and redefine everything (**FIGURE 8.24**).

Now comes the exciting part! Add in all the brightest highlights you can see with a Posca pen or gel pen. This includes little touches of white on the Corinthian columns and a fine white line down the right side of each column (**FIGURE 8.25, NEXT PAGE**).

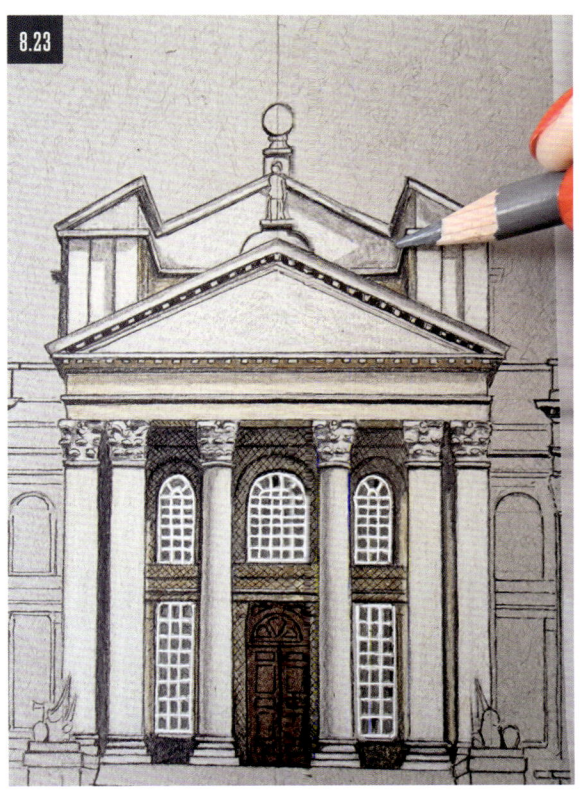

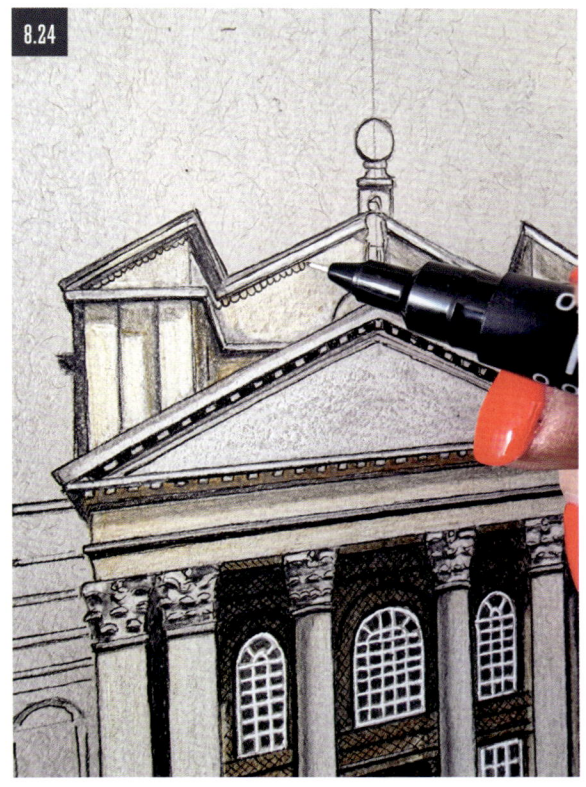

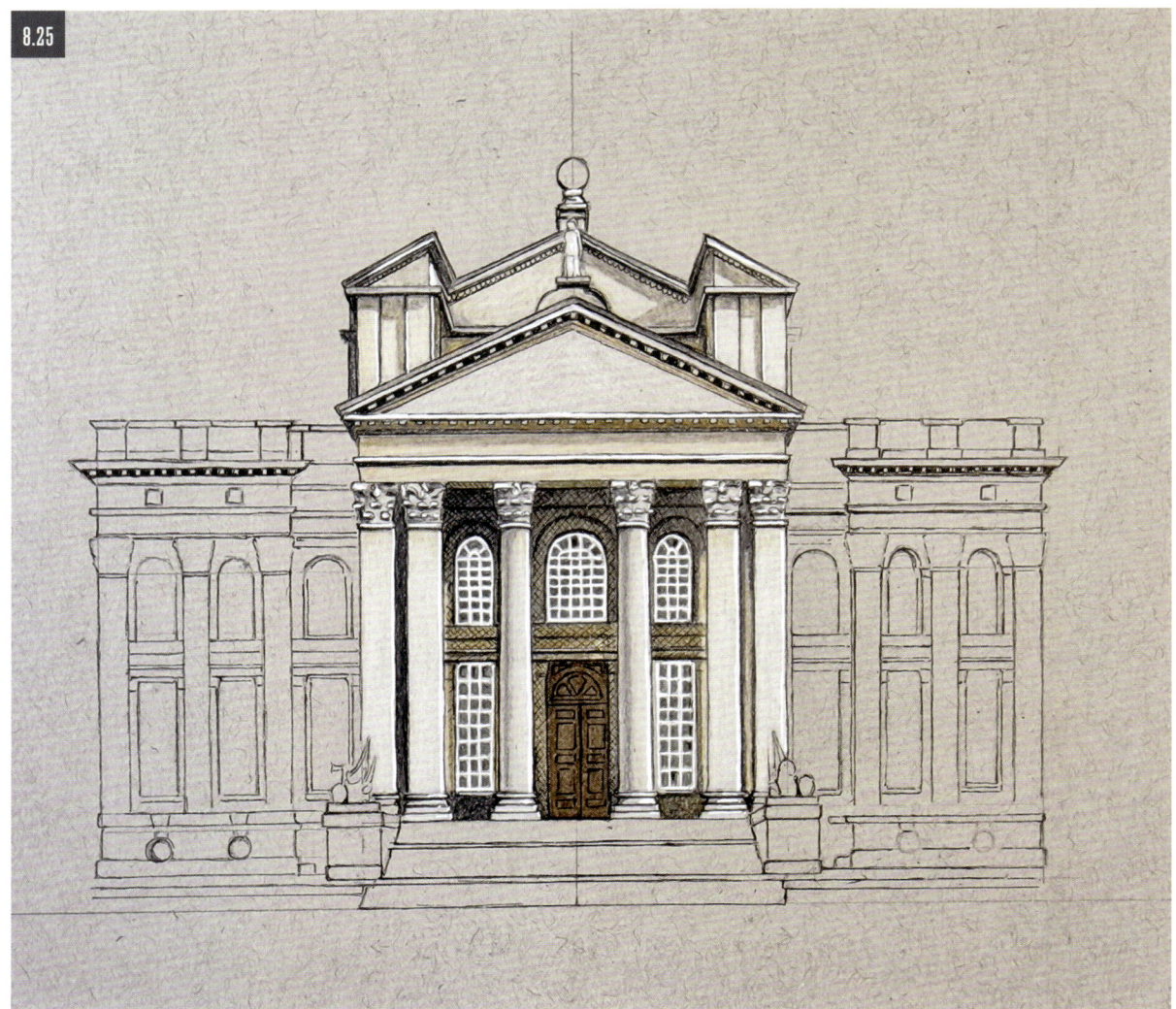

Make sure you place some paper over the central part you have already worked on and begin working on the left side of the palace using the same techniques and colours (**FIGURE 8.26**). However, note that this whole area is covered in shadow, apart from a few chinks of bright sunlight. As before, start with a layer of Ivory, then build further layers of Warm Grey IV, Brown Ochre, and Payne's Grey over the whole area (**FIGURE 8.27**). Continue to look back at the reference photo as you work.

While working on this side, draw in the balustrade by using a series of little straight lines as markers to place each vaselike shape where it should be (**FIGURE 8.28**). You can then draw straight on top of each pencil line with a fineliner so each baluster shape is evenly spaced (**FIGURE 8.29**).

Now move over to the right side of the palace and do the exact same thing again. This side is much lighter, with a big shadow cast right through the middle.

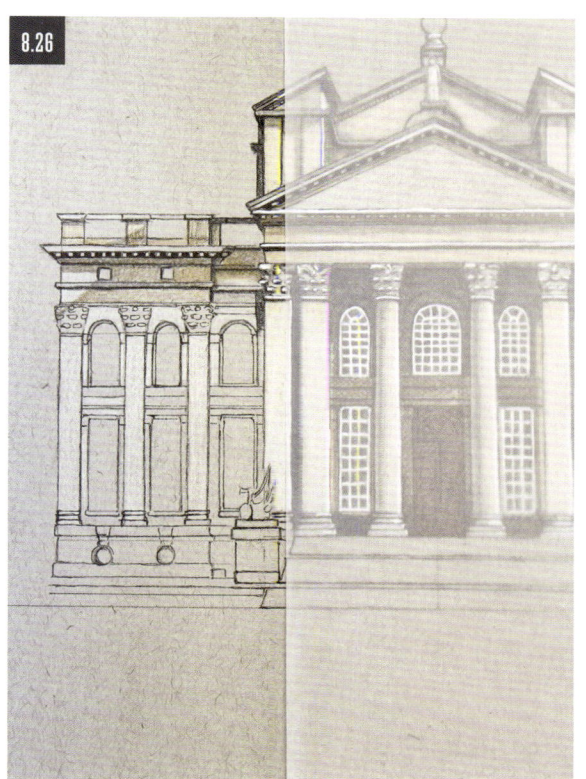

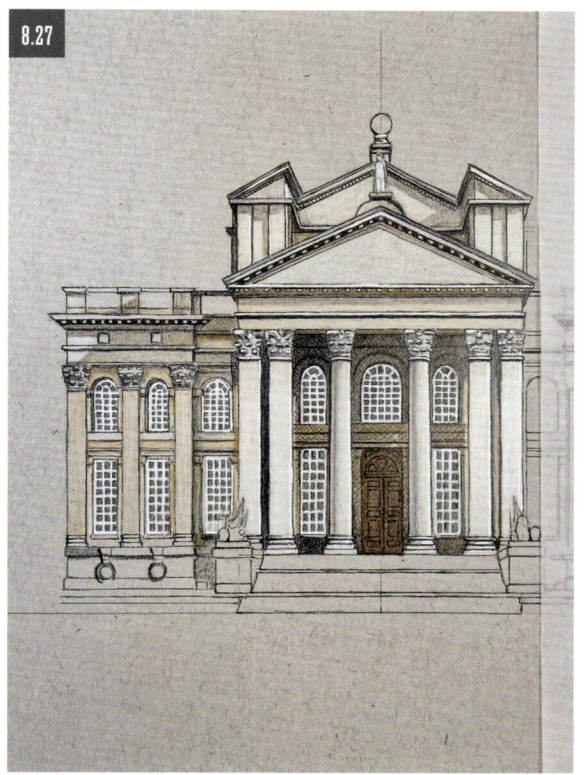

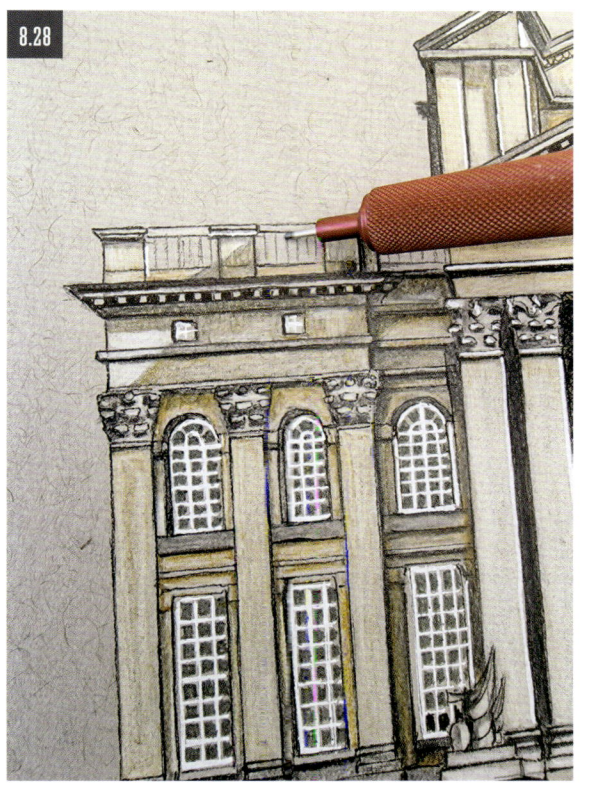

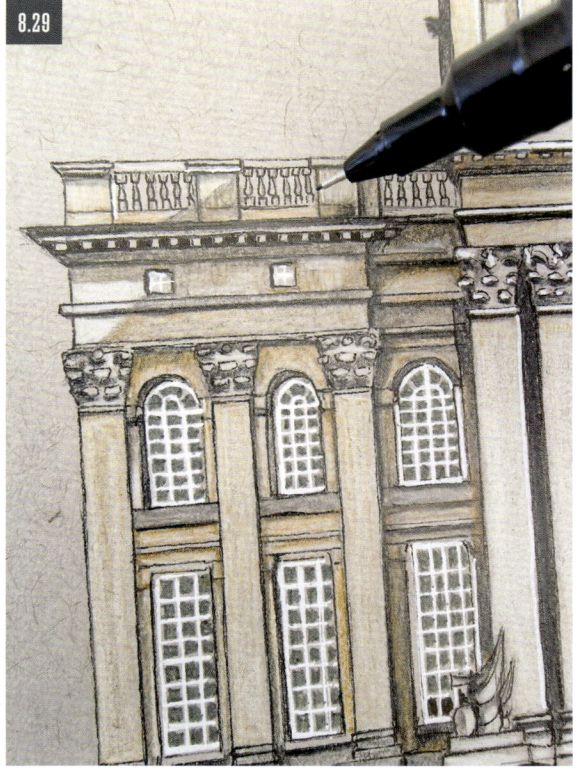

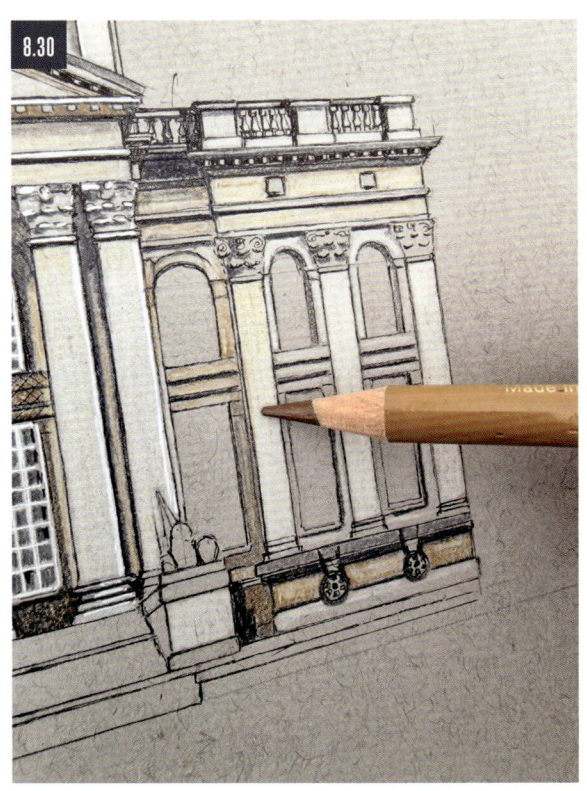

As before, begin with a layer of Ivory, but make the colour brighter and thicker where you can see the lightest parts where the sunlight hits. Now add a layer of Brown Ochre and blend everything together (**FIGURE 8.30**).

Use Payne's Grey to draw in the darkest shadows. As you continue working, periodically redefine everything with your fineliner to sharpen everything up. Regularly blend the colours together as well.

With a nice sharp pencil, carefully add in the all-important Warm Grey IV shadow, observing the line of the shadow as it moves down and across the building (**FIGURES 8.31** and **8.32**).

For the grand entrance staircase, first cover the whole area with Ivory and blend the colour, then draw fine black horizontal lines to indicate the steps (**FIGURE 8.33**). You may want to use a ruler to help you with this.

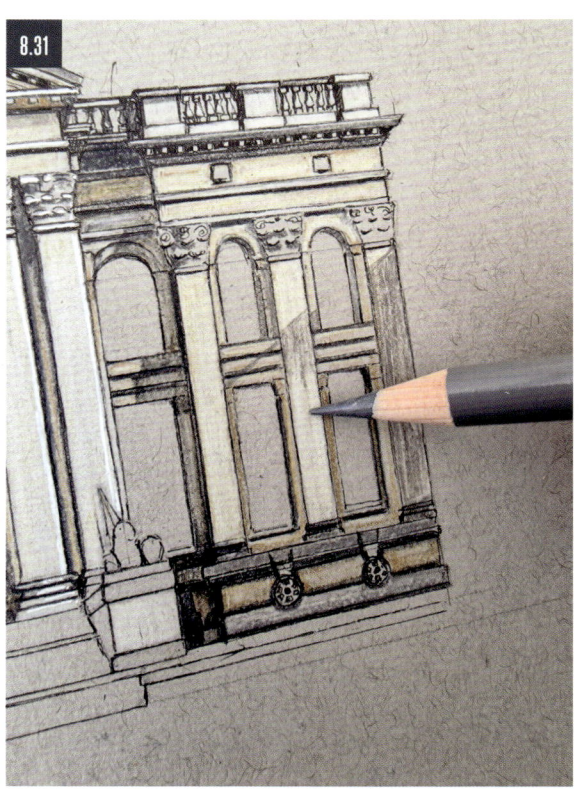

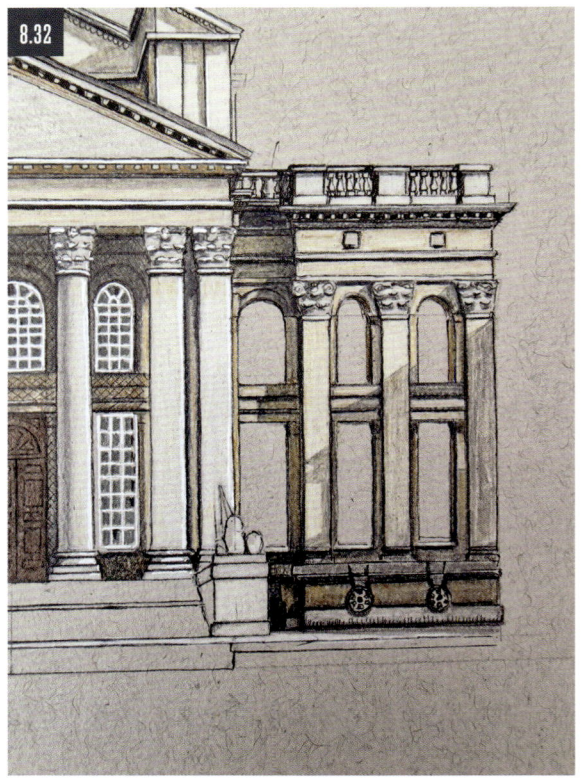

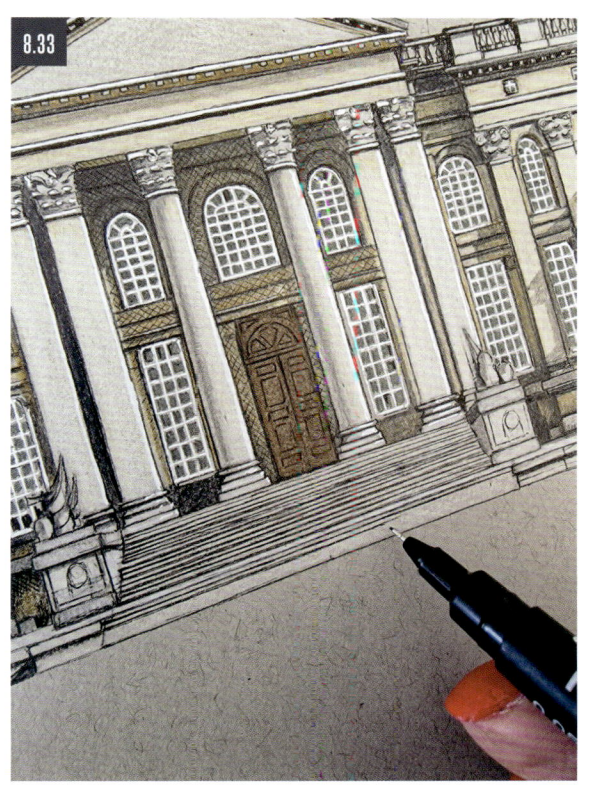

Step 4: ADD FINAL DETAILS

Roughly suggest the statues that are on top of the roof, making sure they are all about the same height. Then outline them in ink and colour them with Ivory, Warm Grey IV, and Payne's Grey.

For the sculpture design on the pediment, roughly suggest the shapes with pencil, and then go over them in ink (**FIGURES 8.34** and **8.35**). It really is hard to see these small details, so just a rough suggestion of what is there is good enough on this size drawing. Colour this in with the same colours used throughout the project, adding in any obvious shadows (**FIGURE 8.36, NEXT PAGE**).

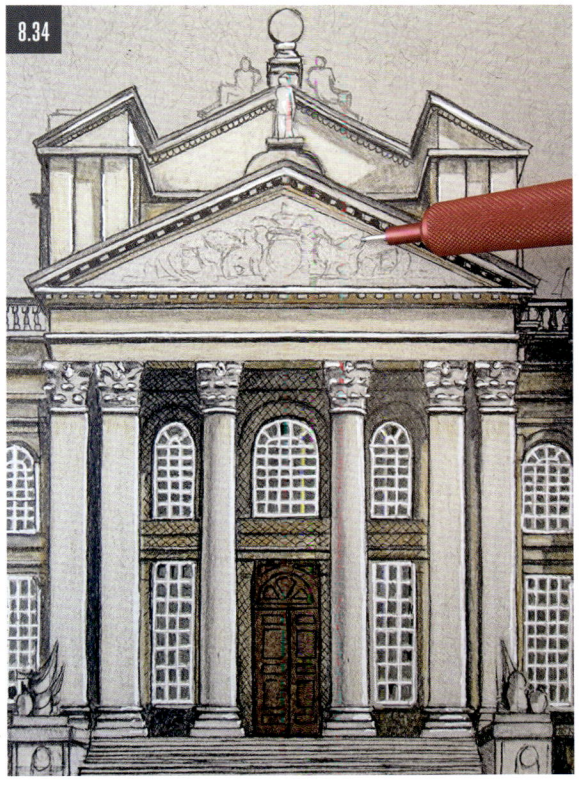

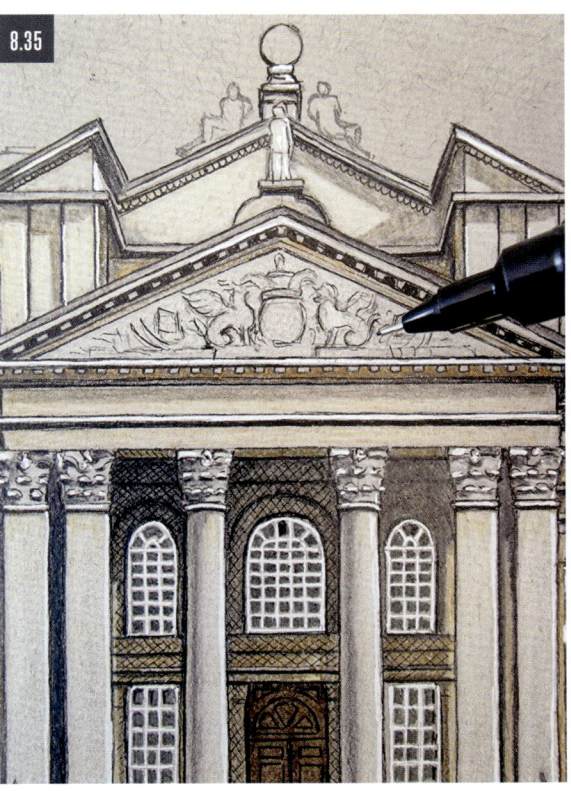

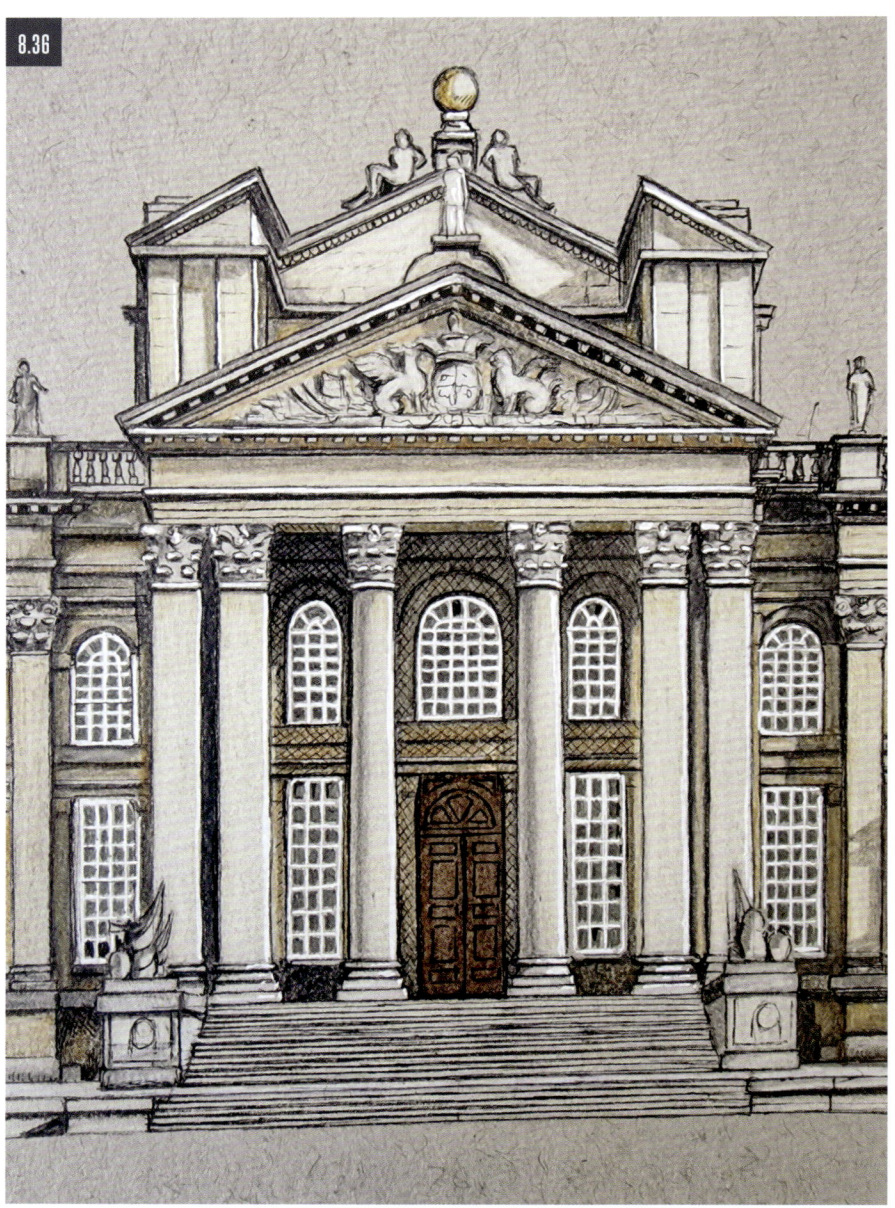

Finally, go over the whole artwork adding in the brightest highlights on the columns, statues, and pediment, and mark in any obvious lines of the brickwork. Check everything over and you are done (**FIGURE 8.37**)!

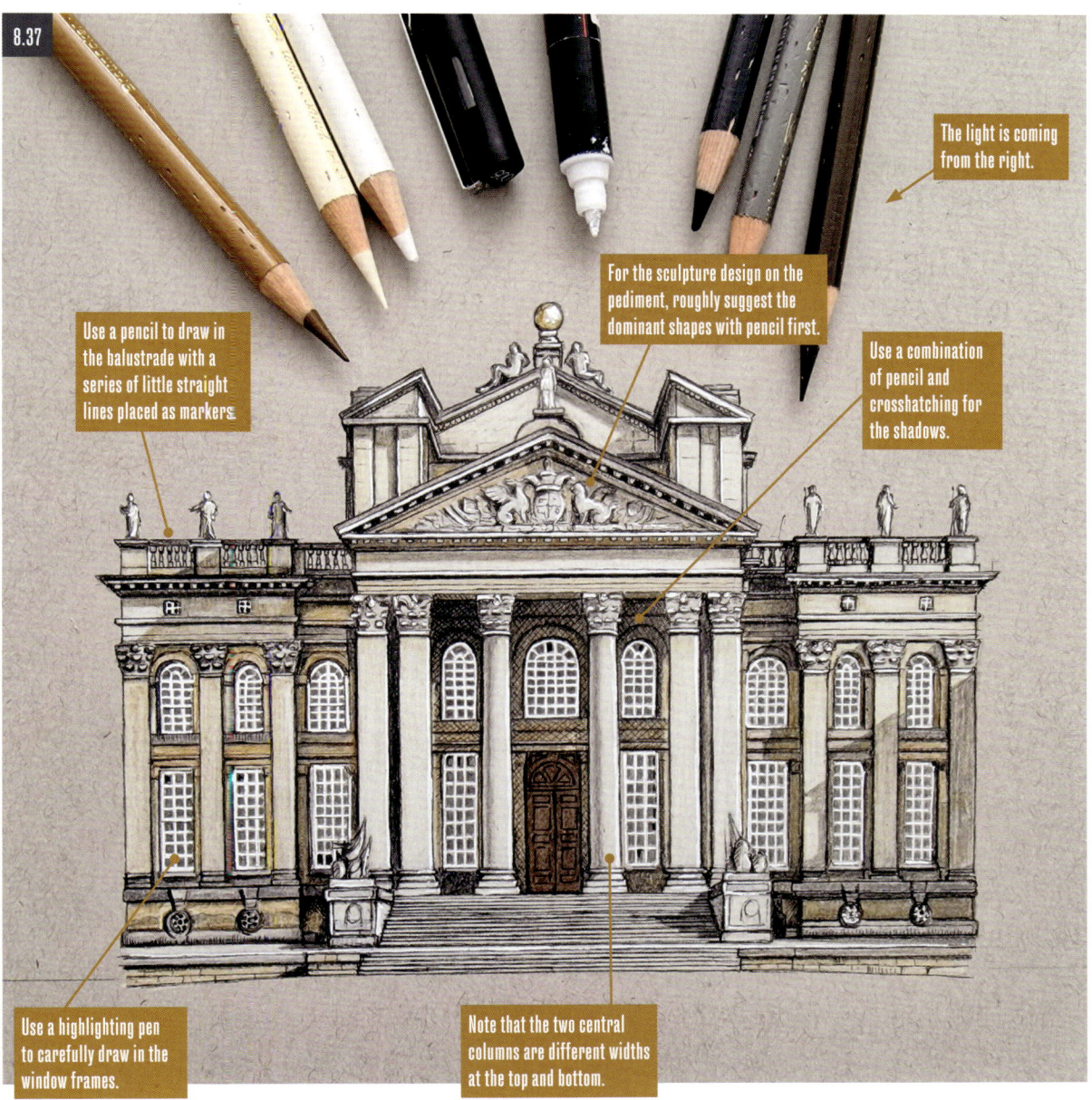

The light is coming from the right.

Use a pencil to draw in the balustrade with a series of little straight lines placed as markers.

For the sculpture design on the pediment, roughly suggest the dominant shapes with pencil first.

Use a combination of pencil and crosshatching for the shadows.

Use a highlighting pen to carefully draw in the window frames.

Note that the two central columns are different widths at the top and bottom.

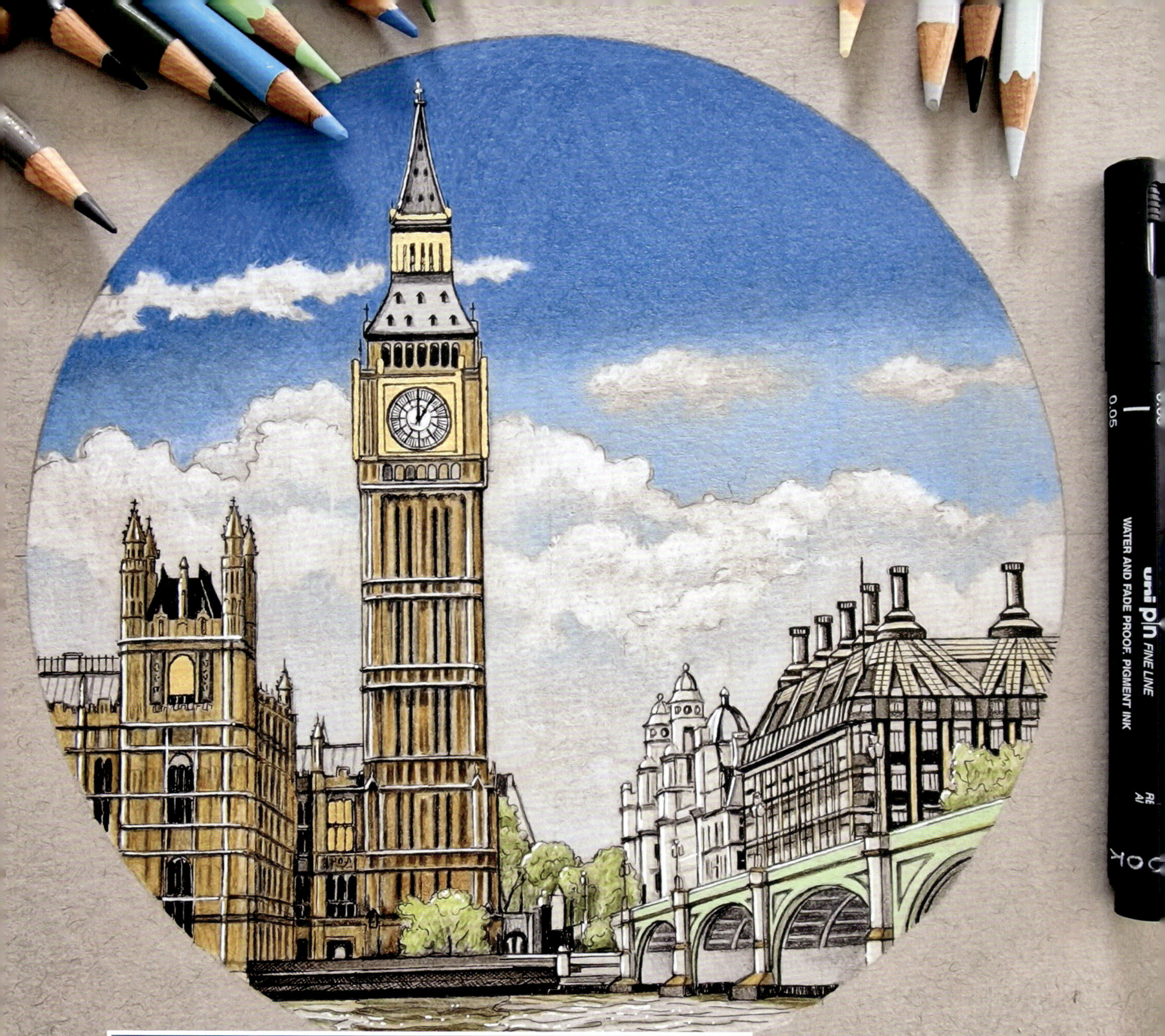

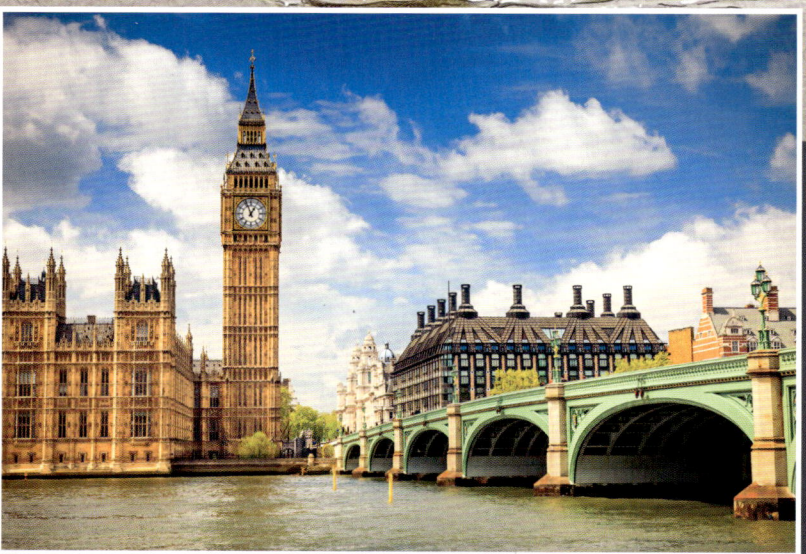

CHAPTER 9

Full-Colour Drawing with Gold

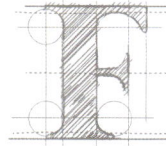

For the final project I have chosen a photo of the London skyline, with the iconic clock tower that is nick-named "Big Ben" as the central feature.

Big Ben is probably the world's most famous clock! It stands as a striking centrepiece and landmark on the River Thames waterfront and is backed by the historic Palace of Westminster, which is home to the Houses of Parliament. The official name for the 316-foot tower is the Elizabeth Tower, after the late Queen Elizabeth II. It is built in a neo-Gothic style and was completed in 1859. To the right of the tower are the green arches of Westminster Bridge.

I thought it would be fun to draw this brightly coloured, iconic scene in a circle, and then at the very end of the project, add some touches of gold using gold leaf or gold paint. This is abso-lutely optional. If you would prefer to complete the drawing in a landscape rectangle just like the photo and not use gold, feel free to do so. The choice is yours! The project will work as either a circle or a rectangle.

There is a nice reflection of the tower on the water as well, which we'll accentuate and bring to life as much as possible.

MATERIALS

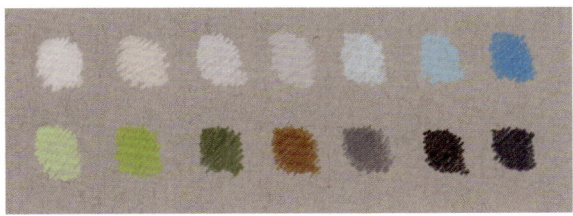

▶ Toned paper
▶ Sharp pencil
▶ Black 0.05mm fineliner pen
▶ Coloured pencils: White, Ivory, Silver Grey, Cold Grey I, Bluish Pale, Sky Blue, Medium Phthalo Blue, Light Green, May Green, Chromium Green Opaque, Brown Ochre, Warm Grey IV, Dark Sepia, Payne's Grey
▶ Ruler
▶ Compass or plate
▶ White highlighting pen
▶ Blender

Step 1: DRAW WITH PENCIL

Draw a circle on your toned paper with a diameter of between seven and eight inches. You can use a compass to do this if you have one, or you could trace around a tea plate or lid.

Then draw the exact same size circle onto your printout. The circle should be positioned so that Big Ben is slightly off-centre. This makes for a better-looking composition that is more pleasing to the eye.

I would suggest using some gridlines to help draw out this picture, as they will be beneficial in determining the exact positioning of the buildings within the circle (**FIGURE 9.1**). It will also help to get the lines of perspective just right.

Begin by drawing a vertical and horizonal line across the exact centre point of the circle on both your printout and drawing paper. If you used a compass to draw the circle, you may be able to see a tiny hole or mark where you placed the point of the compass in the middle. If so, you can use this point as a marker for drawing in the two lines across the centre point.

Now draw another evenly spaced vertical line on either side of the initial central line. Do this horizontally as well. You should now have three vertical lines and three horizontal lines that together create a grid.

Use these grid lines as your guide to draw out the main elements of the whole picture in pencil. As always, keep some paper under your hand to prevent smudging (**FIGURE 9.2**).

In each section, begin with the largest shapes first, then move on to adding the smaller shapes and details.

Some of the details are too small to draw with pencil, so you can add these details in the next step with your fineliner pen. Mark in where the lamps are on the bridge. Draw the square around the clock face, then slot the circular dial into the middle of it.

Once you have reached a stage where you have drawn in as much as possible, move onto the next step of going over the pencil lines in ink (**FIGURE 9.3**).

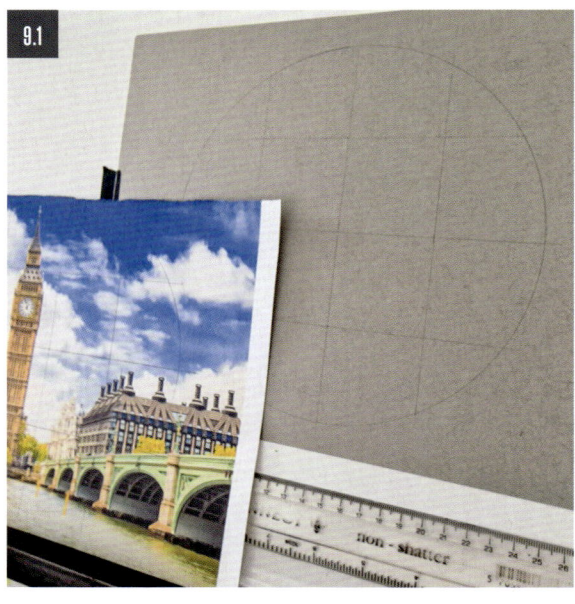

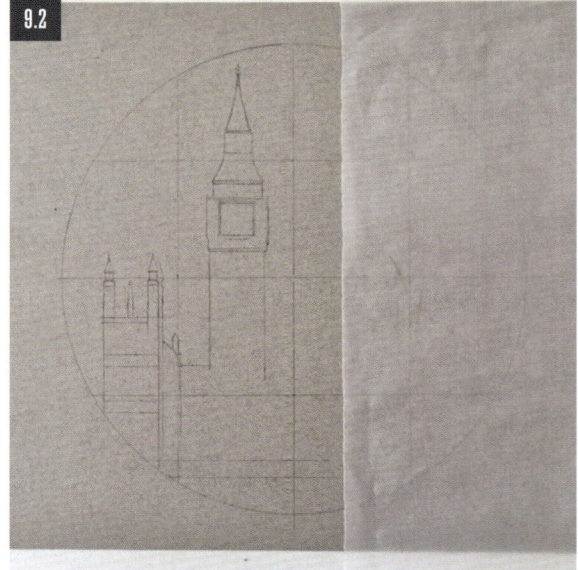

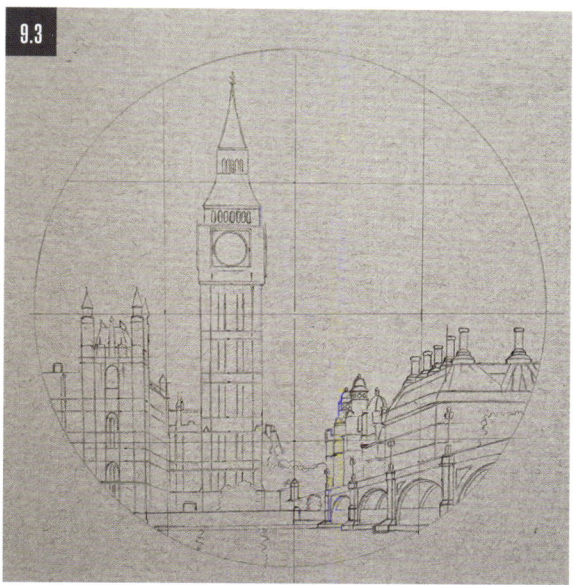

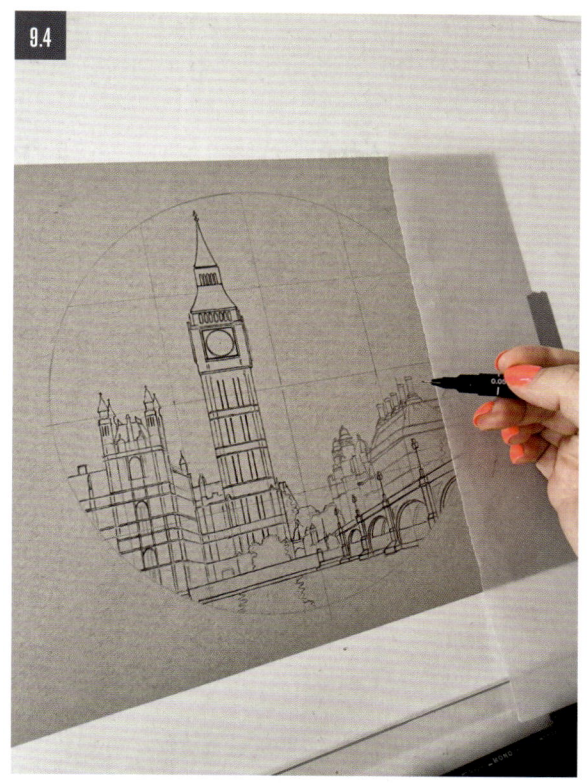

Step 2: COVER THE LINES WITH BLACK INK

Starting from the top, begin covering the pencil lines with ink. Work your way downwards from the top of Big Ben, then work from the left side all the way across to the right (**FIGURE 9.4**).

You will find that some of the details are too small to see clearly, so just draw what you can see and do easily. In step 3, when you add colour, you may find that it is hard to see any very small details drawn with ink once colour is applied, as this drawing is quite compact. Therefore, in these areas, once the colour is in place you can go back and redefine any of the ink lines that have become less visible, or even lost completely, under the pencil work.

For the trees, roughly draw a wobbly outline to show their approximate position.

When it comes to the river water, draw two rough, squiggly lines vertically to show the approximate position of the tower reflection on the water's surface. Then draw in some small and wavy waterlike

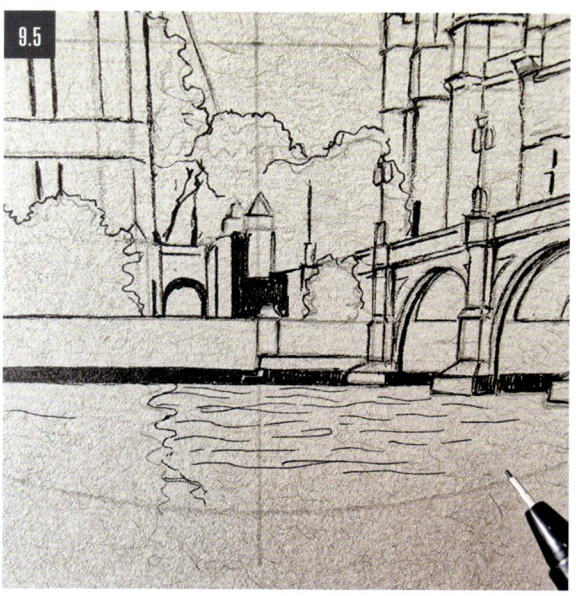

lines to suggest the look and motion of the water (**FIGURE 9.5**). We'll work on the water in more detail later.

Keep going until all the pencil lines are covered. You don't need to cover the pencil line that marks the circle, as the colour from the pencil work in the next step will naturally define this outline.

Finally, block in the very darkest areas, including the tiny Gothic windows (**FIGURE 9.6**).

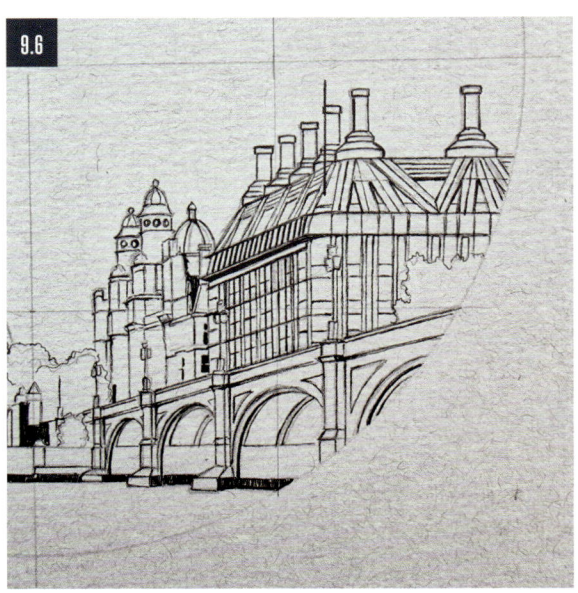

Before you go on to start the colour work, lightly sketch in some puffy cloud shapes in the background using just pencil (**FIGURE 9.7**). Don't ink it in yet, as you may want to adjust the shape later on as the drawing develops.

Step 3: ADD COLOUR

Before we start, please note that in the final stages of the drawing, we will add some gold leaf or gold paint to some of the windows and some small areas of the clock tower. Take a look at the finished drawing on page 195 to get an idea of which areas will be gold so that you can leave these areas blank during the colour process.

We will also add gold to two of the gothic windows at the end. I do sometimes find it easier to make some of these decisions at the end when the picture is finished and I can see the overall look of the work.

Now let's get started with the colour work!

Take a good look at the reference photo—there aren't a great deal of light and shadow contrasts. However, you can see that the light source is coming from the left, as there are lighter areas on the left side of the tower and some small shadows cast to the right.

You can utilise these small observations in the drawing to improve the overall depth of the picture by making the left side of the building slightly lighter than the right.

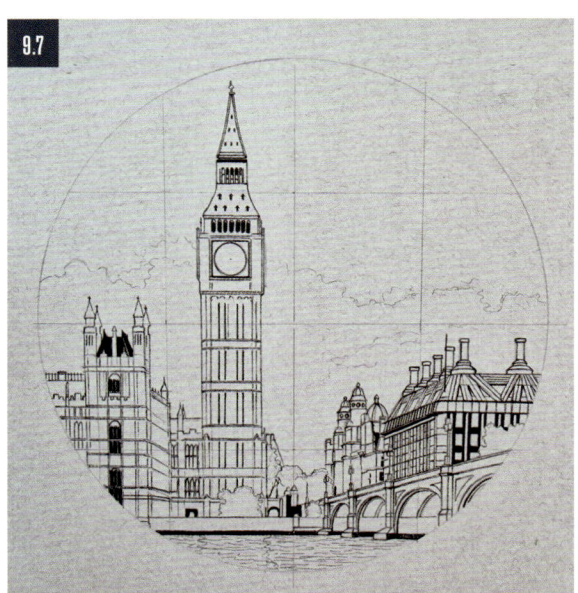

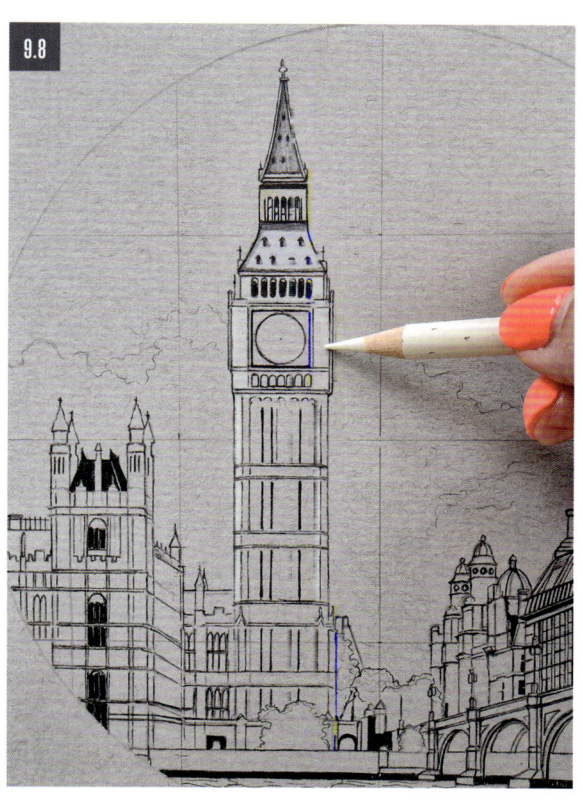

Big Ben

Start at the top of the tower and line the very edge with white. Then use Cold Grey I to colour the grey areas. Next, layer Payne's Grey over the top to create the darker grey areas. Gently rub out any grid pencil lines and pencil work from the initial drawing as you go along.

Now take an Ivory pencil and colour the lightest area of the tower (**FIGURE 9.8**). Apply a few layers to make the colour opaque. Then go over the rest of the tower with a lighter layer of Ivory. Leave the areas that are much darker, like the areas down the left side, free of Ivory.

Next, use Brown Ochre to lightly colour over the Ivory. Deepen the colour by adding more layers where the colour is darker (**FIGURES 9.9** and **9.10**).

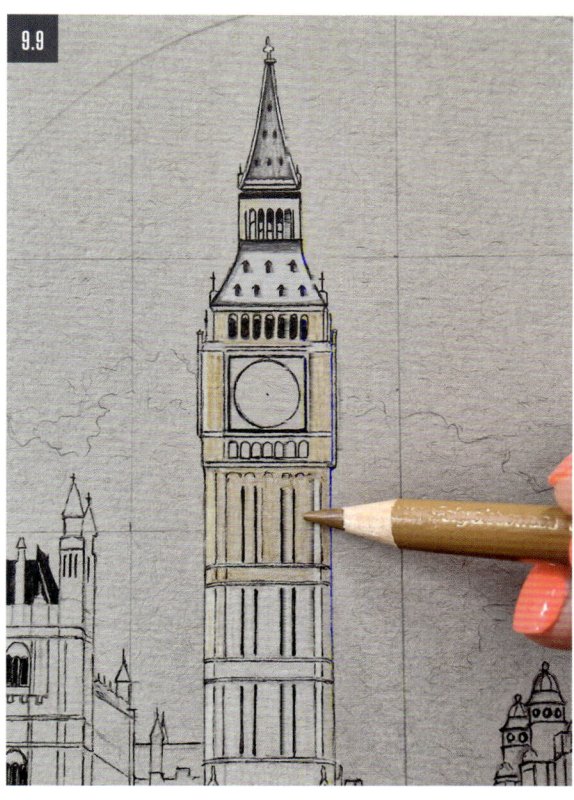

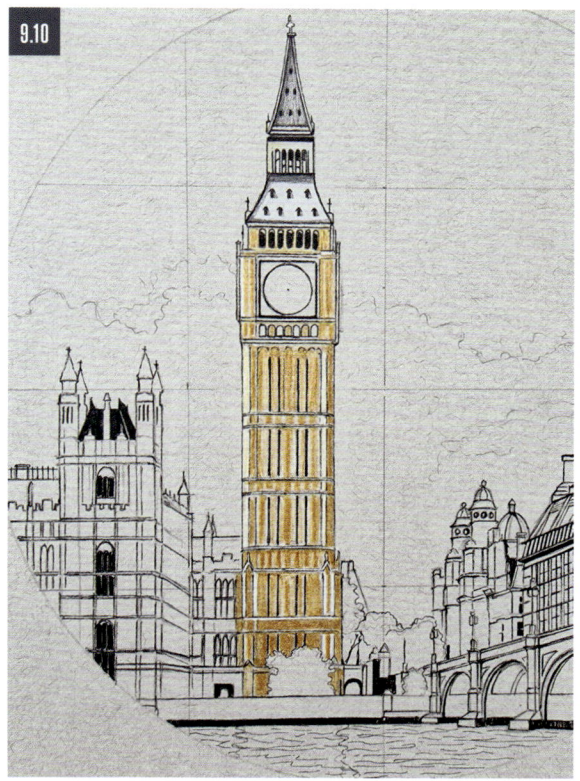

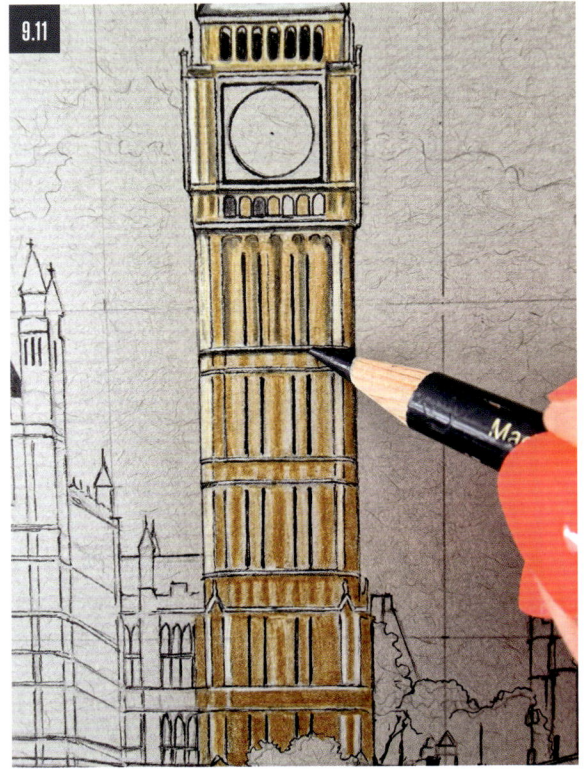

9.11

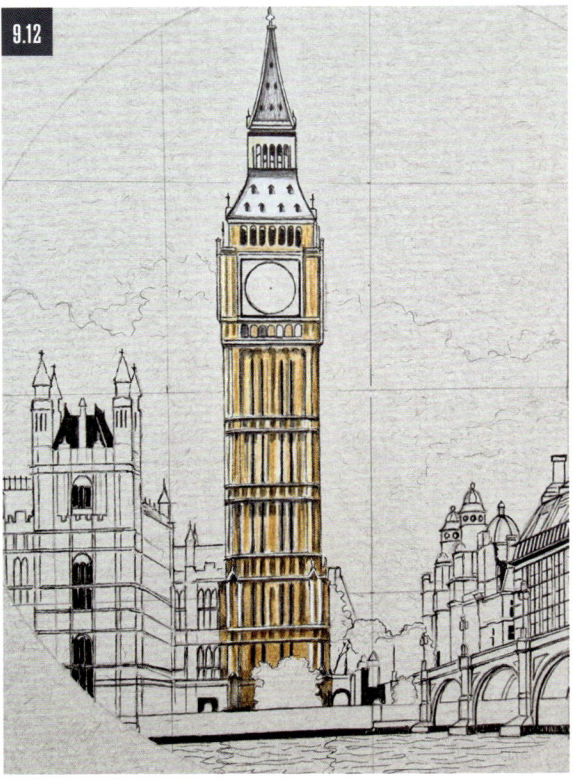

9.12

Once this is done, use a Payne's Grey pencil to add the darkest tones. Work from the top all the way to the bottom (**FIGURES 9.11** and **9.12**). Use the reference photo to observe the darkest areas under the ledges and amongst the carving in the stone on the ornate details.

Now move on to the left side of the building, doing the exact same thing you did on the tower with the exact same colours. Begin by using the Ivory pencil to colour the lightest areas with opaque colour, then cover the whole area with a light layer of the same Ivory (**FIGURE 9.13**).

As before, go over this with a layer of Brown Ochre (**FIGURE 9.14**). You may find that you notice more details that you haven't drawn in yet—I certainly did! You can either add these in as you notice them, using a fineliner on top of the pencil work, or draw them in later as the drawing progresses. To a degree, there are no hard and fast rules with a drawing like this. Use your creativity to do what looks and feels right for you. Adjustments can be made as you go along!

Blend all the colours together, making sure that your blender is clean first so it doesn't muddy the colours.

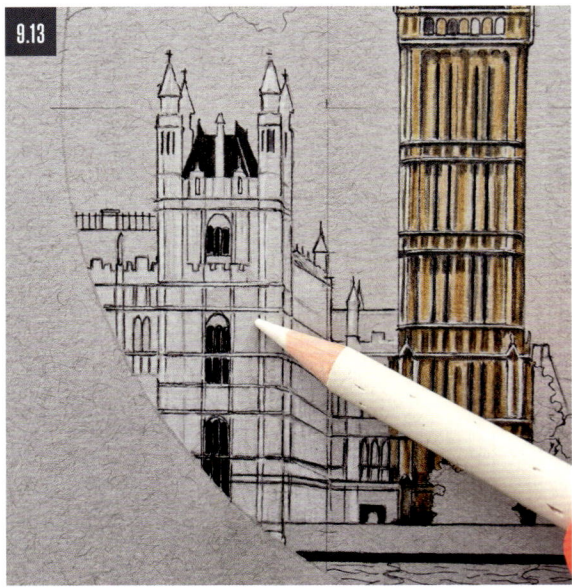

9.13

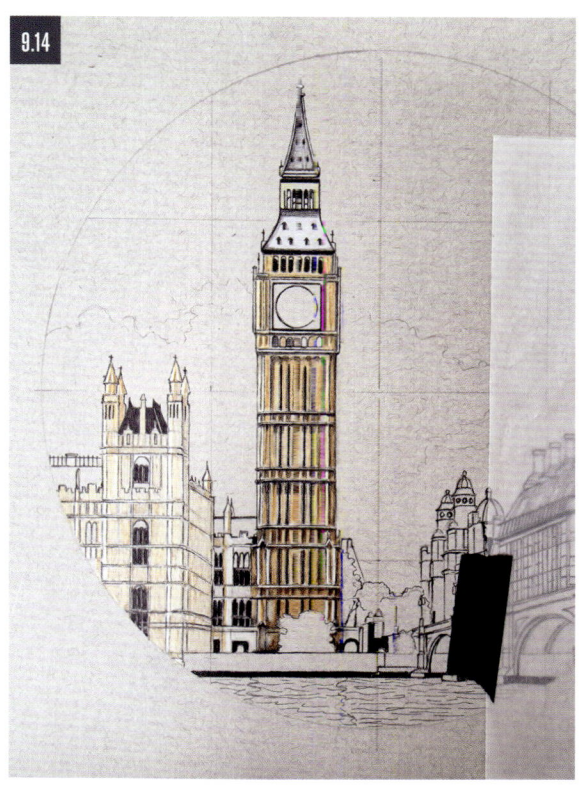

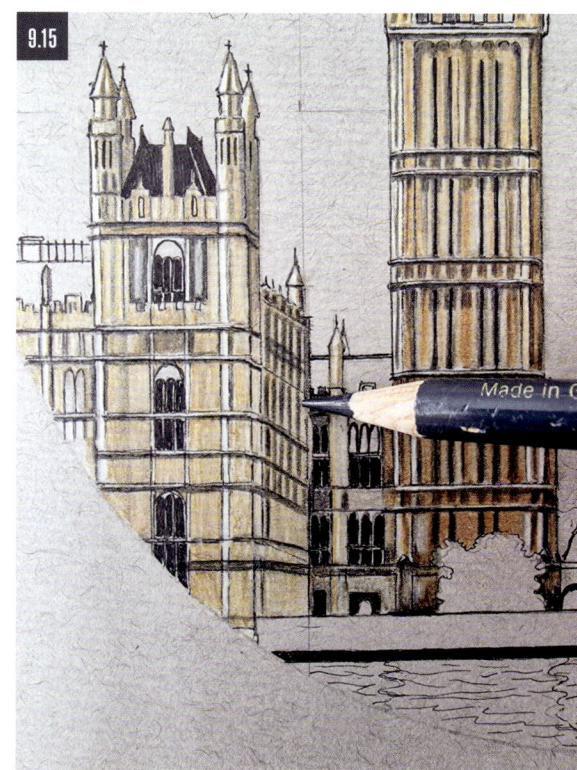

Next, use Payne's Grey once again to add in the darker areas. Vary the depth of colour according to how dark the tones are in the photo. Simply add more layers to increase the depth of the tone.

Use the same colour to draw in the vertical lines on the side of the building where it goes around to meet the tower (**FIGURE 9.15**).

Once that is done, block in the pale grey on the rooftops and add the lines running down them.

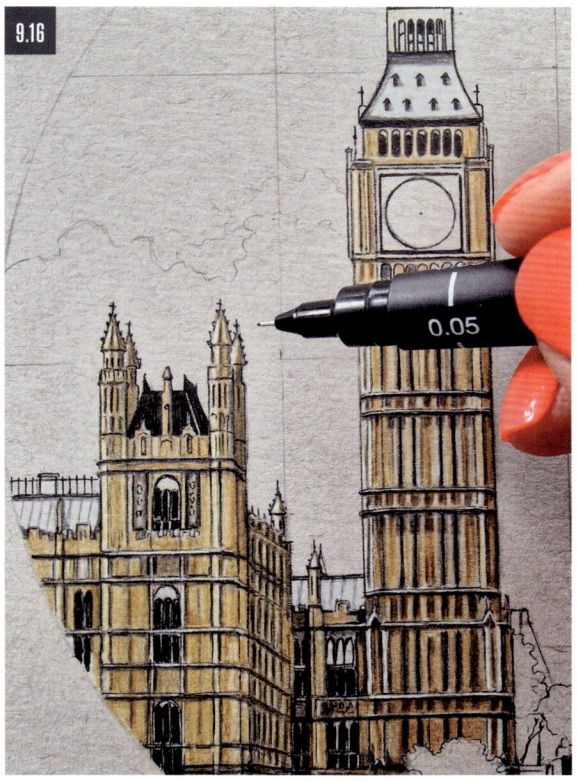

To finish this section, use your fineliner to add in the tiny Gothic details on top of the turrets and any other tiny details you can see (**FIGURE 9.16**). Also use the pen to redefine your ink lines where they have become faded by pencil. I always find that when I do this, everything comes into focus and the drawing starts to come alive and have some impact! It is an important step.

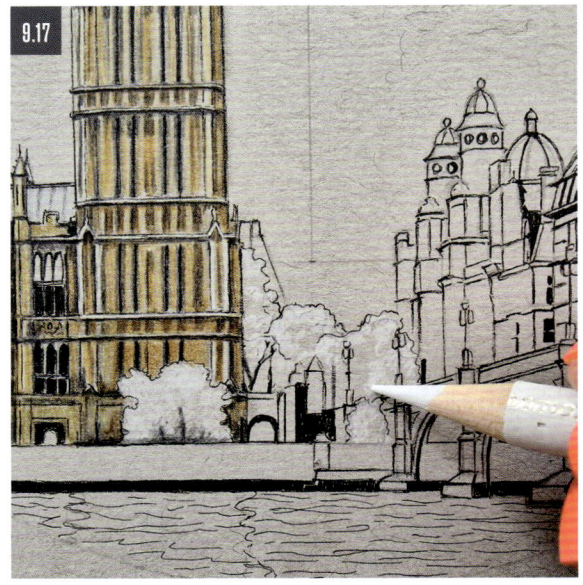

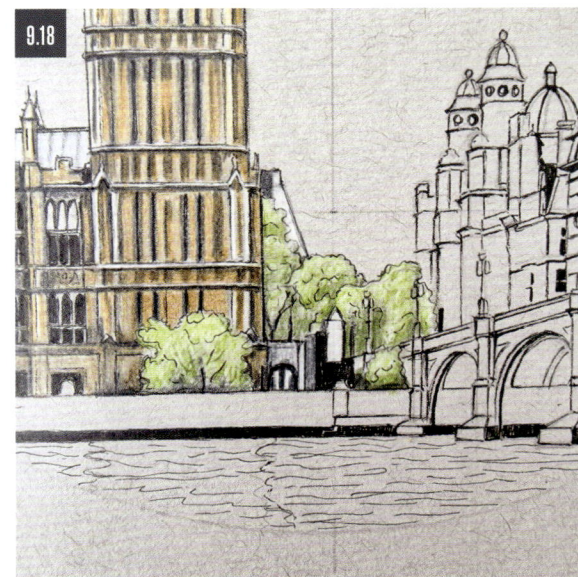

Trees

Go over the tops and lightest areas of the trees with a white pencil, using small circular movements (**FIGURE 9.17**). Cover this with a layer of Ivory, and then introduce some light green (May Green) on top with the same circular movements.

Next, use Chromium Green Opaque to colour the darker areas within the trees. Again, use small circular movements. Follow this by using your fineliner to redefine the area, add some random squiggly lines to describe the shapes within the trees, and add in a few branches to help create the tree effect.

Fill in all the other remaining small shapes around the trees that are still colour-free so that this section is complete (**FIGURE 9.18**).

The Final Buildings and the Bridge

Now move on to the cream-coloured building on the right side of the photo. First, add a quick layer of white on the parts of the building where the light source hits it directly. These areas are slightly lighter. Then cover the remaining parts of the

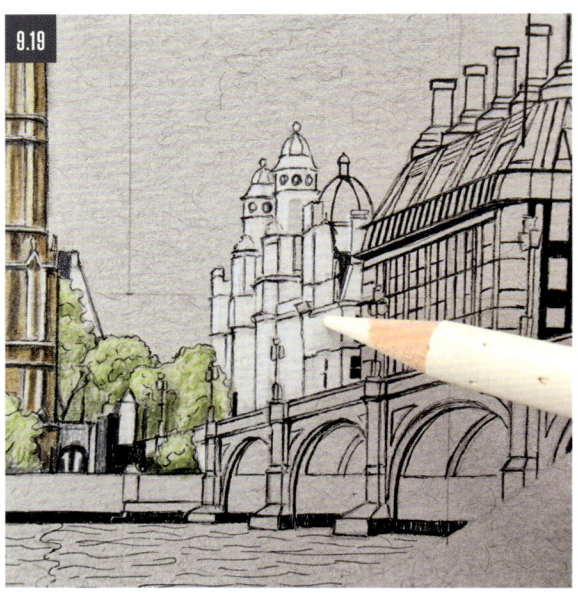

building with Ivory (**FIGURE 9.19**). Now take a Warm Grey IV pencil to draw in the mid-tone colours and shapes. Colour the small dome with Cold Grey IV on the left side where it is the lightest, and then use Payne's Grey to colour the shadows.

Use your fineliner to redefine everything you have just worked on.

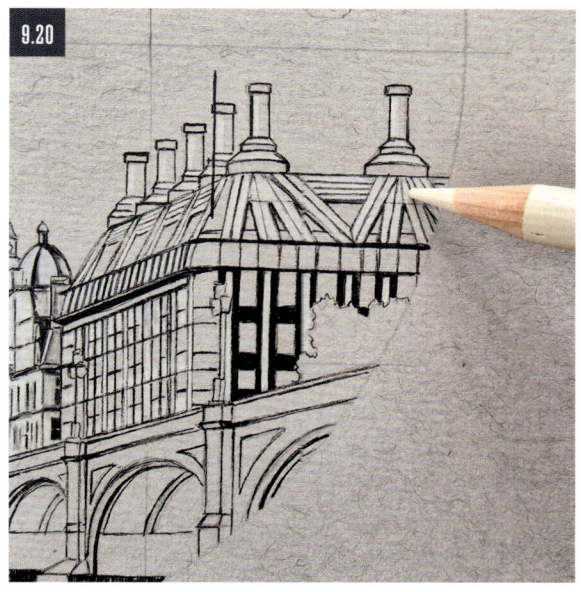

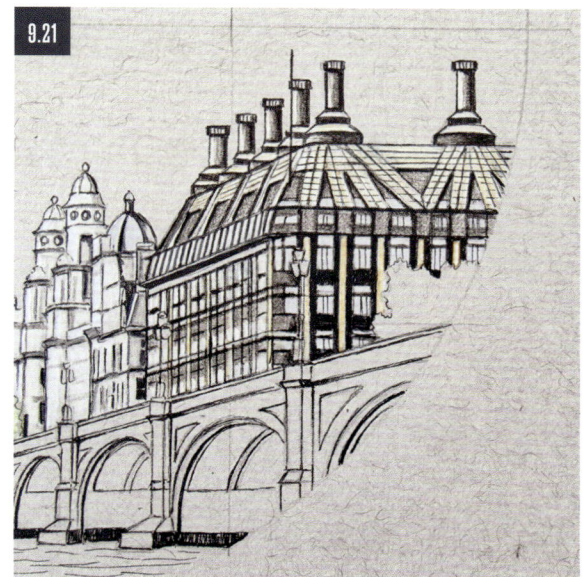

Now move on to the last building on the right with its stacked chimneys. Start by colouring the lightest areas of the building with Ivory (**FIGURE 9.20**). Then use Brown Ochre to go over any of these areas with a slightly warm yellow tone. Next, use Cold Grey I to fill in the light-coloured windows.

Take a Dark Sepia pencil and add in the darkest lines and areas (**FIGURE 9.21**). There are many lines on this building that are very close together, making it quite complicated. Mark in what you can; no one will notice if it isn't perfect!

Once the pencil work is complete here, use a fineliner directly on top of the pencil to draw in the smaller details like the lines on the windows and patterns on the roof.

Now draw in the last tree in the exact same way as the others.

Next, we'll move on to the bridge. The first step is to colour the fronts of the columns with Ivory where the light hits, then the sides that are in shadow with Warm Grey IV.

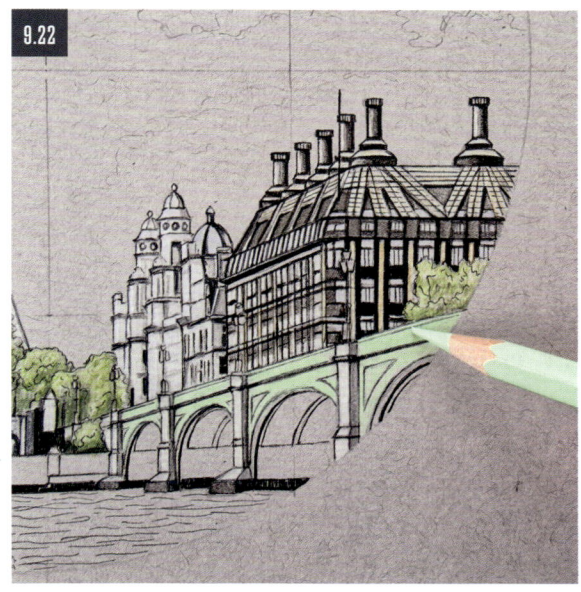

Then cover the green part of the bridge with a base layer of Ivory, followed by a good topcoat of Light Green (**FIGURE 9.22**). Darken the green part of the bridge that is under the arches and in shadow with a layer of Warm Grey IV on top.

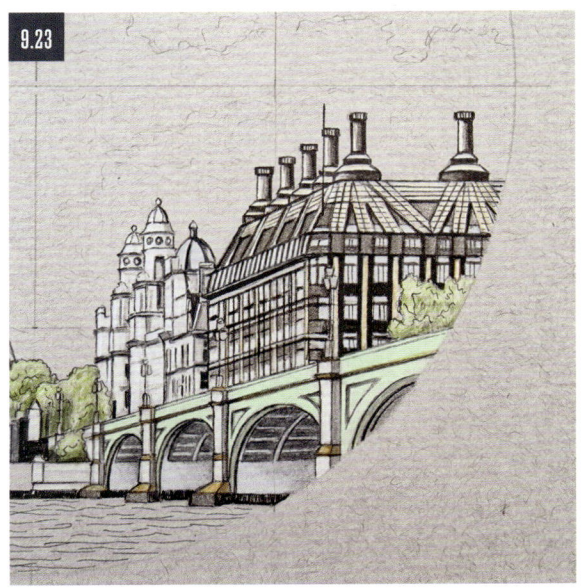

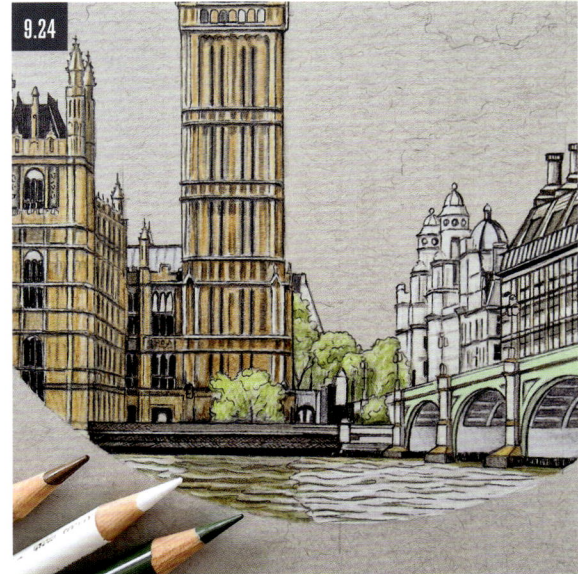

Now let's look at the darker area within the arches. Begin by colouring the lightest areas with Cold Grey I, and then cover the darker areas with Payne's Grey. Once this is done, use Payne's Grey to gently shade over the top of it all to make the area furthest inside the arches darker. Use your blender to gently blend the colours so the gradation is seamless.

Colour the golden-brown parts of the bridge with Brown Ochre, and then redefine everything with your fineliner (**FIGURE 9.23**).

Finally, colour the river wall with a combination of Ivory and Sepia, then crosshatch on top of this where the colour is darker.

River Water

Now let's look at the river water (**FIGURE 9.24**). Water tends to be the colour of the sky, with the colours from any surrounding buildings or trees also reflected onto the water's surface.

The river here is pale in colour, just like the white clouds, with the reflection of Big Ben going across it and some smaller reflections around the edge of the bridge from the arches.

So, for the paler colour, use white and create wave-like marks between the black fine lines that are already in place. Then for the reflections, use a combination of Brown Ochre, Chromium Green Opaque, and a small amount of Sepia. Build the colours in layers using the same wave-like motions you used for the white, and then blend them all together to create a nice, seamless finish.

Sky

Once this water done its time to tackle the sky! There are some lovely white puffy clouds and a brilliant blue sky in the reference photo for inspiration, but you don't have to copy it all exactly. I would suggest creating your own version of the sky and having some fun by working freestyle.

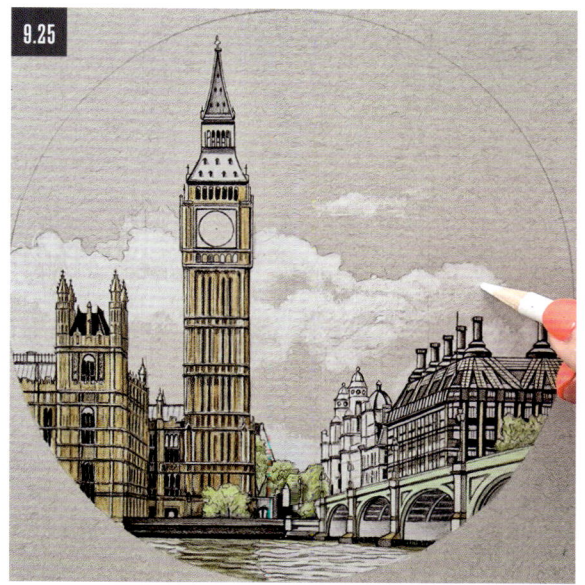

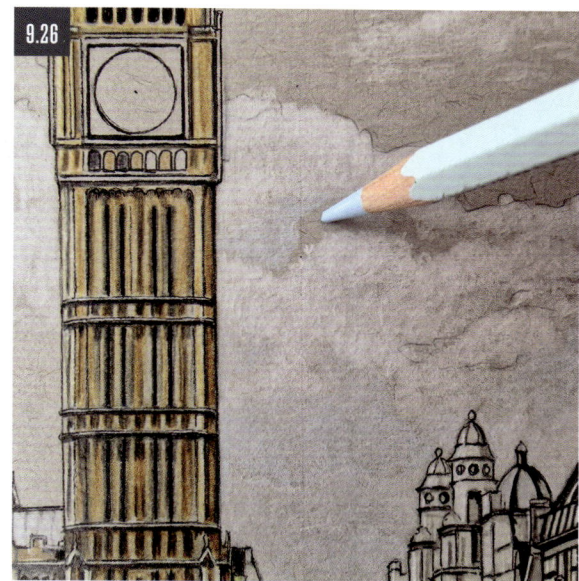

I'll walk you through my version of the sky. After deciding where the whitest, puffy clouds are going to be, take a white pencil and begin adding them (**FIGURE 9.25**). Use small circular movements to help create the movement within the clouds. To make the white more opaque, use firm circular movements. Notice how at the tops of the clouds the white colour is denser and more opaque, so apply this technique there. Vary the density of white layers to replicate real clouds.

Follow the cloud patterns within the photo as little or as much that you want. Just use it as an inspirational guide.

Once the main white cloud shapes are all in place, introduce some Silver Grey. This colour is a very subtle shade of off-white. Use it to lightly fill in the very lowest areas of the sky and to go around the white clouds. Notice how the colour of the sky around the horizon area is softer and hazier.

Next, take Bluish Pale and begin adding some very pale blue around the clouds (**FIGURE 9.26**). The beauty of drawing clouds is that you can literally make them up as you go along!

Once the lower half of the sky is covered in pencil, take a Middle Phthalo Blue pencil and begin colouring the bright-blue sky at the top of the circle. Use circular movements to create a deep blue colour. The idea is that the white puffy clouds will stand out clearly and with impact against the brilliant, deep blue of the sky.

As you are working on the top area, bear in mind that you will graduate the blue colour as you move downwards into the next lighter shade of blue. To graduate the colour, use lighter layers as you move towards the area that is to graduate into the next shade of blue, which will be Sky Blue. Use your blender to push the colour into the paper's surface. Make sure the blender is clean!

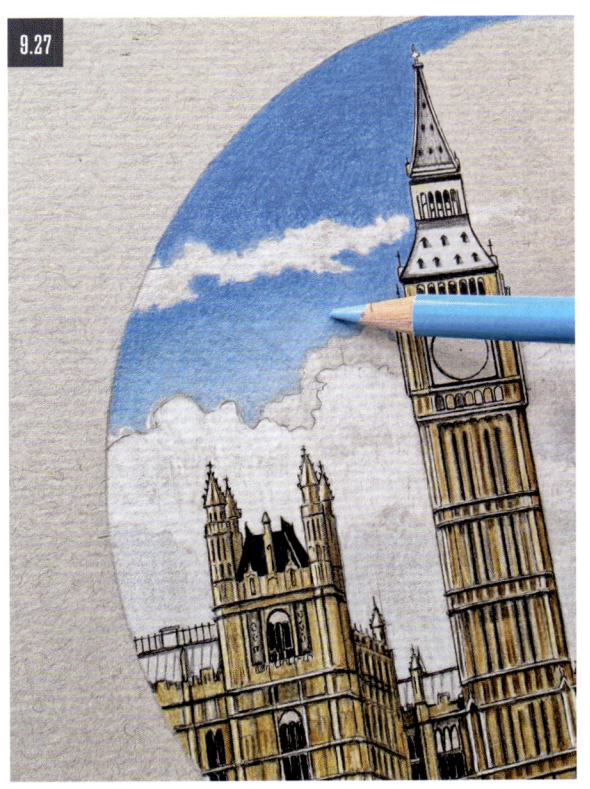

9.27

Now it is time to introduce the Sky Blue colour. This blue is slightly lighter than the first blue we used at the top. Use it in the mid-section of the picture and blend and graduate it up into the darker blue colour above (**FIGURE 9.27**). To do this, crosshatch the two colours over each other in light strokes, blending regularly until the colours are seamlessly blended into each other.

Once the left side of the sky is complete, move on to the right and do the exact same thing again (**FIGURE 9.28**). Sharpen your pencils regularly, as they wear down quickly when covering large areas and a sharp point will give you more control over how the colour goes down.

Aim to match up the graduated line where the two blues meet in a soft horizontal line across the picture.

Once the main blue areas are finished, use Sky Blue to softly add some more mid-blue amongst the clouds (**FIGURE 9.29**).

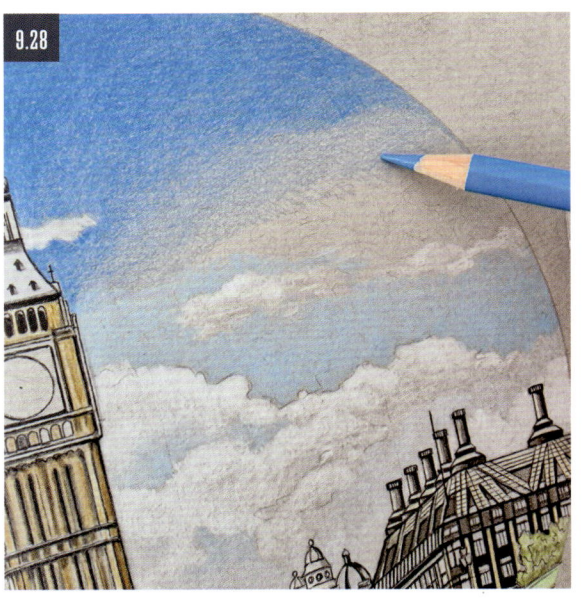

9.28

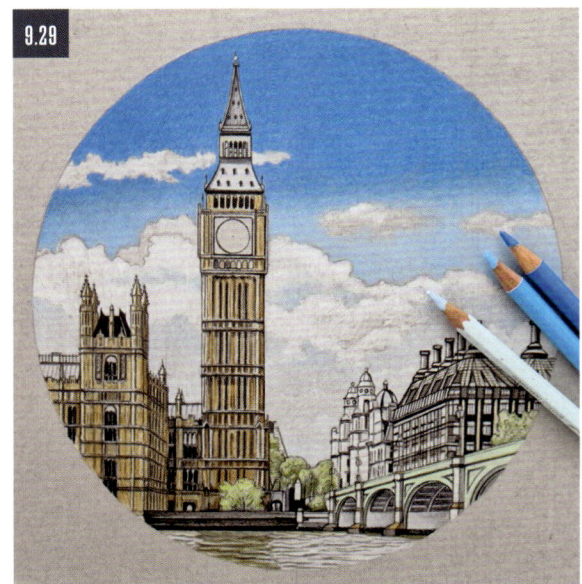

9.29

Clock Face

The next step is to work on Big Ben's clock face. I have left this until last because, for me, a detail like this is the icing on the cake! First, white out the whole circle of the clockface so it is opaque white. Mark in the details on the clock in pencil first, then go over them in black ink with your fineliner (**FIGURE 9.30**). Remember, you can erase ink that is on top of pencil if you make a mistake!

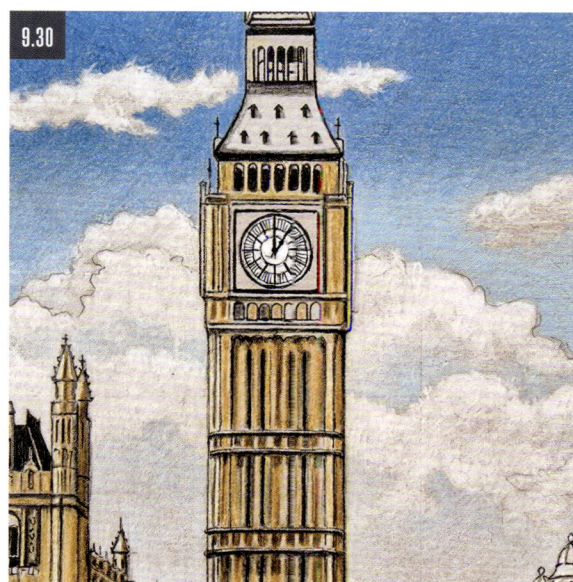

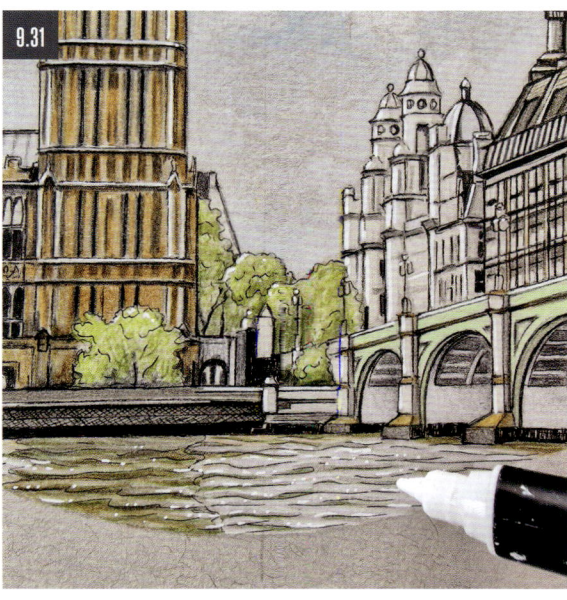

Step 4: ADD FINAL DETAILS

Once this is done, use your white highlighting pen to highlight where the light hits the buildings. Take a good look at your reference photo to help you do this.

Use fine, light lines to do this slowly and carefully, and don't over-highlight. Less is more in this case. Finally, add some sparkles to the river water by adding tiny, random dots and lines along the top of your wavy ink lines (**FIGURE 9.31**).

Now sit back and admire your work (**FIGURE 9.32**)! Check everything over and redefine with your fineliner, if necessary.

The final step is the option to add some gold if you would like to.

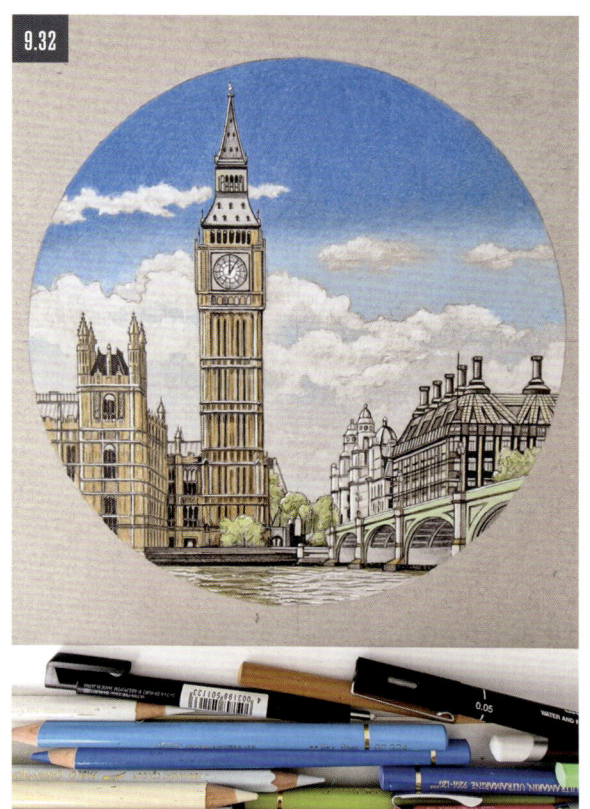

GILDING

Let's talk about gilding. If you would like to go a step further and add something really special to your finished drawing, you can add some gold leaf or gold paint. This works well if added to the sky or specific details within the picture to add a touch of sophisticated bling!

When observing buildings, you will often find that gold is added to architectural details, such as the tops of columns or crests above doors. Sometimes even whole domes are golden.

You can introduce this decorative golden element to your pictures with relative ease either by using some readily available gold paint or by going a step further and applying some gold leaf using the gilding process.

Gilding is the beautifying technique of applying thin metal sheets of gold to a surface. This process has been used in various ways by artisans for thousands of years to add a decorative, bright, and beautiful appearance to different surfaces, including wood, metal, and paper. In this case, of course, it will be paper.

To do this you will need to invest in a few gilding materials (**FIGURE 9.33**). You can buy gold leaf in

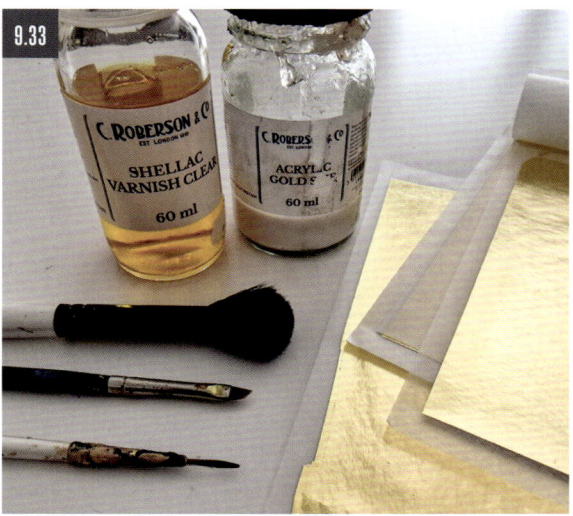

sheets that are either faux gold or real gold. The real gold sheets are quite expensive to buy and use, especially if you are covering a large area.

Faux gold works exceptionally well and is very bright and shiny. It is much more cost effective for larger areas and I think it works just as well as real gold.

For this project I have used faux gold. You will also need to paint the finished gilded area with a layer of protective shellac at the end to prevent it from tarnishing over time. I find that one pack of gold sheets plus the acrylic gold size (adhesive) and shellac lasts me a long time, so after the initial outlay, it's not that pricey, as the products go a long way.

If gilding is not for you, maybe you would like to try an alternative and use some gold paint to apply to the same areas or to create a golden sky. There are many different readymade liquid gold paints available to buy. My favourite are the ones made by Roberson. They come in lots of different metal colours and there are many different shades of gold to choose from. They are also water soluble, so they wash out of your paint brushes easily.

GILDING BIG BEN

You have probably already observed the gold embellishments on the top of Big Ben's tower. These are the areas that we will gild with some gold leaf. We will also apply a small amount of gold to two of the Gothic-shaped windows. Below is the list of materials you will need.

Materials

- ▶ Gold leaf sheets
- ▶ Acrylic gold size (glue)
- ▶ A clean, soft brush (to brush away excess gold)
- ▶ Two fine paint brushes (one to paint on the acrylic gold size and one for the shellac varnish)
- ▶ Shellac varnish (you will need white spirit to clean the brush when you are done)

Drawing and Illustrating Architecture

Step 1: Paint with Acrylic Gold Size

The first step is to paint on the acrylic gold size (**FIGURE 9.34**). This sticky liquid is basically a glue that the gold leaf will adhere to. Start at the top of Big Ben and carefully paint the first area on the clock tower to be gilded. The liquid is quite clear when it is painted on and can be difficult to see, so to make sure you are covering the area properly, hold the area up to the light. You should be able to see the sheen of the liquid and any parts you have missed.

Carefully go around the clock face and the other details. I chose to use gold on two of the windows.

Once this is done, check your watch and note the time. You need to wait fifteen to twenty minutes for the liquid to become dry and tacky. Whilst you are waiting, carry on painting the next areas. Note down the time after each area so you know when it's time to apply the gold leaf.

Finally, move on to the windows. You can add gold to as many windows as you like; it's up to you to decide how you would like it to look.

Step 2: Lay Down the Gold Leaf

Once the time is up, check that the painted area has become dry and tacky. Then take a sheet of gold leaf and place it gold-side down onto the glued area (**FIGURE 9.35**). Gently rub over the back of the sheet with your finger to make sure it has adhered to the surface properly, then pull the gold leaf sheet back to reveal the gold!

Carry on repeating these steps until each area is covered in the shiny gold leaf.

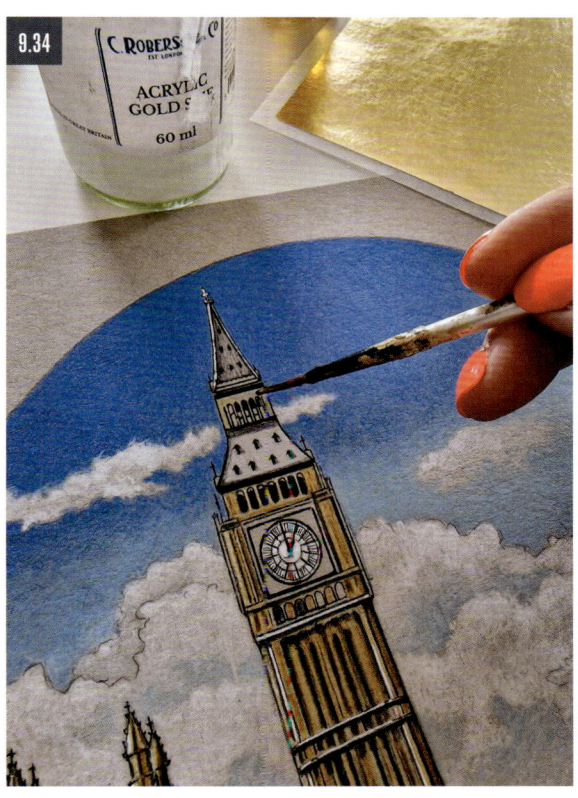

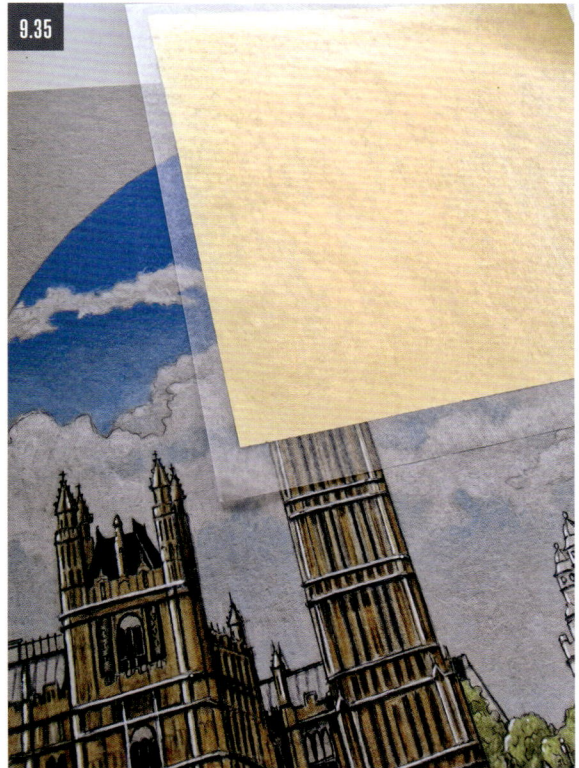

Step 3: Brush Away the Excess

Once each area is finished, take a soft brush and gently brush away the excess gold leaf (**FIGURE 9.36**).

If you have missed any areas, try patting some more gold leaf down onto the gap. If this doesn't work and the gold doesn't stick, carefully paint a dab of the glue into the gap, wait the fifteen to twenty minutes for it to become tacky, and then reapply the gold leaf sheet and brush away the excess.

> ➤ Shake any excess gold off the page into a tub to keep it for future projects.

If the gold leaf has gone over the edges, which often happens, you can usually tidy it up by scraping it back with a craft knife.

Use your fineliner around the edges of the gold to redefine where necessary and tidy everything up.

Step 4: Paint with Shellac Varnish

Once you're happy with how things look, use a fine brush to carefully paint over the gold leaf with a layer of the protective shellac varnish. Allow the shellac to dry, and that's it (**FIGURE 9.37**)!

This type of gilding is actually a simple process, and after you have done it once, you won't look back. Moving forward, you can add gold to any number of areas of your work in many ways. Have fun!

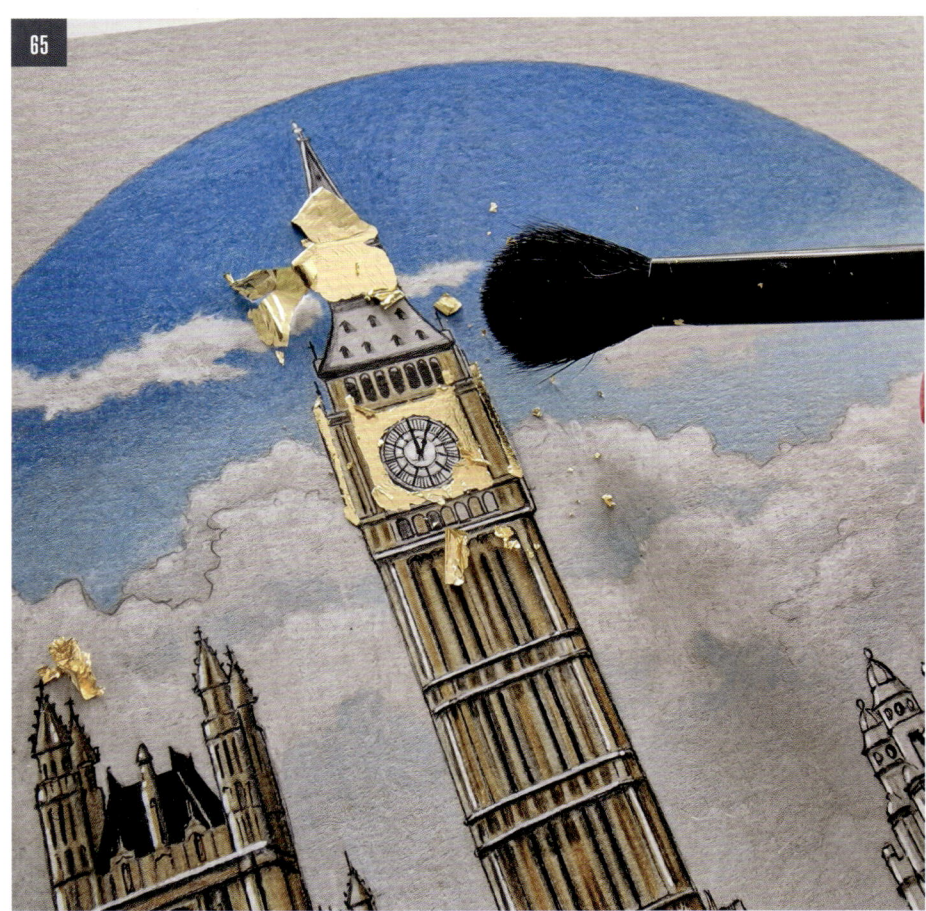

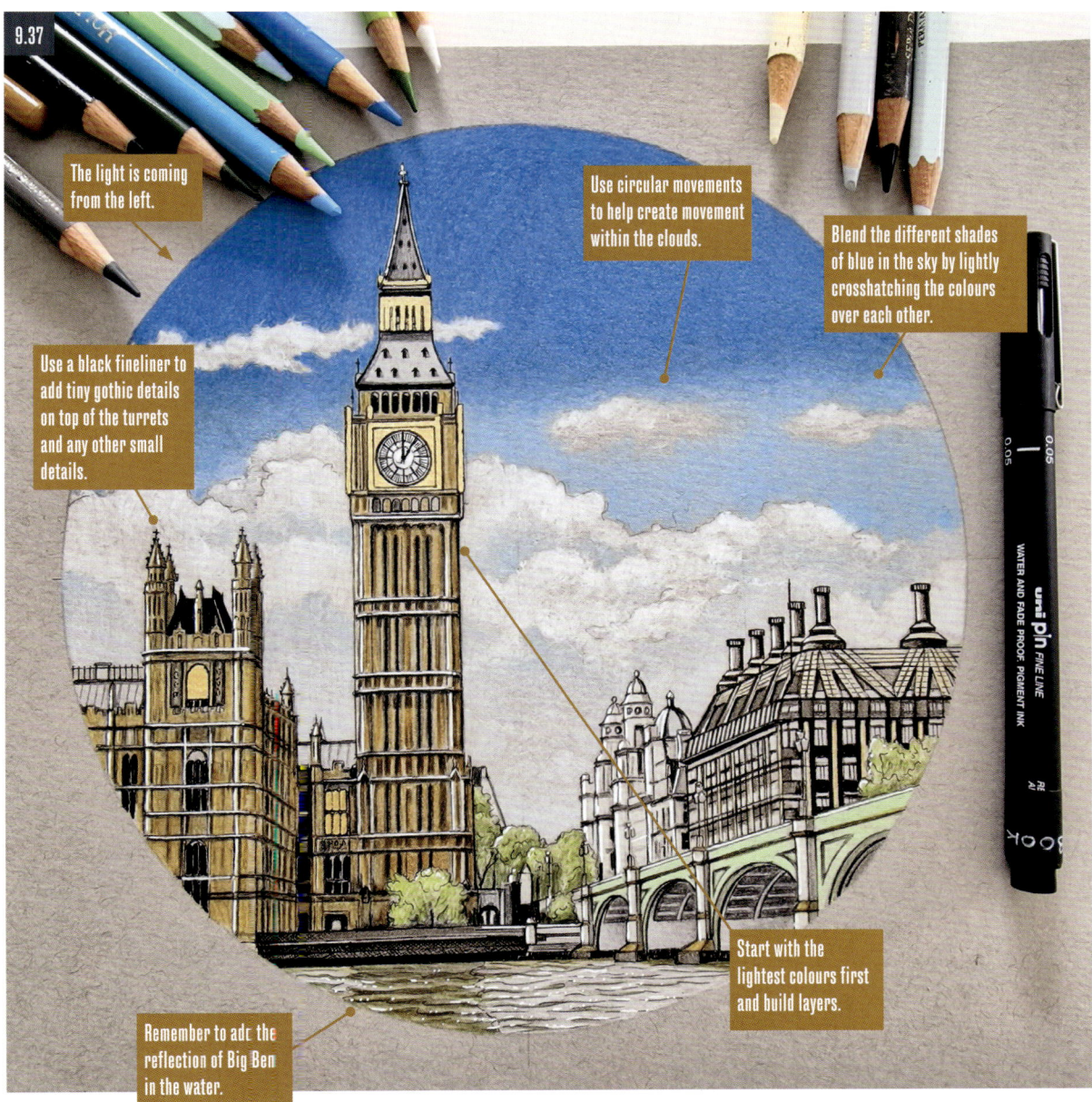

9.37

The light is coming from the left.

Use circular movements to help create movement within the clouds.

Blend the different shades of blue in the sky by lightly crosshatching the colours over each other.

Use a black fineliner to add tiny gothic details on top of the turrets and any other small details.

Start with the lightest colours first and build layers.

Remember to add the reflection of Big Ben in the water.

Full-Colour Drawing with Gold

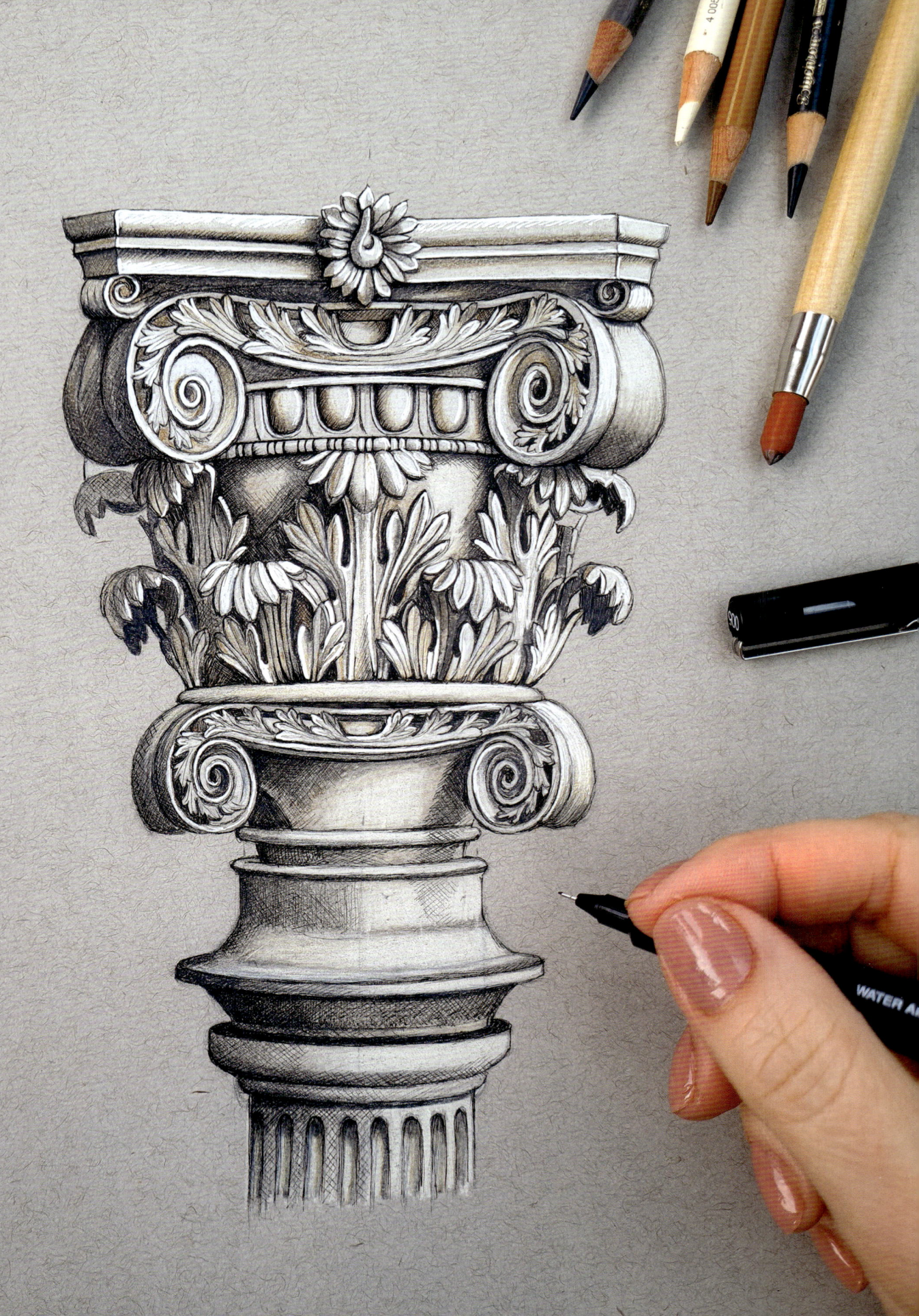

Additional Resources

Here are some additional ideas and resources that you might find useful to help further your art practice.

Getting Out and About!

I recommend visiting exhibitions, galleries, and museums for fresh inspiration.

When you are out in the urban environment, don't forget to look up and all around you. You never know what you will discover that could make a good drawing!

Art Clubs and Societies

Most towns and cities have art clubs and societies where group members can meet up to draw and paint together. It's also a good place to get feedback on your work, share ideas, and hang out with likeminded artistic people! These groups often organise art exhibitions where members can show their work in local venues.

Books

Drawing Architecture: The Beginner's Guide to Drawing and Painting Buildings
By Richard Taylor
A beautiful, inspiring book!

How to See It, How to Draw It:
The Perspective Workbook
By Matthew Brehm
This book is useful if you need a little help with perspective.

Art Classes

There are literally thousands of art classes available online to help further your skills or to do just for fun. I often take a class in a subject I am interested in to gain fresh inspiration and learn new skills. Some popular online courses can be found at:

My Modern Academy
https://academy.mymodernmet.com/

Domestika
https://www.domestika.org/

Social Media

Instagram and Facebook are rich with inspiring art and videos. It's worth taking a look to see what you can find. Use search terms like "architecture illustration" to help you find art you love.

You can find me on social media at:
Instagram: @demilangart
Facebook: DemiLangArt

I would love to see your finished drawings, so feel free to tag me with them on social media.

Art Materials and Stockists

Cult Pens
https://cultpens.com/

Jackson's
https://www.jacksonsart.com/

Amazon
https://www.amazon.com/

Strathmore
https://www.strathmoreartist.com/

Michaels
https://www.michaels.com/

Blick
https://www.dickblick.com/

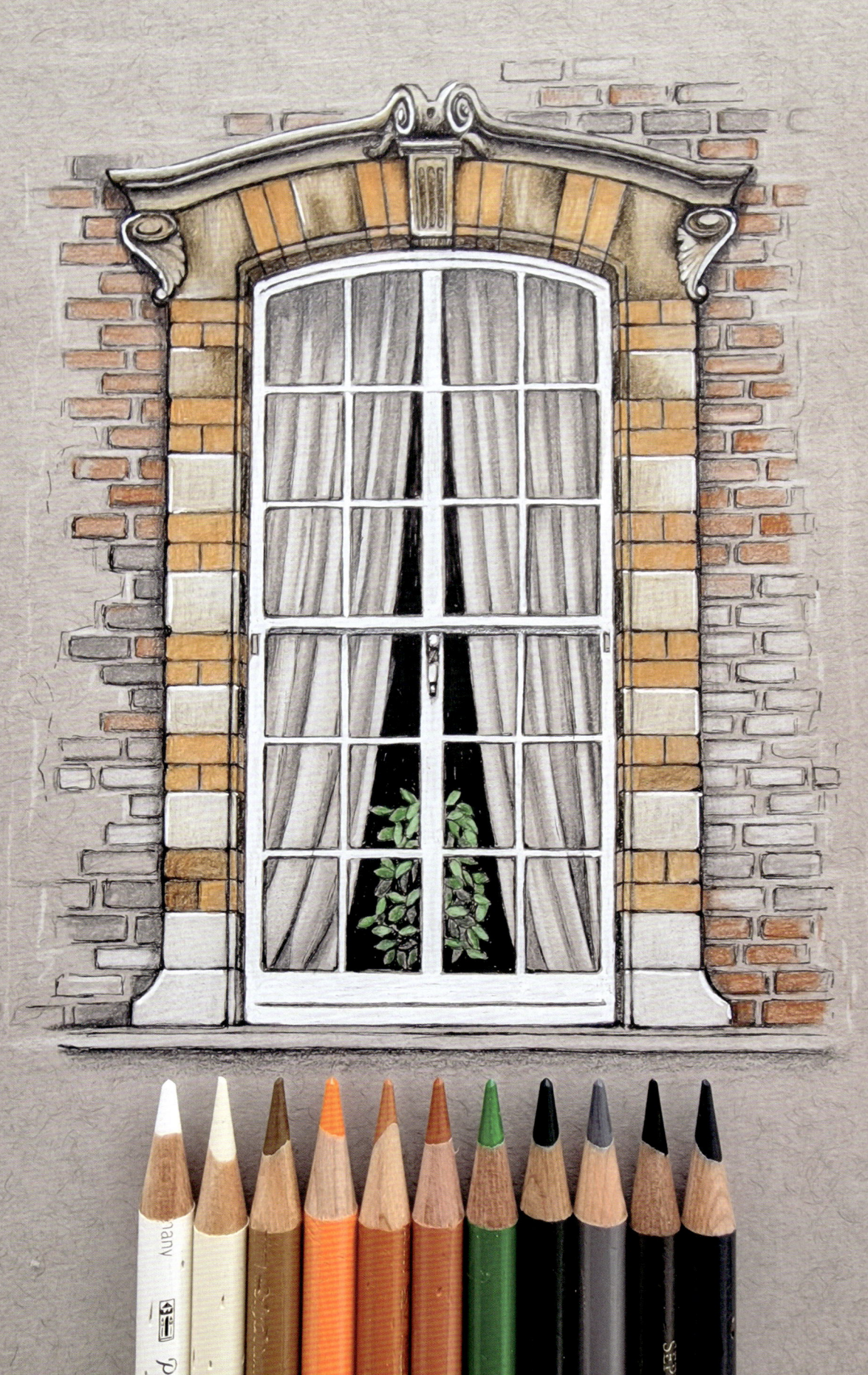

Index